BERGSON AND AMERICAN CULTURE

It is one of the peculiarities of the imagination that it is always at the end of an era. What happens is that it is always attaching itself to a new reality, and adhering to it. It is not that there is a new imagination but that there is a new reality.—Wallace Stevens, "The Noble Rider and the Sound of Words"

Bergson and American Culture

THE WORLDS OF WILLA CATHER

AND WALLACE STEVENS

BY TOM QUIRK

The University of North Carolina Press

Chapel Hill & London

© 1990 The University of North Carolina Press
All rights reserved

Library of Congress Cataloging-in-Publication Data

Quirk, Tom, 1946–
Bergson and American culture : the worlds of Willa Cather and
Wallace Stevens / by Tom Quirk.
p.   cm.
Bibliography: p.
Includes index.
ISBN 0-8078-1880-1 (alk. paper)
1. American literature—20th century—History and criticism.
2. Bergson, Henri, 1859–1941—Influence.   3. Cather, Willa,
1873–1947—Philosophy.   4. Stevens, Wallace, 1879–1955—Philosophy.
5. Philosophy in literature.   6. Vitalism in literature.   7. United
States—Intellectual life—20th century.   I. Title.
PS228.B47Q85   1990
810.9'0052—dc20   89-32355
                                               CIP

Excerpts from the following books have been reprinted with the permission
of the publisher:

From *The Collected Poems of Wallace Stevens* by Wallace Stevens. Copyright © 1954 by
Wallace Stevens. Reprinted by permission of Alfred A. Knopf, Inc.

From *Souvenirs and Prophecies: The Young Wallace Stevens*, edited by Holly
Stevens. Copyright © 1966, 1977 by Holly Stevens. Reprinted by permission of
Alfred A. Knopf, Inc.

From *Opus Posthumous* by Wallace Stevens, edited by Samuel French Morse.
Copyright © 1957 by Elsie Stevens and Holly Stevens. Reprinted by permission of Alfred A.
Knopf, Inc.

From *Letters of Wallace Stevens*, edited by Holly Stevens. Copyright © 1966 by Holly
Stevens. Reprinted by permission of Alfred A. Knopf, Inc.

From *The Necessary Angel* by Wallace Stevens. Copyright © 1951 by Wallace
Stevens. Reprinted by permission of Alfred A. Knopf, Inc.

A portion of chapter 2 has appeared in somewhat different form as "Bergson
in America," in *Prospects: An Annual Journal of American Cultural Studies*,
Volume 11-*Essays* (1987).

The paper in this book meets the guidelines for permanence and durability of the
Committee on Production Guidelines for Book Longevity of the Council on
Library Resources.

Printed in the United States of America

94 93 92 91 90   5 4 3 2 1

Design by April Leidig-Higgins

For my mother Virginia, my wife Catherine,

my daughters Laura and Ann.

My preforensic circle.

CONTENTS

ACKNOWLEDGMENTS

OVER THE LAST SEVERAL YEARS I have accumulated many professional debts owed to many people, and by mentioning them here I cannot hope to repay them or adequately express my gratitude. I wish to thank the staff at the Willa Cather Pioneer Memorial Museum and Education Foundation in Red Cloud, Nebraska; the University of Nebraska Archives at Lincoln; the Newberry Library at Chicago; and the Huntington Library at San Marino, California. Thanks are also due to the staff at the University of Missouri-Columbia Library and to Rebecca Arnold who served as a research assistant and verified my citations. Thanks are also due to the University of Virginia Library for supplying microfilm copies of Willa Cather materials. I am grateful to the Huntington Museum and Library for allowing me to quote from previously unpublished Wallace Stevens materials.

I owe a special debt to the Office of the Provost at the University of Missouri-Columbia for the research leave that allowed me time to do the bulk of the writing for this study. And I am thankful to the University of Missouri Research Council for travel monies.

Then there are those people who read the manuscript. Kermit Vanderbilt at San Diego State University, Paul Boyer at the University of Wisconsin, Jackson Lears at Rutgers–The State University, A. Walton Litz at Princeton University, James Woodress at the University of California at Davis, Edwin H. Cady at Duke University, Albert J. Devlin, J. Donald Crowley, and William Holtz at the University of Missouri-Columbia read part or all of the manuscript and provided many useful suggestions and insightful comments. George Arms and James Barbour at the University of New Mexico patiently and rigorously read the entire manuscript and unfailingly gave me encouragement, direction, and the benefit of their better judgment again and again. The same is true for my friend and former colleague Robert Sattelmeyer. Catherine Parke—wife, colleague, friend—read the manuscript and supplied useful criticisms and commentary throughout the project, but she was also consistently encouraging, interested, and helpful in so many ways that there is simply no way to express my appreciation.

I HAVE TRIED to refer to generally available texts of the works of Bergson, Cather, and Stevens. Both Cather and Stevens read French (and Stevens owned a handsome volume of Bergson's *La Perception du changement* [1911]), and it is possible that they read Bergson in the original. But circumstantial evidence suggests that they did not become acquainted with his works until after they appeared in translation. At any rate, for the most part I have cited Bergson in authorized translations of his work and in editions that were available to American readers before World War I. The University Press of America has recently published a facsimile edition of *Creative Evolution* (1983) with an informative introduction by P. A. Y. Gunter, and the pagination is the same as in the 1911 Holt edition. Rowman and Allanheld republished the Philosophical Library edition of *The Creative Mind* (1946) as *An Introduction to Metaphysics: The Creative Mind* in 1965. I cite this latter edition throughout with the exception of *An Introduction to Metaphysics*, which I cite in the T. E. Hulme translation. Hulme's translation was overseen by Bergson and is of greater interest to literary scholars.

For obvious historical reasons, I cite Willa Cather's 1915 edition of *The Song of the Lark*, now available in a University of Nebraska edition, though I also cite the preface to her 1932 edition of that novel. For the same reasons, perhaps I should have cited the 1923 edition of Stevens's *Harmonium*, but for consistency's sake I refer to *The Collected Poems of Wallace Stevens* (which reprints the 1931 edition of *Harmonium*) and try in the text to make it clear which poems did not appear in the first edition.

While I cite any number of published works about Bergson, Cather, and Stevens, additional secondary materials are extensive. The reader is referred to the following bibliographical texts for a more complete record of works about these authors: P. A. Y. Gunter's *Henri Bergson: A Bibliography*, Marilyn Arnold's *Willa Cather: A Reference Guide*, and J. M. Edelstein's *Wallace Stevens: A Descriptive Bibliography*.

ABBREVIATIONS

Henri Bergson

CE   *Creative Evolution*. Translated by Arthur Mitchell. New York: Henry Holt and Co., 1911.

CM   *An Introduction to Metaphysics: The Creative Mind*. Translated by Mabelle L. Andison. Totowa, N.J.: Rowman and Allanheld, 1965.

D   *Dreams*. Translated with an Introduction by Edwin E. Slosson. New York: B. W. Huebsch, 1914.

IM   *An Introduction to Metaphysics*. Translated by T. E. Hulme. New York: G. P. Putnam's, 1912.

L   *Laughter*. In *Comedy*, edited with an Introduction by Wylie Sypher, pp. 61–190. Garden City, N.Y.: Doubleday and Co., 1956.

ME   *Mind-Energy: Lectures and Essays*. Translated by H. Wildon Carr. London: Macmillan and Co., 1920.

MM   *Matter and Memory*. Translated by Nancy Margaret Paul and W. Scott Palmer. New York: Macmillan Co., 1911.

TFW   *Time and Free Will: An Essay on the Immediate Data of Consciousness*. Translated by F. L. Pogson. New York: Macmillan Co., 1910.

Willa Cather

AB   *Alexander's Bridge*. 1912. Reprint. Lincoln: University of Nebraska Press, 1977.

AB 1922 *Alexander's Bridge*. New ed. with Preface. Boston: Houghton Mifflin Co., 1922.

CSF   *Collected Short Fiction, 1892–1912*. Rev. ed. Edited by Virginia Faulkner. Lincoln: University of Nebraska Press, 1965.

DCA   *Death Comes for the Archbishop*. 1927. Reprint. New York: Random House, 1971.

FS   *Five Stories by Willa Cather*. New York: Random House, 1956.

KA   *The Kingdom of Art: Willa Cather's First Principles and Critical Statements, 1893–1896*. Edited by Bernice Slote. Lincoln: University of Nebraska Press, 1966.

LG   *Lucy Gayheart*. 1935. Reprint. New York: Random House, 1976.

LL   *A Lost Lady*. 1923. Reprint. New York: Random House, 1972.

MA   *My Ántonia*. 1918. Reprint. Boston: Houghton Mifflin Co., 1970.

MME   *My Mortal Enemy*. 1923. Reprint. New York: Random House, 1961.

NUF   *Not under Forty*. New York: Alfred A. Knopf, 1936.

OD   *Obscure Destinies*. 1932. Reprint. New York: Random House, 1974.

OO   *One of Ours*. 1922. Reprint. New York: Random House, 1971.

OP   *O Pioneers!*. 1913. Reprint. Boston: Houghton Mifflin Co., 1913.

PH   *The Professor's House*. 1925. Reprint. New York: Random House, 1973.

PSL   Preface to *The Song of the Lark*. Rev. ed. Boston: Houghton Mifflin Co., 1932.

SL   *The Song of the Lark*. 1915. Reprint. Lincoln: University of Nebraska Press, 1978.

SR   *Shadows on the Rock*. 1931. Reprint. New York: Random House, 1971.

SSG   *Sapphira and the Slave Girl*. 1940. Reprint. New York: Random House, 1975.

WCOW   *Willa Cather on Writing*. New York: Alfred A. Knopf, 1949.

WCP   *Willa Cather in Person: Interviews, Speeches, and Letters*. Edited by L. Brent Bohlke. Lincoln: University of Nebraska Press, 1986.

WP   *The World and the Parish: Willa Cather's Articles and Reviews, 1893–1902*. 2 vols. Edited by William M. Curtin. Lincoln: University of Nebraska Press, 1970.

YBM   *Youth and the Bright Medusa*. 1920. Reprint. New York: Random House, 1975.

Wallace Stevens

CP   *The Collected Poems of Wallace Stevens*. New York: Alfred A. Knopf, 1954.

LWS   *Letters of Wallace Stevens*. Edited by Holly Stevens. New York:
Alfred A. Knopf, 1966.

NA   *The Necessary Angel: Essays on Reality and the Imagination*.
New York: Random House, 1951.

Opus   *Opus Posthumous: Poems, Plays, Prose*. 1957. Reprint. Edited by
Samuel French Morse. New York: Random House, 1982.

SP   *Souvenirs and Prophecies: The Young Wallace Stevens*. Edited by
Holly Stevens. New York: Alfred A. Knopf, 1977.

BERGSON AND AMERICAN CULTURE

A Note on Method and Intent

IN AMERICA, the decade before the outbreak of World War I was, to use Van Wyck Brooks's term, that of the "confident years," charged with bully sentiments and progressive ideals. The old liabilities had suddenly become assets. In politics and history, in religion and sociology, in education and aesthetics, men and women were encouraged to take the "evolutionary point of view." To adopt such a perspective no longer meant resigning oneself to the incontestable truth of a biological determinism or an anonymous and mechanical social and economic order. At the same time that Theodore Dreiser was dramatizing the fate of man as a mere "wisp in the wind," Henri Bergson was urging him to "take life by storm," and the latter attitude had its vocal and articulate partisans and a popular appeal in America. In the public rhetoric of the day, vitality, optimism, confidence, progress, and hope were accepted bywords. And though generalized and often vague, this national mood had its corroborating philosophy in vitalism, particularly as it had been articulated by Bergson.

Vitalism, at least as represented by this French philosopher, was one of the liveliest and most fashionable intellectual currents of the era. Though born in Europe, this import found more than a cordial welcome in America. It had received the endorsement of William James in 1909 and only a few years later was being celebrated in the American press. In 1913, when Bergson traveled to New York to receive an honorary degree from Columbia University and to deliver a series of lectures, automobiles bound for the lecture hall crowded along Broadway (surely one of the first traffic jams in America), and inside well-dressed auditors jostled one another aside to find a seat.

Around 1910–15, there was a sudden and general liberation from a mechanistic worldview, a view epitomized by but by no means restricted to Herbert Spencer. A whole generation had grown up under the Spencerian dispensation but had been made restive by a liberal and scientific progressive faith that had gone sour. During the early years of the twentieth century, however, the world changed; there was a new consciousness and a new reality. And that new reality not only argued for a new stock of assumptions about life; it maintained as well that reality was forever remaking itself afresh. The new reality meant that reality was by its very nature continually new, that one now lived in a world of immanence, a world of incessant and unforeseeable change and possibility, a world always about to be.

This study is an essay in literary history and, to some extent, an experiment in that genre. It is not overly experimental in the theoretical assumptions it makes, however. In that, the book may be considered somewhat conventional. Nor is it revisionist history. For I have not tried to revise anything, although this study does focus upon a certain aspect of the intellectual and social ferment in America just prior to the Great War that has been virtually ignored by literary historians and that played a significant part in reshaping American culture. The evidence I bring to bear upon my subject is also of the familiarly scholarly sort, though I do rely upon testimony (in the form of letters, diaries, and contemporary journalistic accounts) more than similar studies for the simple reason that I want to convey, insofar as is possible, the felt reactions to events and circumstances. No, the originality or experimental quality of this study, to the degree that it is either, exists in the arrangement and emphasis of its argument, not in its logic or methods or critical assumptions. And that arrangement and emphasis have been motivated by a desire, if not to solve, at least to avoid a problem common to such histories.

In a word, by restricting myself to a consideration of direct and demonstrable influence, I want to avoid an in-the-air approach to intellectual and literary history. On the other hand, I am just as anxious to treat that influence as a stimulus to a certain kind of creative vision but not as the cause, however partial, of particular imaginative efforts or calculated literary effects. The first approach, in its radically pure form, assumes that works of imagination reflect the attitudes and assumptions of the time and place in which they were composed, that the political events or intellectual climate of the day determine the character of its cultural artifacts. In this sense, discrete literary works serve as evidence for the generalizations one is able to make about the era itself.

The second approach, familiar in many literary biographies, tends to characterize the historical envelope of circumstance as a gloss on the life as lived or as a stage strangely independent of the literary genius who struts upon it for his or her appointed hour and, just as strangely, delivers an art meant for the ages. To regard a literary work as built up out of its identifiable sources and influences simply reverses the process and is equally atomistic. In either case the actual works are treated as something that happened to an author or as aesthetic wholes that mysteriously passed through the biographical subject, explainable perhaps by sociological, psychological, or political theories, but not as the active, unpredictable, and more or less successful efforts of the imagination. A literature considered to be of its time becomes one of those blocks with which the historian builds up a conception of the time of which it is supposed to be a part. A "timeless" literature, on the other hand, tends to demand that the works of the imagination be given at a stroke, accomplished facts, not the unforeseen results of the creative act itself. Either method implies a certain kind of determinism.

An interviewer once asked Thornton Wilder to comment upon his personal history as a writer. For Wilder, the question posed a special difficulty: "The problem of telling you about my past life as a writer is like that of imaginative narration itself; it lies in the effort to employ the past tense in such a way that it does not rob those events of their character of having occurred in freedom. A great deal of writing and talking about the past is unacceptable. It freezes the historical in a determinism."[1] This study, as I say, is an essay in literary history, and it attempts to avoid the frozen quality Wilder speaks of. But my problem has not been simply a matter of vivifying an era gone by with the scholar's customary advantage of hindsight. One ought to heed Wilder's advice, I suppose, but whether one succeeds in using the past tense in a way that preserves the presentational immediacy for the participants in that era depends almost entirely upon the range of the author's sympathy and imagination; and over *that* one has precious little conscious control. The scholar's imagination is, or should be, perpetually compromised by fact, but his or her success in rendering the past, rather than simply reporting it, proceeds from a capacity to believe in that past and in the participants in it in a way that compromises the scholar, not them. How well or ill I have succeeded in rendering the historical circumstance I have attempted to describe is a matter best left to the individual reader's judgment.

No, the real problem I have had, and in a way that insists upon a caveat, is a methodological one. At some point (five or ten years, say, before the outbreak of World War I), something happened in America that altered in a real way the nation's perception of the world at large and the private understanding and ambitions of its individual citizens. I may say, without hope of explaining precisely what I mean by the expression, that during this period a widespread sense of a "new reality" appeared upon the scene. Whether that alteration was a change of habits and attitudes or of consciousness itself I am not prepared to say; in fact, I am unsure, in my own mind, which is the prior event, which, that is to say, is the experienced and which is the named. But some portion of that new reality had to do with the lively influence of Bergsonian vitalism.

Philosophy "bakes no bread," William James was ready to admit, but the "far-flashing beams of light it sends over the world's perspectives" give it a universal interest; and in 1907 he was convinced that a "kind of new dawn" was breaking in philosophy.[2] James, too, was aware that something was happening during these early years of the twentieth century. I should like to be able to say that this something that happened could be precisely dated—to fix the advent of this new reality at a precise moment—perhaps on the day of Rudolf Eucken's Nobel Prize speech in 1909, or the publication of Bergson's *L'évolution créatrice* in 1907 or James's *Pragmatism* in the same year, or the occasion of Hans Driesch's Gifford lectures in 1907 and 1908. But to do so would be to substitute a symbolic coefficient for an unnameable, but nevertheless real, moment and event, to provide a convenient, but partial, explanation that would as instantly inaugurate a kind of determinism as it would simplify certain complexities.

More abstractly, I should like to be able to say that there was a single historical moment that occasioned in its wake the printed and reliable record of a shifting sensibility, but the evidence will not support such an assertion. Nor, unfortunately, will it support the converse formulation that there was a logical inevitability to events and a consequent intellectual recognition on the part of the cultivated and astute that magically trickled down to the masses and installed in them, if only for a short time, a tardy and bastardized popular response. Nonetheless, something did happen, some new reality was ushered in, but whether in the front door or the back door or both at once, I am unsure. But how chart it? And how get at it?

My solution, such as it is, was not to attempt to write an intellectual history per se, or a social history, or even a pure literary history. Rather I have tried to corral this shift by adapting means to ends and to come at this historical movement, this cultural mitosis, so to speak, from differing angles. The first chapter is, for the most part, intellectual history; the second, cultural and literary history, but literary history that attempts to avoid commenting upon tradition in a way that might, again, implicate me in a kind of determinism. For I have not wanted to say that this era anticipates or constitutes an antecedent for a literary modernism; I wanted instead to try to preserve something of the character of possibility and indeterminacy that gives the moment its own rights and divergent energies.

In the later chapters, I instance two case studies of this transformation as it relates to the unique qualities of the individual imagination. In a word, I attempt to trace the literary careers of two significant American writers, Willa Cather and Wallace Stevens, and to interpret those careers in terms of the revolutionary intellectual currents of the days just before the war. For me, the choices of Cather and Stevens also provide the latitude of tracing the influence of this new reality as it is revealed in two genres (and two genders also, Cather's compulsive manliness notwithstanding). Both read and responded to Bergson in interesting ways, and both were deeply affected by the sudden social changes that occurred between 1910 and 1915. Not accidentally, their own sudden development as artists corresponds to, though it cannot be said to have been caused by, the intellectual and social excitement of those times. I have tried, in short, to involve these writers in their own era, or rather a certain portion of it, and at the same time to allow them their own unique creative visions and artistic resources. The relation between these writers and the period is not incidental, but neither is it causal.

"A cause," wrote Bergson in *Creative Evolution* (1911 translation of *L'évolution créatrice*), "may act by *impelling*, *releasing*, or *unwinding*. The billiard-ball that strikes another, determines its movements by *impelling*. The spark that explodes the powder acts by *releasing*. The gradual relaxing of the spring, that makes the phonograph turn, *unwinds* the melody inscribed on the cylinder: if the melody which is played be the effect, and the relaxing of the spring the cause, we may say that the cause acts by *unwinding*." Only in the first instance can one say that the cause may "explain" the effect; "in the others the effect is more or less given in advance, and the antecedent invoked is—in different degrees, of course—its occasion rather than its cause" (*CE* 73). The logical problem of cause and effect, as Bergson himself knew, is much more complicated than these metaphors suggest, but the distinctions are adequate for my purpose. The intellectual and social significance of Bergsonism in the Progressive Era, however important the philosophy is to an understanding of that time, is that it acted as a causal agent only in the sense that it detonated and released pent-up energies or allowed certain dimly sensed but intensely felt truths to be realized by a relaxation of self-consciousness or anxiety. Even though the Bergsonian philosophy cannot explain much of anything about the era, it can be regarded as the occasion for certain kinds of reactions and happenings; and because Bergson provides a logic and a vocabulary that help to express those reactions, his system offers a framework that makes them coherent. To avoid confusion on this point, I shall not speak of Bergson as a cause, however one wishes to consider the term, but as an epitome of certain tendencies and interests. And although Bergson might epitomize the times, he also serves as an important influence upon the age and upon any number of individuals within it.

The problem of influence, literary or other, presents a different but related difficulty. Carl Becker nicely summed up the problem many years ago in his *The Heavenly City of the Eighteenth-Century Philosophers* (1932):

> It has long been a favorite pastime of those who interest themselves in the history of culture to note the transfer of ideas (as if it were no more than a matter of borrowed coins) from one writer to another; to note, for example, that Mr. Jones must have got a certain idea from Mr. Smith because it can be shown that he had read, or might have read, Mr. Smith's book; all the while forgetting that if Mr. Jones hadn't already had the idea, or something like it, simmering in his own mind he wouldn't have cared to read Mr. Smith's book, or having read it, would very likely have thrown it aside, or written a review to show what a bad and mistaken book it was. And how often it happens that books "influence" readers in ways not intended by the writers![3]

As we shall see, these same diverse results are observable in the changes of American sensibility that occurred when Americans came to contemplate and be influenced by Bergson. Many sophisticated men and women traced the lineaments of their own characters in the pages of *Creative Evolution* and found there a sanction for their peculiar experiences and desires. And they discovered in the new philosophy ideas they recognized as their own, as if these ideas had been inscribed upon them all along. Just as many, it seems, set out to show how bad and mistaken a book *Creative Evolution* was. And, to Bergson's aggravation and dismay, his influence worked on a considerable number in ways that were as remote from his intention as from one another.

However, Becker's identification of the special treachery and irony of influence studies (of which this book is certainly one) does not diminish the interest of such a project or relegate it to a subsidiary and unimportant kind of knowing. Far from it. Instead, influence study, cluttered as it is with the factual, the probable, and the verifiable, leads to the only place it can lead: to the mysterious and infinitely fascinating kinds of responses that human beings have to ideas and events. And in the case of the artist, it leads to the unique and original resources of the creative imagination, rich with the particularity of the actual book read, the concrete event undergone, the emotional or intellectual dilemma solved. "To be at the end of a fact," wrote Wallace Stevens, "is not to be at the beginning of imagination but it is to be at the end of both" (*Opus* 175). The final object of this study is to make statements not about a historical era but about the divergent movements of the imagination, or rather a certain portion of it, as it occurred in two remarkably gifted American writers.

For that reason, the customary emphasis of such histories is reversed in this study. Its structure may be regarded as something of an inverted pyramid. Historical generalizations are set out at the beginning of the book, and little by little they yield, and are meant to yield, to the concrete acts and specific thoughts of individuals whose energies were spent, not in the service of a body of doctrine, but in appropriating and extending in their own lives certain new ways of looking at the world according to their preoccupations. My emphasis, then, is meant to resist homogenizing the mind of the past, a tendency that Daniel Boorstin once disparagingly identified as the "normal psychology of all historians."[4] Thus, I begin with a consideration of one of the liveliest and most abstract controversies of the day—the conflict between naturalism and idealism—and over the course of the book trace the movements of that conflict not to a new set of abstractions or generalizations but to heterogeneous realities and individual imaginative acts that are considered in the light of a new reality that was publicly shared but privately lived.

The opening chapter contemplates the import and significance of such intellectual issues as those suggested by some of the titles I cite there: *Matter, Life, Mind, and God*; *The Riddle of the Universe*; *Knowledge and Life*; *Time and Free Will*; *The Problem of Individuality*. But this study in the end reserves its interest and emphasis for the expressions of a quiet and private equanimity in the face of old age and a world that did not quite turn out as expected. In the case of Willa Cather, I conclude with a brief comment on the last short story she wrote, "The Best Years." In the case of Wallace Stevens, I consider a late and lovely little poem, "The Planet on the Table."

In part, the narrowing interest and emphasis of my argument are meant, in deference to Cather and Stevens, to retreat before the specific performances of the creative imagination itself and allow them their own latitude, in a word to abide by Stevens's recommendation that one ought attend not to "ideas about things but the thing itself." But only in part. For I wanted as well to accent and give space to the individual imagination as a potent and real force, as a power over events, as Stevens once characterized it. Both Cather and Stevens believed in the "creative power," and both in some fashion linked this power to a vital force, biological in nature and primordial in origin. This same linkage gave them a certain confidence and authority in their art and provided them with the assurance that the concerns of art and the claims of life were integrally related. In our own day, one need not believe in an élan vital to yet allow the imagination its earned importance and privileged intelligence.

And certainly we are no longer entranced by the grand, biological vision *Creative Evolution* offered to its readers. The popular influence of Bergsonism died out some time ago. But just as one cannot say precisely when this new reality began, one cannot determine exactly when the authority and fascination of vitalism ended. In the case of Bergsonism, one might say it ended with the increasing interest and influence of Freudian psychoanalysis, to which Bergson gave his endorsement, believing such analysis to portend unlimited possibilities. Or it might have been eclipsed by an awareness of the advances of physics and, particularly, of Einstein's theory of relativity, with which Bergson quarreled.[5] One might say that Bergson's metaphysics was absorbed into and overshadowed by the philosophical methods of phenomenologists and existentialists, who were instructed by his radically new ways of thinking but still found him too much a part of the nineteenth century.

One might be rather more dramatic and say that Bergson's authority ended sometime in August or September 1914. In his fascinating book, *The Culture of Time and Space*, Stephen Kern remarks that one of the most important developments in the history of advancing a homogenous, uniform time was the introduction of standard time at the end of the nineteenth century. Kern further observes that Count Helmuth von Moltke argued, ironically in the interests of peaceful cooperation, that the German parliament adopt standard time to better coordinate military planning.[6] In France, however, as Barbara Tuchman points out in *The Guns of*

August, military strategists took courage from "the idea with a sword"; a Bergsonian élan vital became for them "the doctrine of the offensive."[7] A Bergsonian principle that is involved in this doctrine is the notion that time is heterogeneous not homogenous. And one may suggest, without quite believing it, that Bergson's authority and controversial system were literally tested on the battlefield. At any rate, after the war vitalism no longer enjoyed the widespread interest and enthusiasm it had before.

Nevertheless, the Bergsonian point of view persisted in one way or another well beyond its heyday. For Walter Lippmann, that point of view was modified but not altogether abandoned after the war. For Carl Becker, who was never a complete convert, the adaptation of the new reality to the uses of history occurred belatedly. In Cather and Stevens, the vision they adopted around 1912 or 1913 persisted in some form for the remainder of their lives. The new reality as it was represented by Bergsonism was attractive to them and held their allegiance. Not only did it answer, and continue to answer, the intellectual problems and disturbances they had been brought up on, but because he gave a full and privileged place to the creative imagination, Bergson justified the artistic enterprise as congruent with the general aim of life. And for both, instructed as they were in a time when idealism and naturalism were the reigning modes of thought and in absolute contradiction one with the other, the relation of art to life was a fundamental problem for them and an obstacle to their development as artists.

Harold Bloom has indicated that Wallace Stevens, particularly in his "Notes toward a Supreme Fiction," managed to get a generation ahead of his own time and remains ahead of ours.[8] Willa Cather, on the other hand, is still too often viewed as a writer who remained behind her own generation, fastidiously genteel and aggressively nostalgic. When one considers the historical context in which they both achieved the style and vision that made them writers of continuing significance, one gets a very different picture. And if I seem to display a grand and cavalier indifference to the current theoretical vocabulary, my only answer is that the period I mean to describe had its own idiom for the problems it was most vitally interested in—as sufficient, as technical, and as obscure a vocabulary as one could wish—and I thought it better to learn its language than to make it speak ours.[9]

Other reasons as well argue for keeping as much as possible to the philosophical terminology of the prewar years. In that part of the book where I engage in literary interpretation, I am not so much interested in literary "texts" as I am in literary motivation, in how these two writers appropriated a new vision of reality and made this vision serve the purposes of their art. And although my own methods are typically genetic and biographical, the composing self rather than the biographical self is what interests me.

In two recent biographical studies—*Willa Cather: The Emerging Voice* by Sharon O'Brien and *Wallace Stevens: The Early Years* by Joan Richardson—we learn about the problems of sexual identification in both Cather and Stevens. Cather, we are told, found herself too manly in her manner and her mode of understanding and had to come to grips with her own authentic female identity. Stevens, on the other hand, was apparently troubled by his own sensitivity and believed he was not manly enough. As provocative as these observations may be, they may be applied to the Cather that was a high school teacher in Pennsylvania or an editor in New York or to the Stevens that was an insurance executive in Connecticut as equally and as easily as to Cather the novelist or Stevens the poet.

I greatly admire both Cather and Stevens, but that admiration is reserved for those very human selves who expressed in their art a greater tolerance and sympathy than they might have shown in their daily lives. Cather could be cantankerous and fussy, and Stevens austere and sometimes belligerent. It was in their attachments to an inner self, better than any private or public self, that they found a sanction for their craft. Both believed in some version of Bergson's authentic *moi fondamentale*, a self authorized by an all-encompassing vital principle and all the more human for being allowed to be what it is. In "Chocorua to Its Neighbor," as he does so often in his poetry, Stevens speaks of this composing self:

To say more than human things with human voice,
That cannot be; to say human things with more
Than human voice, that, also, cannot be;
To speak humanly from the height or from the depth
Of human things, that is acutest speech.   [*CP* 300]

In their works of the imagination, because they were profoundly concerned with human things, Cather and Stevens allowed themselves to be more human perhaps than they were.

I should also say that I have avoided classifying Cather and Stevens as certain kinds of writers. Both have been identified as modernist writers, and both have been shown to extend a nineteenth-century romantic tradition into the twentieth. And it has become more and more apparent that romanticism and modernism have more in common than was once thought. I can see no possible objection to labeling Cather as a modernist, so long as the definition of the term unbends enough to include *My Ántonia* or *O Pioneers!*. The same would hold for Stevens, though again one would have to account for the critical remarks he made, both publicly and privately, about moderns and modernism. "One cannot spend one's time in being modern," he wrote in his *Adagia*, "when there are so many more important things to be" (*Opus* 175). And such a limbered-up modernism would have to be able to accommodate the biological features of their respective creative and critical visions.

On the other hand, though it may be true that both were romantic writers, it ought to be recognized that there was an immediate neoromanticism to which they responded and which informed their fiction and poetry. One need not reach back to Emerson or Whitman, to Wordsworth or Coleridge, to define Cather's and Stevens's romanticism. But here too, one has to apply a looser definition of romanticism to make sense of either as romantics. The romanticism of the early nineteenth century generally postulated a transcendent spiritual principle behind natural appearances. Even Melville's dark romanticism struck through the mask to something beyond, albeit something malevolent and terrifying. Neoromanticism, at least as it was identified in Bergsonism, had no such transcendent principle. The Bergsonian universe is a universe of immanence, not transcendence, and not a few of his detractors labeled Bergson an atheist. But for Cather, as for Stevens, to be human in a human world provided its own consolations.

I have taken my epigraph from a passage in an essay by Wallace Stevens. The essay concerns itself less with the new reality I have been describing than with the image of nobility in the modern world, an image he felt to be "conspicuously absent" from contemporary poetry:

> It is hard to think of a thing more out of time than nobility. Looked at plainly it seems false and dead and ugly. To look at it at all makes us realize sharply that in our present, in the presence of our reality, the past looks false and is, therefore, dead, and is, therefore, ugly; and we turn away from it as from something repulsive and particularly from the characteristic that it has a way of assuming: something that was noble in its day, grandeur that was, the rhetorical once. But as a wave

is a force and not the water of which it is composed, which is never the same, so nobility is a force and not the manifestations of which it is composed, which are never the same. [*NA* 35–36]

When we turn toward the past of those few years before the Great War, that "rhetorical once" Stevens himself described as a "much more vital reality" (*NA* 26) than the one that preceded it, we find the time to be neither tired nor ugly. For some at least, it was a time ripe with hope and courage and possibility. For Willa Cather and Wallace Stevens, it was a time when their own creative energies found shape and direction. It was a time when one might actually believe in nobility. (And who, among American writers in the twentieth century, except perhaps William Faulkner, has given us more frequent and more compelling images of nobility than Cather and Stevens?) It was a time when any number of American men and women felt suddenly liberated from outworn attitudes of mind and were ready to take life by storm.

ONE

Naturalism or Idealism?

I

THE FOURTH International Congress of Philosophy was held in Bologna, Italy, in April 1911. The gathering provided no consensus about the prevailing tendencies of the modern philosophical spirit, but it did demonstrate a general impulse to reject or revise the synthetic, system-building philosophies of an earlier era. As characterized by T. E. Hulme, who covered the event as a correspondent for the periodical *Nature* and who was to play his own part in the repudiation of a nineteenth-century intellectual inheritance, this Fourth Congress was most centrally interested in the relations of philosophy and science. Henri Poincaré delivered a paper that examined the hypothetical question of whether the laws of nature may in fact change over time. Paul Langevin, whose reputation rested principally on his work in radioactivity, argued that the laws of mechanics should no longer be considered immutable or absolute. The vitalistic philosopher and biologist Hans Driesch insisted that his concept of the entelechy is scientific not metaphysical. Wilhelm Ostwald applied the second law of thermodynamics to psychology, arguing that the gradual depletion of energy constitutes the framework within which all mental life must operate. Each of these papers, according to Hulme, received considerable attention from the more than 500 participants at the conference. But the lecture "awaited with the greatest curiosity" was the one given by Henri Bergson.[1]

In his address Bergson insisted that the future of philosophy lay in pursuing a method quite different from that of science. Traditionally, the philosopher had followed the route of scientific analysis and had constructed systematic intellectual representations of the world. Such rational structures are destined to failure or diminishment, he claimed, because as scientific inquiry penetrates into the same field explored by the philosopher the discrete and verifiable findings of the scientist overthrow or displace philosophical system. The future of the philosopher belongs not to intellectual analysis but to intuitional knowledge that is, as Hulme remarked in the *Nature* article, "akin to that of the artist, and differing fundamentally from the kind of activity you get in science."

By 1911, Bergson had become the most celebrated thinker of the day. He was an emblem for the age—the focus of hot dispute and lively interest. In Hulme's view, a view shared by innumerable others, Bergson was "the most discussed and the most interesting philosopher in Europe at the present time." The preeminent position Bergson enjoyed at this philosophical congress, and more broadly in the intellectual life of the time, derived from the fresh solutions he gave to longstanding philosophical problems. To that extent, his authority and popularity had been determined by an intellectual context that was busily pondering and redefining philosophical dilemmas and challenging hypotheses inherited from the nineteenth century. Bergsonian vitalism was only one of several philosophical positions then contesting the reigning authority of materialism on the one hand and idealism on the other. The philosophy of life (in all its variety and possibility) was fast replacing the philosophy of the closed system and predictable certainty, and for some the nineteenth century had been but a preamble to this new spirit in philosophy. Bergsonism had become the principal catalyst for the transformation of sensibility and the appropriation of a new reality, but it was not alone in performing its radical revisions of the way one was to understand the world.

II

In the fall of 1908, the German philosopher Rudolf Eucken was awarded the Nobel Prize for Literature. The following March he delivered his Nobel Laureate lecture, "Naturalism or Idealism?" The award was controversial, partly because Eucken was considered by some to be merely a popular writer and partly because most of his work up to that time had been historical rather than analytic and systematic philosophy.[2] In fact, however, Eucken's nomination may have been an act of compromise, an effort to avoid controversy. In his acceptance speech, at any rate, he was something of a meliorist, for as he had in much of his work, he meant there to transcend the terms of the liveliest intellectual debate of the time.

The terms themselves, expressed in the title of his lecture, were unavoidably vague. By *naturalism* he meant to include the whole of a scientific, mechanistic, evolutionary point of view; by *idealism* he intended to convey the spiritual life of ideals and absolutes and the desire for the security of an invisible world, free from contingency and change. Each made equal and opposing demands upon the individual, and each made a heightened appeal to human needs. Together they constituted "divergent and even contradictory attitudes" and seemed to be "irreconcilable" opposites. A forced choice between these "harsh alternatives" characterized the modern dilemma and defined the age as one "undeniably divided against itself" (p. 75).

The naturalistic point of view, Eucken admitted, had undoubtedly wrought many indisputable and powerful advantages, and its technological and scientific innovations had permanently altered the way men and women live in the world. Evidence for such advancement was as common and tangible as the dynamo or an improved postal system. This point of view meant as well that one need not escape to an "invisible" world to achieve exalted goals. Environmental and social improvement, even human perfection, seemed well within reach. But the materialistic foundation of naturalism, philosophically considered, exceeded material advantage. For naturalism also "maintains that man is completely defined by his relationship with the world, that he is only a piece of the natural process" (p. 77). Traditional idealism, on the other hand, was no more satisfactory for Eucken. In its more extravagant efforts to ground reality and existence in the absolute and immutable, idealism removed individuals from the practical concerns and welfare of their own lives and distanced them from their natural environment and from the felt presence of their personal history and experience as agents in the world.

Eucken was often labeled a vitalistic philosopher, but the attribution is inexact. Although his philosophical system emphasized the role of life as a vital organic movement, he did not, as did most vitalists, form his metaphysics on a biological model. Eucken was something of an idealist, though he preferred to characterize his philosophy as an activist idealism.[3] He, like the vitalists, was severely critical of a naturalistic mechanism and did not miss any opportunity to point out its several limitations. A purely scientific naturalism mistakes the nature of its own revelations, he believed, because it ascribes to material nature itself the causes for the effects it discovers there by means of scientific inquiry. The naturalistic method is limited to observation of external objects, and likewise errors are revealed by the transformations of nature into intellectual conceptions and laws. The same translation of sense impressions into intellectual conceptions discloses another and higher level of reality. The spiritual life is discoverable in the operations of science itself, for scientific investigation reveals the transcendent desire to master nature and to meet its challenges. This is but a way of asserting that naturalism is in fact contained in an active and evolving idealism that its adherents too often fail to recognize.

Modern technology proves that human beings are superior to nature, and the social idea and social reform repudiate naturalistic individualism. For life itself is a response to the challenge of the environment and, to the extent that life has evolved beyond mere self-interest and self-preservation, establishes, at a stroke, its own active movement and energy. Because a being is creative, "he is active with the energy of the whole [of life], and so he does not remain a mere part of a given order but becomes a stage on which worlds meet and search for their further development. . . . limitation and freedom, finiteness and infinity, meet in him. The world ceases to be foreign to him, and with the whole of its life it becomes his own and inmost essence" (pp. 81–82).

The intent of these hearty urgings was not merely to displace the naturalistic point of view or to neglect the complexities and anxieties of modern life and to substitute for them an easy faith in the inevitable law of progress. The progressive spirit itself was part of the problem. We have begun to doubt, Eucken argued, whether the "entire range of being can really be turned into an upward movement." The ideal of progress has created new complications, and the release of potent natural and human energies has "conjured up contrasts and passions that are threatening the sanity of our existence." "The restlessness and haste of such progressive activity," he continued, "cannot prevent a growing emptiness and the consciousness of it. Despite the greatness of technical achievements in particular fields, man in the entirety of his existence is doomed to decline: the powerful and individual personality will gradually disappear" (p. 84).

Eucken's antidote to the current malaise was a revitalized idealism, and he detected in the temper of the times an appetite for such a transformation—"there is an urge beyond naturalism in all directions" (p. 86). The rejuvenation of the life of the spirit, however, and the upwelling of the desires of the soul can be accomplished only by the limited and local applications of individuals working in and through the world at hand. The spiritual life must be seen as a personal necessity and an aspect of "intellectual preservation": "Exhilaration, courage, and firm belief can arise only from such an acknowledgement of a binding necessity, not from a hankering after remote and alien goals but from a belief in life as it is active within us and makes us participate inwardly in the large context of reality" (p. 87).

Eucken's lecture is a notable, but single, instance of an expression of discontent with the naturalistic and the idealist inheritance. In fact a manifold reaction against uniform intellectual systems was occurring. Whether such systems appeared as the neo-Hegelian abstractions of Josiah Royce or F. H. Bradley or as the more popular and pervasive cosmic materialism epitomized by Herbert Spencer, whose *First Principles* appeared in 1862, there had been raids upon insular, system-building philosophies for more than thirty years. Personalism, pragmatism, pluralism, humanism, vitalism—all manner of life philosophies sought to displace or undermine the "building block philosophy" that, William James complained, was constantly being "whacked" upon them in radically different forms.[4] Without pausing to examine all the extensive and complicated objections to the naturalistic system that excited controversy and familiar religious, social, and metaphysical debate, I wish to isolate for attention only the mechanistic features of the building block philosophy, for they gave to the age its ruling metaphor: the machine.[5]

Naturalists promoted the view that everything, in the last analysis, could be referred to molecular arrangement. Such an idea, as A. O. Lovejoy observed, was "monstrous" to the imagination and had its inevitable effects on the temper of the times. Reflection upon a "mechanistic cosmology and a quasi-mechanical biology," he remarked in a lecture in 1913, "bred much of that mid-Victorian melancholy which is so conspicuous a phase of the English literature of the past century."[6] The disturbance created by an understanding of a strict determinism and a consequent sense of the meaninglessness of both history and the future contributed to the mood expressed by James Thomson in "The City of Dreadful Night," which Lovejoy cites as evidence of the distress for one who ponders a universe in which all is but "mouldering flesh / Whose elements dissolved and merge afresh":

> Infinite aeons ere our world began,
> Infinite aeons after the last man
> Has joined the mammoth in earth's tomb and womb.

Some could accept a Darwinian world and a simian ancestor[7] but could not accept, or at least were far more troubled by, the idea that the universe is and has been the indifferent mechanical drift of cosmic weather, reducible to the predictable behavior of its atomic parts.

Two distinct nineteenth-century scientific discoveries combined to provide the basis for the mechanistic point of view. The first was the law of
conservation of force, independently advanced by several scientists in the
1840s. This law, along with the related principle of the conservation of
matter, provided a systematic framework wherein enormous scientific advances, not merely theoretical ones, occurred with sufficient frequency
and publicity to establish the law as a practical reality. For scientific discovery and technological innovation enjoy the advantage of not just studying
phenomena but creating them, both in the laboratory and in the marketplace. The machinelike regularity of the heavens was mimicked in the
apple corer and steam engine and constituted not only intellectual truth
but a self-validating environment.

The law of conservation of force had important social, literary, and
psychological implications. Those have been perceptively and instructively
traced by Ronald E. Martin in his *American Literature and the Universe of
Force*. And he has observed that this law had inevitably important cultural
effects, for "one of the most pervasive and oppressive consequences of
nineteenth-century science and its theory of force conservation was the
force-cause-determinism chain it forged out of mechanics and metaphysics."[8] This consequence was the result of complicated and diverse social
and intellectual movements. The law of conservation of force enabled one
to treat inorganic matter with meticulous calculation, for this law allowed
one to suppose that in any particular system the amount of matter and
energy was constant and that change could be considered as the predictable transformation of matter and distribution of force according to demonstrable physical laws.

Organic matter posed a different problem, and chemists and biologists
in particular often found it necessary to bring in some concept of a vital
force or other inner principle to account for the transformations of adaptation, growth, regeneration, and repair. The concept of a vital force was
congruent with an earlier worldview, for, as Howard Mumford Jones
remarks, "among American romantics the universe was not so much inert
matter whirling on invisible circular belts as it was some mysterious entity
filled with life."[9] The publication of Charles Darwin's *The Origin of Species*
(1859) called this view into question by providing a way to reconcile the
apparently incompatible laws of inorganic and organic life. The principle
of natural selection proposed that the evolution and function of life could
be explained in terms of environmental conditions. Life could be studied
empirically and externally and, in the minds of Herbert Spencer and oth-

ers, could be shown at last to participate in the universal principle of redistribution of matter and energy. According to Spencer's interpretation, mental life was merely an adjustment of internal to external relations. In short, he assumed that biological and psychological processes could also be stated in mechanical terms. The formation of species could now be described in terms of natural causation. The assumption was an enabling and legitimate one for scientific inquiry, and it paid cash dividends. As George Herbert Mead pointed out, the inductive leap from particular observations to a universal, mechanistic theory that carried over into biology left a good deal out of its considerations, but this leap nevertheless made the mechanistic assumption a "perfectly legitimate hypothesis for the purposes of research."[10] That same hypothesis was often taken for a doctrine, however, and Spencerian naturalism was promoted as a coherent and synthetic worldview.

The eventual result of these two laws, acting in combination, was to provide room for a vast, materialistic universal philosophy, undergirded by a single principle that moved, or rather evolved, inevitably and progressively forward and could be wholly understood in terms of matter, motion, and force. Such a philosophy was provided by Herbert Spencer, who stated the law of evolution as "*an integration of matter and concomitant dissipation of motion; during which the matter passes from an indefinite, incoherent homogeneity to a definite, coherent heterogeneity; and during which the retained motion undergoes a parallel transformation.*"[11] This definition is as ponderous as it is vague. Josiah Royce identified Spencer as a "philosopher of a beautiful logical naïveté. Generalization was an absolutely simple affair for him. If you found a bag big enough to hold all the facts, that was a unification of science."[12] And William James burlesqued Spencer's law of evolution in particular, for it finally comes to "a change from a no-howish untalkaboutable all-alikeness to a somehowish and in general talkaboutable not-all-alikeness by continuous sticktogetherations and something-elseifications."[13] Be that as it may, in the several volumes of his synthetic philosophy, Spencer magisterially extended his first principles into the realms of biology, psychology, ethics, and sociology and in ways that were particular enough to be convincing and capacious enough to be recognizably harmonious. The law of mechanistic evolution was a universal process observable in the formation of the planets, the growth of organisms, the rise of industrial societies, and the massing of population.

As Ronald Martin has shown, Spencer's philosophy took root and flourished in America in ways that altogether exceeded its influence in

Europe. And according to Jay Martin, authorized editions of Spencer's works sold around 370,000 copies between 1862 and 1903.[14] That same popularity was helped by such influential and eloquent disciples as John Fiske, whose *Outlines of Cosmic Philosophy* (1874) sought, among other things, to reconcile the opposing claims of science and religion, or Henry Ward Beecher, whose *Evolution and Religion* (1885) gave the idea an evangelical tang. But Spencer's philosophy was also popular because it satisfied an American craving for facts and supported the optimistic faith of a country whose future was providentially blessed; it seemed to endorse, scientifically and philosophically, a laissez-faire capitalism whose heroes numbered among the fittest and therefore among fortune's favorites.

"To most Americans," T. J. Jackson Lears observes, "Spencerian positivism was not a bleak necessitarianism but a secular religion of progress, a social scientific version of the optimistic, liberal Protestantism which pervaded the educated bourgeoisie."[15] Spencer himself, and necessarily his followers also, blinked altogether another "law" that absolutely contradicted such progressivism—the second law of thermodynamics, the law of entropy. This law was formulated separately by Lord Kelvin and Rudolph Clausius in the 1850s and demonstrated that energy inevitably dissipates in every conversion process and gradually becomes unusable to man. Spencer ignored the implications of this physical law and remained content to believe the evolutionary law led toward a final, blissful human state.[16] According to the law of entropy, however, the future held no such felicitous promise but an inevitable lethargy.

William James examined the "theory of mechanical evolutionism" in his *Pragmatism* (1907) and cited the statesman and philosopher Lord Balfour to give his readers a vivid picture of the future such a theory foresees: "The energies of our system will decay, the glory of the sun will be dimmed, and the earth, tideless and inert, will no longer tolerate the race which has for a moment disturbed its solitude. Man will go down into the pit, and all his thoughts will perish. The uneasy consciousness which in this obscure corner has for a brief space broken the contented silence of the universe, will be at rest. Matter will know itself no longer. 'Imperishable monuments' and 'immortal deeds,' death itself, and love stronger than death, will be as if they had not been." This, as James remarked, is the "sting" of such a theory; the lower, not the higher, forces in the universe will prevail. A scientific materialism so conceived predicts, utterly and inevitably, a "final wreck and tragedy."[17]

Clearly, the popular appeal of a mechanical materialism was backed by a cheerier emphasis of the sort promoted by Spencer and his advocates. And to a degree that optimism was institutionalized for a time. But it also provided a foundation for a more rugged imaginative vision and for severe social criticism. Several American writers—Hamlin Garland, Frank Norris, Edgar Lee Masters, Theodore Dreiser, and Jack London, among them—responded to a Spencerian philosophy with the elation of discovery. In part, this philosophy provided a harmonious view of the world, however gross and fatal in its particulars, ruled by a comprehensible purpose. And the same influence was adapted to conventional American life in ways that had little to do with the "vulgar" productions of literary naturalists.

Spencer, himself an agnostic, began his *First Principles* (1862) with a grudging recognition of what he termed the "Unknowable." Behind the world of observable scientific fact, inscrutable and absolute powers may indeed reside, but those are forever beyond human comprehension. The concept of the Unknowable was really a conciliatory gesture on Spencer's part, and he was surprised to find that critics of his system often deplored this notion for its implicit agnosticism. In America, just as surprisingly, as Ronald Martin has shown, the concept seemed "to bridge the most dangerous chasm of the age, that between science and religion," and therefore to recommend itself to a multitude of readers (p. 45). Such bridging can be observed close up in an American high school textbook that, even though it does not mention Spencer by name, participates in this special breed of optimistic faith.

J. Dorman Steele in his *Fourteen Weeks in Natural Philosophy* (1875), one of a series of his books in the sciences, insisted that nature is "interwoven everywhere with proofs of a common plan and a common Author."[18] Steele moves effortlessly from the explanation of particular laws of mechanics to spiritualized observations such as that the "confused" noises of nature, softened by distance, adjust to the key of F and therefore combine in an "anthem of praise which Nature sings for His ear alone" (p. 182). And in the concluding paragraphs of the book, Steele echoes the synthetic philosophy (or rather a peculiarly spiritualized version of it): "No force can be destroyed. A hammer falls by the force of gravity and comes to rest, but its motion as a mass is converted into a motion of atoms, and reveals itself to the sense of touch as heat. Thus force changes its form continually, but the eye of philosophy detects it and enables us to drive it from its various hiding-places still undiminished." The "Correlation of the Physical Forces" is the grand and inspiring law of nature and evidence of a "Divine Hand" at work in the universe (p. 316).

The cosmic idealism expressed in this high school textbook betrays an unstable but appealing alliance between naturalistic truth and transcendent purpose, and a generation of America's youth was instructed in some version of this materialistic philosophy, liberally sprinkled with references to moral purpose and ethereal security. An earlier Emersonian intuition of nature, from which an immediate perception of natural fact issues a revelation of active spiritual truth, has been displaced. The natural world is understood only mediately by means of a coordinate system of mechanical law and by the intellectual discriminations of mathematical or scientific calculation. Personal experience and human agency are left out of the equation, and the romantic claims for the potency of a creative self are rendered meaningless.

For some, an evolutionary point of view was profoundly disturbing, not just because it challenged conventional pieties but because it modified experience and nullified human purpose. Emerson proclaimed an "occult relation" between man and the trees, "They nod to me and I to them." Half a century later, in "The Menagerie" (1901), William Vaughan Moody, who resisted Darwinian determinism, could nevertheless jocularly recognize that nature returned his gaze. But it made one squirm:

Helpless I stood among those awful cages;
The beasts were walking loose, and I was bagged!
I, I, last product of the toiling ages,
Goal of heroic feet that never lagged,—
A little man in trousers, slightly jagged.[19]

Moody's fellow poet and friend, Edwin Arlington Robinson, put the matter more solemnly in "The Man against the Sky" (1915) when he sardonically considered the man who built "A living reason out of molecules / Why molecules occurred" and then took especial pride in "being what he must have been by laws."[20] As early as 1891 while at Harvard, Robinson had been influenced by Royce and in his poetry betrays something of that idealist philosopher's tough-minded optimism.[21] At any rate, in "The Man against the Sky" Robinson questions the wisdom of the man who sees with "mechanic eyes":

Are we no greater than the noise we make
Along one blind atomic pilgrimage
Whereon by crass chance billeted we go
Because our brains and bones and cartilage
Will have it so?   [p. 66]

In the 1880s, Mark Twain had adopted a deterministic point of view as personal conviction and confessed his belief that there is no such thing as "personal merit": "man is merely a machine automatically functioning without any of its help. . . . I observed that the human machine gets all its inspiration from the outside and is not capable of originating an idea of any kind in his own head."[22] Although Twain contended such a "gospel" secured a certain human happiness, his fable of progress in *A Connecticut Yankee in King Arthur's Court* (1889) raised this philosophy to the pitch of comic disaster. And *The Mysterious Stranger* (posthumously published in 1916) continued the theme and pushed it, illogically, into solipsism. Twain's acquired gospel of happiness in no way abated his own progress toward a personal bitterness and despair.

Joseph Conrad spoke more suppositiously and more desperately than Twain in a letter in 1897:

There is a—let us say—a machine. It evolved itself (I am severely scientific) out of a chaos of scraps of iron and behold!—it knits. I am horrified at the horrible work and stand appalled. I feel it ought to embroider—but it goes on knitting. You come and say: "this is all right; it's only a question of the right kind of oil. Let us use this—for instance—celestial oil and the machine shall embroider a most beautiful design in purple and gold." Will it? Alas, no. You cannot by any special lubrication make embroidery with a knitting machine. And the most withering thought is that the infamous thing has made itself; made itself without thought, without conscience, without foresight, without eyes, without heart. It is a tragic accident—and it has happened. . . . It knits us in and it knits us out. It has knitted time, space, pain, death, corruption, despair and all the illusions—and nothing matters.[23]

Images such as these testify to a darkening pessimism at the end of the century.[24] The mood was not general of course, though it was widespread among writers, and its causes could not be wholly attributed to a naturalistic worldview. For a variety of literary response to the prevailing evolutionary and deterministic point of view existed, and the reactions corresponded, roughly, to the three great branches of subjectivism, as James characterized them—sentimentalism, sensualism, and scientificism.[25] For a quarter of a century, led by William Dean Howells, American literary realists had combated the sentimental and falsely sanguine in literature. The sentimental and homiletic survived, nonetheless, and were as grandly indifferent to expressions of a despairing pessimism as they were to the practical counsel of Howells and other realists.

In 1904, for example, the *National Magazine* issued a call and promised a cash award for "heart throbs": literary examples of "wholesome good cheer, humor, comfort, hope—those things that make dark days endurable and sunny days enduring." And the readers responded, sending original compositions, anecdotes, and clippings they had saved of some of America's favorite fireside philosophers—Eugene Field, Frank L. Stanton, Ella Wheeler Wilcox, and Hezekiah Butterworth. The collection was published as *Heart Throbs in Prose and Verse: The Old Scrapbook* (1905), and readers were told that they were not apt to find within its pages any of the "artificial, and 'advanced' views of life and duty": "Agnosticism, destructive evangelism, the iconoclasm of faith, may attract attention, but do not awaken the loving loyalty of Anglo-Saxon, Celt and Norseman, and the races who have affiliated with these to build up the American people."[26]

Less ardent, and a good deal less nationalistic, was fin de siècle aestheticism. The art-for-art's-sake movement never flourished in America, partly because of traditions that demanded that art must have something to do with the uses of life. Americans, nonetheless, turned out to hear Oscar Wilde lecture, and they read Walter Pater and John Ruskin. The machine Conrad described continued to knit, however; it would not embroider. Neither the celestial oil of sentiment nor of aesthetic rebellion could make it turn out a design in purple and gold. The oppositions of fact and the ideal, life and art, were only a more restricted statement of the wider dilemma Eucken and so many others were addressing at this time. For the young Harvard student, Wallace Stevens, who desired to be a poet but whose practical inheritance counseled law or business instead, a personal conflict mirrored the larger cultural one and he recorded his dilemma privately and succinctly in a journal: "I must try not to be a dilettante— half-dream, half-deed. I must be all dream or all deed" (*SP* 71). Like so many others at the time, Stevens was caught between the harsh alternatives that defined the era.

Still a third reaction was possible—to accept and dramatize a universe of force and mechanical law. Literary naturalism, as advanced by Zola in "The Experimental Novel" (1880), took its cues from science and most particularly from Claude Bernard's *Introduction to the Study of Experimental Medicine* (1867). Such a novelist would maintain the detachment of a scientific observer and seek out the determinism of social behavior—this method in its capacity to master nature and reform society, Zola insisted, invested the naturalistic writer with a superior morality. The naturalist would remain largely indifferent to literary form and proceed according to proved facts and thereby "dissect piece by piece this human machinery in order to set it going through the influence of the environment."[27] "The metaphysical man is dead," wrote Zola; "our whole territory is transformed with the advent of the physiological man. No doubt 'Achilles' Anger,' 'Dido's Love,' will last forever on account of their beauty; but today we feel the necessity of analyzing anger and love, of discovering exactly how such passions work in the human being" (p. 54). American literary naturalists seldom conformed absolutely to these principles; nevertheless, theirs was a vigorous response to the times. Circumstance, however, conspired against the best of them—Stephen Crane and Frank Norris died young, and a publisher's delicate feeling delayed Dreiser (the limited printing of *Sister Carrie* in 1900 amounted to suppression). Besides, for most Americans, literary naturalists were still indecent and vulgar. Those artists who could not find inspiration in the physiological man or woman or could not treat experience with the necessary clinical detachment, those who still loved beauty and form, could, if they chose, embroider. But the machine would continue knitting. The ambitions of art and the requirements of life, of dream, and of deed seemed to run in opposite directions.

A mechanistic materialism, shorn of its optimistic and progressive features, contributed its share to the disillusionment of artists at the turn of the century, yet that mood was on the verge of dramatic if momentary change. In 1913, the neo-Hegelian philosopher Bernard Bosanquet delivered the Adamson Lecture at Manchester and sought to describe the new situation for philosophy. The situation was indeed new by 1913, but the essential conflict between scientific materialism and an absolutist idealism persisted. Bosanquet was responding in particular in his lecture to the "new realists," the most recent group of philosophers to advance a materialistic philosophy. He cited James Hinton on the meaning of materialism: "What a world is that which science pronounces real; dark, cold, and shaking like a jelly."[28] This was the view that the British idealist Bosanquet and others like him meant to transcend and that expressed the same sort of discontent Eucken addressed in his Nobel lecture.

III

In 1912, Rudolf Eucken analyzed the relation between the problem of knowledge on the one hand and the problem of life on the other. The result was a volume published, naturally enough, under the title *Knowledge and Life* (1913) and prepared, he said, when his approaching visit to the United States was very much on his mind. That latter fact may account for the special attention he paid to the modern conceptions of life as they were represented by pragmatism and the "biological view" (vitalism). For those were the philosophical positions enjoying particular favor in America in 1913—the first finding its native advocate in William James and the second, as an import of unprecedented popularity, being advanced by Henri Bergson. In any event, Eucken was troubled by the direction the current life philosophies were taking: "The incessant expansion of Life towards the inclusion of what is great and what is small shows Life as being far too rich and coloured—far too mobile and variable—to be reduced into the forms and formulas of Thought. The stream of Life breaks through the dam which was meant to enclose it, and flows out of its limited enclosure into the open and the boundless. At the same time, there springs up a strong antipathy towards all attempted adjustments of Life to Thought: stronger and stronger grows the aspiration after more immediacy, more intuition and more originality."[29]

Although Eucken found much to admire in both pragmatism and vitalism, his own view was that life itself implied far more than could be discerned in the narrow attention these philosophies gave to it. The first method seemed content to connect life with the individual and society, the second with nature. Both converted the idea into mere utility (pp. 96–97). He who would study life by analyzing consciousness undervalues the *"deed-character"* of life revealed in a "universal history." Such a history teaches that thought and life are superior to time and contingency: "He who presents no counter effect to the flux of Time falls inevitably into a destructive relativism" (pp. 302–3). The whole history of life revealed to Eucken a spiritual world and a spiritual life that entered into human consciousness at the level of the act but were in no way dependent on it, an eternal promise that could be furthered by concrete activity in a living present.

Eucken was openly Christian and unashamedly optimistic, though still urgent in his pleas for a rejuvenation of a spiritual reality. However, his philosophical statements were but a single ingredient in the intellectual chowder that characterized the pre–World War I years. Only months before Eucken delivered his Nobel speech, the Third International Congress of Philosophy was held in Heidelberg and became an arena for a heated contest between German rationalists and Anglo-American pragmatists. It was the meeting of two distinct worldviews—the first, the most recent example of a noble tradition of rationalistic thought reaching back to Kant and Hegel; the second, aggressively anti-intellectual and (despite William James's claim that pragmatism was but a new name for an old way of thinking) of fairly recent origin. The Third Congress marked a significant event in intellectual history; for as Oron J. Hale remarks, "Here the nineteenth century encountered the twentieth. To the former life was thought and truth was absolute; to the latter life was action and truth was psychological."[30] This observation may be an oversimplification, but Eucken's philosophical position, at any rate, represented a philosophical merger of the terms of the recent conflict in Heidelberg.

The Fourth International Congress of Philosophy, held in Bologna in 1911 and in which Bergson figured so centrally, continued, in its essentials, the same debate. For the moment, a discussion of Bergson's own philosophical position is not necessary. I need only note that for several reasons he is a preeminently important figure to this study. First, he seemed to exalt the role of the artist both as a master of intuitive and absolute perception and knowledge and as a specimen of the truly free and whole individual. I say seemed because Bergson only incidentally elevated the artist to this status. He often suggested that the philosopher might take his or her cues from the example of the artist, and he drew lavish analogies between philosophical intuition and creative experience. And he emphasized the role of creative activity as central to historical and evolutionary development. But Bergson consistently argued that philosophical knowledge of the sort he advocated was altogether superior to aesthetic intuition. Nevertheless, the Bergsonian philosophy gave to certain artists a sense of authority and confidence in their vocation and reconciled the activity of art to the uses of life.

A second and more immediately significant reason is that Bergson challenged the overwhelming dominance of the naturalistic point of view that was the cultural inheritance of the nineteenth century. Pragmatists such as William James or F. C. S. Schiller might continue to worry and aggravate rationalists and, to a lesser degree, scientists, but Bergson baffled and outraged them. William James impishly delighted in clearing up the fuzzy thinking of those he disdainfully referred to as the "intellectualists." Bergson, on the other hand, challenged the authority of the intellect itself. He particularly seemed to deprive scientists of their method and their analytic tools, or at least he relegated their findings to a certain subordinate kind of knowledge. Again, I say seemed because Bergson himself earnestly sought an active cooperative effort between science and philosophy. But, as we shall see in the next chapter, Bergson's historical and popular significance has at least as much to do with what he seemed to be saying as with what he actually said.

A third and related reason for the centrality of Bergson in this study is that he served as a kind of deliverer from an oppressive, mechanistic point of view that lingered in the popular mind well beyond the time when scientific evidence provided a proper foundation for the synthetic philosophy of Herbert Spencer or the materialistic monism of Ernst Haeckel. For scientists, this view had years before begun to break down at several points. Studies of light and electricity had disputed the assumption of classical physics that there existed a cosmic ether through which light must travel. The laws of conservation of energy and the indivisibility of matter also had been recently tested and found wanting. And several papers delivered at the Fourth International Congress of Philosophy challenged the once secure view that scientific laws were themselves immutable.

Henry Adams, who was more troubled by the onset of the evident chaos that was to be the twentieth century than by the material uniformity that was the nineteenth, made it his business to study this scientific renovation of the world. As a historian, he could comprehend the movements and shifts of the past so long as the "swerves" were part of a continuous movement. But, as he wrote in his *Education* (privately printed in 1907), in 1900, the "continuity snapped":

> Vaguely conscious of the cataclysm, the world sometimes dated it from 1893, by the Roentgen rays, or from 1898, by the Curie's radium; but in 1904, Arthur Balfour announced on the part of British science that the human race without exception had lived and died in a world of illusion until the last year of the century. The date was convenient, and convenience was truth.

The child born in 1900 would, then, be born into a new world which would not be a unity but a multiple.[31]

At the same time that Adams looked to the future with a trembling sympathy, Ernst Haeckel, very nearly Adams's exact contemporary, looked back over the scientific advances of the nineteenth century with a self-satisfied equanimity. For the zoologist/philosopher Haeckel was unregenerate, and his *The Riddle of the Universe* (1899) reaffirmed that the world was still very much a unity, not a multiplicity. All natural phenomena, including the soul, are governed by the "law of substance," the "highest cosmological law."[32] Religious faith is fetid superstition. The age-old debate between the determinist and indeterminist has been settled once and for all and absolutely in favor of the determinist (p. 131). "The anthropomorphic notion of a deliberate architect and ruler of the world has gone forever. . . . the 'eternal, iron laws of nature' have taken his place" (p. 261). The law of mechanical causality rules the universe and life and the human mind; "it is the steady, immovable pole-star, whose clear light falls on our path throughout the dark labyrinth of the countless separate phenomena" (p. 366).

Haeckel's book was an anachronism. Despite the confident assertions of the concluding paragraphs that his materialistic monism was supported by all modern scientists with the "courage" to accept a "rounded philosophical system" (p. 382), modern science, it appears, was craven. The German scientist who boldly undertook to explain all of human history spoke from a foundation science itself could no longer support. And the American historian who timidly attempted to trace the tendencies of modern science found that historical continuity had snapped under the strain. Between the poles of these attitudes existed innumerable others, and if in fact a nineteenth-century naturalistic philosophical view was fast collapsing under the accumulating weight of discrete scientific discoveries, it remained nevertheless a living intellectual issue.

Certainly, this view was vital enough for Eucken to address it in his Nobel speech. Bergson concluded his popular *Creative Evolution* with a criticism of Spencer's evolutionism, though by that time Spencer's intellectual dominance and popular appeal had long since faded. Anachronism or not, *The Riddle of the Universe* was widely translated and sold some 300,000 copies by 1914.[33] As Thomas Cochran and William Miller have shown, a Spencerian philosophy fit American cultural and political ideals so well that it was often enlisted by industrialists as a point from which to attack the reforming policies of the New Deal.[34] In the 1920s, George Herbert Mead in his lectures at the University of Chicago (posthumously published as *Movements of Thought in the Nineteenth Century* [1936]) was perfectly right to remind his students again and again that the postulates of science in no way constitute a dogma. But his very insistence on the point indicates a recognition that it *felt* like a dogma. In England, in lectures addressed to the business and industrial community on "contemporary tendencies of thought," R. F. Alfred Hoernlé wrote in 1923: "Every student of the influence of natural science, and more especially physics, upon philosophy is aware that, next to the concept of 'matter,' the concept of 'machine' or 'mechanism' has presented the greatest obstacles to a synoptic theory of the universe. Or, rather, we should say that 'materialism' and the 'mechanical theory of nature,' going hand in hand, have themselves claimed to be the one all-sufficing synopsis."[35] Yet, as Hoernlé attempted to demonstrate throughout his lectures, physical theories of nature have been tested against the actual data of living experience and have required radical modifications in the way one thinks about the world. In fact, attempts at a renovation of the worldview had been most vigorous at least a decade earlier, when the nineteenth-century machine was being dismantled piece by piece.

In part, the philosophical controversies that flourished in the first years of this century and commanded the attention of nonspecialists with surprising urgency derived from the repeated use of terminology made equally available to the layman, the scientist, and the philosopher alike. Charles Peirce often lamented the "inexactitude" of William James's phrasing of difficult philosophical questions, considering it "downright bad morals so to misuse words." In order for philosophy to become a science, Peirce remarked to his friend, it ought to have a "recognized technical vocabulary, composed of words so unattractive that loose thinkers are not tempted to use them."[36] Such "inexactitude" was not restricted to James, however, and many intellectuals, without his genial verbal facility, meant to carry the debate into the streets and to make their thinking attractive to large numbers.

A remarkable fact about the philosophical literature of this period is how much of it was originally delivered as public lectures. As a result, complex philosophical concepts were often simplified and diluted for general consumption. To a significant degree, a lively interest in ideas thrived on the sort of available, nontechnical vocabulary Peirce deplored. Antino-

mies such as "inheritance and environment, naturalism and supernatural-
ism, mechanism and organism—all these and other considerations," writes
Robert Scoon, "formed a welter of ideas that somehow were coherent
enough to conflict and yet incoherent enough to permit a fresh systemati-
zation in religion and philosophy."[37] As we shall see, fresh systematiza-
tions proliferated in America during the prewar years and were by no
means restricted to religion and philosophy. *Life, modernism, personality,
idealism,*[38] *individual, evolution,* and any number of other terms had an
intellectual vogue at the time and the capacity to tease one into thought or
to irritate one's prepossessions.

The term modernism is of particular interest in this regard because it
had a special currency during this era and, historically considered, bears
only a faint resemblance to the literary modernism associated with Pound
and Eliot. And considerable historical misunderstanding may result when
one applies, retroactively, the term modern, as Eliot and others defined it,
to its earlier and rather frequent appearance. In *Main Currents of Modern
Thought* (1909), Eucken declared the concept to figure so centrally in
current thinking and to so divide men's minds that it required some pro-
longed consideration. He traced the word back to the sixth century and
showed its various historical significations. In his own day, he found the
term to have acquired an alarming popularity and to be identified for the
most part with a "merely human thirst for newness."[39]

A genuine modernism, he said, was one that sought to revitalize the
spiritual life and set it working in the present moment, but a simple
appetite for novelty wore the label modern as well. This latter attitude, for
the philosopher, was but a superficial modernism, though it claimed the
interest of a considerable number: "Thus we have an exaggeration and
overvaluation of the new. The new is valued merely because it is new,
however empty or foolish it may be in itself." This superficial modernism
has contributed to a "wretched pseudo-culture, an attempt on the part of
the semi-educated mass to dominate the spiritual movement of humanity"
(p. 339). (The last thing Eliot and Pound wanted to do, of course, was to
associate themselves with the "semi-educated" masses or to promote a
"pseudo-culture.")[40] A superficial modernism rejects the past because the
past is dead; it is loud and aggressive; it asserts the claims of the individual
personality over and above historical tradition.

Generally, modernism tended to be associated with religious controversy and especially with a philosophy of immanence rather than transcendence (which, as Eucken also points out, the contemporary world seemed

to favor).[41] Though it rejected mechanism and was inclined to deny miracles and ritual, the modernist movement in religion accepted the findings of science. And this movement had a wider and vaguer application as well. For modernism meshed nicely with the movement and claims of *youth* (another term that had a certain intellectual currency and weight). Youth was often associated less with guileless charm than with a certain potency, a biological force, active and authoritative by virtue of its own radical energies. The European emphases and consolidating authority of youth, coupled with a confused sense of identity and purpose, have been impressively traced by Robert Wohl in *The Generation of 1914*.[42] In America, the emphases were different, but the culture of youth found a leading and most articulate spokesman in Randolph Bourne, at once an ardent feminist, political radical, and acute literary critic.

In a sense, to be a modernist in the superficial way Eucken declaimed meant one had opened an intellectual charge account and could shop around among the several modes and schools of thought available from 1910 to 1916. If the modern world had indeed become a multiple, surely some liberality ought to have been allowed to those making the adjustment. The challenge of modern life, as Wallace Stevens put it years later but referring to this era of enormous intellectual and social change, was to find "what will suffice" (*CP* 239). And in America, one's choices were naturally guided by familiar national predispositions. Henry May isolates three articles of common faith as dominating the Progressive Era of 1912, and each was a survival from the nineteenth century.[43] Each, too, had been somewhat modified or compromised to accommodate the new consciousness and the new reality.

The first of these articles of American faith was a steadfast conviction in the eternal reality of moral values. The big words—justice, patriotism, charity, decency, and so forth—were a strongly felt and unquestioned part of the American vocabulary. As we have already seen, an idealized morality might look in opposite directions for support. Bastardized or diluted notions of idealism and evolutionism were ready partners in the genteel tradition. The first, idealism, had its origins in the moral strenuousness of the Puritans, usually as it had been cheerfully and eloquently recommended by Emerson or as it survived for Americans in their own day, most notably and intelligently, in Josiah Royce. This idealism found popular expression in the fireside philosophers whose homilies made one's heart throb. The second possibility, as we have also seen, was to adapt or to accept the adaptations of a Darwinian evolutionism and apply them to moral and social progress. By 1912, a strict evolutionism had loosened up enough to allow some creative principle to figure in one's biological destiny, and Bergson in *L'évolution créatrice* (1907; translated as *Creative Evolution*, 1911) had gone farther than most in establishing a creative life impetus as absolutely fundamental to the evolutionary process.

The same allowance enabled one to sustain a belief in May's second article of American faith—the belief in progress from which the era took its name. Virtually from the time of colonialization, Americans had been willing to believe in some form of manifest destiny (whether authorized by a community of saints, the beneficence of "Nature's God," or a universal and mechanical law of progress) without succumbing, absolutely, to feelings of doubt or despair about their own part in the process. Yet by 1912, a paradoxical progressive faith that openly manifested itself as an urgent appeal for reform at the same time that it celebrated longstanding American ideals had been eroded, whether or not the mass of men and women consciously recognized it. A moralistic progressivism was, as May has noted, an "unstable compound," and the confidence of Americans tended to ride upon the surfaces of life, unmindful of or unworried by the several contradictions of their faith. Somehow, there remained a general air of triumph and security; critics and doubters, such as Thorstein Veblen, Charles Beard, or Lincoln Steffens, only nibbled at the margins of that popular confidence.

The third article of American faith was a belief in culture—a devotion to the arts and literature (mostly British) that revealed and supported those same indestructible values. But the available and agreeable avenues of literary endeavor at least tended to draw readers and writers alike away from the active experience of life as lived. In 1907, William James announced that "the earth of things, long thrown into the shadow by the glories of the upper ether, must resume its rights,"[44] and Wallace Stevens, who had grown up under this shadow, only a few years later engaged in a lifelong project to become a poet of the earth. Stevens's poems would attempt to do away with the "vast ventriloquism" of intellectualism, as he wrote near the end of his life, to give "not ideas about things, but the thing itself" (*CP* 534). In 1912, however, there was still a standard literary tradition, tarnished but holding fast to its severe authority in American culture. Literature, it was popularly held, was meant to uphold certain standards of conduct, belief, and refinement. That a certain restlessness and dissatisfaction with this tradition existed is cogently revealed, albeit in blustering overstatement, in Van Wyck Brooks's essay "America's Coming of Age" (1915).

Brooks identified a Puritan moralistic inheritance as anathema to the creative imagination. In vain, he looked back over a native literary tradition that possessed the force of the human personality. Except in Whitman, Brooks saw no organic relation between the American artist and the social community. Art and life kept only a superficial acquaintance, and the reformer's zeal suggested to him the hypocritical frame of mind of the businessman who retires at sixty and collects pictures.[45] The average American of this generation has grown up surrounded by "a sort of orgy of lofty examples, moralized poems, national anthems and baccalaureate sermons; until he is charged with all manner of ideal purities, ideal honorabilities, ideal femininities, flag-wavings and skyscrapings of every sort,—until he comes to feel in himself the hovering presence of all manner of fine potentialities, remote, vaporous and evanescent as a rainbow" (p. 24).

In America, the "hovering" of beauty and the satisfaction of the ideal as somehow existing above or beyond human experience had been characteristic of literary expression for some time and were part and parcel of the genteel tradition Brooks and others came to deplore. However, as Howard Mumford Jones points out, this same tradition performed a valuable and double service by preserving an important and usable romantic tradition and by yoking it to the technical demands of craft and form.[46] The result nevertheless was all too often a strain of artificial sentiment decked out with mere literary ornament. But the same tradition challenged the crass materialism of the day and opposed to it a poetry that spoke from "soul to soul." Late nineteenth-century Americans, as T. J. Jackson Lears remarks, were starved for real life, and "the decline of autonomous [sic] selfhood lay at the heart of the modern sense of unreality."[47] Idealists created appetites for the eternal only eternity could supply. And the implicit scarcity psychology of naturalists demanded that psychic resources be thriftily husbanded against depletion. Both stood in dramatic opposition to the psychology of possibility and abundance.

When Brooks called for the establishment and reassertion of personality in America's literature, he was requiring of art an active force that, a generation earlier, had no solid intellectual foundation. The self, from a purely naturalistic point of view, could eventually be reduced to a complex chemical compound or more immediately be identified as a series of affective psychological states—in both cases reducible to familiarly mechanical operations. From the idealist point of view, the essential self, or soul, was immaterial substance hovering above contingency, uncontaminated by temporal experience. These were the harsh alternatives Eucken and others had been rethinking for some time. For William James, both presupposed closed systems that prohibited the introduction of time, chance, or possibility. "Is not the notion of eternity being given at a stroke to omniscience," he asked, "only just another way of whacking upon us the block-universe, and of denying that possibilities exist?"[48]

Whatever *life* might mean, whether for naturalist or idealist, it did not seem to be something in which the force of human personality might take an active part. And where was one to find it? In the determining circumstance that made Stephen Crane's Maggie a prostitute, or in the surfacing of ancient and brutal instincts that made Frank Norris's McTeague a murderer? Did it consist of those common experiences and smiling aspects William D. Howells defended and, a generation later, H. L. Mencken and Sinclair Lewis would deride? Did life and personality consist of so many discrete affective states strung like beads upon the string of consciousness, existing wholly within the realm of scientific calculation? Or in an earth-freed soul, generally intolerant of the cynical complaint of an Ambrose Bierce or the lowbrow humor of a Mark Twain? Whether life and personality were considered as a mechanism or an idealism, they were part of a unitary principle describable without reference to the currency of human experience. In America, William James in particular had fashioned his large and tolerant *Principles of Psychology* (1890) by challenging both positions, though he tended to give rather more play to the idealists than most scientists were inclined to do and rather less to the naturalists than they had come to expect. And he did so in a lucid and enjoyable prose that made this book an assigned text in the classroom and a popular favorite in the marketplace.

Of the numerous and various strands of influence that contributed to the cultural mitosis of these prewar years, the genial and gentlemanly voice of William James is surely one. With the appearance of his two-volume psychology, which was twelve years in the making, James's reputation was well launched, and the briefer version two years later extended his influence. In his psychology James had already begun to unstiffen conventional ways of thinking about reality and thought, something he particularly insisted upon in his *Pragmatism*. With regard to human identity, or "self" (the authentic personality Brooks demanded in literary effort), James in his *Principles of Psychology* had placed a premium on feeling and experience as a positive and legitimate part of knowing. He postulated, on scientific grounds, that thought must occur as a stream (thus disarming the associationist of his intellectual construction of consciousness as occurring in discernible states); that the "mind dust" theory was logically and empirically indefensible, admitting the "soul" theory to be a hypothesis that better accommodated the facts of psychological observation and was more amenable to solving a variety of psychological difficulties; and that a persistent methodological problem he named the "psychologist's fallacy" (which resided in a *"confusion of his [the psychologist's] own standpoint with that of the mental fact* about which he is making his report")[49] called into question the objectivity of scientific psychological investigation altogether.

Each of these observations in the *Principles of Psychology*, and a dozen others besides, limbered up psychological investigation and permitted one to acknowledge a plurality of selves both actual and potential. James never reduced the "I" to the man who wears my hat, but neither did he exclude that fact from legitimate consideration. Nor did he exclude the possibility of a "Self of selves," but if it existed it was not in the condition of a timeless absolute but in the "collection" of the "peculiar motions in the head or between the head and throat" (p. 301). For such a self is felt and, as with an empirical ego, is known by its "warmth and intimacy" of relation with the individual consciousness.

As Ralph Barton Perry noted, the *Principles of Psychology* had established for James a "half-finished" theory of knowledge.[50] The direction he began there was a movement toward an organic and scientific metaphysics, but the direction he took was more purely philosophical, moving over the years from his psychology to his pragmatism on to his pluralism and culminating finally, late in his life, with his essays on radical empiricism. There were others who pursued the course of a scientific or, in a more restricted sense, a biological metaphysic. And James's *Principles of Psychology* had helped prepare the American public to accept such a system.

IV

Part of the "half-finished" quality of James's epistemology involved his allowance for a certain "empirical parallelism" (usually referred to as a psychophysical parallelism) in determining the relation between physiological occurrences in the body and the brain and metaphysical operations of the soul and the mind. This, as he admitted, was a middle road, not meant to establish a dualism so much as a pluralism entitling materialists and idealists alike to believe as they will, so long as each party limbered up their relative positions enough to accept the facts of experience. James still intended his psychology to be "positivistic and non-metaphysical" (p. 182), but only in a properly provisional way.

The same popularity that gave James's philosophy currency also prevented him from attempting to construct and elaborate a systematic metaphysics until late in his life. Constant requests for public lectures, along with other demands on his time, limited the necessary and sustained attention he could give to the purer philosophical enterprise he engaged in when he began to develop the implications of "pure experience" and a radical empiricism.[51] In 1902, James characterized his own philosophical development as a kind of "intellectual higgledy-piggledyism."[52] It was surely not that, but his pluralism (implicit in his *Principles of Psychology* and explicit in later lectures and essays) proved too disturbingly relative and arbitrary for many of his readers.

The "pluralistic and restless" universe James described impressed one of his friends as sickening, "like the sight of the horrible motion of a mass of maggots in their carrion bed." James cordially accepted the analogy and pushed it further—any determinism, with its necessary carrion, and "with no possible maggots to eat the latter up, violates my sense of moral reality through and through."[53] In fact, a universe without possibility was, for James and others, a carcass universe. Several vitalistic philosophers of the time, Bergson among them, shared this view and were attacking a materialistic mechanism at just that point.

The naturalistic philosophy, they felt, was excluding life from its determinations. Even in their methods, it seemed, naturalists were seeking out the dead in order to establish a foundation for observations about life. The English vitalist Marcus Hartog noted that the chemist typically isolates the organism he proposes to study. He "resorts to crystallisation, precipitation, filtration, evaporation, and congelation; he utilises temperatures ranging far above the 30–40° C of living beings, and solvents such as pure alcohol, petrol, benzol, and ether, which are deadly to the organism."[54] Is it any wonder, then, that the naturalists should envision a universal husk of mechanical relation, having so meticulously excluded the living principle from their considerations? Such a method, to borrow an analogy from James made in another connection, was like attempting to study the dark by turning up the lamp very quickly.

To an extent the vitalistic school attempted to reaffirm the cogency of an earlier, romantic principle of a vital force operating in and through all of organic life. And vitalists tended to do so by examining ever more critically and minutely the concept of the machine as a model for living organisms. If the metaphysical man were indeed dead, the physiological man could not be sufficiently explained, they thought, without some recourse to a metaphysical principle. For living organisms are capable of certain adjustments that violate, both logically and experimentally, the assumptions of mechanism, and machines, by their very definition as structures composed of parts, can neither reproduce nor repair themselves. Both machines and organisms may raise energy to a higher and more concentrated type, but the machine cannot store energy within itself. Machines, in a limited sense, may be said to possess a teleology, but they are not self-directing and are limited in their capacity to adjust to circumstance. These are among the more obvious limitations vitalists found in the mechanistic model when it was applied to biological organisms.

Hans Driesch, the German biologist-turned-philosopher, became the most authoritative spokesman for a new and pure vitalistic movement and may serve as an adequate representative for it. Unlike Bergson, who came by his biological metaphysic less from laboratory experiment than philosophical inquiry, Driesch derived his vitalism from systematic scientific investigation. Driesch developed a highly technical biological metaphysic that further challenged the mechanistic hypothesis, and he did so most extensively in his Gifford lectures for 1907 and 1908, which were subsequently published as the massive, two-volume *The Science and Philosophy of the Organism* (1908). There and elsewhere in his writings Driesch tested the mechanistic theory wholly within the experimental tradition of scientific induction and drew from his own experiments and those of others certain metaphysical conclusions.

In *The Problem of Individuality* (1914), Driesch outlined the three proofs of vitalism he had established more elaborately in the Gifford lectures. The first proof considered the question of whether or not there are in organisms "*whole-making processes* sui generis, i.e. *processes not reducible to the forms of inorganic becoming.*"[55] To this end he revived the study of morphogenesis, or the study of the physiology of form, which, according to Driesch, had been all but abandoned half a century earlier under the reigning influence of Darwinian mechanism.[56] Driesch conducted experiments on the embryo of a sea urchin at the four-cell stage. After destroying three of the four cells, he found that a complete, though smaller, embryo might be developed out of the remaining cell.

He concluded that such a process cannot fit the mechanistic thesis, which assumes a systematic arrangement of parts, but that the embryo instead constituted what he called a "harmonious equipotential system." In such a system each of the four cells possessed equal "prospective potency" to develop a complete embryo. Driesch observed the same phenomenon not only in the regeneration of other organisms but also in the restitution and repair of certain life-forms. Such potentialities in living structures, he concluded, cannot come from outside the organisms but must be localized within them. In what he termed "harmonious equipotential systems," "*every* cell of the original system can play *every* single role in morphogenesis; *which* role it will play is merely a function of its position."[57] This conclusion renders the machine theory an absurdity in embryology at least because the very concept of the machine is as a specific arrangement of parts.

This first proof enabled Driesch to assert a fundamental principle of vitalism—the autonomy of life. His second proof supported this conclusion from a different angle. Harmonious equipotential systems are typically simple forms of life, such as the blastula or the infusorian. In "complex equipotential systems," observable in the cambium layer of higher plants and in almost the complete organism of some lower plants, innumerable cells develop from a single ovary, and each cell is capable of further development. One cannot imagine a miniature machine within each of these eggs because the egg has divided any number of times before becoming what it is; and how, asks Driesch, "could a 'machine' be divided and divided and—*always remain the same?*" (p. 22). This observation further combines with the problem of inheritance. Because an egg cannot be regarded as bearing within itself an "embryological machine," some "agent that arranges" the functions and systems of organic life and that is passed from generation to generation is necessary. That agent, he insists, "*cannot* be of a machine-like, physico-chemical character" (p. 23).

Driesch's third and final proof has to do with the "physiology of movements" and more particularly with concrete actions. Considered as a biological rather than a psychological phenomenon, action derives from the historical basis of the organic system (that is, the history of individual experience) and the specific stimuli that elicit a reaction. But this historical basis merely defines the limits and possibilities of an action and is not to be considered as the mechanical sum of remembered psychic occurrences or stored-up sensorimotor reactions. In human beings, at least, reaction is not the exact reproduction of a former action in all its specificity; something more is added. One's history provides the basis for future action not for the repetition of past actions in the present. Moreover, stimuli and reactions are themselves unities, not parts as in a machine, and cannot be related to one another part by part.

Together, these three proofs provided the biological foundation for Driesch's central metaphysical proposition. Since there are whole classes of facts in organic life that cannot be accounted of the mechanical or physicochemical type but seem to have an autonomy of their own, an autonomous agent must be at work in these vital processes. He gives to this principle the Aristotelian name entelechy. Because this principle helps explain certain organic processes, he asserts that entelechy is an agent or factor in and of nature. In this concept one has a name for specific happenings in organic becoming that are peculiarly nonmechanical in their operations: "Entelechy is bound to material conditions, not for its existence but in its effects. The so-called material *continuity* of life now means simply that there are certain areas of matter, certain material systems, embracing an enormous number of possibilities of happening in the form of differences or 'potential'" (p. 38).

As for the origin of this principle, Driesch can only say that it is unknown. We are "*absolutely unable to say anything whatever about the origin of life*. Life is there, and is transferred from generation to generation in material continuity; and this material continuity means a continuity of systems under control" (p. 38). Moreover, entelechy is a supersensual agency without the character of energy or force; it has wholly to do with the arrangement of systems and is not to be confused with an earlier hylozoism, for the living principle is not distributed evenly throughout the universe. Nor is Driesch's entelechy an unmodified version of a romantic life force, considered as an independent form of energy. Somehow, though, this principle works in and through organic life at the cellular level and makes possible individuals as coherent, self-directing biological systems.

Driesch's entelechy permitted him to argue for a dynamic teleology of organic life that is distinct from the static teleology of physicochemical processes. And he was representative of other vitalists in insisting that the concept in no way violated the law of conservation of energy because it is a supersensual, nonenergetic entity that occurs in connection with physical life and is limited by natural contingency. It is an agency of arrangement not of alteration. Driesch went even further in declaring that entelechy is a part of the "givenness" of nature itself. However, vitalistic doctrine did attempt to dislodge or at least drastically modify the second, and more disturbing, law of thermodynamics, the law of entropy.

Because the entelechy of organic life can "suspend" or "redirect" the operations of mechanical causality,[58] this agency introduces a supervening principle that repudiates mechanism and also disallows the application of the law of entropy to the realm of organic becoming. *"Entelechy,"* writes Driesch, "though *not capable of enlarging the amount of the diversity of composition of a given system, is capable of augmenting its diversity of distribution in a regulatory manner,* and it does so by transforming a system of *equally* distributed *potentialities* into a system of *actualities* which are *unequally* distributed."[59] Such a principle, in other words, constantly introduces new and productive tensions into life processes, and new and heterogeneous realities are the result. It does so through the coordination and arrangement of existing energies and in that role contributes to a nonmechanistic becoming that is nonetheless teleological.[60]

Further summary of Driesch's system is unnecessary. He is representative of the larger vitalistic movement, and the general implications of his philosophy, which he termed a "subjective idealism," indicate the contours of the whole school. Because Driesch was devoted to keeping the connections and, as a rule, the methods of philosophy and science closely tied, his system was vulnerable precisely for the reasons Bergson identified in his lecture at the Fourth Congress in Bologna. One can easily see how fundamentally altered, if not completely demolished, the concept of entelechy and the "proofs" of vitalism are by the introduction of the scientific discovery of DNA, for example. Moreover, even though his metaphysics did serve to scrutinize and criticize the mechanistic synthesis on its own grounds, his philosophy did not lead to the formulations of new scientific hypotheses or to scientific discovery. The assumptions of mechanism remained more valuable in the laboratory.

Nevertheless, the new vitalism loosened up the strict determinism of naturalism by forcing it to recognize the activity and existence of autonomous life-forms acting in coherent ways altogether beyond the determinations of mathematical calculation and capable of slipping the bonds of mechanical necessity. Vitalism inserted its own version of pluralism into the carrion host of the universe, for entelechy appears only here and there in organic processes. But where it does appear, the principle introduces possibility and freedom into the scheme of things. More importantly, vitalism attempted to do so wholly within the realm of scientific principles and methods. Driesch admitted at least the possibility of an encompassing "primary entelechy." Even so, such a unitary principle could not be considered to have created an absolute reality but merely to have ordered certain parts of it. For he insisted that entelechy was a scientific, not a metaphysical, concept and observable only in organic life-forms. Though Driesch perceived in his system certain "windows" to God or the Absolute, they were clouded by obscurity that only science could cleanse. He concluded his *Science and Philosophy of the Organism* by noting that the concept of God remained the "eternal task" of science itself and ought to direct and call forth its best efforts and energies.[61]

German and Anglo vitalism was never popular in America, though it did have a detectable influence in England and may have contributed something to a developing modernist literary theory.[62] Despite the meticulous avoidance of the antirational aspects of an earlier vitalism, it nevertheless suggested to some a reemergent romanticism. Driesch recognized this tendency and was careful to distinguish his system from pantheism, for example. He constructed an elaborate vitalistic logic of becoming that kept it somewhat within the positivistic tradition. In the vitalistic scheme of Henri Bergson, however, a full-blown neoromanticism surfaced and captivated a considerable number of men and women happy to be rid of the legacy of mechanism but still anxious for a unitary and comprehensible philosophy of existence. In America and elsewhere, as we shall see in the next chapter, the Bergsonian influence amounted to a popular craze.

Bergson cannot be precisely identified with the vitalists per se, and he is perhaps best described as a maverick vitalist. The Bergsonian philosophy was, and is, difficult to label and characterize. In the prewar years, when Bergson was at the height of his influence and popularity, his philosophy was variously referred to as temporalism, evolutionism, neoromanticism, modernism, vitalism, and, perhaps most accurately because it was so uniquely his own, as "Bergsonism." Only as a matter of convenience and convention shall I refer to him from time to time as a vitalist. Still, there are several points in which he was in essential agreement with the vitalistic philosophers.

Bergson, too, tied much of his system to physiological and biological evidence, but he tied it with the slipknot that was his metaphysical method. Like the vitalists, he was profoundly interested in life as a self-evident and comprehensive evolving force that could not be explained by a materialistic mechanism, yet here too he separated himself from conventional vitalistic assumptions by rejecting internal finality (or teleology) and individuality as adequate representations of this principle. Organized elements may indeed constitute self-directing individuals in a special sense, he thought, but individuals are never sufficiently independent to possess a vital principle unique to themselves—one cannot mark exactly where an individual begins and leaves off. If there is a fundamental harmony in life, it exists behind its manifold appearances, in the original, unitary push of a life impulse that has continually divided and subdivided and sought to realize itself in innumerable manifestations of particular life-forms. And Bergson, like other vitalists, attacked with a marvelous grace and ingenuity the mechanistic point of view, not only in psychology and biology but even in physics.

Along with the vitalists and the later James, Bergson resisted a psycho-parallelism that put matter on one side of the metaphysical equation and mind on the other. He did posit two distinct principles (spirit and matter), but they so interpenetrate one another and exist in pure states only by hypothesis that he avoided, or attempted to avoid, any sort of dualism. Because these principles were the psychological conditions of acting and thinking, they resembled what James referred to as "experience," immediately given to consciousness and requiring no transcendent and higher unifying agency to explain them. Bergson likewise shared with James the belief that, in James's words, "the directly apprehended universe needs, in short, no extraneous trans-empirical connective support, but possesses in its own right a concatenated or continuous structure."[63]

Bergson also argued that organic life is largely exempt from the law of entropy. Such a law, he said, is "as irrefutable as it is indemonstrable" (*CE* 244). Physicists consider energy as extended in space, and particles act as reservoirs for this force. Organisms, however, can store energy and release it in explosive surges. The movement of matter is continual descent, inert and relentless; the movement of spirit is constant ascent, the attempt to remount the slope of matter. Life cannot stop the course that matter would have it take according to material necessity (expressed as mechanical laws), but it can retard and redirect that course. For Bergson, this effort to prolong and realize the initial impulsion of life by seeking ever more efficient means to prolong itself in time is what a true evolutionism means: "The impetus of life, of which we are speaking, consists in a need of creation. It cannot create absolutely, because it is confronted with matter, that is to say with the movement that is the inverse of its own. But it seizes upon this matter which is necessity itself, and strives to introduce into it the largest possible amount of indetermination and liberty" (*CE* 251).

Life-forms, then, are not the caused result of a past determination but a prolongation of the past in the present; in a word, life endures in manifold appearances and evolves not at a steady, uniform rate but in alternating periods of relative rest and dynamic, eruptive bursts. Matter is not the condition of existence; it is the medium through which life asserts itself. Everything, including matter, rises up out of the original life impulse and takes on a multiform material character by virtue of the creative impetus. But this same impulse (which Bergson sometimes calls spirit, sometimes the élan vital) is "riveted" to the same material world it struggles to escape. Life itself emerges out of the tension between spirit and matter and occurs at those very points where these two principles intersect and compete for dominance.

The vitalistic features of the Bergsonian philosophy are implicated in a grander, more capacious vision of life and evolution and experience, and this vision derives principally from his earlier thinking about time and memory. But I have emphasized the biological character of Bergsonism because it best provides a context for understanding his historical significance. Whether one considers Bergsonism as a neoromanticism or a protomodernism (modernism here understood as a later intellectual and cultural movement and not a contemporaneous thirst for newness) perhaps makes little difference. The latter attitude has often yielded an interesting angle of vision on modernist literature,[64] yet it necessarily tends to highlight the epistemological and psychological qualities in Bergson, and especially his views on intuition, time, and memory. This emphasis is peculiarly appropriate to an investigation of the antecedents of modernism, but it gives insufficient attention to the reasons for Bergson's enormous influence and popularity in or around 1912. Such a method, in fact, attempts to analyze the evolution of a literary school out of the identified characteristics of modernism itself. Although useful for interpretation of certain texts, this method is not particularly useful for the sort of literary history I am describing here. To analyze the evolution of modernism out of the constituent parts of the already evolved is just the kind of mistake Bergson identified in the Spencerian version of evolution. Bergson's historical importance does not reside in the fact that he may have been coincidentally contributing to a twentieth-century philosophical or literary movement but in the fact that he seemed to be liberating the twentieth century from the nineteenth while at the same time restoring certain longstanding values and attitudes. He was attempting to solve the intellectual dilemmas of his own era in radically new ways.

In 1909, William James advised the public to read Bergson directly: "new horizons loom on every page you read. It is like the breath of the morning and the song of birds." Bergson had this stimulating effect because he seemed to free men and women from the closed system of the world as represented by either idealists or naturalists. Bergson "annuls the intellectualist veto," James said, "so that we now join step with reality with a philosophical conscience never quite set free before." Once readers have adopted the Bergsonian point of view, James continued, "they can never return again to their ancient attitude of mind."[65] Bergson was promoting a new multiform reality and a new progressive consciousness made all the more attractive by their liberating features rather than by a precise metaphysics or an alternate and rigid philosophical synthesis.

The world Bergson offered was alive with possibility; it was a universe animated with a creative power that was not remote from human experience and, in fact, was an intimate part of that experience. For A. O. Lovejoy and others, however, Bergson represented not an advance into future possibility so much as a return to an earlier romantic worldview. In a lecture delivered in 1913, Lovejoy tried to place Bergson in the history of ideas:

Bergson's chief significance, then, in relation to the history of modern thought, lies in this: that after a century's scientific progress, and after the intervening alliance of an evolutionary with a mechanistic philosophy of nature, he has revived this hypothesis of Romantic, activistic, or radical, evolutionism, as a serious philosophical doctrine; has once more insisted that the notions of evolution and of mechanism are not natural allies, but rather irreconcilable rivals for the primacy in our interpretation of the nature of things; and has declared that it is to the idea of real evolution that the primacy should be given. He has thus seemed to exorcise that spectre of a "block-world" which to much nineteenth century reflection had come to seem intolerable. He has presented to us the picture of a world which is at bottom alive; in which in truth there is at every moment "something doing" and something to do; in which there is a striving in progress which all *our* strivings help or hinder; in which, finally, the future contains the possibility of unimaginable fresh creations, of a real and cumulative enrichment of the sum of being.[66]

Though the romantic qualities Lovejoy discerned in Bergsonism typically found their analogues in German romanticism, and especially in Schelling, other Americans, particularly journalists, often likened Bergson to American romantics. Comparisons to Emerson and Whitman were strained but not altogether gratuitous. His emphasis upon experience and the self, as the true measurement of the real, and creative activity, as an active and beneficent principle in human progress and a participant in a universal movement, was familiar to the American sensibility. And the philosophical program he seemed to be offering was consonant with longstanding American philosophical interests.

As Charles Hartshorne has shown, creativity is a major theme in the American philosophical tradition, a philosophical category of cosmic significance,[67] and at the beginning of this century Bergson was the principal philosopher of creativity. Perhaps for this reason, among others, many Americans responded to Bergson with particular zest and fitted his system snugly into American traditions and preoccupations. But Bergson arrived at the comprehensive position he took when he published *Creative Evolution* only by degrees. He had formed his vitalism along different routes than the biological philosophers such as Driesch. The spaciousness he achieved in 1907 had been prepared for several years before by his address of two particular philosophical problems that are succinctly expressed by the titles of his earlier works—*Time and Free Will* and *Matter and Memory*. "Admit plurality," observed William James in *The Will to Believe* (1896), "and time may be its form."[68] Bergson's pluralism, at any rate, took this form in his first philosophical work, *Essai sur les données immédiates de la conscience* (1889; translated as *Time and Free Will*, 1910).

Attempting a comprehensive summary of Bergson's philosophy would be pointless for several reasons. First, it is a difficult system, highly metaphoric and resistant to easy synopsis; second, Americans tended to give it their own special interpretations; and finally, because I will refer to particular features of his philosophy throughout this study, there is little reason to give a detailed description of it here. Nevertheless, the general contours of his philosophical development can be sketched out easily enough.

The underlying method in Bergson's most significant books proceeds from the conviction that many philosophical problems derive from a common and historically conditioned mistake: philosophers and scientists alike err when they treat becoming as being, a process as a state, a movement as a fixity, time as space, though this tendency is habitual and, to a degree, natural to human thinking. His own perception of this mistake, Bergson recalled, occurred when he began to think about and attempted to refine the mechanics of Spencer's *First Principles*. He discovered, to his surprise, that the notion of time as lived completely eluded mathematical treatment:

> Ever since my university days I had been aware that duration is measured by the trajectory of a body in motion and that mathematical time is a line; but I had not yet observed that this operation contrasts radically with all other processes of measurement, for it is not carried out on an aspect or an effect representative of what one wishes to measure, but on something which excludes it. The line one measures is immobile, time is mobility. The line is made, it is complete; time is what is happening, and more than that, it is what causes everything to happen. [*CM* 12]

From this sudden revelation Bergson evolved a radically new philosophical method to accommodate it. Number and language, he discovered, are necessary but inadequate representations of the real, which is eternal flux; they are static symbols for a dynamic reality. Such intellectual substitutions, however, are absolutely necessary for the analytic operations of the intellect. For the intellect by its very nature can only operate on the already made; it cannot deal with real duration. For this reason, Bergson insisted that metaphysics is actually the "science which claims to dispense with symbols," whether they be numerical, logical, or linguistic (*IM* 9). A true empiricism is also a true metaphysics because it attempts to comprehend the absolute as it exists in duration and is perceived as change. In doing so, Bergsonian metaphysics completes the operations of the intellect, which studies an object from without, by engaging intuition, which attempts to seize the reality of an object from within by means of a certain "intellectual auscultation" (*IM* 36). Reality can never be adequately expressed in the rigid and static forms of symbols because symbols reify what is in its very nature a flowing. If we are to seek the real, then, as it lives in us and is perceived as change, we must by an effort of intellectual "sympathy," or intuition, immerse ourselves in this flux. Only by that means can we come to comprehend the real not as the made but as the being made.

This fundamental premise underlies Bergson's criticism of associationist psychology in *Time and Free Will*. Affective sensations cannot be reduced to multiple psychic states; for to do so is, quite simply, to mistake time for space, to arrange mentally side by side in space what, as felt in duration, varies in intensity not sequence, in quality not quantity. Time is heterogeneous not homogenous, he claimed, internally felt not externally observable. Time is the "fourth dimension" of human experience, but it is a psychological not a physical reality, varying according to the rhythms of individual becoming. Scientists, psychologists, and philosophers alike create false problems when, for the convenience of abstract thought, they make mechanical (and therefore predictable) what is fundamentally organic and fluid and, for all intents and purposes, unforeseeable and therefore free.

A free act, wrote Bergson, consists in the outward manifestation of an inner state, and "the self alone will have been the author of it," for the whole self exists at any moment (*TFW* 165–66). Freedom in its several acts repudiates the Spencerian notion of becoming as internal adjustment to external circumstance, for it seeks to preserve the felt continuity of the individual life. Thus, he might consider an ethical act as a certain authentic ripeness of personality that proceeds from a *moi fondamentale*, an inner self as opposed to the parasitic, social self that acts according to ideas received from without rather than those generated from within. For this reason, too, he might claim elsewhere that laughter is a natural response to automatic and mechanical behavior, a reaction to the artificial, stylized, and habitual modes of life that contradict an intuited sense of reality as change and possibility.[69]

Having abolished an associationist psychology in *Time and Free Will*, Bergson next contemplated the metaphysical relations of psychic life to the world in which it acts. He wished to affirm the reality of both spirit and matter and to this extent was admittedly dualistic, but he attempted to overcome this dualism by submitting his inquiry to the "verdict of consciousness" and of common sense (*MM* xi). His method was to that extent analogous to William James's, for it considered experience as a real principle of understanding. What common sense dictates, however, is an original conception of matter—it is neither "representation" as idealists would have it nor a "thing" as realists insist. Matter is "an aggregate of images," and the image is that independent existence somewhere between thing and representation. Considered in this way, matter does indeed possess color and grace and form, but because we know it by virtue of our acts upon it and feel its recalcitrance and resistance, we know it to possess as well an existence independent of the mind. Interestingly, spirit or mind is known, at least inferentially, by those same images, for perceptions are stored in the form of memory images for the purpose of contemplation or future action. And memory, argues Bergson, is just that "intersection of mind and matter" (*MM* xvi).

Thus he might argue in *Matière et Mémoire* (1896; translated as *Matter and Memory*, 1911) that the whole of memory (which is nothing less than the self) is present at any moment, that, like an inverted cone, our personal past presses into the future, that indeed memory forever attempts to drive out perception. By the counsel of memory, we feel and know the presence of spirit, for the brain is an instrument of action not of representation (*MM* 83); its function is something like a "central telephone exchange" (*MM* 19). Our representations of the past act through the material organ of the brain, but the cerebral state cannot be considered as the complete condition of memory. Memory, in a word, is the activity of spirit, not matter, and it mysteriously and automatically preserves itself and stores its images as a plant stores nutrients. The fullness of memory constitutes the historical basis for future action and prepares the ground for human freedom. Consciousness, therefore, gives value and richness to life by perpetually calling upon the past to direct a future act, ideally not as a sensorimotor response but as an expression of the continuity of human personality. It is in this way that experience of the world acquires its subjective character.

In *Matter and Memory*, Bergson argued that neither perception nor memory is ever pure in the normal activity of living; they interpenetrate one another in a process resembling endosmosis and always with a view toward action. The past is life itself and that of which we are actually conscious. The pure present is merely that "invisible progress of the past gnawing into the future": "Consciousness, then, illumines, at each moment of time, that immediate part of the past which, impending over the future, seeks to realize and associate with it. . . . It is in this illuminated part of our history that we remain seated, in virtue of the fundamental law of life, which is the law of action" (*MM* 194). In this sense, consciousness possesses the "warmth and intimacy" of experience William James described; the individual's lived past, stored as memory images, is linked to present perception. To designate this quality as the fundamental law of life was to give, suddenly, power and large importance to the individually lived experience and the human personality.

In the final chapter of *Matter and Memory*, Bergson seemed to be looking forward to a much wider application of his thought, almost epic in scope, that would eventually be called *Creative Evolution*. Pure memory resides in the domain of spirit, he suggested, and he concluded *Matter and Memory* with this sentence: "Spirit borrows from matter the perceptions on which it feeds, and restores them to matter in the form of movements which it has stamped with its own freedom" (*MM* 332). Here was suggested the vital force that would become the generalized principle of the élan vital in his most popular and widely read book. When he came to contemplate biological becoming in *Creative Evolution*, he was already equipped with a metaphysical method that enabled him to investigate scientific evidence without being inextricably tied to the positivistic method.[70]

Bergson's thought always had a biological cast to it, however. Indeed, Ralph Barton Perry suggested that the essential difference between William James and Bergson is that the former sought to construct a biological philosophy whereas the latter sought to develop a philosophical biology.[71] In *Creative Evolution* this ambition reached its fullest expression. Spirit and matter are treated as dramatic personae in the evolution of life: the first is always ascending, seeking to perpetuate its past in the future; the second is always descending, content to remain what it is and to drag spirit down with it. The burden of necessity is that spirit must always express and organize itself in matter and conform to physical law, but evolution is creative in that spirit asserts its rights in and through matter, always seeking simpler, more efficient means to express itself. To a familiar Spencerian, mechanistic, unilinear, and progressive evolution, Bergson opposed an evolution that developed certain indeterminate tendencies along several lines at once, as in a "sheaf," and is given not to steady acceleration (or depletion) but to varying eras of complacent inertia and explosive surges. To the timeless, transcendent reality of an idealistic Absolute, he opposed duration, felt from within, and implicated the real in an immanent world of ceaseless becoming.

The answer Henri Bergson gave to the question Eucken posed in his Nobel speech, "Naturalism or Idealism?," was uniquely his own. But for any number of people who were discontented with naturalism or who felt that the time had come for the earth to resume its rights, Bergsonism was appropriated as a common property. For a time, if only for a short time, Bergson was a cultural phenomenon, and for some he articulated a vision of the world that spoke of their own best hopes and corroborated their experience. Bergson cannot be said to have caused the mood, at once restless and confident, so widespread in America just before the war, but he serves as an epitome of it. And in that capacity, he provides access to the shape of its preoccupations and energies.

Max Beerbohm once described his own attempts to fathom the new philosophy of James and Bergson:

> M. Bergson, in his well-known essay on this theme [laughter], says . . . well, he says many things; but none of these, though I have just read them, do I clearly remember, nor am I sure that in the act of reading I understood any of them. That is the worst of these fashion-able philosophers—or rather, the worst of me. Somehow I never manage to read them till they are just going out of fashion, and even then I don't seem able to cope with them. . . . Time passed; M. Bergson appeared "and for his hour was lord of the ascendant"; I tardily tackled William James. I bore in mind, as I approached him, the testimonials that had been lavished on him by all my friends. Alas, I was insensible to his thrillingness. His gaiety did not make me gay. His crystal clarity confused me dreadfully. I could make nothing of William James. And now, in the fullness of time, I have been floored by M. Bergson.[72]

Though the gaiety and thrillingness that were William James and Henri Bergson eluded Beerbohm, there was a moment when an extraordinary number of men and women (including, presumably, Max Beerbohm's friends) were infused with and excited by the new spirit in philosophy. This was particularly true of America during the prewar years. But to understand the extent and nature of Bergson's cultural significance, we must turn from intellectual history to cultural history.

TWO

A New Reality

I

"O MY BERGSON, you are a magician," wrote William James shortly after he had finished reading *L'évolution créatrice* (1907), "and your book is a marvel." He continued to praise the book in the letter, finding it "pure classic in point of form," with its persistent "flavor of euphony" oddly reminding him of the "aftertaste" of *Madame Bovary*. If he were not in the mood to make any definite comment about the content of the book, James vaguely recognized certain coincident features between his pragmatism and what had already come to be called Bergsonism, and this shock of recognition was personally gratifying. (In this respect, James was rather backward, for Bergson had read and been influenced by James's work long before the American had fully grasped the relevance of Bergson's thought to his own.) James felt they were "fighting the same fight" against what he called in the letter the great "beast," "Intellectualism," but what Bergson would have variously described as a pernicious Spencerian mechanism or the stubborn and habitual claims of a Platonic idealism. In any event, in James's mind, the much younger French philosopher had delivered the "death wound," and James was personally content to serve modestly "in the ranks" behind such an exquisite "commander."[1]

Despite his enthusiasm and the magical spell *Creative Evolution* had cast over him, James was an acute and critical reader, one whose acceptance and agreement Bergson personally desired. Four years earlier James had expressed his reservations about the operations of memory as described in *Matière et Mémoire*, and the point was well taken. Nevertheless, despite his characteristic modesty, we should have taken James at his word, I think, when in 1908 he delivered his Hibbert lectures at Manchester College, Oxford, and told his audience that Bergson had made him "bold,"[2] that "without the confidence which being able to lean on Bergson's authority gives me I should never have ventured to urge these particular views of mine upon this ultra-critical audience" (p. 215). His sixth lecture was entitled "Bergson and His Critique of Intellectualism," and there James not only offered a summary of Bergsonism (still one of the best) but alerted his audience to the seductive features of Bergson's thought and style. Above all else, Bergson has a "peculiar" way of looking at things, and therein lies his originality, an originality so profuse, James confessed, "that some of his ideas baffle me entirely. I doubt whether any one understands him all over, so to speak." Bergson possesses a "flexibility of verbal resource," he said, "that follows the thought without a crease or wrinkle, as elastic silk underclothing follows the movements of one's body. The lucidity of Bergson's way of putting things is what all readers are first struck by. It seduces you and bribes you in advance to become his disciple. It is a miracle, and he a real magician" (pp. 226–27).

When this lecture was published, along with the other Hibbert lectures, in *A Pluralistic Universe* (1909), it constituted an invitation to Americans to read Bergson directly, as James had urged his audience at Oxford to do. And coming, as it did, from America's favorite philosopher, the invitation was well heeded. James's own reaction to Bergsonism, though more sophisticated, was a preamble to the national reception of Bergson between 1910 and 1915; like James, many Americans were soon to become emboldened, if somewhat baffled, disciples, disposed to lean on him in expressing their own views. Bergson the magician was soon to cast his spell over prewar America and to work his influence in ways that no one, least of all Bergson himself, could have properly foretold.

As Henry F. May has observed, "the most authoritative spokesman of the new vitalism, and for a brief spell the most influential thinker in the world as well as the rage in intellectual America, was Henri Bergson." No philosopher had excited as much enthusiasm or controversy in America as did Bergson when he visited in 1913. Not even William James himself had enjoyed such widespread and fashionable popularity. When Bergson came to New York to deliver a series of lectures and to receive an honorary doctor of laws degree from Columbia University, May records that "a line of automobiles (still the vehicles of the well-to-do) clogged Broadway, one lady fainted in the crush at the lecture-room door, and regular students were crowded out of their seats by well-dressed auditors."[3] Applications for tickets to his lectures on "Spirituality and Liberty" were reported as "record breaking"—numbering over two thousand. Similarly large crowds clambered into the auditorium of the City College of New York, where he lectured in French on the duties and functions of a college, and some two thousand male students greeted him with two or three choruses of the "characteristic American 'college yell.'" From New York, Bergson traveled to Harvard where he had occasion to honor publicly and remember fondly his friend, William James, who had died a few years before. All in all, his visit was, as one journalist commented, a "nine days' wonder."[4]

To a degree, this extraordinary reception was probably due to calculated planning. Columbia had published a 417-item bibliography of articles, monographs, and books about Bergson before his visit, and the *New York Times* printed a special article on him the week before his arrival. The article did not offer any summary views of the man or his thought—apparently by 1913 Bergsonism was already familiar to American readers. What it did do, however, was to effectively dismiss the argued relation between Bergsonism and the syndicalism of Bergson's disciple Georges Sorel. Though the two schools have a few points in common, the author contended, they are basically divergent streams, and Bergson's philosophy has a "fundamentally individualistic character."[5]

While the author of the *New York Times* article attempted to sever the link between Bergson and syndicalism (and by extension, in this country, between Bergson and the notorious Industrial Workers of the World), he also portrayed Bergsonism as basically congenial to conventional democratic tastes. But he did not dispute other, perhaps more specious, associations that had been proclaimed in any number of periodicals. Advocates of contending schools of thought and ambition, notable for their almost random variety, were also apt to lean on Bergson for authority. Still others, whose hopes and fears were less well defined, found in Bergson the cheering uplift necessary to face the future with steady optimism. For the appeal of Bergsonism cut across competing interests and convictions, and, simply put, for the popular mind Bergsonism was nearly anything one wanted it to be. Bergson was more often regarded and frequently identified as a prophet than as a philosopher, and his philosophical writings were sometimes interpreted as parables for the new age.

Woodbridge Riley, writing in 1915, chose to conclude his survey of American thought from Puritanism to the present, not with a discussion of an American philosopher, but with a brief synopsis of *Creative Evolution*. Himself a philosopher, Riley found it difficult to classify Bergson or to get beyond the antithetical claims made for his system. As Riley pointed out, opinions about Bergson were as "varied as the persons who propound them": he was seen as a pragmatist and an antipragmatist, as a rationalist and an antirationalist, as a religious leader and someone who had no religious message, as a conservative and a political radical, and so forth. To these attributions, Riley observed, might be added those opinions that associated Bergson with Emerson and William James. "Like Emerson," he wrote, "Bergson may be called a prophet of the soul, a friend and aider of those who would see with the spirit and enter into the mystery of creation through intellectual sympathy or intuition, instead of making the vain attempt to do so through the logical and scientific understanding."[6] Bergson was, like James, more a poet than a philosopher, whose insistence on taking the immediate point of view and seeking reality in the flux of experience is analogous to the pragmatic method. All of which is to say that, on the one hand, Bergsonism was easily adapted to prevailing modes of thought and, on the other, that there was something vaguely familiar about it, that somehow the latest French fashion was in this instance fundamentally American after all.

When William James wrote his letter praising *Creative Evolution*, he modestly announced that Bergson would soon be receiving his own "little 'pragmatism' book." "How jejune and inconsiderable it seems in comparison with your great system," he continued. "But it is so congruent with parts of your system, fits so well into the interstices thereof, that you will easily understand why I am so enthusiastic."[7] In a real way, Bergson's own system, or parts of it, fit into the interstices of the prevailing modes of American thought and life: it encouraged many Americans to believe what they already believed or wanted to believe, and it must have appeared to them, perhaps subconsciously, as perfectly consonant with their national aspirations and historical traditions. Bergson also exerted a particularly significant influence on literary sensibility, an influence that was sometimes repudiated, sometimes carefully qualified, by those once profoundly affected. Moreover, Bergsonism served as an epitome for the new reality that dramatically, if quietly, altered literary manner and ambitions and installed a new consciousness in the literary artist. These are points we will return to later, but first it is necessary to sketch the contours and extent of the Bergsonian influence in this country.[8]

II

Bergson's reputation as a philosopher rested principally upon three book-length studies—*Time and Free Will, Matter and Memory*, and *Creative Evolution*—each investigating different philosophical problems but clearly signaling a consistency and progression to his thought. Almost certainly the majority of his readers did not read his works in this order, however, and this was probably unfortunate for his permanent reputation as a serious philosopher, though ironically it likely enhanced his popular reception. Not until after the publication of *L'évolution créatrice* in 1907 was Bergson's work generally available in English, and much of it immediately followed the publication of this work in translation in 1911. Attention was typically lavished on the later work, and more than one popularizer suggested that one should read *Creative Evolution* before tackling the "more difficult" *Time and Free Will* and *Matter and Memory*. More unfortunate still, the London correspondent who had maintained that *Creative Evolution* might be read as a "poem" was often quoted approvingly by American journalists. Reviews of this sort fostered an interest in Bergsonism at the expense of solid understanding, and in part the seductive style that James had identified and warned his auditors about a few years before formed the basis for Bergson's popular appeal.

For Bergson, like James, believed philosophy had a practical importance for the man and woman in the street, and he was not content to let it seep down to them through normal academic channels; he sought to clarify his own position in such a way that nonexpert readers could understand and appreciate it for themselves. This tendency was complicated by the equal conviction that language, like number, was a static symbol system and essentially inadequate to describe actual realities, that words could never "express" but only "suggest" the real as it was experienced in duration. These impulses were seductively combined in a richly metaphoric prose style, especially suggestive in *Creative Evolution*, yet his thought was further complicated by the fanfare that attended the introduction of Bergson to the American reading public. If casual readers did not get their Bergson directly but consulted one of the two or three dozen books that were devoted in part or in whole to rendering an explanation of Bergsonism or one of the nearly one hundred magazine articles about his system that were published during these years, those same readers nevertheless would have been eventually urged to read Bergson firsthand.

The range of these sometimes effusive endorsements or alarmed critiques of Bergson may be suggested by a sampling of some of the titles: *Bergson for Beginners* (1913), "Bergson's Wonder-Working Philosophy" (1911), "Is the Bergson Philosophy That of a Charlatan?" (1912), *Bergson and the Modern Spirit* (1913), "Playboy of Western Philosophy" (1913),

"Prophet of the Soul" (1913), "The Most Dangerous Man in the World" (1912), "Christ and Bergson" (1913). Henri Bergson was news; his influence is the proper concern of social as well as intellectual history. In fact, Bergsonism in America is most intriguing at that point where the popular and the intellectual meet, or perhaps more properly divide. The degree of his popular appeal is difficult to measure precisely, but we can guess at it.

The reader who dropped *Time and Free Will* or *Matter and Memory* as too obscure and difficult and took up *Creative Evolution* rather than one of the popular summaries would likely have come away with a confused notion of what Bergson meant by the terms *intuition* or *metaphysics*, partly because the author more often exhibited his metaphysical method in *Creative Evolution* than argued it. More than once in that book, Bergson took the point of view of the lowly, single-celled infusorian by means of the "intellectual sympathy" that he called "intuition" and that, as he himself had defined it in the *Introduction to Metaphysics*, is remarkably close to, perhaps synonymous with, the literary term *identification*. One sees and can identify with the infusorian as a dramatic character in the pageant of life—a microscopic Christian in a divine and constantly evolving, biological *Pilgrim's Progress*. Santayana astutely, if contemptuously, identified Bergson's psychology as an essentially "literary" one and described *Creative Evolution* as a "universal biological romance,"[9] and the feel, as opposed to the significance, of *Creative Evolution* is that of a novel or perhaps a grand, biological epic. This same reader, if unable to follow the intricacies of Bergson's arguments at every point, would surely have acquired an epigrammatic understanding of his philosophy. Bergson did not, like Nietzsche, develop an aphoristic style, but his metaphors sometimes have that effect.

The average reader might have come away from reading *Creative Evolution* with, if nothing more, a conviction that intuition is superior to intellect and a pocket full of cheering aphorisms, separated from their argument and divorced from a sometimes edgier, less-heartening context. One might recall, for example, that men and women are in a special sense "the 'term' and the 'end' of evolution" but overlook, as Bergson explicitly pointed out, that "the rest of nature is not for the sake of man: we struggle like other species, we have struggled against other species" (*CE* 265). That the tone of *Creative Evolution* is decidedly uplifting cannot be denied, but Bergson himself was not blind to the darker implications of life. Indeed, part of A. D. Lindsay's stated motive in writing *The Philosophy of Bergson*

(1911) was to establish that Bergson was a systematic rather than simply an aphoristic philosopher, known too widely as the author of occasional and brilliant aperçus but no real and comprehensive point of view.[10]

Fortunately, we do not need to depend entirely upon speculations about our hypothetical average reader to establish the unreserved optimism that attended a casual reading of *Creative Evolution*. If anything, our guesswork is a good deal more cautious than some of the extravagant claims made for the significance of this remarkable French philosopher. Our casual reader would have likely developed an encapsulated understanding perhaps best expressed by the sinister and tautological aphorism of our own day—"get in touch with your feelings." This essentially was what Louise Collier Willcox suggested when she tried, rather more sensibly than most commentators, to assess the reasons for Bergson's popularity in the United States. People have a natural willingness to believe in their own feelings, she observed, and "in reading Bergson they identify their spontaneous emotions with Bergson's intuitions." Mankind cannot and will not live without hope, she added, and "so far as they can follow Bergson's theory of evolution they derive hope from it."[11] "The average interested reader," she concluded, "will come from him consoled and strengthened, realizing that he has had restored to him faith in the intuitions which have always seemed to him to lie deeper than his logical reason; belief in freedom and responsibility, and finally rescue from a hopeless isolation. He has, indeed, given men more power to act and to live" (p. 451).

Willcox's evaluation of Bergson's appeal was a balanced one. These were the confident years, however, and Americans as a whole were probably less inclined to feel in the need of rescue than to hear bullier, more-charged sentiments of enthusiasm and optimism. Other journalists were more apt to see in Bergson something grander, even something divine. Thus, Alvan F. Sanborn, in the conservative magazine *Century*, felt Bergsonism offered a "rehabilitation" of God and the soul, a reconciliation "of science and metaphysics with religion, of knowledge with life, of law with conduct, of liberty with authority, of the ideals of the Occident with the ideals of the Orient, of the present with the past and with the future."[12] Charles Johnston, writing in *Harper's Weekly*, felt Bergson's philosophy should "wake us from the torpor in which most of us pass our lives": "The nineteenth century was the golden age of experimental science, bringing marvelous practical results, but leading to philosophic materialism. The twentieth century seems destined to be remembered as an epoch of spiritual thought and life, one of the greatest, perhaps, in the history of the world."[13] For

Johnston, Bergson was the great "bridge builder" between these epochs. And John Burroughs thought Bergson a latter-day Emerson, a "prophet of the soul," and even detected in him an Emersonian look, lacking only the "powerful Emersonian mouth."[14]

Commentators like Burroughs often considered Bergson the most significant philosopher since, depending on their predilection, Kant, Descartes, Aquinas, or Plato. But no one, I think, offered as extravagant a comparison as did Albert Whittaker in the *Forum* when he contended that "the modern kindly philosopher of Jewish extraction reinforces the lesson of the gracious Nazarene who nineteen centuries ago spoke to the noblest there was in his fellow man. Like that great teacher, Henri Bergson comes that we may have life and that we may have it more abundantly."[15] To think that Bergson's system met with universal and unqualified praise, however, even if less farfetched than Whittaker's, would be a mistake. Readers might well divide over his philosophy—indeed Bergsonism had something to do with the dissolution of two of the most famous intellectual friendships of the twentieth century: that of Alfred North Whitehead and Bertrand Russell and of Carl Jung and Sigmund Freud.[16] And, to be sure, there were detractors, but they too reveal something about Bergson's significance as a social phenomenon.

Bergson's Jewishness was undoubtedly an issue for some, and adversaries occasionally resorted to anti-Semitic innuendo.[17] For the most part, however, critics attempted to oppose the threat of Bergsonism through calculated argument, albeit on differing grounds, and many of the objections were predictable. For Irving Babbitt, Bergson was no "humanist" but a Rousseauistic primitivist, and his philosophy would "seem to encourage rather than correct the two great permanent maladies of human nature—anarchy and irrationality."[18] A. O. Lovejoy took a lively and enduring, if somewhat ambivalent, interest in Bergson and fitted Bergsonism into the history of ideas, believing him to be "a sort of modernized Heraclitus."[19] Though he granted that Bergson's observation about duration as experienced rather than measured was a significant contribution to philosophy, Lovejoy was uneasy with Bergson's florid style. Too often, Bergson lets "a simile do duty for a syllogism," he wrote, and a luxuriant prose style is a "perilous possession" in the hands of a philosopher and obtrudes upon rigorous, systematic discourse (p. 300). On the other hand, the impressionist critic James Gibbons Huneker admired Bergson's "loops of golden prose" but believed the philosopher managed his opposition the way John Millington Synge's playboy of the western world managed his competition. Huneker was quick to add, however, that he could not dispute Bergson's earnestness.[20] But these individual retorts were insignificant compared to the Catholic Church's concerted effort to banish Bergsonian vitalism.

The story of Bergson and the Catholic Church is an interesting one, fraught with ironies, but only a sketch can be offered here. Led by Éduoard Le Roy (whose book on Bergson was published in English translation by Holt and Company in 1913), the neo-Catholicism movement was built upon Bergsonian principles, perceiving in the Divine Immanence inferred from *Creative Evolution* an antidote to the scientific scholasticism or intellectualism of the nineteenth century. This tendency was soon systematically quashed by the church itself—Pope Pius X issued an encyclical against modernism in 1907; two French Catholic modernists were excommunicated; the antimodernist oath was later imposed; and by 1914 Bergson's works were indexed. Yet by the 1940s Bergson himself was prepared to convert to Roman Catholicism; however, after the Nazis invaded France, he decided not to do so as a symbolic protest.

Pius X's encyclical, "Pascendi Dominici Gregis," of 8 September 1907 is an especially interesting document. He advised the patriarchs of the church that it was their solemn duty to prevent works "infected" with modernism from being read and, wherever possible, from being printed.[21] Modernism, which he defined simply as an infatuation with things modern, but which was obviously identified with the spread of vitalistic ideology, was the "synthesis of all heresies," and the adoption of this system "means the destruction not of the Catholic religion alone but of all religion" (p. 89). Adherents of modern Catholicism were the "most pernicious of all adversaries of the Church" (p. 72), and their chief principle, "vital immanence," tended to make "consciousness and revelation synonymous" (p. 74) and to reduce dogma to "symbols" subject to evolutionary change. "With regard to morals," Pius X added, these modernists "adopt the principle of the Americanists, that the active virtues are more important than the passive, both in the estimation in which they must be held and in the exercise of them" (p. 89).

Other critics judiciously attacked Bergson on purer philosophical grounds, but the most revealing and interesting criticism is in George Santayana's *Winds of Doctrine* (1913). Santayana's objections are various and to a degree confused. This very confusion, I think, is what makes Santayana's essay so revealing an assessment of Bergson's significance in America, for Santayana is never clear, and perhaps was not clear in his own mind, as to whether he is objecting to the Bergsonian philosophy as philosophy or to it as a social phenomenon, foreboding and personally distasteful.

Santayana begins his book with the resigned observation that "the shell of Christendom is broken": "Our whole life and mind is saturated with the slow upward filtration of a new spirit—that of an emancipated, atheistic, international democracy" (p. 1). This vitalistic upsurgence is, simply put, vulgar, yet its persuasive fascination is for a time virtually assured because it makes its mistaken appeal to the "sturdy animality" at the heart of human nature. Against this background of Santayana's personal preoccupation, Bergson becomes, symbolically at least, the dire villain presiding over the dissolution of the age, and Bertrand Russell emerges as the prospective redeemer, the harbinger of a "new scholasticism" in which the life of reason may once more find sustenance.

Had Bergsonism been simply a philosophical position for which Santayana had little sympathy, he would have been eminently qualified to dispute it on purely philosophical grounds. But the threat Bergson posed to the life of reason (exhibited, no doubt, by the uncritical popularity he had excited at the time and the position of the church regarding him) probably made it a cultural and personal problem for Santayana. At any rate, Santayana was unsure how to dispense with the Frenchman, and his criticism is replete with contradictory positions of attack. At one point, he speculates that some unknown scientist in some laboratory was at that moment making a discovery that might wholly undermine Bergson's position (p. 92). At another he indulges in a frank misreading of Bergson, making of him a pure idealist, but later intimates that for Bergson the intellect is a "petrifying blight" (p. 19). He attempts to reduce Bergson's philosophy to a "myth or fable" because Bergson begins where science ends (though Santayana had earlier suggested that the Bergsonian position was contingent upon scientific discovery). He attempts to psychologize Bergson, making of him a victim of "cosmic agoraphobia," afraid of "non-human immensities" (p. 63); yet he later concluded that Bergson was essentially a "mystic" and admitted that "it is hard to be a just critic of mysticism because mysticism can never do itself justice in words" (p. 88).

As a systematic examination and criticism of Bergson, Santayana's essay is a sorry muddle. Yet apart from rational inquiry, an emotional coherence and ethical point of view is displayed apropos of Bergson, as it were, that is honest and searching, and Santayana does provide penetrating insights into the basis of Bergson's popularity. But for Santayana the true villain is the age itself, the whole modern tendency, and the danger lies not in the Bergsonian doctrine so much as in the public's ready willingness to accept it. As easily as Bergson might be made a latter-day saviour for some, for others he might become a tempter and corrupter. For Santayana, as for many others, Bergson was a fit emblem for the age, and the greatest influence of Bergsonism resided not in the assimilation of it as a body of thought so much as in the application of selected Bergsonian principles to preexisting, progressive concerns and impulses. Ironically, in those very disciplines that Bergson himself worked—philosophy, psychology, and science—his contributions were either quietly absorbed or simply ignored.

American philosophers, rather patriotically, tended to regard William James as the more genuine and original thinker and to see in his pragmatism and pluralism an indigenous American philosophy that shared with Bergsonism a certain preoccupation with experience as occurring within a constant flux and antagonisms toward the intellectualist point of view. Ralph Barton Perry and Horace Kallen, both former students of James, agreed upon not only the priority of James in his philosophical and psychological inquiries in this respect but also his preeminent position in the American philosophical tradition that should not be overthrown by James's own enthusiasm for and deference to Bergson.[22] At best, Bergsonism was absorbed into the new realism of Perry and others, shown to have overlapping concerns, and perfunctorily dismissed. Woodbridge Riley, on the other hand, writing in 1915, adopted a more tentative, wait-and-see attitude and was personally content to "allow it the right of self-determination." Their intellectual hesitation probably derived from an unwillingness to be drawn into the fadism of the Bergson mania, and they, like Santayana, though more self-consciously cautious, were at odds to distinguish between his popularity and his significance, between his style and his substance. Riley observed, "by the fundamental thesis of his philosophy he encourages us to take the pictures and let the thinking go."[23] Perry astutely remarked that "having rejected the reason as a means to metaphysical insight, Bergson has exposed himself to the discipleship of every man with an intuition or a cause for which he can assign no reason."[24] Professional philosophers were understandably reluctant to be so compromised, and, in effect, Bergson's national popularity probably worked against his acceptance as an authentic philosopher.

American psychologists were less hesitant to accept the Bergsonian point of view, even if only as providing a more respectable ground to endorse recent developments in psychoanalysis. As Nathan G. Hale has pointed out, "several American psychoanalysts would interpret Freud through Bergsonian assumptions." Hale instances James Jackson Putnam, whose own inheritance was that of a Boston Brahmin schooled in transcendentalist Unitarianism, as one such devotee. For Putnam, argues Hale, Bergson revived the Emersonian moral universe in which the mysterious operations of spirit prevailed.[25] (It is amusing to note that Putnam wrote Freud himself and, despite his enthusiasm for the Vienna school, announced that he considered Bergson the "keenest psychologist alive.")[26] Another disciple was William Alanson White, whose enthusiasms were more in keeping with the temper of the times than with New England moralism. White was a popularizer of psychoanalysis whose reformist impulses were girded by a Bergsonian faith in creative evolution. It was the very fullness of the Bergsonian vision that enabled it to easily accommodate Freudian analysis, and Hale is surely right when he suggests that "the enthusiasm for Bergson swept together several currents: Freud and abnormal psychology; a sanction for radical change in morals and society; a benediction for instinct and intuition."[27] But the popular reception of psychoanalysis was no doubt eased by Bergson's own benediction of Freud at the conclusion of Bergson's monograph on dreams.[28]

For the most part, Bergson's controversial objections to the fallacies of the scientific method were debated in Europe, and Americans were more often acquainted with the thrust of the dispute conducted in England as it filtered through the sensational press. As a rule, scientists themselves tended to ignore Bergson. A. J. Balfour, the statesman and philosopher, found Bergson more interesting as a psychologist than a biological scientist and timidly registered his objections to Bergson's criticisms.[29] Yet the biologist James Johnstone, in *The Philosophy of Biology* (1914), found the vitalistic principles espoused by Bergson and Hans Driesch better able to account for the most recent discoveries in biological research than the physicochemical view held by the mechanists.[30]

The most vehement and, at the same time, the most supercilious attack upon Bergson's criticisms of the scientific method came from the unregenerate Spencerian Hugh S. R. Elliot in *Modern Science and the Illusions of Professor Bergson* (1912). Predisposed as he was to view all metaphysics as "foolish puerilities" and confessedly mechanistic in his outlook, Elliot objected to Bergsonism on the grounds that Bergson had not produced "facts" in support of his claims about the nature of time, memory, and intuition.[31] Admitting neither logic, common sense, nor experience as satisfactory methods of inquiry, believing consciousness to be the insignificant motor accompaniment to thought, and accepting "facts" only in the narrowly scientific sense as testable and verifiable, Elliot's argument was a form of sustained question begging. If Bergson had delivered a death wound to the intellectualist tradition, Elliot seems not to have felt it. Elliot myopically looked forward to the day when positive science would supplant philosophy altogether, when psychology would become a branch of "nerve physiology" and ethics would be derived from scientific inductions (pp. 220–21).

Sir Oliver Lodge was virtually the only scientist of reputation to find the Bergsonian method compatible with scientific aspirations. Balfour registered his objections in the English philosophical periodical the *Hibbert Journal*, and Lodge replied to them in the same publication. Lodge made it clear that he was speaking as a scientist, not a philosopher, and that he was something of an interloper in the debate but undertook to speak for Bergson until such time as the Frenchman might speak for himself. He found Bergson's philosophy "peculiarly acceptable and interesting to men of science."[32] Lodge admitted that when the scientist steps out of the realm of certainty of mathematical propositions one enters the realm of "probable inference, the domain of pragmatic conviction, of commonplace intuition, of familiar faith" (p. 293). For Lodge, the Bergsonian system opened out "one avenue" toward a comprehensive scheme of unifying experience and science. The reports of this altogether serious and decorous exchange, however, were reported in the American journal *Current Literature* under banner headlines: "Balfour's Objections to Bergson's Philosophy" and "Bergson's Intuitional Philosophy Justified by Sir Oliver Lodge." This is yet another example of Bergson's philosophy being transformed into a bastardized media event.

H. Wildon Carr of King's College, with Bergson's approval, undertook a book-length study of Bergson's fundamental principles and stressed their significance to scientific inquiry. He argued that the recent theory of relativity was no less a metaphysical principle than a scientific one. Such a theory does not "rest on anything we are able to observe in the external world but on the nature of conscious experience itself. It belongs to philosophy because it is only the method of intuition that reveals it."[33] On the other hand, this theory is clearly "a scientific advance" (p. 12). For Bergson, science and metaphysics ran a parallel course and were mutually dependent, and he rankled under the spurious attributions to his thought that science and mathematics were subordinate to philosophy. Edwin Slosson, interviewing him for the popular "Twelve Major Prophets of

Today" series appearing in the *Independent* in 1911, questioned him on this point: "In short," Bergson replied, "all my researches have had no other object than to bring about a rapprochement between metaphysics and science and to consolidate one with the other without sacrificing anything of either."[34]

In philosophy, psychology, and science, then—those disciplines in which one might say Bergson properly "worked"—his positions were frequently reported inaccurately or diluted for popular consumption. Those qualified to interpret him and to assess his intellectual contribution to modern thought were probably hesitant to do so for two reasons. First, they would have to concede from the beginning that in matters of style and exposition Bergson was in no way obscure; in fact he had no peer. Rather, they would have to admit some presumption, as did one expositor, in stripping his ideas of the "brilliant metaphorical dress in which Bergson himself has clothed them." Nor could they offer any better defense for doing so than he did when he reminded his readers that "metaphor is not always conducive to clearness, and that illustration is apt to be confused with argument."[35] A second, and related, reason is that a popular exposition of Bergsonism, or a balanced criticism of it, ran counter to the customary direction of such commentaries. That is, these expositors were not charged with bringing Bergson out of the ivory tower but with putting him back in. Bergsonism was already in the streets, and they faced the double difficulty of dampening enthusiasm and correcting popular misunderstanding and of returning to the public a philosopher essentially less attractive than the one they had already embraced.

Ironically, one finds that during these years the Bergsonian philosophy exerted its greatest influence in matters about which its author personally had little to say. Bergsonism, half-digested though it may have been, was popularly accepted; and causes so various as mysticism and feminism, political radicalism and scientific management, literary criticism and history could all find a portion of the Bergsonian philosophy to lean upon.

III

Shortly after Bergson's lectures at Columbia University, a journalist for *Current Opinion* tried to sum up Bergson's influence in America. "If keen interest in a new message, manifested by the most widely varying schools of thought, constitutes proof of the greatness of the exponent of that message," he surmised, "then Bergson is indeed great." Quoting at length from an article in the *New York Evening Post*, this journalist argued that there was a distinctly American flavor to Bergsonism and speculated that it would probably prove more popular in America than abroad. For Bergson's is a "doctrine for pioneers," and those "rebels" we have always had with us now have "the sanction of an entire philosophical system behind them." He quoted with approval the observation of the writer for the *New York Times* that pragmatism is really too "high brow" for most Americans, but that once the conception of "creative evolution" is translated into familiar "inspirational terms," "many readers of Walt Mason, of Frank L. Stanton, and of Elbert Hubbard, before he gave up philosophy for the advertizing business, will be surprised to find they have been reading and thinking in Bergsonian terms all their lives."[36]

No doubt there was some truth in these remarks. Bergsonism provided a respectable undergirding for a progressive spirit that developed almost randomly. One might survey the tendencies of the time and find them developing much as Bergson's evolutionary sheaf—some impulses doomed to run their brief course, and others to prevail as satisfactory and creative solutions to existing problems. The article in *Current Opinion* quoted the observation of the writer for the *New York Times* at length: "M. Bergson's theories must have their strong appeal to a generation that is fond of describing itself as a restless, searching, groping, questioning age. The modern mind is a mass of struggling contradictions. Irreconcilable tastes and aspirations find entertainment there and shelter. . . . To reconcile such contradictions there is evident virtue in a philosophy which lays stress not on final purposes, but on mere agitation."[37]

Bergson's conviction that we were artisans before we were either artists or geometers would have had a definite appeal for the arts and crafts school, for example. For Bergson, the activity of the artisan in its historical attempts at repetition of forms was prior to, and indeed an indispensable antecedent to, mathematical abstraction and formulas. The work of the artisan was more fundamental than disinterested art, which for Bergson was a luxury, because it adapted means to ends and was "fashioned for the needs of human action." But the editor of the *Craftsman* found in Bergsonism especial authority for the endorsement of simple freedom in constant activity, which confirms the place of family and brotherhood and love in honest toil, which "keeps our vital contact with nature and our consciousness of the common lot."[38] And as late as 1917, *Art World* would report Bergson's appreciation of that journal and print a poem that identified the philosopher as the "clairvoyant of true life."[39]

Bergsonism was also easily adapted to a purer aestheticism. More than one reviewer had compared *Creative Evolution* to the famous conclusion to Pater's *Studies of the History of the Renaissance*. Indeed, Bergson had maintained in *Time and Free Will*, much like Oscar Wilde in *The Decay of Lying*, that "in a certain sense art is prior to nature" (*TFW* 14); that nature can only express feelings whereas art can suggest them; that, unlike nature, which is but a series of simultaneities, the artist possesses the resources of "rhythm." Yet, one could hardly have maintained with any consistency that the Bergsonian philosophy, directed as it was toward life and action, endorsed a doctrine of art-for-art's-sake. The creative impulse, especially as it was represented by imaginative artists, was at the center of the Bergsonian vision and expressed long before the publication of *Creative Evolution*, but its most authentic embodiment was more complicated than a simple aestheticism.

American feminists were disposed to cite Bergson for support of their cause as well. Marion Cox, writing for the *Forum*, began her inquiry into the appropriateness of Bergsonism to feminism thus: "It is Bergson's hour. Is it because he brings us a needed message? Those who see only the mysticism in his philosophy claim that it is convertible into any and every significance; but a definite message is in his insistent demand that we turn away from the intellectualism of life to life itself, and this also is the aim of Feminism."[40] Hers was a shrewdly rhetorical adaptation of Bergson, even if a misleading one, to the feminist movement. Through him, Cox undertook to convert a liability into an asset; the realm of intuition, to which women had conventionally been consigned, was from this point of view the "depository of the life-essence" (p. 552). The intellectualistic male principle follows the configuration of matter into "disintegration, finalities, the *made*, which in the Bergsonian sense is the dead" (p. 551). By contrast, the female principle is intimately involved in living realities and human sympathy: "The woman-movement is but the movement of life—toward the human. One cannot repeat this too often, for the salvation of the future race depends on it" (p. 553).

Cox's conversion of Bergsonism into a "definite message" was opportune, for it was, indeed, Bergson's hour. She had, however, the French philosopher's own authority and heartiest endorsement of the feminist cause, whether she knew it or not. A few months before, in an interview for *Harper's Weekly*, Louise Collier Willcox queried Bergson on his reaction to feminism: "I consider *the present feminist movement*," he replied, "*the greatest event in the history of civilization since the promulgation of the*

Christian ideal." "Not till women have every right that men have, equal political power, the same opportunity to make their opinions felt and acted upon in every realm of life," he added, "can we hope for a further development of the race."[41]

Bergsonian optimism, at least as it had been expressed in *Creative Evolution*, would no doubt have had a cloying effect upon the popular sensibility were it not for the sheer variety of its influence and application in America and abroad. Piecemeal appropriation and general misapprehension of Bergsonism probably did much to sustain its popularity. The most comprehensive assimilations of Bergsonism, however, were in theology and political analysis.

The Catholic Church despised philosophical vitalism, but Bergson seems not to have represented such a pernicious challenge for Protestants. In "Bergson's Reception in America," the writer for *Current Opinion* reported that the Baptist publication *Watchman* identified Bergson as a "fundamentally conservative" thinker and that the *Biblical World* believed Bergson was working toward a "'higher synthesis' of pantheism and deism, of immanence and transcendence, preserving the values of each, while yielding to the faults of neither." The *Methodist Review* printed an approving exposition of *Creative Evolution*, and the contributor argued in an article (and later in a book) that Bergsonism was consistent with, indeed anticipated by, the doctrine of philosophical methodism known as personalism.[42] More obscurely, Evelyn Underhill argued that Bergsonism, with its emphasis upon intuition, validated ancient mystical truths and the currency of mysticism for the new age,[43] and more generally, Theodore Roosevelt claimed that every truly scientific and truly religious man will turn with relief to the "lofty" thought of Bergson and James.[44]

If we may judge from the studies of Bergsonism by George Rowland Dodson in *Bergson and the Modern Spirit* (1913) and Emily Hermann in *Eucken and Bergson: Their Significance for Christian Thought* (1912), Bergson was acceptable to conventional Christian doctrine as long as one did not take a "'hard' view" of creative evolution but indulged in a "more intuitional reading." Thus understood, argued Hermann, one discovers, "between the lines," the "Father who worketh hitherto."[45] This less than rigorous approach enabled them to make of Bergsonism a "gospel" (p. 165). The difficulty in converting creative evolution into a Christian vision, of course, was that Bergson allowed for no teleological development of the élan vital, for the very nature of human freedom consisted in inserting some "indeterminacy" into matter. Yet, both Dodson and Hermann tended to glide over this problem—the first arguing that Bergson implicitly endorsed the teleology he explicitly rejected and that Bergson's effort to avoid finalism was futile; the second claiming that the élan vital was purposive in the sense of expressing desire and direction. And both insinuated that Bergson would, sooner or later, occupy the philosophical position they had preemptorily taken for him.

These are examples of rather specious conversions of Bergsonian principles into Christian doctrine, yet there can be little doubt that *Creative Evolution* did much to restore the realm of spirit as a complementary principle to the development of the physical universe. Whether or not Bergsonism could be made to conform to conventional dogma, Bergson himself certainly seemed to liberate the individual spirit from mechanical necessity and to involve this spirit in the larger workings of the cosmos. And his philosophy of intuition was often construed so as to make divine knowledge immediately and equally available to all. Emily Hermann deplored the idea, but the fact, as she herself pointed out, that Bergson was known "in not a few quarters" as "a translator of Yankee philosophy into metaphysics" (p. 167) probably came closer to explaining the spiritual basis of his attraction in this country than did the argued notion that his creative evolution was actually good Christian doctrine. Moreover, Bergson himself was sometimes identified as a prophet, and his relevance to religious thought might be more accurately sought in the general faith he inspired and, like Emerson, delivered broadcast than in any special theological position.

One of the most original and well-schooled applications of Bergsonian thinking was political, not theological, in character. As they were articulated in *A Preface to Politics* (1913), Walter Lippmann's political analysis and proffered solutions to the nation's ills represented a skillful blend of Freudian, Fabian, and Bergsonian principles that in their adroit application and concrete illustration established him as an important commentator upon, and discerning critic of, American life. This young writer for the *New Republic* had inquired searchingly into the mainsprings of human motivation and had articulated their relevance to political activity, and as Henry May has pointed out, Lippmann's incorporation of the findings of psychoanalysis into shrewd political analysis was a pioneering effort—though Lippmann, like some professional American psychoanalysts, tended to filter his Freudianism through Bergsonian assumptions. In any event, I see no reason to doubt Lippmann's own hesitation regarding a blanket application of psychoanalysis to political life. Freudian psychoanalysis may represent "the greatest advance ever made toward the understanding and control of human character," he wrote. "But for the complexities of politics it is not yet ready."[46]

The political needs of a nation could not wait for the laboratory findings of these analysts in any event. Thus, Lippmann stressed the need for "creative statecraft," best embodied in Theodore Roosevelt and anxiously hoped for in Woodrow Wilson. For Wilson, however, as a contemplative man, "the world has to be reflected in the medium of his intellect before he can grapple with it" (p. 81). In other words, he fails to enlist his intuition in the completion of the operations of analysis. The country needs a leader whose experience with and sympathetic instincts for common men and women enable that individual to "speak their discontent and project their hopes" (p. 77), and this leader must be able to translate their agitations into meaningful social programs. This, in effect, was a plea for modern political leaders to think and act metaphysically, in the Bergsonian sense, to recognize through "intellectual sympathy" the needs of citizens, and to act creatively in breaking through encrusted habits and stultifying tradition.

"When we recognize that the focus of politics is shifting from a mechanical to a human center we shall have reached what is, I believe, the most essential idea in modern politics," Lippmann maintained (p. 67). And his charting of this shift and his own recommendations were informed by Bergsonian principles more profoundly than even his extensive citation indicates. "It has been said," he wrote, "that every genuine character an artist produces is one of the characters he might have been" (p. 85). Lippmann need not have been mysterious about the source of this notion; he was paraphrasing a Bergsonian observation in *Laughter*. Similarly, his claim about the inadequacy of language, that it must be vivified by "the sympathetic imagination" (p. 130), and his assertion that "art enlarges experience by admitting us to the inner life of others" (p. 86) and, therefore, has a fundamental place in our social life were also unlabeled echoes of Bergson.

Moreover, the overarching theses of Lippmann's book—that we should keep our habits of mind flexible, that there is a destructive tendency toward the hypostasis of instruments of government and a subsequent tendency to cling to the vessels through which life flows rather than to life itself (p. 129), that the real dichotomy of political life resides in an antagonism not between Democrat and Republican but between "routineers" and "inventors"—were applications of essentially Bergsonian ideas to political analysis.

We should not, however, minimize Lippmann's originality. He was probably right when he said that "no matter how much we talk about the infusion of the 'evolutionary' point of view into all of modern thought, when the test is made political practice shows itself almost virgin to the idea" (p. 16). His own eager plea that the practical business of politics is to harmonize divergent tendencies and to provide adequate "channels" (p. 114) and "fine opportunities" (p. 225) for fundamental human impulses was less a modification of syndicalist principles than an original and inspired reaffirmation of a traditional democratic mode of thought, neither beguiled by a "superficial homogeneity" nor diverted by a petrifying, institutionalized propriety. Ethical questions are simply beside the point in the management of the national life, he argued; our faith in the mechanism of democracy has tended to "blot out human prestige, to minimize the influence of personality" (p. 18). Lippmann's politics may have been radical, but his values were conventionally democratic.

A Preface to Politics is a brilliant and natively optimistic reassertion, à la Bergson and others, of our national credo. Confident in the goodness of the average citizen when the individual personality is allowed to ripen and creatively express itself in daily life rather than made to conform to national pieties, Lippmann attempted to probe behind superficial rivalries and divisions and to bundle together the sheaf of natural tendencies. In sum, he endeavored to see in the diversity of our communal life a single impulse striving to express itself—to make, of the many, one.

To some extent, Van Wyck Brooks shared Lippmann's complaints, as they were expressed in *A Preface to Politics* and reiterated in *Drift and Mastery* (1914), about the quality of American life, and Brooks extended them in his analysis of our literary tradition. Though from time to time he displayed a nodding acquaintance with philosophical vitalism in "America's Coming of Age" and "Letters and Leadership" and wished to place the creative impulse at the center of the country's preoccupations, Brooks's methods were rather more derisive than constructive. His early essays were something of a disenchanted filibuster against American culture and ambitions. Like Lippmann, he believed that the pioneer spirit survived in the form of simple acquisitiveness and that the outlets for the expression of human personality were stopped up. But, save his celebration of Whitman as a poet who transcended the inherited cultural oppression of the creative personality, Brooks expressed little of the Bergsonian optimism of the time; rather, he foreshadowed and to a degree helped shape the mood of the 1920s.

We find a more direct, if less familiar, application of vitalistic principles to literature in Edwin Björkman. Björkman, best known, if he is known at all, for his English translation and promotion of August Strindberg, was inspired by the vitalistic movement and applied its spirit to the principles of literary criticism. Though later critical theory was greatly influenced by Bergsonism and appropriated its subtler, more useful logic, we glimpse in the progressive spirit of Björkman a more accurate reflection of the times.

Actually, Björkman was well read in vitalistic writings, and his philosophical and literary essays, collected in *Is There Anything New under the Sun?* (1911) and *Voices of Tomorrow* (1913), provided a schematized amalgam of pragmatic and evolutionary principles. Nevertheless, the dominant impress of Bergson is observable in the development of his thought, and appropriately so, for Bergson more than other vitalists stressed the significance of artistic creation to the development of the race.

Himself a Swedish immigrant, Björkman began his journalistic career in Minneapolis in 1892 and later moved to New York, where, as a reporter for the *New York Sun*, the *New York Times*, and the *New York Evening Post* and as an editor for the *World's Work*, his literary acumen seems to have developed in spite of, rather than because of, his vitalistic convictions. At best, his progressive optimism created a broad tolerance and enthusiasm for the innovative, and he instanced John Galsworthy, the "serious" George Bernard Shaw, Strindberg, Björnstjerne Björnson, and Hjadman Söderberg as possessors of the new spirit. Yet, Björkman found the reformer's impulse anathema to art, its main symptom being an "exaggerated faith in the efficacy of precept,"[47] whereas true art was nothing more or less than "experimental creation" (p. 203) that flourished independent of ethical and social concerns.

Björkman's own version of vitalism is expanded in the first section of *Is There Anything New under the Sun?*, and his series of proclamations must appear slightly ridiculous to a modern reader. His belief that before our "rapt eyes life flows by like a mighty, restless, all-embracing current of energy" (p. 17) led him to plot the course of this flow. Thus, he identified four "cosmic tendencies" (p. 39) that for humanity, because one is always both an individual and a member of the race, translate into four "master instincts"—"the *will to be*, the *will to love*, the *will to do*, and the *will to rule*"

(p. 43). These competing impulses foster an irresistible impulse toward self-expression and the exercise of the emotional faculties, leading ultimately toward an ever-sought state of perfection, the residue of which is simply the cultural reward of evolutionary progress. The stronger that inner voice is in some individuals, the more it turns them from "well worn grooves." And "out of such individuals comes poetry—whether it be made *by* them or *about* them" (p. 64). The changes wrought by these individuals ultimately result in the healthy and cooperative advancement of the quality of life. Our own age, Björkman claimed, is at a turning point in evolutionary progress: "No longer does the old chasm yawn between our intellect and our senses, or between our 'noble' sentiments and our 'degrading' needs and desires" (pp. 75–76).

The exhilarated convictions and high-flown purposes argued in the opening chapters of his book translated into the duties and practices of criticism in the two concluding chapters. The most valuable resource of the creative artist for Björkman, as for Bergson, is the power of "suggestiveness." "By stopping short of exhaustive explanations, it enlists the imaginative cooperation of our minds," he claimed (p. 225). He also adopted the Bergsonian point of view when he maintained that art "appears as an instrument forged by life for the promotion of its most essential purpose—its own perfection"; art is a "messenger and missionary of a great life force" (p. 229). The true artist must master technique and consult artistic tradition for inspiration, but the muse is, simply put, life itself. The "outward form" of art is a "vessel," but it must have content as well. That content derives from the artist's spirit: "It is the inspiration of the artist that counts, not his intention; it is the spirit speaking *through* him, often independently of his conscious reason, that stamps his work in its relation to the forward urge of Life" (pp. 252–53).

The great artist, Björkman added, "absorbs into his own soul the essence of what the race has thought and felt and aspired up to that time. To this he adds something that is wholly his own" (p. 249). The critic, however, works from the other, or social, side. The critic must attempt to determine the artistic form, its formal antecedents, and its subject matter and to relate them to both the past and the future. The significant artist is someone who "roots himself most firmly in the past while reaching farthest into the future" (p. 249), and the critic identifies the scope and implication of great art. Though Bergsonian principles were applied to critical theory more rigorously and in more subtle and interesting ways by

others (most familiarly in the "speculations" of T. E. Hulme), I have
lingered over Björkman's exuberant applications as representative of
American excitement for Bergson.

Whatever Bergson contributed to the dominant faith in the progressivism of the time, he also seems to have suggested to some, however
vaguely, a furtherance, an evolutionary continuity of existing American
traditions as they had been expressed by such men of good hope as Emerson and Whitman or as might be found in the pioneering tradition itself.
These were at best hastily drawn and strained analogies, however. Some
journalists discerned faint echoes of democratic truths in this French philosopher, but nothing systematically pertinent to that tradition. Yet if the
past itself is life, if memory bends over the future with love, as Bergson
said it did, here was a philosophy of nostalgic remembrance and personal
continuity that modified present perceptions and conditioned the expectations of the future. This point is relevant to the "literary psychology" (as
Santayana termed it) Bergson provided for the creative writer, but we may
glimpse its relevance more clearly in the American historian Carl Becker.

As early as 1913, in an essay prepared for the *American Journal of Sociology*, Becker announced that "philosophy, which natural science, in the
heyday and flush of its tawdry intolerance, so carefully interred forty years
ago, has come to life again; and its first conscious act has been to an-
nounce, in metaphysical and poetical form, a definition of time which
frees the will from deterministic shackles, and a conception of history
which liberates the present from slavish dependence on the past."[48] The
effacement of the boundaries between history and philosophy and the
social sciences, he believed, provided a happy augury for the history that
was yet to be written.

Historians are beginning to recognize "very slowly" that the past must
be regarded in a "new way, or perhaps in an old way," Becker maintained
(p. 664). He was echoing the claims of James Harvey Robinson, under
whom he had studied during his graduate years at Columbia University.
Robinson, in "The New History," published only a few years before
Becker's essay, had suggested that history is neither as remote nor as
objective a subject of study as historians would like it to be. History might
be viewed "as an artificial extension and broadening of our memories and
may be used to overcome the natural bewilderment of all unfamiliar situations."[49] Thus regarded, history is personally intimate and significant to
activity in the present.

Another Columbia University professor, Frederick J. E. Woodbridge, himself a philosopher, would adopt a Bergsonian perspective in articulating *The Purpose of History* (1916).[50] Historians, no less than scientists, he maintained, are apt to represent time spatially. The result is the distortion whereby historians read a purpose into history by their selection of facts but believe they have found it there. History, Woodbridge concluded, is "not only the conserving, the remembering, and the understanding of what has happened: it is also the completing of what has happened. And since in man history is consciously lived, the completing of what has happened is also the attempt to carry it to what he calls perfection."[51] Becker himself would take up this theme years later in his 1931 presidential address to the American Historical Association, which he titled "Every Man His Own Historian."

Bergsonism, for Becker, was at best a tributary influence; it was not a formative one. He made many shifts in his historical perspective during his career, and the vicissitudes of his thought and feeling are sensitively and suggestively traced by David Noble in *Historians against History*. But, as late as 1931, Becker enlisted Bergsonian psychology to define the social role of the historian and the relevance of history to modern life, and he furnishes a telling example of how Bergsonism might be fittingly appropriated to regard the past as well as the future.

"It is impossible to divorce history from life," he maintained in his address—impossible because of the nature of time and memory, both aspects of human knowing and human nature. To explain the significance of time and memory to the historian, Becker drew upon a blend of Jamesian and Bergsonian principles: "We must have a present, and so we create one by robbing the past, by holding on to the most recent events and pretending that they all belong to our immediate perceptions."[52] He clarified his point by a simple example (one of Bergson's favorites): "If, for example, I raise my arm, the total event is a series of occurrences of which the first are past before the last have taken place; and yet you perceive it as a single movement executed in one present instant. The telescoping of successive events into a single instant philosophers call the 'specious present'" (p. 240).

The terminology was doubtless drawn from James's *Principles of Psychology* (though James himself had borrowed it from E. R. Clay), but the conclusions Becker drew from the example are distinctly more Bergsonian than Jamesian. Shrewdly expanding the notion of the specious present beyond the bounds of the simple psychological perception of philosophers to present hours, years, and generations, he thus made the present a primary concern for historians. History, in its simplest terms, is "the memory of things said and done" (p. 235), and since memory is the most essential ingredient in knowledge, "history may become any artificial extension and enlargement of human memory perpetuating itself in this present" (pp. 234–35). The past, however, must always be directed toward a future action; the more complete and stable our memory of the past, the more we are provided with a "hypothetical, patterned future" necessary for human orientation in the world. Since memory makes no distinction between the actual and the artificial recollection, a good deal of human knowledge is sheer fancy that must be adjusted according to the recorded and objective fact. However, our memory does not need to be true so much as it needs to be useful to some practical and purposive action in the present. Because of the nature of this reconstruction of remembered activities and things, those who would imagine their past always retain "something of the freedom of the creative artist" (p. 245). The professional historian's charge, therefore, is a very old one—to be the "bard" or "soothsayer" of the tribe entrusted with keeping, and keeping alive, the "useful myths" (p. 247).

History, in this sense, is always a story, and historians, in fact, must use the normal devices of literary narrative. Historians, no less than Mr. Everyman of "Every Man His Own Historian," are disposed to view the past in terms of their immediate situation as they understand it and necessarily delude themselves when they characterize history as objective or scientific. History is the same blend of fact and fancy (or, in the case of historians, of fact and interpretation) as goes into all story making. The mere selection of one set of facts over another is the beginning of a pattern-making process, and, said Becker, historical facts have a "negotiable existence only in literary discourse" (p. 251). Histories have a practical purpose only insofar as they enrich the present of Mr. Everyman and enable him to direct his activity toward a meaningful future. Sooner or later, Becker concluded, professional historians must adapt their "knowledge" to Mr. Everyman's "necessities" (p. 252).

Nowhere in this address does Becker mention Bergson by name, but clearly he had adopted the Bergsonian epistemology and made it serve his purpose of defining a living history and the social role of the historian. Certainly, an antiquarian's objective interest in the past neither outfits one to become a historian nor comes to grips with the evolutionary character of history itself. Perhaps, Becker in his address was transforming Frederick Jackson Turner's frontier thesis into a psychological and humane process rather than a social and economically determined dialectic. For what, after all, is the frontier thesis but the past moving into the future? And what is the pioneering experience and history itself but, as Willa Cather had intimated in *O Pioneers!* (1913), the old story writing itself over with the best that we have? In any event, Becker converted Bergson's "literary psychology" to the uses of narrative history. In so doing, he found that the past, as was the historian, was indeed "usable."

Becker's progressive faith, like that of so many others, foundered upon the shoals of the Great War. And if it were never entirely regained, if the great social changes to be wrought by liberal political reform later seemed an idle hope, by 1931 he seemed content to pin his hopes on nothing grander than the historically minded Mr. Everyman endeavoring to get along in the world. This was a mundane faith, and the purpose of history, at best, was to enlarge the personal present of the common citizen. Historians must resign themselves to living in whatever future Mr. Everyman might create for them. This was no blind faith in an élan vital (which as early as 1914 Becker had sarcastically described as "the measure of virtue")[53] but a reaffirmation, still along democratic lines yet informed by a Bergsonian psychology, of the Jeffersonian common man and woman.

In an essay published in 1927 and entitled simply "Frederick Jackson Turner," Becker had spelled out the appropriateness of the novelistic approach to history, even if he had not yet explicitly endorsed it as he did in his presidential address. The difficulty for the historian who would deliver us a "comprehensive history" is both methodological and generic. The proper task for the historian is to make "a synthesis of social forces" and to "trace the evolution of society":

> The point is that for the "synthesis of social forces" one must employ the method of generalized description; while for the "evolution of society" (in the chronological sense that is) one must narrate the forward march of events. Well, the generalization spreads out in space, but how to get the wretched thing to move forward in time! The generalization, being timeless, will not move forward; and so the harassed historian, compelled to get on with the story, must return in some fashion to the individual, the concrete event, the "thin red line of heroes."[54]

In the historical consciousness of Carl Becker we see clearly a turn toward the literary psychology and the creative integrity of the novelist and poet. In order for the past to be at all usable, it must serve the purposes of life, and events do not march of their own accord. Becker seems to have recognized, as Woodbridge did before him, that the italicized *t* is as problematic for the historian's formula as Bergson had argued it was for the mathematician and the scientist, that time as a fourth dimension is psychologically conditioned and internally felt. History, like the universe itself, is, from a certain point of view, a heterogeneous mass of simultaneities, of dead facts, ordered, if they are ordered at all, within an intimate and personal memory that meets the future through purposeful activity. The historical fact that the Declaration of Independence was signed on 23 August 1776 matters not at all to Mr. Everyman when his memory tells him that it was signed on 4 July. The remembered event, however grossly false it may be to documented fact, "will have for him significance and magic, much or little or none at all, as it fits well or ill into his little world of interests and aspirations and emotional comforts."[55]

The duty of historians is always, argues Becker, to be true to their facts insofar as they can ascertain them, but in delivering the verifiable past to the exigencies of the present, historians, knowingly or unknowingly, narrate the past into existence, promote their own legends, which may or may not displace more familiar ones. In either case, historians who would make a generalization "move forward" must fall back upon the resources of the novelist, or bard, and locate it in the individual character and concrete event. For Carl Becker, Bergson's literary psychology, if not a wholly satisfactory solution, provided a means, however temporarily he might claim it, of retrieving a personal past from the welter of desiccated fact and generalization.

IV

The Bergsonian influence in America is a largely unchronicled and, I think, significant episode in our social history, and I have meant merely to sketch the general contours and dimensions of that influence. Those who might read *Matter and Memory* or *Creative Evolution* today would likely find little there either to excite such giddy enthusiasm or to provoke such nervous opprobrium as is discernible in the published reaction during these years. Although we have the authority of at least one journalist, writing in 1914, that Bergson's "influence is in the air nowadays" and, referring to the recent indexing of Bergson's work by the church, that the Catholic laity "cannot be sheltered from it if they read at all,"[56] his influence was more than simply an atmospheric one. Curious and sometimes brilliant blendings and collocations of Bergsonism with unrelated disciplines, with equally new doctrines, or simply with private prejudices, various and original intellectual transactions, sustained and often dissolved his thought into the temper of the times, but always in concrete and interesting ways.

The imaginative applications of Bergsonism by men such as Lippmann and Björkman; its enthusiastic promotion in the popular press; its admiration and endorsement by such diverse but revered worthies as John Burroughs, William James, and Theodore Roosevelt (himself an American institution); its argued relevance to a variety of political and social causes —all of these tended to make Bergsonism appealing to the progressivism of the age, in both the dominant and radical modes. Thus conceived, it was an uplifting and encouraging philosophy, full of hope and confidence in the individual personality and fully connected to the larger workings of the universe. Walter Lippmann would complain as late as 1929 that certain "far-reaching conclusions" had been arrived at "by half-understood popularizations of Bergson or Freud."[57] Lippmann was himself secure in his understanding of Bergsonian principles, and his application of them in *A Preface to Politics* was one of the most legitimate and original adaptations in prewar America. Yet, his own appropriation was itself selective and partial; he tended to look to the future and to place his faith exclusively in the progressive ideal, in an evolutionary impetus creatively expressed and properly channeled to the uses of democratic life. Atavistic and nostalgic ingredients were in the Bergsonian psychology (indeed Ralph Barton Perry detected an "*aboriginal*" quality in Bergson's thought).[58] Lippmann may have slighted or simply neglected them, but they made their equal appeal to the historically minded, to antimodernists, or to the simply nostalgic.

In a real sense, the philosophy of Bergson inadvertently inserted itself into the interstices of traditional American prepossessions. He displayed immense erudition and subtle powers of reasoning, but, in the end, Bergson appeared to be uttering familiar democratic truths. He was commonly compared to Emerson, and sometimes to Whitman. Like Emerson, he seemed to preach a "poetry and philosophy of insight and not of tradition"; he was one who would have us clear away the received ideas that float upon the surface of consciousness like so many dead leaves and obscure a more fundamental spiritual life. Like Whitman, he seemed to celebrate the "procreant urge of the world" and the "ever push'd elasticity" of youth, wherein resided the fundamental author of free acts. He would restore to the individual, in Emerson's phrase, "an original relation to the universe," unfettered by habit and accommodation. And, like Emerson too, Bergson was sometimes thought to have promoted a religious pantheism. Yet fundamentally, their philosophical positions were antithetical—Bergsonism is a philosophy of immanence, not transcendence. Nevertheless, it was a philosophy especially attractive to the creative artist, in America and Europe. And when we turn our attention to the appeal of Bergson to the literary sensibility, we find the same ambivalence that characterized the reactions of the population at large. Moreover, we find an emerging awareness of the entrance of a new reality that would have its inevitable effects upon the literary consciousness and of a neoromanticism that would underwrite new literary forms.

It may or may not be true that, as Santayana observed, Bergson's philosophy offered its readers little more than a "literary psychology." It is true that Bergsonism was a widespread popular phenomenon that possessed a special fascination and appeal for the literary artist. There are too many particular instances (sometimes acknowledged by the writers themselves, sometimes detected by scholars) of an indebtedness to Bergson's system as a salutary and liberating influence upon individual creative temperaments to dismiss his importance to literary history. To establish the point, one need only review the names of a few of those who were in some measure influenced by Bergson: Marcel Proust, Nikos Kazantzakis, Paul Valéry, Virginia Woolf, Thomas Wolfe, Wallace Stevens, James Joyce, William Faulkner, T. S. Eliot, Robert Frost, Willa Cather, T. E. Hulme, and Wyndham Lewis.[59] Kazantzakis, Hulme, and Lewis studied under Bergson; T. S. Eliot, as did Gertrude Stein[60] (whose philosophical preferences seemed to remain nevertheless with her former teacher William James), attended his lectures at the Collège de France; and Edith Wharton, in her autobiography, recalls a stimulating dinner conversation with the man.[61]

Even F. Scott Fitzgerald, not notable for his interest in ideas, devoted the summer of 1917 to reading William James, Arthur Schopenhauer, and Henri Bergson.[62] If Fitzgerald took that reading very seriously, it does not show in his comic reference to Bergson in *The Beautiful and the Damned* (1922):

"What'd you talk about" [asks Anthony Patch]. "—Bergson? Bilphism? Whether or not the one-step is immoral?"

Maury was unruffled; his fur seemed to run all ways.

"As a matter of fact we did talk on Bilphism. Seems her mother's a Bilphist. Mostly, though, we talked about legs."[63]

"Bilphism" is apparently Fitzgerald's invention, and the linkage of Bergson with this imagined school is meant to convey something of the quality of faddish enthusiasm surrounding Bergson in 1913, the year of the action of the novel. "Bilphism," we learn later, is not merely a religion but the "science of all religions"—Shakespeare was a bilphist, Fitzgerald has Mrs. Gilbert proclaim. "If you've read 'Hamlet,' you can't help but see it" (p. 76).

Fitzgerald's satirical and casual dismissal of Bergsonism as something quite as preposterous and unlikely as "Bilphism" epitomizes a similar, if far more sophisticated, tendency in other writers who were more disposed to take Bergsonism seriously but equally loathe to be identified with such bourgeois enthusiasm. We have already noticed a like reaction in philosophers and psychologists. Nevertheless, the fact remains that Bergson was significant to a considerable number of accomplished twentieth-century writers, but in ways that are often difficult to assess or chart. As we have seen, Bergsonism could be appropriated easily enough to the uses and designs of various and divergent creeds and disciplines. This was as true for literary creeds as it was for others; Bergson had something to do with the formation of such literary programs as imagism and, more broadly, modernism. He may even be linked to the aesthetic principles of postmodernism.[64]

Among the first in England to promote Bergsonism and its special application to literature and art were F. S. Flint, John Middleton Murry, and T. E. Hulme. Murry, in 1911, proclaimed that the artist lifts the veil that separates us from the "great divinity immanent in the world" and that the philosophy of Bergson reestablishes the primacy of the artist as the advocate for a new, fluid reality.[65] Murry was the first in England to apply the new metaphysic to the uses of literary theory, yet even he would qualify his endorsements by insisting that "Modernism is not the capricious outburst of intellectual dipsomania" (p. 57) and, thereby, separate himself from those stricken by the current Bergson mania.

T. E. Hulme's interest in Bergson was originally more purely philosophical than aesthetic, but Bergsonism contributed its share to his thinking about imagism and to his significant "A Lecture on Modern Poetry."

Hulme's interest in Bergsonian vitalism stemmed as much from inner necessity as from intellectual curiosity, however. He declared forthrightly in a five-part essay for the *New Age*, entitled "Notes on Bergson,"[66] that the philosopher had released him from a "nightmare": "If I compare my nightmare to imprisonment in a small cell, then the door of that cell was for the first time thrown open" (p. 30).

These "Notes" attempted to define the nature and the terms of that release. Hulme's sense of imprisonment derived in part from a sense of the claustrophobic and oppressive implications of a Spencerian, mechanistic weltanschauung, but it also derived from the terrible exclusiveness and power that vision enjoyed. What was disturbing in this worldview was not the materialistic philosophy itself but its dominance, the almost total want of balance, unrestrained by a countervailing force. So heavily armed was the mechanistic philosophy that dethroning it with any feeble or illogical notions of spirituality or the soul seemed impossible. Bergson did not, for Hulme, drive out the prevailing intellectualism of the day, but he did right the balance. Hulme did not discover in Bergsonism that he had a soul, but he was able for the first time to "meet fairly without any fudging the real force which was opposed to it. It would have been sheer silliness on my part to pretend that this force did not exist, for I knew very well that it did and affected me powerfully" (p. 42). This affective power of Bergson rather than his contribution to the development of a modernist or imagist aesthetic is our concern here, and Hulme offers one of the most articulate and thoughtful assessments of that transforming and exhilarating power.

For Hulme, Bergson could be empowering without requiring discipleship. As did William James, Hulme seemed to see in Bergson an "exquisite commander" around whom one might gather in opposition to the dominant intellectualism of the day. Throughout his "Notes on Bergson," Hulme was careful to describe the influence Bergson had upon him in a way that exonerated him from any accusation of youthful enthusiasm, sentimentality, or "romanticism"—the last an accusation Hulme regarded with "peculiar horror" (p. 32). There is nothing "comic" in those people who found in Bergson that they had "suddenly discovered their souls," he said, "but merely an admirable sense of reality" (pp. 42–43).

T. S. Eliot shared Hulme's dread of the imputation of anything that smacked of the romantic. However, whereas Hulme sought to qualify his reaction to Bergson, Eliot came to deny or repudiate it. Eliot, indeed, seems to have suddenly discovered that he had a "soul" when he first encountered the philosopher. He attended seven of Bergson's lectures at the Collège de France in January and February 1911, and according to his mother, Eliot was so affected by the man that he opted for graduate study at Harvard in philosophy instead of literature.[67]

Eliot's philosophical enthusiasm soon turned from the neoromantic vitalism of Bergson to the sceptical idealism of F. H. Bradley, however. The two schools of thought could not have comfortably shared his allegiance, for as Eliot himself once noted, Bergson and Bradley have virtually nothing in common except the possession of an exquisite prose style peculiarly suited to their respective points of view.[68] Nevertheless, Eliot's temporary enthusiasm for Bergson was probably more ardent than it ever was for Bradley, and his subsequent repudiation of Bergson at times resembled the mordant satirical strategies of Fitzgerald rather than the closely reasoned criticism of someone trained in philosophy.

In 1948, Eliot confessed that he had temporarily been a convert to Bergsonism (the only such "conversion" he had ever been liable to).[69] How temporary his conversion was is a matter of some dispute. According to F. O. Matthiessen, Eliot, in an essay written in 1913 while he was still at Harvard, had been openly critical of Bergson. A. D. Moody believes that Eliot's conversion lasted only a few months in 1911 and that he weaned himself of his enthusiasm in unsatisfactory poetic experiments in the Bergsonian vein in that year. More recently, Paul Douglass has argued that Eliot was permanently affected by Bergson and Bergsonism.[70] At any rate, by 1917, when he published a two-part sketch called "Eeldrop and Appleplex," Eliot was sufficiently disaffected to lampoon such romantic philosophical enthusiasms in the culture and, presumably, in himself.

The sketch, in its essentials, is a comic dialogue on the temper of the times, and Eeldrop appears as a version of Eliot himself. Eeldrop is a "sceptic, with a taste for mysticism," who also happens to be learned in theology; he is, as well, as was Eliot at the time, a "bank-clerk" whose tastes and interests run toward the literary.[71] According to William Skaff, Eliot first became interested in Bergsonism because it provided a means for him to rationalize his own youthful mystical experiences, but when Eliot's scepticism overruled his mysticism, he turned to Bradley.[72] In any event, by the time he came to write "Eeldrop and Appleplex," Eliot had become merely sardonic toward Bergson. "The question is," says Appleplex, "what is to be our philosophy?"

"This must be settled at once. Mrs. Howexden recommends me to read Bergson. He writes very entertainingly on the eye of the frog."

"Not at all," interrupted his friend. "Our philosophy is quite irrelevant. The essential is, that our philosophy should spring from our point of view and not return upon itself to explain our point of view. A philosophy about intuition is somewhat less likely to be intuitive than any other. We must avoid having a platform."[73]

Eeldrop goes on to observe that, whatever one's philosophy, one must attempt to resist a label—such labeling cannot be totally escaped, but one may define oneself in a way that "carries no distinction" and therefore "arouses no self-consciousness" (p. 11).

However much Eliot wished to dissociate himself from labels, and especially the label of being a Bergsonian romantic, he does not in this sketch seriously question Bergsonian philosophical assumptions. It seems likely that he was more interested in simply separating himself from pedestrian enthusiasms than in criticizing particular philosophical systems. Eeldrop and Appleplex wish to escape the "too well pigeon-holed, too taken-for-granted, too highly systematized" (p. 8); they wish to assert their iconoclasm and the superiority of their desire over "generalized men." In a word—expressed "in the language of those whom they sought to avoid—they wished 'to apprehend the human soul in its concrete individuality'" (p. 8). Eliot further distances his characters (and himself) from the masses when he has Appleplex say, "The majority of mankind live on paper currency: they use terms which are merely good for so much reality, they never see actual coinage" (p. 10). Ironically, the notion and the language are reminiscent of Bergson himself: when language, especially poetic language, transcends its pedestrian functions of labeling and categorizing and somehow evokes a more fundamental, fluid reality, it could be said that the poet has got "hold of the gold coin, instead of having the silver or copper change for it" (ME 160).

My point here is not to question Eliot's authenticity or to revise the commonly accepted notion that the course of his intellectual development led him away from the vitalism of a Bergson and toward the neo-Hegelianism of a Bradley or, more generally, the antiromanticism of an Irving Babbitt. I want, instead, to note merely the possibility that Eliot was as reluctant as was Hulme to be labeled an enthusiast or a romantic. Having discovered that he possessed a soul, Eliot may have been anxious to disguise the fact or, at least, to appear tough minded about the newly discovered property. And certainly something of this sort of motivation and strategy is discernible in Eliot's fellow modernist Wyndham Lewis.

Wyndham Lewis had studied under Bergson in 1910 and, like Eliot, was for a time a convert. Whether or not he discovered in the Bergsonian metaphysic that he too had a soul, Lewis nonetheless sought to distance himself from his teacher by mocking and denunciation in *Time and Western Man* (1927).[74] If he acknowledges that Bergson more than any other figure is "responsible for the main intellectual characteristics of the world we live in,"[75] Lewis equally regards him as a diminished figure whose personal and direct influence upon that world perished with the Great War. If Bergson was the first philosopher to take time seriously, his is also a "brutal" world and he a "philosophic ruffian, of the darkest and most forbidding description: and he pulls every emotional lever on which he can lay his hands" (p. 170). Lewis might privately confess in a letter written more than twenty years after the publication of *Time and Western Man* that he had embraced Bergsonism with a youthful earnestness and add that "when one is young *on fait des bêtises, quoi!*"[76] Nowhere in the book, however, does he betray any of that earlier enthusiasm, nor does he display any of his former susceptibility to the attractions of the "sickly ecstasies of the *élan vital*" (p. 210).

One may, perhaps unkindly, characterize the sort of distancing from Bergson observable in Eliot and Lewis as merely symptomatic of the anxiety of influence. But the motives for such dissociation may in fact be more complicated than a simple resistance to doctrine or a declaration of aesthetic independence. For, as we have seen, Bergson was as much a popular phenomenon as he was a serious philosopher. What Lewis and Eliot and no doubt others might be moved to resist, as much as the system itself, is the association with a broad public for whom the Bergsonian system had a considerable appeal. As we have seen, many were cynical about the popularity of Bergson's thought, and even adherents, such as Walter Lippmann, despised a promiscuous and uninformed application of Bergsonian principles to private desires and interests. Eeldrop and Appleplex wish to avoid the lot of "generalized men" and superciliously regard labeling and cataloguing as "not only satisfactory *to other people* for practical purposes, it is sufficient for *their* 'life of the spirit'" (p. 10; italics mine). Apart from any intellectual or ethical quarrels that Eliot and Lewis might have had with Bergson and the fact that they may have come to regard vitalism as démodé, they may have been equally moved to reject the taint of the popular and conventional.

In Hulme's "Notes on Bergson," a like motivation to separate himself from common intellectual belief, but performed in a more cautious and discriminating way, operates throughout. For Hulme recognized, in fact insisted, that Bergson is "not the only philosopher who has refuted mechanism"—that that point of view can be traced back to Coleridge or even earlier.[77] The real question concerns the sudden obsession with Bergson's particular brand of refutation. The kind of "mental debility" that expects to find in any new philosophy the excitement that makes one believe one is on the "verge of an entirely 'new' state of society" is common enough and is to be found in any age. With the Bergson mania of Hulme's own time, this expectation approaches a "hysterical pitch which can almost be called a disease" (p. 34). As had William James, Hulme identifies the seductive powers of Bergson's style as a contributing cause: "It is not so much anything definite that Bergson says that moves them to enthusiasm as the fact that certain sentences perhaps give a pretext for this enthusiasm to empty itself in a flood" (p. 33).

Bergson articulated for a great number of men and women notions that existed in "embryo" already and must have been "present in the mind of this generation ready to be developed" (p. 37). In this sense Bergson serves the modern spirit, for his originality was that of articulating an ancient impulse. Bergson's widespread acceptance is attributable to the "only originality left to a philosopher—the invention of a new dialect in which to restate an old attitude": "This, then, is the sense that I might safely say that Bergson had presented a new solution to an old problem. I should restate the thing, to avoid any suspicion of romanticism, in this way: Bergson has provided in the dialect of the time the only possible way out of the nightmare" (p. 36).

Hulme treats Bergson and Bergsonism as the epitome of the emerging new reality, not as its cause but as its occasion. And it seems to me that this is the proper and most profitable way to inquire into the matter of Bergson's role in these historical circumstances. If by cause we mean something that will explain its effect, then Bergson cannot be considered as the "cause" of the new reality. If, on the other hand, we consider him as a cause in the sense of releasing pent-up energy, then Bergson can indeed be seen as having a causal influence upon this transformation of reality. It is through Bergson, rather than because of him, that Hulme obtained the key to unlock the mechanistic prison that held him. But that key "corresponded to the type of key which I had always imagined would open it" (p. 30). Because Bergson's philosophy corresponds to a felt solution to those vague, inarticulate fears and enables one to oppose them, he may be considered a central and defining influence on the age.

Not as the formative influence upon a literary style or program nor even as one who provided a fashionable literary psychology is Bergson central to this study. Rather, through him, and through individual responses to him, we may chart in the literary imagination a historical phenomenon— the movement away from nineteenth-century naturalism and toward the new consciousness of the twentieth century—without restricting our inquiry to aesthetic categories or literary schools or even particular sources of literary influence, though these last are plentiful enough. For Bergson existed both as the most significant philosopher of the day (one whose idiom and structure of thought are especially useful for our inquiry) and as something of a social institution. The substance of his thought and the amazingly diverse and ranging reaction to him as the avatar of this new reality provide a means to focus our investigation and to coordinate otherwise heterogeneous and extraneous materials. In a word, he enables us to speak intelligibly about something so grandiose as the transformation of reality.

Sometime in 1910 or thereabouts, the world changed, and Bergson served as an integrating and luminous intelligence in this change. That the world, or rather (to borrow the language of Wallace Stevens) one's "sense of the world," did indeed change is a matter of recorded testimony. That the imaginative artist's sense of the world is (to borrow the intent of Stevens's language) supremely important and, finally, the poet's truest subject is a matter that reveals itself in the investigation of individual artistic ambitions and achievements. An artist's sense of the world is a private and idiomatic affair, but the transformation of a weltanschauung is a generalized condition. I have already noted the often effusive and far-fetched statements of popular belief in a new reality on the wing. But we have not yet identified this sense of a new reality with particular reference to the literary mind.

Hulme is once again helpful in characterizing not only this transformation from one vision of the world to another but also the vague and stealthy way in which such a transformation enacts itself. "For some people," he writes, "by a kind of slow and gradual change, and not by any definite conscious process, the difficulty [of dealing with the nightmare of mechanism] vanishes" (p. 56). Such a gradual transformation "is like the dissolving pictures that one used to see in the pre-cinema age, where one scene melts away into the next and is not shifted to make room for its successor. In your view of the cosmos the things which at one time seemed the solid things melt away, and the flimsy, cloud-like entities gradually harden down till they become the solid bases on which the rest of our beliefs are supported. Whereas at one time you felt sure that matter was the only permanent thing; you now find that you are equally convinced, without any necessity of proof, of the permanent existence of individuals." The sense of this change, Hulme insists, "takes place on the plane of quality and feeling, rather than that of clear representations" (p. 57).

But T. E. Hulme was not the only artist to note this change. Virginia Woolf, too, records the transformation, and she is as exact as she is arbitrary when she declares in her lecture "Mr. Bennett and Mrs. Brown" that "on or about December, 1910, human character changed." The date probably refers to the opening of the Second Impressionist Show, and the assertion is dramatic. But she is quick to qualify, if not to completely withdraw, the assertion: "I am not saying that one went out, as one might into a garden, and there saw that a rose had flowered, or that a hen had laid an egg. The change was not sudden and definite like that. But a change there was, nevertheless; and since one must be arbitrary, let us date it about the year 1910."[78]

The way was paved for this change, she remarks, by Samuel Butler's *The Way of All Flesh* (1903) and the dramas of George Bernard Shaw, writings that emphasized the evolutionary character of reality and the dramatic force of the life urge. And if Woolf openly yearns for a recognizable code of manners that would enable the writer to render characters in fiction adequately, she does not intend to deliver herself of regret or nostalgia. What is at stake for the writer in this time of change is the preservation of ordinary character in fictions that are responsive to these transformations of human personality. She offers her hypothetical Mrs. Brown as palpable example of what is to be gained or lost, and Woolf at once sympathizes with and depreciates modernist literary techniques. Joyce is too indecent and Eliot too obscure for her tastes, but she recognizes that the literary tools of a past generation will not serve the literary purposes of the present. She divides her attention between the outmoded and unserviceable literary manner of the Edwardians and the fragmentary attempts of the Georgians to forge a new aesthetic. The writer (or at least Virginia Woolf), after the change of human character in 1910, is deprived of the first and sceptical of the second. Still, she is sanguine about future prospects at the conclusion of her lecture: "For I will make one final and surpassingly rash prediction—we are trembling on the verge of one of the great ages of English literature" (p. 119).

William Carlos Williams, in his *Autobiography*, recalls his belated recognition that at some point the world had changed, and he too, perhaps in imitation of Woolf, tentatively locates the change in the occasion of an exhibition of modern art, the Armory Show, which opened in New York in February 1913:

> There had been a break somewhere, we [poets] were streaming through, each thinking his own thoughts, driving his own designs toward his self's objectives. Whether the Armory Show in painting did it or whether that also was no more than a facet—the poetic line, the way the image was to lie on the page was our immediate concern. For myself all that implied, in the materials, respecting the place I knew best, was finding a local assertion—to my everlasting relief. I had never in my life before felt that way. I was tremendously stirred.[79]

The reactions of Woolf and Williams to this undefinable event are quite different, however—Woolf hopes for a new social consensus that will insure that the writer will not abandon her Mrs. Brown to the artifice of technique; Williams, by contrast, affirms the possibility of a new poetry and a new regionalism that allow for the local assertions of the self. Elsewhere, Williams elaborates upon the artistic difficulty in making such assertions in terms remarkably close to those Hulme used in his "A Lecture on Modern Poetry." Hulme had insisted that modern poetry "has become definitely and finally introspective and deals with expression and communication of momentary phases in the poet's mind."[80] Williams, in his "Prologue to *Kora in Hell*," remarks that "the thing that stands eternally in the way of really good writing is always one: the virtual impossibility of lifting to the imagination those things which lie under the direct scrutiny of the senses, close to the nose."

> It is this difficulty that sets a value upon all works of art and makes them a necessity. The senses witnessing what is immediately before them in detail see a finality which they cling to in despair, not knowing which way to turn. Thus the so-called natural or scientific array becomes fixed, the walking devil of modern life. He who even nicks the solidity of this apparition does a piece of work superior to that of Hercules when he cleaned the Augean stables.[81]

For Williams, the new reality involved him in a new poetic task—to cleanse the vision, to attend to the senses. Floyd Dell also sensed a change in the world and felt a command to see afresh. Dell, then living in Chicago and helping edit the *Friday Literary Review*, noted an urgency in the times and recalls his own perception of a change in the world in his autobiography, *Homecoming* (1933). He committed himself to his own generation and, in a New Year's resolution for 1912, formalized the commitment to slough off acquired habits and routines:

> I lived—so I reflected—in an interesting time, full of its own peculiar scenes, with sounds and colors all its own; and yet I had been content to read about it in the newspapers. . . . so I resolved to break up some of those regular habits which had kept me in a path as it were, between my apartment and the El, the El and the office, the office and the restaurant. I would resist that instinct of conservatism which had been keeping me in a pattern and making me old before my time. I would use my faculties, see and explore life, and so "on this short day of sun and frost, not lie down before the evening."[82]

Dell recalls that the occasion for his resolution followed a rereading of the conclusion to Pater's study of the Renaissance, yet such inspiration hardly encouraged the soon-to-be editor of the *Liberator* and the *Masses* in the direction of a detached aestheticism. Nor is his resolve merely indicative of the temper of the Chicago Renaissance. If the impulsions moved inward—to the precinct of individual perception and experience—the mood was general. "In the year 1911 there were signs that the world was on the verge of something," he writes. "It was thought to be new life":

> The London Athenaeum—we quoted in the Review—said: "Few observant people will deny that there are signs of an awakening in Europe. The times are great with the birth of some new thing. A spiritual renaissance may be at hand." The Contemporary Review said: "We are face to face with a new world teeming with wonders unknown," and prophesied a "European renaissance," "a thing of wonder and beauty, and supreme achievement." And George Cook, writing in the Friday Review, expressed the hope that America, as an intimate part of modern life, would be "moved by the same new perception of the beauty and wonder of the world, and not be voiceless."
>
> Something was in the air. Something was happening, about to happen—in politics, in literature, in art. The atmosphere became electric with it. [pp. 216–17]

One might cite still other instances of this felt sense of enormous and energizing change. Wallace Stevens, for example, identified the onset of a new, "vital" reality and remarked upon its attendant productive "tension" for the artist (*NA* 26). We will more closely inspect Stevens's participation in this shift of consciousness in a later chapter; our present purpose is simply to establish that such a vitalizing change of the world did in fact take place somewhere around 1910 or 1911 and that that change elicited in the literary mind, as it had in the popular mind, a seemingly inexhaustible variety of responses. The literary careers of Hulme, Woolf, Williams, and Dell, to name only those few, describe divergent, not unitary, courses of development, though each was affected by the indefinite something that happened around 1910 or 1911.

In the face of such diverse accumulated testimony, one must take seriously what otherwise might be deemed a patent absurdity: that the world (or, what amounts to the same thing, one's sense of the world) did indeed change—was radically transformed in ways that invaded one's sense of things at the level of perception and feeling—before the metamorphosis had acquired an accepted logic or science to correct or corroborate it.

V

What I mean to illustrate, or to at least suggest, by this brief review of isolated and individual instances of attention and reaction to the temper of the times in the years just prior to World War I is not that the sudden infusion of a soul in the consciousness of an age occurred. Nor do I even mean to insist that Bergson played any causal or defining role, positively or negatively, in the shift from one stock of assumptions or order of understanding to another. Whatever Bergson's actual historical significance may in fact be (and it seems to be considerable), Hulme's qualified assertions about the philosopher—that he provided a vocabulary and a logic for understanding larger historical purposes and forces—are perfectly adequate to this study. Through Bergson, I wish to hint at the larger reshaping of consciousness and, more particularly, the reformation of artistic ambitions testified to by a considerably diverse mass of evidence. But for that, Bergson is by no means incidental to my purposes. He is in one sense a convenience, but he is also an absolutely necessary departure point for any subsequent discussion of how particular creative intelligences might be implicated in this historical moment in important ways and yet be allowed their own unique and inimitable voices.

In the following chapters, I offer case studies of two original and important American writers: Willa Cather and Wallace Stevens. Both read and responded to Bergson in different but important ways that deeply affected their art. This is not to say that Bergson was the sole, or even the most significant, influence upon them—merely that he provides for this study a common denominator, a figure whose articulate voice and cultural importance were, finally, enabling to their own artistic expression. Nevertheless, he provides access to a sense of the "new reality" Cather and Stevens absorbed and, according to their own gifts, promoted in their art. The following pages, therefore, inspect and emphasize literary motivation over and above historical circumstance, and I bring a distinctly different approach to my subject from here on.

Wallace Stevens, speaking in 1942, remarked upon the pressure of reality and the function of the imagination as it relates to that pressure. Certain pressures (such as daily news of the events of World War II) may so forcibly invade the consciousness that the possibility of contemplation is eclipsed. The power of the imagination confronted by extreme circumstance is paralyzed. But not all events are so extreme or so disastrous to the imagination, and not all people are alike in their responses to events. Nevertheless, says Stevens, "the pressure of reality is, I think, the determining factor in the artistic character of an era and, as well, the determining factor in the artistic character of an individual" (NA 22–23). The degree and extent of this pressure, he claimed, is "incalculable and eludes the historian" (NA 21).

Doubtless, Stevens is right if the historian's calculations reduce the exertions of the imagination to so many formalized reflexes in response to the pressure of reality, for the imagination continually reaches beyond mere presence. Ideally, the dislocations of the modern poet slip the bonds of historical necessity in their poetic enlargements and metamorphoses. "It is one of the peculiarities of the imagination that it is always at the end of an era," Stevens insists. "What happens is that it is always attaching itself to a new reality, and adhering to it. It is not that there is a new imagination but that there is a new reality" (NA 22). I do not mean to give Stevens any special authority here, but it does seem to be true that the stabilizing gestures of the artist do not measure the pressure of reality so much as they disclose, in works of the imagination, individual resistance to such pressure. My case studies, then, are not meant to provide collective evidence for an eventual literary or historical generalization. Instead, the generalizations of the first part of this study are designed to provide evidence for a social and historical context in which the uniqueness of certain literary personalities might be made comprehensible.

Memorable literature typically springs from the struggle between self-expression and form. Particular forms, whether they be poems or fictions, are ordinarily the imperfectly realized residue of that struggle. But the individual creative personality lies behind its works, and I shall be more interested in the energies of literary motive than in the specifics of particular literary accomplishment. For that reason, too, I shall place a greater emphasis upon those years when the world changed and when the artistic motives and means of Cather and Stevens were transformed. Wallace Stevens identified the indefinite character of the creating self in his poem "Motive for Metaphor":

> The obscure moon lighting an obscure world
> Of things that would never be quite expressed,
> Where you yourself were never quite yourself
> And did not want nor have to be,
>
> Desiring the exhilarations of changes:
> The motive for metaphor, shrinking from
> The weight of primary noon,
> The A B C of being.
>
> The ruddy temper, the hammer
> Of red and blue, the hard sound—
> Steel against intimation—the sharp flash,
> The vital, arrogant, fatal, dominant X.   [*CP* 288]

My methodological approach to these artists shall be a typically genetic or biographical one, but the composing self is not identical with a self inscribed by events, the self of conventional literary biography, because it neither wants nor has to be. And the "obscure world of things" (which is also the world of the poet's literary subjects) is "never quite expressed." But poetry, as distinct from individual poems, may be considered a resistance to or a shrinking from the dominance of "X," an escape not from the thing itself but from the arrogance and brutal fatality of it. Stevens's poem suggests at least three items of belief about the creative motive that were points of conviction for both of my case studies: that language possesses a suggestive rather than a denotative power, that literature is fundamentally "escapist" in an honorific sense, and, finally, that the creating self mediates between a world of fact and feeling. I shall allude to these concepts at length in later chapters; for now, noting that my case studies do share certain defining characteristics, these among them, is sufficient. In short, there are aesthetic reasons for putting these figures together, even if we are determined to preserve a sense of their artistic individuality.

But there are also historical reasons for isolating Cather and Stevens for attention. From a historical point of view, they belong to the same generation. Both were born in the 1870s and grew up in a world dominated by the mechanistic philosophy that Hulme deplored and that, as Lovejoy claimed, generally was so monstrous to the imagination. The "new reality" of around 1910 was for them, therefore, all the more revolutionary and, perhaps, more liberating. Significantly, their most important work appeared after the advent of this new reality and when the writers were themselves in middle age. Cather's *O Pioneers!* was published in 1913; and though Stevens's first book of poems, *Harmonium*, was not published until 1923, "Peter Quince at the Clavier," his first really significant poem, was published in 1915. And as we shall see, these works bear discernible traces of the effects of reading Bergson and of the new philosophy.

Theirs was a generation altogether distinct from that of many familiar modernist writers. In 1900, Willa Cather was twenty-seven years old, Robert Frost (who was also profoundly influenced by Bergson and might as easily be included as another case study) was twenty-six, and Stevens was twenty-one. That same year, T. S. Eliot was twelve, and Ezra Pound fifteen; E. E. Cummings was six, F. Scott Fitzgerald four, Faulkner three, and Ernest Hemingway was just learning to walk and talk. When Gertrude Stein, also born in the 1870s, dismissed Hemingway's generation as lost, the gesture was in part an avuncular one. And when both Faulkner and Hemingway somewhat subversively declared their literary independence from Sherwood Anderson, it was in part youthful assertion. Cather and Stevens were a few years older than Van Wyck Brooks, H. L. Mencken, and George Jean Nathan, members of what Frederick J. Hoffman, in his book *The Twenties*, called the "old gang."[83]

One should not make too much of this distinction, I suppose, but it is at least worth noting that in 1920, say, the fund of memories (which for Bergson is nothing less than the creating self) available to Cather or Stevens was larger and qualitatively different from that of writers of a younger generation. They would have been old enough in 1886, for example, to have been disturbed by reports of the Haymarket Riots and perhaps old enough to have read a fictionalized account of them in *A Hazard of New Fortunes* (1890) by W. D. Howells (who was then the dean of

American letters). They might have read in newspapers about the massacre at Wounded Knee in 1890. Robert Frost, had he chosen to do so, could have voted for William McKinley. So could have Willa Cather, if women had had the vote in 1896; as it was, she would be forty-seven years old before the nineteenth amendment was ratified in 1920.

Cather had met Stephen Crane (only two years older than she) when he traveled west in the 1890s, and Wallace Stevens attended Crane's funeral in New York in the summer of 1900. Howells's *Criticism and Fiction* was not published until 1891, Twain's *Puddn'head Wilson* in 1894, and James's *The Ambassadors* in 1903. Cather reviewed, unsympathetically, Kate Chopin's *The Awakening* when it was published in 1899. In 1898, Stevens, who was at Harvard, elected to buy a two-volume set of the letters of James Russell Lowell instead of spending the money to go to the Harvard-Princeton football game.

Both were in their forties at the beginning of the Roaring Twenties and in their fifties in 1929 when Joseph Wood Krutch's assessment of the era appeared as *The Modern Temper*. They were not immune to the stimulations of the decade; however, neither was an expatriate, and both felt as intensely as certain nineteenth-century writers the claims of nature as poetic subject and transcendent authority. The term modernism likely would have been first familiar to them in the way Pope Pius X or Rudolf Eucken understood it, as something newfangled and vaguely associated with neo-Catholicism. T. S. Eliot would have to argue, in 1916, that modernism was an intellectual, not a religious, movement[84] and in doing so would have been expressing an unconventional view. This, apparently, was the imprecise label he chose to avoid the self-consciousness of labeling. And if we understand the term as Eliot would have us, neither Cather nor Stevens can be strictly identified as modernist writers.

It is not surprising that they were not as excited by the revolutionary concepts of Freud, to give only one example, as were so many younger men and women. The popularization of Freud in this country was essentially a phenomenon of the 1920s, and as Frederick J. Hoffman has shown, Freud received nearly as much attention then as Bergson had a decade before.[85] Willa Cather, preferring the psychology one got from reading Tolstoy to the latest news from Vienna, rejected Freud out of hand. In a lecture given in 1948, Wallace Stevens characterized Freud as a "realist" and therefore an enemy of the imagination. But thirty years earlier, when he was approaching his fortieth birthday, Stevens wrote "Le Monocle de Mon Oncle" in which he remarked more than a bit sardonically that, "If sex were all, then every trembling hand / Could make us squeak, like dolls, the wished for words" (*CP* 17). For a Cather or a Stevens, at least, a literary psychology was sufficient to their art. For them too, as we shall see, a psychology of resemblance advocated by James and Bergson and others—a psychology that may be loosely characterized as "literary," I suppose—had a lasting effect upon the conception and creation of that art.

I offer this arbitrary and haphazard chronology merely to establish a sense of possible historical circumstance. Actual circumstance, or the individual's sense of reality and of time and place, must be approached indirectly and minutely. But it may be said in advance that Cather and Stevens, among others, participated in and were influenced by the new reality, particularly as it was revealed in the writings of Bergson, in ways that transformed and legitimized their craft. I intend in the following pages to chart that artistic development and to implicate these writers in their own era, or at least a special portion of it. But I mean to do so without ceasing to recognize in them their own unique talents of accommodation or resistance to the pressures of their own peculiar present and their own unique gifts as imaginative writers.

THREE

The Road Home

I

"It makes one exceedingly weary to hear people object to football because it is brutal," wrote Willa Cather in 1893. "Of course it is brutal. So is Homer, and Tolstoi; that is they all alike appeal to the crude savage instincts of men. We have not outgrown all our old animal instincts yet, heaven grant we never shall" (*KA* 212). The piece was written for the University of Nebraska student publication the *Hesperian*, and its author was not yet twenty years old. No doubt Cather's attitude toward football reveals some normal portion of collegiate enthusiasm, and her exceeding weariness is in part the rhetorical pose of the young student aesthete. But, in its essentials, her column discloses a view characteristic of her aesthetic stance during her long literary apprenticeship from the early 1890s until the publication in 1913 of *O Pioneers!*, the novel in which she claimed she had finally hit the "home pasture."[1] A survey of Cather's growth as an artist during this period reveals a preference for a literary naturalism, on the one hand, and a psychological realism, on the other, until she came to embrace the neoromanticism of the modern era.

In some measure, Cather's disposition in this and a second piece on football published in the *Nebraska State Journal* a year later is typical of the times. It is well that sport arouses primitive emotions in us, she wrote, "all great emotions are essentially animal." Football provides an antidote to the "growing tendencies toward effeminacy so prevalent in eastern colleges," for it "renders distasteful the maudlin, trivial dissipations that sap the energies of the youth of the wealthier classes" (*KA* 213). In that, it is a democratic, character-building sport that outfits young men for the rigors of life beyond the campus. Privilege does not exist on the playing field; there, no man's life is "better than any other man's." Surely, she insisted contemptuously, "it doesn't do Cholly or Fweddy any harm to have his collar bone smashed occasionally." Rather, football is the healthy surfacing of ancient, virile impulses—"one of the few survivals of the heroic." It is a peculiarly Anglo-Saxon expression of that "bulldog strength which is the bulwark of all the English people" (*KA* 213).

The attitude Cather expresses here epitomizes the vogue the martial ideal enjoyed in the 1890s—it is extremely race and class conscious, it is informed by fashionable if vague notions of evolutionism, and it ritualizes and celebrates a universe of brutal force. The 1890s were a muscular decade. The "new woman" of the era had been urged toward a manly athleticism, and the "new man" toward a martial aggressiveness years before Theodore Roosevelt formalized the attitude in 1900 with his aptly titled book *The Strenuous Life*.[2] It should not be especially surprising, therefore, that Willa Cather claimed to despise the woman writer and the feminine imagination as too soft and too given to "hobbies and missions" (*KA* 408). She excepted from her condemnation George Eliot and George Sand (who were "anything but women"), Charlotte Brontë (who kept her "sentimentality" under control), and Jane Austen (whose "common sense" made her the greatest of them all). Until that time when women write stories of adventure—"a stout sea tale, a manly battle yarn, anything without wine, women and love" (*KA* 409)—she could not hope for any great art from them. Instead, Cather reserved her praise for the adventurous romances of a Stevenson or a Kipling and her contempt for the novels of an Ouida or a Marie Corelli.

Cather had herself taken the manly view of things almost from the beginning. She was the oldest of five children and perhaps expected to be the most courageous when her family moved in 1883 from their comfortable farm house in Back Creek, Virginia, to the plains of Nebraska to seek finer opportunities. She recalled her arrival in that as yet untamed prairie country in an interview in 1913:

> The land was open range and there was almost no fencing. As we drove further and further out into the country, I felt a good deal as if we had come to the end of everything—it was a kind of erasure of personality.
>
> I would not know how much a child's life is bound up in the woods and hills and meadows around it, if I had not been jerked away from all these and thrown out into a country as bare as a piece of sheet iron. I had heard my father say you had to show grit in a new country, and I would have got on pretty well during that ride if it had

not been for the larks. Every now and then one flew up and sang a few splendid notes and dropped down into the grass again. That reminded me of something—I don't know what, but my one purpose in life just then was not to cry, and every time they did it, I thought I should go under. [*KA* 448]

She did not "go under," however. In this interview, she attributes to the territory the qualities she had recently described in "The Wild Land" section of *O Pioneers!* and to herself the kind of "grit" and survival of personality she had dramatized in the heroine of that novel, Alexandra. Nevertheless, there is no reason to suppose that she had not shown the kind of courage her father expected of her. Later, when the family moved from the farm into Red Cloud, Nebraska, she asserted her personality with a manly determination that revealed itself in her dress and in her manner.

By the age of fifteen she was wearing her hair shorter than a boy's, and she often signed her name "William Cather." At the university in Lincoln she sometimes wore suspenders and adopted the nickname "Billy."[3] She defiantly announced her atheism at college and in one of her columns praised Colonel Ingersoll. She claimed to despise sentiment, and she was not squeamish—as a girl, she once assisted a local doctor in the amputation of a young man's leg, she delighted in dissecting frogs in those early years when she dreamed of becoming a doctor, and she argued in favor of vivisection.[4] She was to win the Pulitzer Prize for her own "battle yarn," *One of Ours* (1922), and her rendering of the grisly business of war in certain passages of that novel are as tough minded as anything John De Forest, Ambrose Bierce, or Stephen Crane had written.

Willa Cather is not remembered for such disturbing realism, however, nor, for that matter, for stirring romances of adventure. Nevertheless, she was devoted to the genre of the romance, "the highest form of fiction" (*KA* 232). From her first publication, a student theme on Carlyle in 1891, to her last novel, *Hard Punishments*, uncompleted at the time of her death in 1947, she was a romantic. Bernice Slote demonstrated that Cather drew heavily from her reading of romantic literature in formulating her earliest critical convictions, and, more recently, Susan Rosowski has convincingly shown just how complete and thoroughgoing Cather's romanticism was.[5] For Cather, as much as for Wallace Stevens, the imagination was a primary faculty and a value. And she exalted it above intellectual system or scientific truth.

The scientist and economist see "falsely," she claimed: "They see facts not truths. The only things which are really truths are those which in some degree affect all men. Atoms are not important; the world would be just as happy if we did not know of their existence. The ultimate truths are never seen through the reason, but through the imagination" (*KA* 143). For Willa Cather, at this time, the imagination was rather more of a holy office, not yet, as she would define it in 1915, a "composition of sympathy and observation" (*KA* 452). This latter conception was, as we shall see in the next chapter, partly inspired by her reading of Bergson in 1912. But during her literary apprenticeship, the creative imagination, for her, more nearly resembled a liberating force than metaphysical intuition.

Like Stevens too, though at the age of twenty we should suppose a bit naively, she would push the principle of the imagination to its ultimate conclusion. The author must have great and profound experiences, she said, must live "deeply and richly and generously, live not only his own life, but all lives." The creative writer must in the end "know the world a good deal as God knows it" (*KA* 143). The tendency toward the sort of conclusions Stevens would draw many years later—that poetry is a kind of metaphysics, that God is a "supreme fiction"—was in Willa Cather as early as the 1890s. But only after a long literary apprenticeship would she find a philosophical system (or, more broadly, a vision of the world) that satisfactorily reconciled the seemingly antagonistic realms of art and life and encouraged her to draw upon her own native talents and materials in the confidence that the greatest art sprang from the most familiar resources. When memory became her muse, Willa Cather suddenly vaulted into the first ranks of American novelists. And when she came to believe that artistic desire participated in a universal living principle that extended back to a prehistoric people and reached forward into the future, she was freed, just as suddenly, from what T. E. Hulme had called the "nightmare" of mechanism. For the time, however, she would persist in the belief in a transcendent and perfect realm of beauty and truth, forever opposed to the world of fact and federation.

Willa Cather was never a friend to the conventional American myth of progress. Political arrangements, biological improvement, and social reform tended to obscure or distort rather than correct those vitalizing and age-old impulses. The artist's duty runs counter to the notions of technological innovation and social advancement, or so she felt in these early years. "The further the world advances the more it becomes evident that an author's only safe course is to cling to the skirts of his art," she wrote in

1894; "the artist should be able to lift himself up into the clear firmament of creation where the world is not. He should be among men but not one of them, in the world but not of the world" (*KA* 407).

James Woodress, in his biography of Cather, has sensitively traced her allegiance to her art.[6] The muse is severe and demanding, and Cather committed herself wholly to this master with a will and a purpose that her college classmates sometimes mistook for offishness or superiority. But she was following "Our Lady of Genius," as she said Edgar Allan Poe had done: "What matter that one man's life was miserable, that one man was broken on the wheel? His work lives and his crown is eternal" (*KA* 387). For all her intoning the transcendent glory of art and the artist's calling, however, Cather had little patience with or feeling for what she termed the "aesthetic school," whose archvillain she located in Oscar Wilde. As John H. Randall has argued, Cather absorbed the doctrines of Pater, but she found Wilde's tribe of decadents repellent[7] and characterized this school that maintained that nature imitates art as "the most fatal and dangerous school of art that has ever voiced itself in the English tongue" (*KA* 389).

Instead, Cather's conviction was that that "Spartan mother," nature, superintends human destinies, and in ways that bear directly upon her early aesthetic. Ornament, refinement, and artifice, in art, may beguile for a time, but sooner or later nature spawns some "scion who reverses all this dreary artificiality and goes desperately back to the native." Such an artist returns to "first principles," and nature is revenged. "We cannot with impunity rise entirely above her [nature] any more than we can sink below her," Cather wrote in 1895 (*KA* 230). She would repeat this conviction five years later in her short story "Eric Hermannson's Soul." In that tale, a woman's kiss releases the passionate, subterranean self of a husky Norwegian farmer who finally exults in the guilty knowledge that his soul is forever damned and that he would go proudly and fearlessly "down to the gates infernal" (*CSF* 378). The woman, a young easterner named Margaret Elliot, is equally affected by the kiss. She "belonged to an ultra-refined civilization which tries to cheat nature with elegant sophistries. Cheat nature? Bah! One generation may do it, perhaps two, but the third—Can we ever rise above nature or sink below her? . . . Does she not always cry in brutal triumph: 'I am here still, at the bottom of things, warming the roots of life; you cannot starve me nor tame me nor thwart me; I made the world, I rule it, and I am its destiny'" (*CSF* 377).

This story makes vivid what Cather had often averred in her early criticism—that the soul thirsts for life more than redemption from life and is the inspiration for all great art. One often meets with the word *soul* in Cather's critical writings, and she defined it variously and broadly. It is a "peculiar balance of vital forces," the "unison of all one's powers into one lambent flame which men call genius" (*KA* 143). Elsewhere she describes it as the "power of idealization" (*KA* 416)—Zola's work fails despite his craft, she once wrote, because it lacks the "impress of the human soul" (*KA* 371). This same lack in the novelist Edgar Saltus makes him a failed artist and a "lost soul." The truth about Saltus, she claimed, is that his "soul—it's too bad we have no word but that to express a man's innermost ego—is completely lost among his many accomplishments and rattles feebly about among them like a dried pea in a bladder" (*KA* 416).

Cather, like many others, detected in the materialism of the age that the world was inhospitable to the claims of the soul and of art. Civilization conspires to make us too introspective; when we become nothing more than a "bundle of nerves," then some savage people will come along and "burn our psychologies" and teach us, once again, that "nature is best" (*KA* 232). She would complain that "this is becoming such a mechanical age that pretty soon we may have a little ticker that will keep correct count of our deeds done in the body and estimate the exact state of our souls and save St. Peter the trouble" (*KA* 225). But these are merely cynicisms; they do nothing to reconcile the opposing tendencies of science, philosophy, and psychology to the higher claims of art.

Nor would they ever be entirely reconciled in Cather's mind. Nevertheless, we can discern in her early critical statements, if only in embryo, certain Bergsonian notions about the relation of art and life; of intuition and intellect; of a *moi fondamentale* (what Cather had to call "soul" in 1896 because there was no other term for the "innermost ego") and an inauthentic, socialized self; of the internal pressure of a divine life urge and the refined, artificial boast of civilization; of the "unanalysable" quality of artistic feeling and the clever stratagems of the intellect; of paralyzing introspection and creative passion. Even in her earliest critical statements, one may discern a body of convictions, but they have not yet consolidated into a useful point of view, a unified vision that would serve as the foundation for her mature art. Bergsonian vitalism, as we shall see, provided that point of view.

The record of Cather's apprentice years is a record of poising in dramatic conflict the oppositions of art and life, of East and West, of civilized refinement and ignorant provincialism. Like Nathaniel Hawthorne, whom she greatly admired and much resembles, she devoted herself to the high calling of art and for two decades wrote short stories in which she experimented with literary possibility and developed her craft. The process culminated in a small but ambitious novel, *Alexander's Bridge*. It was a disappointment to her, however, and Cather later claimed that *O Pioneers!* was her "first" novel emotionally.

The enabling circumstances that encouraged the creation of *O Pioneers!* were several, but it is not incidental that the "inner explosion" that produced it occurred shortly after she had acquired firsthand her own sense of the new reality as it was revealed in an excited reading of *Creative Evolution* in 1912. The publication of *O Pioneers!* in 1913 marks the beginning of Willa Cather's career as a significant American novelist, but the achievement of this novel was prepared for by a long literary apprenticeship—the gradual discovery of her native themes and peculiar talents, and the sudden liberating confidence to exploit them.

II

Cather begins an introduction to *The Best Stories of Sarah Orne Jewett* (1925) with a passage from a letter she had received from Jewett many years before: "*The thing that teases the mind over and over the years, and at last gets itself put down rightly on paper—whether little or great, it belongs to Literature*" (*WCOW* 47).[8] Her comment on Jewett's observation is particularly interesting because it necessarily looks back to that time when the encouragement and criticisms contained in Jewett's letters vitally interested a writer who had as yet written nothing, or virtually nothing, that belonged to "Literature," but the essay itself was written with the full knowledge and authority of literary achievement. By 1925, she had received the Pulitzer Prize for *One of Ours* (1922) and had published seven novels, including *O Pioneers!* (1913), *My Ántonia* (1918), and *A Lost Lady* (1923), and had just recently completed *The Professor's House* (1925). In this sense, her introduction to the best of Jewett serves as revealing commentary on Cather's own growth as an artist as well as, more generally, the creative process.

If the writer is ever to achieve the high order of literary effects of a Jewett at her best, she claimed, one must give oneself completely to the material and allow it over time, through its "persistence" and "recurrence" in the memory, to get "rightly" down on paper. Neither the "vigorous transfer of immediate impressions" (*WCOW* 47–48) nor improvements upon subject matter (especially the introduction of dramatic "situation") nor "good writing" and "clever story-making" can produce anything more than a "brilliant sham" at last (*WCOW* 49). These are merely journalistic stunts and not really implicated in the imaginative process at all (which by this time she had come to believe was intimately connected to the process of memory). Cather's remarks here, as elsewhere in her later criticism, point to an essential quality in her mature fiction. She was, first to last, a romantic, but she became a patient romantic, one who would neither indulge herself in bulletins from the heart or nerves nor deliver herself of an urgent social conscience.

Much of Cather's early fiction, however, strives for instant effects, and she herself was often guilty of merely "good writing" and "clever story-making." Still, several of the stories sometimes reveal in surface detail and incidental episode the things that would tease Cather's imagination and eventually find their way into her mature fiction, and thereby belong to "Literature." The most familiar example of this imaginative compulsion is the stubborn persistence in her memory of the story of a suicide she had heard not long after the Cathers had arrived in Nebraska—the story of a Bohemian farmer, Francis Sadilek, who had one day smashed his violin and shot himself.[9] The local story became the basis for her first published piece of fiction; this work appeared in a Boston weekly in 1892. "Peter" was twice revised and republished, but she did not get the story down rightly until Peter appeared as Papa Shimerda in *My Ántonia* and his suicide was subordinated to the purposes of that longer work.

Another familiar example of this sort of imaginative persistence is observable in her transformation of the title character in "Lou, the Prophet" (1892) into Crazy Ivar of *O Pioneers!*. Lou is a Danish immigrant who is sufficiently aware of his own mental weakness to identify it, but he does not relate it to the sources of his prophetic dreams or his religious zealotry. His apocalyptic vision causes him to run away, but to avoid the "Sword of the Lord and Gideon" rather than the townspeople who would have him committed as insane. "Lou, the Prophet" is, like many of Cather's early tales, a case study designed to show, in this instance, that "the most blunted mechanical people, the youths and the aged always have a touch of romance in them" (*CSF* 535).

When Lou reappears in *O Pioneers!* as Crazy Ivar, he appears not as the exemplar of the possibilities of romance erupting on the prairie but as a living character. Ivar, like Lou, has a distorted religious sensibility and a degree of self-consciousness about his own limitations and vulnerability that enables him to perceive his own situation clearly. But Cather had imagined Ivar more completely, for he also possesses a practical intelligence and at times is worldly wise. Though he speaks as a madman, Alexandra Bergson knows that "some days his mind is cloudy. But if you can get him on a clear day, you can learn a great deal from him" (*OP* 33). Children may sometimes believe he has the ability to communicate with birds and beasts, but we, as readers, are to understand that his pragmatic intelligence comes from keen observation and sympathy rather than transcendent gifts. Ivar's supposed craziness derives from the mistaken authority he assigns to his intelligence—he is a figure whose superstitions and special knowledge a child may find romantic, but whose clear awareness of his own situation and how to get along in the world is entirely realistic and practical.

Ivar, like Lou, remains something of a study in temperament, but he is subordinated to the larger design of the novel in a way that reveals Cather's artistic patience and her willingness to suggest rather than to explain her meanings. "A good workman can't be a cheap workman; he can't be stingy about wasting material, and he cannot compromise," she wrote in 1920 (*WCOW* 103). This is the statement of a writer who has acquired a deeper wisdom about her craft than the young woman who wrote "Lou, the Prophet," and in *O Pioneers!* she achieved the kind of literary art that she said Jewett had in her best stories. One can find in Jewett's early writing sketches and impressions that later "crystallized" into "almost flawless" art (*WCOW* 48).

If some of Cather's early stories were sacrificed without compromise to her mature literary purposes, others served as germs for later literary development. And many dramatize her lifelong interest in the essential doubleness of human personality, but she could not yet see this conflict as anything more than the result of the free soul at odds with a restrictive environment. Some of these stories teased her imagination over the years and contributed to the accomplishment of longer fictions. Such is the case with "The Joy of Nelly Deane" (1911) and "The Professor's Commencement" (1902). The first suggests the inchoate beginnings of Cather's persistent preoccupation with the tragic implications of a young woman's capacity for joy that would eventuate in one of her last novels, *Lucy Gayheart* (1935). The second establishes a created character with whom the author had some special sort of identification and through whom she might contemplate her own situation; it has a germinal relation to *The Professor's House*.

Nelly Deane dies young (in childbirth), but her tragedy, as are the

tragedies of so many of the characters in Cather's early stories, is attributed to the cramped and narrow influences of her small western community. Her romantic vigor and capacity for joy, rather than Nelly herself, are
the victims of the tale. But by the time Cather came to write *Lucy Gayheart*, she recognized that youthful assertions of the soul (which she had
once described as the "power of idealization"), especially if they are mis-
guided, are themselves potentially tragic.

Professor Emerson Graves, by contrast, has squandered his youth and
vitality teaching high school, attempting to "secure for youth the rights of
youth; the right to be generous, to dream, to enjoy, to feel a little of the
seduction of the old Romance" (*CSF* 287). At a commencement ceremony
he recognizes that his colleagues are "cases of arrested development" (*CSF*
289), but Graves's sister has to tell him the terrible truth about himself:
"Here you have buried yourself for the best part of your life in that high
school, for motives Quixotic to an absurdity . . . all your best tools have
rusted" (*CSF* 285). "The Professor's Commencement" suggests, in germ,
the story of Professor Godfrey St. Peter.[10] But, significantly, it also suggests such a strong identification between the author and the created
character that returns in the novel that James Woodress could call *The
Professor's House* a "spiritual autobiography."[11] The short story, by contrast,
might be seen as a spiritual prophecy.

When she wrote this story, Cather, like her professor, was teaching high
school in Pittsburgh. She seems to have liked her new job well enough; at
least it afforded her more time than had editing the *Home Monthly* or
writing drama criticism or, later, writing wire copy for the *Pittsburgh
Leader* had done before. Writing for magazines and newspapers, she knew,
and was to know again when she later took a job with *McClure's*, saps
one's energies and imaginative resources and it spends one's time. High
school teaching freed her for writing during the summer months and,
potentially, might have left her with enough energy in the evenings to
devote herself to writing. But she may have thrown herself too completely
into her new job (she lost twenty pounds in only three months of that
year),[12] and she may have detected in her temperament, rather than in her
situation, that she might well become a Professor Graves. Generous and
sympathetic energy spent in the service of youth and romance might be
heroic, but it might also be the symptom of "arrested development."

Cather often complained in her letters to friends that she was too inclined to become disturbed by trivial matters and sometimes worried that
she might become fussy. More importantly, she, like Professor Graves, had

a gift for getting "all the possible pain out of life" (*CSF* 285). She once wrote that she felt things more deeply than most people and, as a result, was dented and bruised inside.[13] This was the artist's liability, a "gift of sympathy" (*WCOW* 51) that exacts its price. She had written in a review in 1896 that to preserve an idea with all its "original feeling," "preserving in it all the ecstasy which attended its birth," is what art means after all (*KA* 417). But by the time she came to write "The Professor's Commencement," if not before, Cather recognized that that same sharp sensitivity could as easily defeat one's purposes as promote them.

At the conclusion of the story, Cather has Graves say to his sister, "I was not made to shine, for they put a woman's heart in me" (*CSF* 291). This is an admission that he too is a case of arrested development, and he recognizes that to scatter one's sympathies in the service of youth, however noble, is, nevertheless, a dissipation. At any rate, the autobiographical element in "The Professor's Commencement" is an introspective one, and the author seems to be assessing her present situation and contemplating her future in terms of the fate of her character. She may or may not win the admiration of her colleagues and students at last, but this much is sure—her own best work is at hazard and may remain unwritten until such time as she has neither the energy nor the will to complete it. She, too, might suffer private disappointments that public approval cannot assuage.

Again and again in her early fiction, Cather was to explore the fate of art and the soul at odds with circumstance, but her manner alternated between the psychological realism of "The Professor's Commencement" and the romantic naturalism of "The Joy of Nelly Deane." Sometimes her naturalistic treatment of this theme succeeds brilliantly, as in "A Wagner Matinee" (1904) or in "The Sculptor's Funeral" (1905). In the first, the narrator discovers in his aunt's reaction to a concert that the soul "withers to the outward eye only" (*CSF* 240), but he is unable to gauge "how much of it had been dissolved in soapsuds, or worked into bread, or milked into the bottom of a pail" (*CSF* 241); in the second, the student discovers that the real tragedy of his master's life was that he suffered from "a shame not his, and yet so unescapably his, to hide in his heart from his boyhood" (*CSF* 180). These stories have an affective quality that makes them two of Cather's best early tales. More often, when she struggled too anxiously for her effects, Cather's treatment of the same theme drifted into pure sentimentality.

This is the case in such stories as "Jack-a-Boy" (1901) or "On the Gull's

Road" (1908), stories of the soul stricken dumb by sickness and death. "A Death in the Desert" (1903) is perhaps another example, but it is more interesting because it combines a plotted sentimentality with a more serious psychological interest. The central story concerns the fate of the once famous singer, Katherine Gaylord, who has fallen ill and returned to her home in the deserts of Wyoming to live out her final days with her brother, remote from the glamour and excitement of the world she loved. Her tragedy of the soul is that she, like the heroine of "On the Gull's Road," has become a shadow of her former self. But this story of desire cheated by circumstance is supplemented by the psychological element in the secondary story of the two brothers, Everett and Adriance Hilgarde.

Katherine Gaylord had studied under Adriance and had been in love with him; the younger Everett had seen her at the studio and had fallen in love with her. Adriance is the contemptible genius whom women nevertheless find charming. Everett is his brother's virtual double, but the resemblance is entirely physical, for he belongs to that "lovable class of men who never accomplish anything in particular" (*CSF* 213). Everett tries to comfort Katherine during her illness, and they often speak of Adriance's genius and fame and possibility. Katherine says she wants the composer "to grow wholly into his best and greatest self even at the cost of the dear boyishness that is half his charm" (*CSF* 212). Adriance seems to have achieved this best self in his latest sonata, which Everett plays for her, and has grown enormously since the days when she knew him. Everett's tragedy, which is finally more poignant than Katherine's, is that he has not grown and is reminded of the fact every time he is mistaken for his brother.

Everett Hilgarde, like Professor Graves, is a case of arrested development, and his story belongs to that group of several such stories Cather wrote between 1901 and 1907. The souls of many of Cather's characters are defeated by circumstance, but as many are self-defeated because they do not attend to that inner impulse within them. This is true of Margie Van Dyck in "The Treasure of Far Island" (1902) who discovers that it is she, and not her childhood friend Douglass Burnham, a successful playwright, who has failed to "grow up" (*CSF* 281) and, by too passively accepting life's realities, has become a case of "arrested development" (*CSF* 273). Caroline Noble, in "The Garden Lodge" (1905), is another instance. She resolves to live only amid realities but discovers there lives within her an "undercurrent of consciousness," a primary self she had tried to suppress but had developed within her nonetheless: "Whatever she might be doing or thinking, it went on involuntarily, like her breathing; sometimes welling up until suddenly she found herself suffocating" (*CSF* 192). The young tragic hero of "Paul's Case" (1905), however, suffers from the opposite condition. As the subtitle indicates, this is another "study in temperament." Paul denies the harsh realities of his pinched and predictable existence and rebels against the adult world of his father and teachers. The world Paul believes in exists on the stage beyond the footlights in Carnegie Hall where he works as an usher. The music and the singing release a "potent spirit" (*CSF* 246) in him and take him far away from the ugly world of getting and spending. But he is merely stagestruck, and Cather locates his problem not in his romantic temperament but in his immature and limited romantic vision.

Cather explored still other cases of arrested development in her early fiction—in Harriet Westerfield of "Eleanor's House" (1907), who clings so desperately to the past that she cannot understand the eventual growth of her friend Harold Forsythe beyond it; in Flavia Malcolm of "Flavia and Her Artists" (1905), who supposes her husband has "held her back" (*CSF* 169), when in fact she is a child playing house by collecting her artists and providing for them a refuge "where the shrinking soul, the sensitive brain, should be unconstrained" (*CSF* 152); and in the painter Aaron Dunlap of "The Profile" (1907), whose harsh upbringing has made him so "morbidly sensitive" (*CSF* 126) that he becomes overly delicate in his art and painfully grotesque in his life. And she explored the "inverse development" of the artist in the novelist Kenneth Gray of "The Willing Muse" (1907), whose "distressing leakage of power" (*CSF* 114) perplexes his friends who believe him a great genius only a single step away from glorious achievement but who instead becomes his wife's secretary.

Willa Cather had investigated in her fiction, almost from the beginning, the relations between art and life, between the soul and society, and had found them in irreconcilable opposition. Her preoccupation with this theme verges on obsession, and it indicates just how powerfully she was absorbed by this dilemma of modern life and its special relation to her own artistic ambitions. Often, as in her psychological stories about cases of arrested development, the failure of the individual personality to assert itself truly was due to misapprehension or personal weakness.[14] In such naturalistic stories as "A Wagner Matinee" or "The Sculptor's Funeral," however, the sources of tragedy are located in the repressive environment of the frontier community.

These two stories, along with five others, were included in her first collection of short fiction, *The Troll Garden* (1905).[15] As the title and the epigraphs taken from Christina Rossetti and Charles Kingsley made clear, the stories included in the volume defined the paradoxical relations between art and life. The garden is the rich and sensuous precinct of art, but it is inhabited by trolls who would corrupt simple desire and contaminate the artist. Outside the walls of the garden, according to the parable Cather had borrowed from Kingsley, are the rude and unfashioned forest children—a barbaric and ignorant tribe, but pure and brimming with "animal health" (*KA* 443), who find life in the forest dull and poor. One may become deprived and crude by avoiding the garden fruit or become self-satisfied and weak by tasting it.

E. K. Brown notes that *The Troll Garden* "closed the door" on Cather's formative years and opened another to her future.[16] This remark is certainly true biographically: S. S. McClure had agreed to publish the stories in a single volume, and the attention she received from him eventually won her an appointment on the staff of his magazine. But she was far from solving the fundamental problem implicit in most of her early fiction and emphasized in *The Troll Garden* itself. Living and working in New York placed her within the walls of the garden and provided her with better opportunities than Pittsburgh had done, but the primary impulse of the soul belonged outside, on the western prairie. It was there, she came to recognize, that the sources of her art resided.

Cather's revolt against the village was never so complete that she could despise its people rather than their attitudes. And there was, after all, the land itself issuing out of itself some strange pull and appeal that claimed Cather's loyalty. Life on the Divide, at least, was as yet unspoiled by the corruption of progress and industry, and those brutal and primitive energies of the pioneers were still heroic for her. The public manifestation of raw force in this age of energy, however, was hideous beyond belief. The same year that Henry Adams was privately circulating his *Education*, Cather published "The Namesake" (1907) and through her character Lyon Hartwell made her comment on the temper of the times in terms every bit as distressed and despairing, though in a different way, as had Adams:

> The great glass and iron manufactories had come up and up the river almost to our very door; their smoky exhalations brooded over us, and their crashing was always in our ears. I was plunged into the very incandescence of human energy. But, though my nerves tingled with the feverish, passionate endeavor which snapped in the very air about

me, none of these great arteries seemed to feed me; this tumultuous life did not warm me . . . everywhere the glare of that relentless energy which followed me like a searchlight and seemed to scorch and consume me. I could only hide my self in the tangled garden, where the dropping of a leaf or the whistle of a bird was the only incident. [*CSF* 141]

If Adams sought to ease his disturbance by reconciling the claims of history to the truths of science, Lyon Hartwell found consolation in his namesake and, by extension, some blood force working in and through him. Hartwell's sensed union with his dead uncle stirs him with a violent emotion: "It was the same feeling that artists know when we, rarely, achieve truth in our work; the feeling of union with some great force, of purpose and security, of being glad that we have lived. For the first time I felt the pull of race and blood and kindred, and felt beating within me things that had not begun with me. It was as if the earth under my feet had grasped and rooted me, and were pouring its essence into me" (*CSF* 146).

Lyon Hartwell is suddenly thrown back to the "native," and in this instance the native is, for the artist, the appropriation of a peculiarly American subject matter. To borrow the language of Jewett's advice to Willa Cather that so impressed the younger writer, Hartwell has known the "world" (for he grew up and was educated in Europe), but he has to discover the "parish."[17] So authentically American is Hartwell that the students who listen to his story and are themselves transplanted Americans believe him "more than any other living man" to have absorbed and to "mean" America, all of it, from "ocean to ocean" (*CSF* 137). That quality was acquired, the students learn, by a visit home to a land he had never known.

Hartwell uncovers in his aunt's attic artifacts of his uncle's identity—clothes, letters, boots, a riding whip—but the object that triggers his knowledge of his namesake and of a past that is present within him is an inscribed copy of the *Aeneid*. On the back flyleaf of the volume, Hartwell discovers a pencil drawing of the federal flag and two lines from the national anthem copied in his uncle's unsure hand. It is the application of a Greek and Roman spareness and directness to American materials that inspires Hartwell's bronzes with a special dignity and force and that prefigures Jim Burden's recognition in *My Ántonia* that it would be a fine thing to be the first to bring the muse into one's own country.[18] But "The

Namesake" was written before Cather herself had acquired the firmness of artistic purpose that would guide her in *My Ántonia*, and Hartwell's discovery of a native muse is rather more vague and mystical than familiar and intimate. The story itself serves as yet another counterstatement to the dominant cultural tendencies of the age. Cather gave a different emphasis to the motive power of a life force in a later story, "Behind the Singer Tower" (1912). In tone and intent, this story participates in the kind of muckraking social criticism for which *McClure's* was famous. It does, in its way, call into question the "New York idea," but it also poses a different problem, one at odds with the dramatic conflict and resolutions of "The Namesake."

In "Behind the Singer Tower," six men on a launch discuss the implications of a fire in the Mont Blanc Hotel. One of these men, Fred Hallet, had worked under the engineer, Stanley Merryweather, who had constructed the hotel. Hallet recalls a rather trivial episode (compared with that day's disaster): the death of an immigrant laborer. These three figures represent different types of men and each has contributed his share to the great idea of the skyscraper. Hallet is a "soft man for the iron age" (*CSF* 50), sensitive but ineffectual. He complains to the engineer about his cost-cutting practices, but he cannot beat the Merryweathers of the world, who possess certain "racial characteristics." They are "quick and superficial, built for high speed and a light load" (*CSF* 47), unencumbered by conscience or feeling. The common laborer Caesarino, however, pays the price. He is crushed beneath a load of earth when a cable snaps. Hallet observes that our civilization, "built on physics and chemistry and higher mathematics" (*CSF* 49), must have been incomprehensible to this man from a remote Italian village, and he wonders why Caesarino should have abandoned his simple life and familiar traditions and traveled so far to "cast his little spark in the bonfire" (*CSF* 53). Hallet concludes that "wherever there is the greatest output of energy, wherever the blind human race is exerting itself most furiously, there's bound to be tumult and disaster" (*CSF* 53). The age and its idols require a sacrifice, and we respond—"helping, with every nerve in us, with everything our brain cells can generate, with our very creative heat, to swell its glare, its noise, its luxury, and its power" (*CSF* 53). He might have said nothing exists but matter and the motion of matter, a furious and irresistible force advancing recklessly and tragically to some end we neither desire nor comprehend.

The consolation provided by an awareness of those survivals of an ancient and dignifying past and of one's own place in the design of things is the discovery of the artist Lyon Hartwell. The all-consuming, self-immolating absorption in some great idea yet to be born partakes of the same impetus, driving relentlessly, progressively forward. These stories restate the terms of Cather's familiar dilemma. Hartwell makes his separate peace with the world, retreats to the "tangled garden" of art; Merryweather, who possesses the truly "journalistic mind" (*CSF* 52), unthinkingly and imperturbably advances in the race, at once its hero and its victim. These two stories identify the twin intellectual inheritance of the times, and Cather attempted to chronicle its effects upon the individual personality in her first novel, *Alexander's Bridge*. For her, the experiment was disappointing, but she was to follow *Alexander's Bridge* with a novel that more perfectly realized her ambition to reconcile the antithetical claims of art and life. She would call it *O Pioneers!*.

III

As Susan Rosowski so aptly notes, Willa Cather was more interested, finally, in the "way" than the "what" of our seeing.[19] This concern may have persisted in Cather from the early 1890s and may have derived, as Rosowski believes, from her romantic tendencies. Nevertheless, Cather's inclinations and her achievements did not, from the beginning, coincide. The congruence of her life and her art reveals itself in the achievement of *O Pioneers!*, when she found a way to render reality as a felt and natural quality instead of as a collection of dramatic situations. This shift in artistic mode was due to several factors, but we are concerned here with how the author exchanged a late nineteenth-century vision of the world for another, how the emergent new reality provided her art with a certain enabling authority and confidence and entered it at the level of craft and conception rather than intellectual conviction.

Cather, no more than Virginia Woolf, did not go out one morning to discover that a rose had bloomed, that a new order of understanding and perception had suddenly inserted itself. Her explosive growth as an artist, however, did occur sometime around 1912, and it owes something to her conversion to the new reality and to a new way of seeing. Cather herself made the distinction between artistic ambition and artistic achievement in her preface to the 1922 edition of *Alexander's Bridge*: "There is a time in a writer's development when his 'life-line' and the line of his personal endeavor meet" (*AB* 1922 vi), and when this happens, it provides a deeper thrill than manufactured tales about exciting subjects. The remark looks back to that critical moment in her artistic development when there was a convergence of her pursuit of the beautiful with the familiar and intimate attachments of her own experience.

That moment cannot be located precisely, but the publication of Cather's two "first" novels surely bracket the event. *Alexander's Bridge* represents the culmination of the writer's twenty-year apprenticeship; *O Pioneers!*, a new beginning. She commented upon this sudden shift on at least four occasions—in two early interviews, in a preface to the second edition of *Alexander's Bridge*, and in a 1931 essay. Each sheds some light on her advance as an artist, but the shift is more precisely and immediately discernible at the level of style. The two following passages disclose at a glance the substantive differences in her craft and aspiration:

> The yellow light poured through the trees and the leaves seemed to burn with soft fires. There was a smell of acacias in the air everywhere, and the laburnums were dripping gold over the walls of the gardens. It was a sweet, lonely kind of summer evening. Remembering Hilda as she used to be, was doubtless more satisfactory than seeing her as she must be now—and, after all, Alexander asked himself, what was it but his own young years that he was remembering?
>
> [*AB* 35–36]

> No living thing had ever seemed to Alexandra as beautiful as that wild duck. Emil must have felt about it as she did, for afterward, when they were at home, he used sometimes to say, "Sister, you know our duck down there—" Alexandra remembered that day as one of the happiest in her life. Years afterward she thought of the duck as still there, swimming and diving all by herself in the sunlight, a kind of enchanted bird that did not know age or change.   [*OP* 205]

In the first passage, it is evident that Cather was not yet free of what she described in an interview in 1915 as her "florid," "adjective spree period" (*KA* 450). Once, in 1896, she had cited a passage from John Ruskin that begins "that scarlet cloud may, indeed, melt away into paleness of night, and Venice herself waste from her islands as a wreath of wind-driven foam their beach." "Who can write such English now?," she asked (*KA* 401), as though the imitation of such floridness were the highest artistic ambition. By 1926, however, she would claim in a preface to *Wounds in the Rain* that Stephen Crane is the best of our descriptive writers because he is the "least describing" (*WCOW* 70). The passage from *O Pioneers!* participates in this later aesthetic and signals how far she advanced in a single year toward a spare and direct idiom and how far behind her was the appetite for eloquence and "clever writing."

But these passages do more than illustrate a shift of literary manner, for they project and proceed from a different conception of mind. Bartley Alexander's memory of Hilda Burgoyne is a memory of his own youth. The idea of youth, for which she is the palpable if evanescent emblem, dogs him and stimulates him. And, as he is described early in the novel, Alexander is not so much "introspective" as he is a "tremendous response to stimuli" (*AB* 7–8). Bartley Alexander's yearning for his past (which in the novel exists more as internal stimulus than memory) is poised against his successful, but disappointed, middle age, and Cather does get some dramatic, and sometimes melodramatic, effects out of the contrast. Alexandra's mind is defined differently, and it is rendered differently.

"Her mind," we are told, "was a white book, with clear writing about weather and beasts and growing things. Not many people would have cared to read it; only a happy few. She had never been in love, she had never indulged in sentimental reveries" (*OP* 205). The contents of her consciousness are resistant to dramatic treatment, and even at its deepest levels are of simple, familiar things. Her memories exist as images and recur as images, not as ideas. They persist and modify present experience, not as rational introspection or stimuli, but as the atmosphere of mind itself.

Alexandra's "think stuff" (what William James liked to refer to as the *denkmittel* of the mind) is neither categorically organized nor introspectively urgent. Her recollection of the wild duck comes unbidden from what Bergson described as that "immense zone of obscurity," the "fringe" of her consciousness (*MM* 97), and steps forward as an emblem of happiness and youthful vitality. James made an analogous statement when he argued in his *Pragmatism* that sense impressions and memories constitute a "perceptual weather."[20] Cather renders the "weather" of submerged innocence and primary perception in Alexandra not by insisting on it nor by dramatizing it, much less by providing the stream of Alexandra's consciousness. She evokes it by suggesting an intermittent recollection and moving the image along the corridors of Alexandra's memory, by transporting it from one past to another—from the first perception to her brother's occasional reference to it afterward to its persistence in her memory years later. The memory of the wild duck has endured for her and, at last, has become an enchanted thing, free from age or change. Alexandra does not remember her youth; she merely recalls a youthful perception that exists for her as a romantic, transcendent symbol. The effect of the wild duck upon Alexandra's limited imagination is wholly romantic, but Cather's literary presentation is matter-of-fact and realistic.

After completing *Alexander's Bridge* but before beginning *O Pioneers!*, Cather made her first trip to the American Southwest, a land that was to have a lasting effect upon her fiction. She did no writing there, but she did recover from the "editorial point of view" (*WCOW* 92) she had brought to her first novel. Part of this recovery meant doing away with too exclusive a reliance upon "rules and theories" (*KA* 451); another part probably meant developing the ear and rhythm necessary to good fiction, the confidence to speak without accent or insistence. The two books were written in different artistic modes, and she identified the differences in an apt figure: Writing *O Pioneers!* "was like taking a ride through a familiar country on a horse that knew the way, on a fine morning when you felt like riding. The other was like riding in a park, with someone not altogether congenial, to whom you had to be talking all the time" (*WCOW* 92–93). She made a similar claim in 1922 when she wrote that once a writer discovers one's own natural material, "he finds that he need have little to do with literary devices" (*AB* 1922 viii–ix). Rather, "he comes to depend more and more on something else—the thing by which our feet find the road home on a dark night, accounting of themselves for roots and stones which he had never noticed by day. This guide is not always with him, of course. He loses it and wanders. But when it is with him it corresponds to what Mr. Bergson calls the wisdom of intuition as opposed to that of intellect" (*AB* 1922 ix)

If *O Pioneers!* was the product of intuition, *Alexander's Bridge* was, in many ways, a thing of intellect, for its intent and design were calculated. In part, the book was inspired by a trip to London where Cather had met some "interesting" people in an interesting city (*WCOW* 91), but it was as well the ambitious attempt to examine in fictional terms the opposing claims of art and science. As Elizabeth Ammons has instructively demonstrated, the engineer was something of a cultural hero at the end of the nineteenth century—a popular image of the Progressive Era. Cather was working in the tradition of Richard Harding Davis, Harold Bell Wright, Rudyard Kipling, and others when she created Bartley Alexander.[21] However, argues Ammons, Cather, unlike the others, intended to demythologize the figure in her own treatment of the engineer as cultural hero. Kipling's story "The Bridge Builders," in particular, has a germinal relation to Cather's own story of a famous and powerful bridge builder.

She reviewed Kipling's volume of tales, *The Day's Work*, in 1899 and instanced this story as proof that the author's exceptional talents lay in his ability to appropriate the subject matter of science and convert it to the purposes of art: "He finds energy the most wonderful and terrible and beautiful thing in the universe; the energy of great machines, of animals in their hunt for prey, of men in the hand-to-hand fight for a foothold in the world. He has found in this energy subject matter for art, whereas it has previously been considered the exclusive province of science" (*WP* 558). This is what she would attempt in her first novel.

Cather's Professor Graves divides his library between works of art and works of science, and the narrator notes that this dual interest is customarily considered a peculiar "form of bigamy" (*CSF* 283). Cather herself, however, wanted to bring them into fruitful conjunction. Kipling's bridge builder and her own Bartley Alexander combine a technical mastery of construction with an active creative intelligence in a way that brings these mutually exclusive realms into close contact. She resisted Alfred de Musset's belief that "poetry and mechanics" are "forever incompatible and antagonistic" (*WP* 557), and in *Alexander's Bridge* Cather would, as she claimed Kipling had done, build her hero's "life into the bridge" (*WP* 558) in a way that would explore and attempt to define the place of the soul in a mechanistic world that celebrated the creations of force.

Her romance is the story of a middle-aged bridge builder whose public success and domestic happiness prove disturbingly insufficient for him. He lives in Boston but is building a cantilever bridge in Canada. He is required to travel to London periodically to consult about British building codes and there attends a play where he sees the actress Hilda Burgoyne, the woman with whom he had been in love when they were students at the Beaux Arts in Paris. Alexander revives their love affair but is all the time aware that what he seeks in the relation is some youthful, vital image of himself he has lost along the way. The "dead calm of middle life" (*AB* 38) frightens him, and he yearns for the "wild light-heartedness" (*AB* 39) of youth. When Hilda travels to New York, he meets her in an apartment he keeps for business purposes. The diversion of Hilda causes him to miss a telegram from his assistant superintending work on the Moorlock Bridge. A second telegram advising Alexander of structural problems in the foundation reaches him, and he rushes to the construction site and orders the workers off the bridge. But he is too late. The bridge collapses, and Alexander drowns in the river he had attempted to span.

This, in its essentials, is the plot of the novel. Rather too deliberately, Cather had attempted to link her engineer's fate to that of his creation, mostly by intrusive commentary or obvious symbolism. Like his bridge, Alexander's character possesses a "weak spot where some day strain would tell" (*AB* 12). And the river beneath seems to him to mean love and, its equivalent, death: "only those two things awake and sleepless; death and love, the rushing river and his burning heart" (*AB* 118). These are the fluid eternals that divide Alexander against himself, and he, like many of Cather's case studies, may be understood, finally, in an epigram: "The mind that society had come to regard as a powerful and reliable machine, dedicated to its service, may for a long time have been sick within itself and bent upon its own destruction" (*AB* 131). Bartley Alexander is more than another case study, however. Like Merryweather, Alexander is an emblem of an age of energy and a Spencerian, optimistic faith, but his public identity contradicts his private impulses, and Cather gives to her character a tragic self-awareness. For he epitomizes his age and its ambitions and becomes a self-destructive version of Everyman in a universe of force.

Throughout, Cather characterizes Alexander as raw, mechanical energy. To his former professor Lucius Wilson, he is a "natural force" (*AB* 15), and beyond that not much of anything. For Wilson, Alexander is a "powerfully equipped nature" possessing "the fascination of a scientific discovery," a "force" at work in the world (*AB* 17). The engineer has become the engine, a powerful machine performing the "functions of a mechanism useful to society" (*AB* 39) and existing as a mere "public utility" (*AB* 38). Alexander feels himself caught in the net of social necessity, "built alive into a social structure" he cares nothing for (*AB* 13). The "machinery" is always "pounding away" inside him; even after dinner, "when most men achieve a decent impersonality, Bartley had merely closed the door of the engine-room and come up for an airing. The machine itself was still pounding on" (*AB* 13).

His success and his despair alike are due to the severance of his familiar past from the "fiery moment" of the present (*AB* 8); Alexander is a man little given to reflection or contemplation, and thus his dreams "always took the form of definite ideas, reaching into the future" (*AB* 40). "Force" is the "thing we all live upon," observes Winifred Alexander. "It is the thing that takes us forward," and her husband's bridges are "bridges into the future" (*AB* 17). But, like the cantilever bridge he is erecting, there is a structural weakness in him, something inside has "broken loose" (*AB* 68). The result, in the same gesture, is the destruction of Alexander and his creation.

Like Jay Gatsby, for whom he seems to have served as something of a model, Bartley Alexander rushes into the future in an effort to retrieve his past.[22] What he longs for is not love but freedom, the "one thing" he has always desired (*AB* 38). But his success and influence have brought him only an unanticipated restraint. Alexander, like so many of Cather's characters, has become a shadow and a fragment who desires the "continuous identity" of youth—"that original impulse, that internal heat, that feeling of one's self in one's own breast" (*AB* 40). What he acquires, however, is a double, not a single, identity: "I feel as if a second man had been grafted into me. At first he seemed only a pleasure-loving simpleton. . . . But now he is strong and sullen, and he is fighting for his life at the cost of mine" (*AB* 102). Nature, at last, has revenge. The bridge builder, a "tamer of rivers," cannot subdue the torrential currents within him. His tragic misjudgment ends in catastrophe, and sixty men drown along with him.

One can easily see why Cather considered *Alexander's Bridge* to be an "external" story (*AB* 1922 vi). It expressed and, to a degree, refined the concerns of many of her earlier short stories. Alexander possesses the decisiveness of a Merryweather and the sensitivity of a Hallet of "Behind the Singer Tower"; he has the same vague and impossible desires of the Paul of "Paul's Case." Like Caroline Noble, Alexander is victimized by a submerged second self. Like Lyon Hartwell, he cannot in the end draw a vitalizing strength from the energy of the age. But unlike Hartwell, the "garden is closed" to him (*AB* 101), and he is drawn into a constraining social structure. These were all authentic and longstanding concerns for the author, and her ambitions for her novel were high ones. *Alexander's Bridge* is, as David Stouck has described it, a "secondary" or literary epic,[23] and Cather gave to her story a vastness and to her hero legendary capacities that might contain and comment upon the times. However, her purposes were too much at variance one with the other; her literary manner was external to her experience and too contrived to have fashioned a tale equal to her ambitions.

Alexander's Bridge was a "built" tale, and she borrowed, rather than discovered, the means to construct her narrative. Cather's appropriation of the contemporary worship of force to the purposes of art was in imitation of Kipling, but she appears to have been rather more interested in examining, through the actions of her hero, the deficiencies of the age than in celebrating its accomplishments. For Alexander's heroic and creative energies cannot find satisfaction or release in the exalted monuments of the era. She herself acknowledged the unhappy influence of James and Wharton upon the novel—that she, like so many young writers of the time, "followed their manner, without having their qualifications" (*WCOW* 93). That influence can be exaggerated, however, and apart from certain stylistic similarities, the most conspicuous Jamesian quality is the superficial use of an international setting. Cather moves her character back and forth across the Atlantic with almost absurd frequency and rapidity. Her hero was not so much an American innocent abroad as he was a powerful public exemplar of the tendencies of the age, but one privately pursued by his own peculiar "imp of the perverse," and the psychological dimension of her book took more of its cues from Poe than it did from James.[24] Professor Wilson says to Alexander, "I always used to feel that there was a weak spot where some day strain would tell. . . . The more dazzling the front you presented, the higher your facade rose, the more I expected to see a big crack zigzagging from top to bottom . . . then a crash and clouds of dust" (*AB* 12). Cather built Alexander's life into his bridge in the same way that Poe connected the fate of Roderick Usher to the fate of his house and developed, by means of a romantic symbolism, the psychological crack in him.

It is a strange turn of events that, by 1937, Lionel Trilling could claim that Cather's career had degenerated into an indefensible, if artful, snobbishness and that "her mystical concern with pots and pans" did not amount to much more than an "oblique defense of gentility" or seem very far from the "gaudy domesticity of bourgeois accumulation glorified in the *Woman's Home Companion*."[25] The accusations of escapism and rarefied gentility leveled at her in the 1930s could not have been predicted for a writer who, in 1912 in *Alexander's Bridge*, had imaginatively engaged in contemporary preoccupations with energy and materialism and had attempted to examine and measure the popular American success story against primitive psychic desires for wholeness and liberty. A "Ragged Dick" or a "Tattered Tom" of her own inventing became, under her imaginative management, an inverted version of James's Spencer Brydon in "The Jolly Corner." Alexander's alter ego is not that of the capitalist entrepreneur but that of a boy whose "potentialities" have not been "lived out" (*AB* 13). His second self is not so much a pernicious and destructive force, as some critics believe, as it is a "resolute offshoot" (*AB* 114) in him who wishes to merely live but whose natural impulses are perverted by the deadening opportunities offered by the world at large. His inner impulse is perverse, not because it is parasitic, but because it is indifferent to the social attachments and associations that constitute a public happiness but a personal despair.

Cather could identify with her hero to the extent that, like him, she sought adventure and success in the world of the present but carried within her the strong voice of a familiar past. That is the implication of her comment, recorded in the preface to the 1922 edition of *Alexander's Bridge*, on her sudden growth as an artist in 1912: "I think usually the young writer must have his affair with the external material he covets; must imitate and strive to follow the masters he most admires, until he finds he is starving for reality and cannot make this go any longer. Then he learns that it is not the adventure he sought, but the adventure that sought him, which has made the enduring mark upon him" (*AB* 1922 viii). The adventure that seeks the adventurer is the reassertion of native material and acquaintance, the unsought recognition of the rights of the local and familiar.

There is a glimmering of this recognition even in *Alexander's Bridge*. Hilda Burgoyne is a successful artist who keeps a "mite of a hut" (*AB* 51) in her native Galway, and she understands, even if she does not herself possess it, the courage required to resist the attractions of the "fiery" present—"It doesn't take pluck to fight for one's moment," she says, "but it takes pluck to go without" (*AB* 93). The pull of the local and the native are also affirmed in a Nebraska story, "The Bohemian Girl" (1912), that Cather wrote not long after *Alexander's Bridge*. Clara Vavrika, who is about to run away with Nils Erickson (the younger brother of her husband Olaf and the only man she has ever loved), hesitates before her flight: "The great, silent country seemed to hold her as if by roots. She felt as if she could not bear separation from her old sorrows, from her old discontent. They were dear to her, they had kept her alive, they were a part of her" (*CSF* 37). But Nils lifts her bodily into the saddle, and together they escape the severity of the Divide. The final section of the story, however, shows that the author's admiration belongs at last to those who stay and have the "pluck to go without." For, a year later, the youngest Erickson boy on his way to join his brother and Clara in Europe has a change of heart and returns to the farm and his mother, who reaches out and caresses the boy's hair. "His tears splashed down on the boards; happiness filled his heart" (*CSF* 41).

In "The Bohemian Girl," Cather was beginning to relocate her interests and sympathies in the human personality that endures and asserts itself in and through the near at hand. But in *O Pioneers!*, she was to do so by relating her characters to large and ancient, though still particular and creative, evolutionary forces that underwrite and elevate her subject far above local-color writing. She dedicated *O Pioneers!* to Sarah Orne Jewett, and the book was an example of the sort of regionalism Cather admired in Jewett. It was as well a grand and ambitious attempt, or a second attempt really, to write on an epic scale. She concealed that design, however, beneath a quiet and elegiac mood in a way that allowed her to describe the book as a "two part pastoral."[26]

O Pioneers! may be fairly characterized as a vitalistic novel, and the author clearly took much of her inspiration for it from Henri Bergson. In the preface to the 1922 edition of *Alexander's Bridge*, she as much as says that the mode of creation she followed in composing *O Pioneers!* was a Bergsonian one. However, the effect Bergson had upon her is only one of several factors that made these years what Sharon O'Brien has called a "watershed" period for the author.[27] The most immediate and the most liberating causes of her sudden creative growth were changes in her literary situation. Due to a reorganization at *McClure's*, Cather was able to take a leave of absence from the magazine in order to write. She traveled to Cherry Valley, New York, and there completed the revisions of *Alexander's Bridge*, for Houghton Mifflin had agreed to publish the serialized *Alexander's Masquerade* as a novel. Cather was now a full-fledged novelist. Her first impulse, however, was not to write another novel but to write one short story and write and rewrite another.

While she was in Cherry Valley, she wrote the long story "The Bohemian Girl" and began a story she called "Alexandra"; that story was eventually to become "The Wild Land" section of *O Pioneers!*. According to Edith Lewis, "Alexandra" originally included "The Wild Land" section of *O Pioneers!* pretty much as it appears in the novel[28] but with the significant difference that Cather concluded the tale with Alexandra's dream of a mysterious lover who carried her away, a "strong being who took from her all her bodily weariness" (*OP* 207). As it was first conceived, this story was the complementary opposite of "The Bohemian Girl," a story of endurance not of escape, a story of the woman who was never rescued from the monotony or fatigue of prairie life. The Alexandra of the original story endured but despite her material success and spiritual attachment to the soil dreamed of release. *O Pioneers!*, however, was to alter the context of Alexandra's strivings and make her a triumphant and heroic figure.

Soon after completing "The Bohemian Girl," Cather traveled to Arizona to visit her brother. On her return trip, she stopped by Red Cloud, and then to visit her friend Isabel McClung, she traveled on to Pittsburgh where she wrote another Nebraska story called "The White Mulberry Tree." It was a tale of star-crossed lovers and yet another version of "The Bohemian Girl" and was to become the fourth section of *O Pioneers!*. In it, Marie Shabata sleeps beneath a white mulberry tree. Emil Bergson, the man whom she loves and who has asked her to run away with him, finds her and lies down beside her. "I was dreaming this," she says, "don't take my dream away!" (*OP* 259). Her husband returns and, wild in his grief and anger, shoots the couple in their embrace. After she finished this story, Cather read it along with "Alexandra" and reported to Elizabeth Sergeant that there came to her a "sudden inner explosion and enlightenment."[29] "Alexandra" and "The White Mulberry Tree" constituted, in germ, the "two parts" of her pastoral novel—the first a story of a young girl's reconciliation to her father's death and her subsequent resolution to carry out his final wish to hold on to the land; the second the tragic story of the lovesick Emil and Marie. But the creative excitement of combining these two tales in the longer narrative had the scope of epic, and this excitement marks that moment when Cather fully accepted her material, when the adventure found the adventurer.

IV

The experience of writing *O Pioneers!*, according to Cather, "was the first time I walked off on my own feet—everything before was half real and half an imitation of writers whom I admired."[30] Her own creative voice was suddenly liberated in this book, and it spoke with a naturalness and poise that recovered the rhythm and the feel of her own Nebraska experience and provided release for her own native talents. But the novel must have satisfied her for other reasons as well, for it seemed to reconcile the oppositions that had long concerned her and are recurrently dramatized in her fiction—the conflict between art and science, the claims of the soul and the requirements of the world, her own romantic temperament and the materialistic philosophy of the day. Such reconciliation was achieved, not by retreating from the world of the present, but by enlisting a neo-romanticism that argued for a new reality and a new consciousness but that at the same time reached back, it seemed, to the very origins of life. *O Pioneers!*, at any rate, was not an escape. Though it was set in Nebraska ("distinctly déclassé as a literary background" [*WCOW* 94]) and though it rejected a universe of force and mechanical energy, it was nonetheless progressive insofar as it looked hopefully to the future and feminist to the extent that it located its hopes in a pragmatic and inspired heroine. And surely by giving that heroine the name "Bergson," Cather meant to suggest that her new novel was evolutionary and progressive in a way that reflected the new organic philosophy of the era.

Part of the author's sudden creative inspiration must have involved a recognition that the land itself might play a dramatic role in the development of her novel, might indeed have the force of character. The country, Elizabeth Sergeant recalls, "insisted on being the Hero and she [Cather] did not interfere."[31] The place the land was to have in the design of her book is indicated by "Prairie Song," the poem that introduces her narrative. Her novel would be the story of youth, with its "insupportable sweetness," set against the silent and "sombre" prairie land. The theme was familiar to her, but she was not to be conventionally naturalistic in her treatment of it. Hers was not the same old story of the pitifully small man or woman opposed to an "unresponsive sky," for the "fierce necessity" and "sharp desire" of youth would issue out of the land itself and return to it as part of a grand and vital urge. Cather would treat the subject of youth as she said Arnold Bennett had done in his play *Milestones*: "Mr. Bennett takes the biologist's rather than the poet's view of both youth and age. Youth is the only really valuable thing in the world, not because it is 'youth,' a pretty name, a charming quality, but because it is 'force,' potency, a physiological fact."[32] The song of youth and the song of the prairie merge and participate alike in the energies and push of an élan vital. Cather borrowed her title from Whitman, but her novel would reflect the popular neoromantic attitude of the day and would render the evolutionary character of the new reality as it had been revealed in Bergson's *Creative Evolution*.

In a letter dated 12 September 1912, Cather wrote to Elizabeth Sergeant and noted her agreement with Sergeant's enthusiasm for *Creative Evolution*.[33] Evidently, the two had talked before about the book, and Sergeant claims with some authority in her memoir of Cather that "mind and invention were not her tools; the decisive element was intuitive, poetical, almost mystical perception. Though she rejected Freud, she was a reader of Henri Bergson."[34] Something akin to a mystical perception seems to have inspired the creation of her first significant novel. With apparent reference to the naturalness of the writing of *O Pioneers!* and to Bergsonian intuition, Cather wrote in 1922 that the "true" artist has "seen" the "essential matter" of her story, "has been enlightened about it in flashes that are as unreasoning, often as unreasonable, as life itself" (*AB* 1922 ix).

How extensive a "reader" of Bergson Cather was is uncertain. Certainly, her study of him extended well beyond an excited reading of *Creative Evolution* alone. Leon Howard, Edward and Lillian Bloom, and, most recently, Loretta Wasserman have detected a profound Bergsonian influence in her writings, particularly in her imaginative preoccupations with time, memory, creative intuition, and history, subjects Bergson developed most completely in other books.[35] Cather, like Wallace Stevens, preferred the psychology of William James and Bergson to that of Freud,[36] and that preference is revealed in her later fiction. However, not much has been made of Cather's interest in the scientific character of Bergson's philosophy, and this appears to be the element that first interested her and so pervades *O Pioneers!*.

Cather's letter to Sergeant makes clear that, from an intellectual point of view, she was rather more attracted to the scientific than the purely philosophical dimensions of *Creative Evolution*.[37] In that, she was unlike T. S. Eliot, who had sarcastically remarked that Bergson wrote very "entertainingly" about the eye of the frog. Cather thought the early chapters of the book to be magnificent, but the final one (which is essentially a critique of the "mechanistic illusion" and a history of philosophical systems) she found considerably less interesting. From a literary point of view, however, the book seems to have suggested to her a means to coordinate and integrate imaginative materials in a way that supplied her two-part pastoral with an epic design and an intellectual currency.[38]

Cather was responding to a Spencerian rather than a Bergsonian worldview in *Alexander's Bridge*, and this new reality had little to do with the making of that book.[39] As an editor, she would have been familiar with, and perhaps a bit skeptical of, Bergson as a commercial literary property as early as 1910 and no doubt would have read one or more of the journalistic accounts of his system. Indeed, in *Alexander's Bridge*, she seems to be making a slighting reference to the current fascination with Bergson when she has her narrator describe an incidental character as a "very genial and placid old scholar who had become slightly deranged upon the subject of the fourth dimension. On other matters he was perfectly rational" (*AB* 47–48).[40]

Cather's own interest in Bergson was enthusiastic, though hardly "deranged," and it was personal, though not at all idiosyncratic. Certain of her friends and acquaintances, among them Dorothy Canfield Fisher, Hartley Burr Alexander, and Edwin Björkman, had been or would be affected by the spell Bergson had cast on prewar America.[41] And the American critic Cather came to admire above all others was Randolph Bourne, a man deeply influenced by James, John Dewey, and Bergson.

Elizabeth Sergeant had directed Bourne's attention to O Pioneers!, and he read it with enthusiasm and admiration.[42] Though a decade older than he, Cather came to trust Bourne's critical perceptions to be always instantaneous, authentic, and correct, and she grieved his untimely death in 1918 as a great loss to American letters.[43] Bourne was an eloquent and spirited spokesman for the new generation, and he undertook to defend the claims of youth in his first book, Youth and Life (1913), published in the same year as O Pioneers!.

Coincidentally, Bourne's characterization of the times has a special appropriateness to the purposes of Cather's novel. "A settled conviction that we live in a mechanical world," he wrote, "with no penumbra of mystery about us, checks the life-enhancing powers, and chills and depresses the spirit": "In this scientific age there is a call for youth to soar and paint a new spiritual sky to arch over our heads."[44] Youth "must think of everything in terms of life," he insisted, and the artist ought confidently to affirm the mystery and assertions of the life urge and to reveal them in one's work. What is the literary gift, after all, he asked, "but an absorbing interest in the personality of things, and an insight into the wonders of living? . . . the epic of the humblest life, told in the light of its spiritual shocks and changes, would be enthralling in its interest."[45] Bourne's call for an "epic of the humblest life" and a "new spiritual sky to arch over our heads" had already been answered in O Pioneers!. It was a novel infused with a "penumbra of mystery" that implicitly rejected a dead and mechanical world.

Cather's story is a simple one—a tale of the pioneering spirit and eventual triumph of Alexandra Bergson and of the tragic consequences of the illicit passion of Alexandra's brother Emil and the young and pretty Marie Shabata. These events were dramatized in the original short stories that inspired the longer work, and Cather included enough about the routine and customs of frontier life on the Divide for some reviewers to praise the book for its realism and local color but at the same time to complain about its lack of incident and loose construction. Many reviewers recognized the novel as an American success story, and a few found it to be in part a feminist work. None, however, perceived its philosophical currency or its epic scope.[46] But the transformation of the landscape provided her novel with an overarching structural principle and absorbed her two short stories in a larger design that was anything but formless or exclusively regional.

How completely Cather exchanged a mechanical for an organic world-view is evident in the very feel of *O Pioneers!*. Its tone is quiet, almost elegiac, but the novel is everywhere stirring with life and motion and mystery. Images of germination and organic growth and life are as frequent in *O Pioneers!* as images of the machine are in *Alexander's Bridge*. The shadows of clouds run across the prairie to the horizon; banks of soil crumble under hooves; snowflakes curl and eddy in the air and gather in drifts against the fence rows; "brown waves of earth" roll away to meet the sky (*OP* 307). The following passage conveys the fluid and vital texture Cather gave to her book:

> Carl sat musing until the sun leaped above the prairie, and in the grass about him all the small creatures of day began to tune their tiny instruments. Birds and insects without number began to chirp, to twitter, to snap and whistle, to make all manner of fresh shrill noises. The pasture was flooded with light; every clump of ironweed and snow-on-the-mountain threw a long shadow, and the golden light seemed to be rippling through the curly grass like the tide racing in.
>
> [*OP* 126–27]

The lives of her characters, at once abundant and starved, are mysteriously tied to this pervasive life impulse, and their fates are as strange and unfathomable as the seed corn Alexandra tests every spring: "From two ears that had grown side by side, the grains of one shot up joyfully into the light, projecting themselves into the future, and the grains from the other lay still in the earth and rotted and nobody knew why" (*OP* 164). But the ceaseless change and vigor of the life about her are at times for the impatient and impulsive Marie monotonous necessity: "The years seemed to stretch before her like the land; spring, summer, autumn, winter, spring; always the same patient fields, the patient little trees, the patient lives; always the same yearning, the same pulling at the chain—until the instinct to live had torn itself and bled and weakened for the last time, until the chain secured a dead woman, who might cautiously be released" (*OP* 248). A mysterious, energetic life impetus drives upward, and patient and relentless necessity pulls this same life urge downward. These are the essential and opposing forces at work in the novel, and they correspond to the two opposing forces at work in biological development that Bergson had elaborated in *Creative Evolution*—the ascension of spirit and the descent of matter.

The assertions of life and the blessed release of death, fierce necessity and youthful desire, the "great operations of nature" (*OP* 70) and the impulsive affirmations of human freedom—these are the familiar human stories that "go on repeating themselves as fiercely as if they had never happened before" (*OP* 119). The remark is an early observation of Carl Linstrum, but Alexandra Bergson qualifies it in the final chapter when she says to him, "You remember what you once said about the graveyard, and the old story writing itself over? Only it is we who write it, with the best we have" (*OP* 307). This is the human element in Cather's evolutionary epic, and Alexandra epitomizes a Bergsonian heroine, one who has a mysterious intuition of the great operations of nature and by giving herself completely to the soil and listening to its promise at once shapes its destiny and expresses that innermost self Cather typically referred to in her early criticism as the soul. In part, *O Pioneers!* is the story of the evolution of a soul, but the evolutionary character of the novel is most comprehensively revealed in the transformation of the land itself.

The novel is composed of five sections—"The Wild Land," "Neighboring Fields," "Winter Memories," "The White Mulberry Tree," and "Alexandra"—and each moves inexorably away from furious and chaotic life energy toward a comprehensible human achievement finally located in the figure of Alexandra. The design of the novel is something of an inverted pyramid—a massive, biological past penetrating the future at a single point, in Alexandra herself.[47] The efforts of true pioneers do not subdue the wilderness so much as they channel an organic force every bit as potent and far more ancient than the mechanical energy so conspicuous in *Alexander's Bridge*.

At its simplest and most fundamental level, the land in *O Pioneers!* is symbolic of matter itself, and during the course of the novel, it passes through those phases Spencer had defined as the essential nature of evolutionary change. The land, that is, moves from an "indefinite, incoherent homogeneity" to a "definite, coherent heterogeneity." But Cather added the creative force of personality to her story in a way that affirms the evolutionary character of the new reality and liberates the soul from mechanical necessity.

"The Wild Land" section of the novel begins at a time when buildings "huddled" together against the howling Nebraska winds. The land is the "great fact of life" on the frontier, and it "seemed to overwhelm the little beginnings of human society that struggled in its sombre wastes" (*OP* 15). Carl Linstrum feels even in his youth that men are "too weak to make any mark here, that the land wanted to be let alone, to preserve its own fierce strength, its peculiar savage kind of beauty" (*OP* 15). The "Genius" of the Divide seems unfriendly, and the "record of the plow was insignificant, like the feeble scratches on stone left by prehistoric races, so indeterminate that they may, after all, be only the markings of glaciers, and not a record of human strivings" (*OP* 19–20).

The savage strength of the land is in its death throes, however, and the first section of the novel describes "the last struggle of a wild soil against the encroaching plowshare" (*OP* 47). "Neighboring Fields" is set sixteen years later, after the land has been tamed and its energies made coherent and geometrically definite. The "shaggy coat" of the prairie has become a vast "checkerboard, marked off in squares of wheat and corn"; roads run at "right angles," telephone wires hum above the fences, and windmills tremble as they harness the energy of the wind that blows across that "active, resolute stretch of country" (*OP* 76). Cather, at the same time that she conveys the patterned effects of settlement, renders the incessant, active power one feels in the very "atmosphere" of things, "the same tonic, puissant quality that is in the tilth, the same strength and resoluteness" (*OP* 77). "Order and fine arrangement," the impress of human personality, are everywhere observable on Alexandra's farm—in fences and hedges, windbreaks and sheds; in the "symmetrical pasture ponds," the white rows of beehives, and the neat orchards. These are the signs of the directing creative intelligence of Alexandra, and we are told that "it is in the soil that she expresses herself best" (*OP* 84). Alexandra is an artist of the soil who possesses a superior sensitivity to the vital forces about her and directs their energies.

The third section, "Winter Memories," reemphasizes the presence of a vital impulse in the country, hidden but abiding beneath the prairie snow. Winter is the time nature "recuperates" and "sinks to sleep" (*OP* 187); the torpor is so absolute one could almost believe the "germs of life were extinct forever" (*OP* 188). The atmosphere is close, and people keep indoors. But Cather floods this chapter with invigorated nostalgias and emblems of growth and life and continually reminds her readers that "down under the frozen crusts, at the roots of the trees, the secret of life was still safe, warm as the blood in one's heart" (*OP* 202).

"The White Mulberry Tree" and "Alexandra" continue and sharpen the focus of this pattern by emphasizing the human element in a world of incessant change. The first three sections render the evolutionary development and settlement of the frontier in a way that corresponds to a universal design, a movement from unorganized and indefinite homogeneity to organized and coherent heterogeneity. But the formulaic and abstract quality of this design might have provided her novel with no more than an intellectual coherence, without making it a thing of feeling, had not Cather's recent experience corroborated and made vivid just this sort of development.

After she had been in the Southwest for a time, she suddenly suffered an unaccountable depression. She was sitting by the Rio Grande at Santa Domingo pueblo when she saw written in the dust a line from Honoré de Balzac: *Dans le désert, voyez-vous, il y tout et il n'y rien—Dieu, sans les hommes.*[48] The revelation that so vast a land might contain everything and nothing, might be divinely and lastingly indifferent to human effort, was a disturbing one, and soon after she fled the New Mexico desert for her native Nebraska.

The train trip east would have provided her with a view of just the sort of transformation that defined the character of evolutionary progress. Cutting through the Sangre de Cristo Mountains, across the arid plains of eastern Colorado and western Kansas, little by little she would have seen the landscape transformed into something comprehensible, something human—the checkering of farm lands and the stretch of dirt roads, church steeples and train stations. She arrived in Nebraska in time to witness a wheat harvest in the Bohemian country, an event that partly inspired the story "The White Mulberry Tree." Then she traveled on, through villages and towns; as she approached Pittsburgh, she would have seen black clouds of smoke issuing from furnaces and hanging over the city.

Here was the lived example of something that quite reversed the conventionally understood pattern of an East/West development of American civilization: for the old world was behind her, in the southwestern deserts; the new, in whatever future Bessemer converters were constructing for her. This is speculation, of course, but the characters of *O Pioneers!* stand in just this sort of relation to the cultivated land and to a past that antedates even the potsherds and petroglyphs of those cliff dwellers who so intrigued Cather. This kind of relation Eudora Welty has astutely identified as the absence of a "middle distance" in Cather's fiction—"the perspectives of time and space run unbroken, unmarked, unmeasured to the vanishing point." "Willa Cather saw her broad land in a sweep," Welty continues, but "she saw selectively too. . . . Her eye was on the human being. In her continuous, acutely conscious and responsible act of bringing human value into focus, it was her accomplishment to bring her gaze from that wide horizon, across the stretches of both space and time, to the intimacy and immediacy of the lives of a handful of human beings."[49] The concluding sections of *O Pioneers!* tell the stories of human lives, but they do so without ever severing the vital relation between individual destinies and resolute organic impulses.

"The White Mulberry Tree" takes place at harvest time, and the section dramatizes in a different way the equivalency of love and death that marked Bartley Alexander's strivings in Cather's first novel. The yearnings of the youthful soul are juxtaposed to Whitmanesque notions of a "procreant urge" and the "knit of identity." This fourth section dramatizes the unthinking desires of youth, and Cather renders the thought of Emil, Marie, and, particularly, Frank as sensorimotor response or vague longing uncorrected by reflection. Human intelligence, as Bergson had defined it, is reserved for the more mature Alexandra. The function of intelligence, he wrote, is not "to look at passing shadows nor yet to turn itself round and contemplate the glaring sun": "To act and to know that we are acting, to come in touch with reality and even to live it, but only in the measure in which it concerns the work that is being accomplished and the furrow that is being plowed, such is the function of human intelligence. Yet a beneficent fluid bathes us, whence we draw the very force to labor and to live" (*CE* 191).

Youth and maturity, the ideal and the real, are the subjects of these final sections, and the conclusion Cather reaches (implicit in the "Alexandra" section) is analogous to that reached by Wallace Stevens in "Sunday Morning"—that natural human desire for an "imperishable bliss" is a false hope. *O Pioneers!*, too, endorses a pantheistic, or at least pre-Christian, spirituality. Her pioneers also "live in an old chaos of the sun," "unsponsored, free." In this sense, it is appropriate that Cather should have begun "The White Mulberry Tree" with a description of the French church standing upon a hill, "powerful and triumphant there on its eminence, so high above the rest of the landscape, with miles of warm color lying at its feet" (*OP* 211). The Church of St. Agnes is an emblem of the hope for the eternal and immutable, and it figures importantly in this section. It is the place for human rituals of hope and desire—the church fair (where the boys conspire to kiss their sweethearts), christenings, confirmations, and the funeral mass for Emil's friend Amédée. Emil responds to the choir's song at the mass with a "rapture" that takes hold of him, but this is only the "equivocal revelation" (*OP* 256) of aesthetic feeling and leads him unthinkingly to Marie, who sleeps under the mulberry tree. Emil and Marie are the impatient "wooers" of death; for the young, the grave is but a "doorway to forgetfulness." "The heart," we are told, "when it is too much alive, aches for that brown earth, and ecstasy has no fear of death" (*OP* 257).

This fourth section of the novel belongs to the insupportable desires of youth. Their lives are composed of so many hopes (of Amédée's exuberant joy at the birth of a son and his wish for twenty more or of Emil's exalted sense of himself conveyed by Charles-François Gounod's "Ave Maria") and of so many inexpressible sadnesses (of the "unhappy temperament" of Frank Shabata (*OP* 261), the death of Amédée, or the disappointments of the young lovers Marie and Emil). Alexandra is content to believe that Emil's advantages have made him the first of his father's children to not be tied to the plow and, therefore, to possess "a personality apart from the soil" (*OP* 213). She fails to recognize that that same life impulse in the soil moves in the blood of her brother and Marie. Alexandra has about her "the impervious calm of a fatalist," and her family is surprised by her decision to marry Carl Linstrum. Her composure is also disconcerting to the young, who "cannot feel the heart lives at all unless it is still at the mercy of storms; unless its strings can scream to the touch of pain" (*OP* 226).

The dramatic impulses of youth are epitomized by Marie's despair and her contemplation of suicide: "But she did not want to die. She wanted to live and dream—a hundred years, forever! As long as this sweetness welled up in her heart, as long as her breast could hold this treasure of pain!" (*OP* 250). Hers is a transcendent desire for a perfect and eternal love. The unmeasured, irresponsible robustness of youth is as ripe as Amédée's wheat, but its felt sense of immortality is vain deception. Angelique is secure in her belief that only good things can happen to her husband, a man "with a new baby in the cradle and a new header in the field" (*OP* 242), but Amédée dies of a ruptured appendix. Alexandra is happy in her hopes for her young brother's future, but Emil dies beneath the mulberry tree.

Ivar discovers the bodies of the lovers and cries out that "it has fallen! Sin and death for the young ones! God have mercy upon us!" (*OP* 271). Their deaths are meant to be humanly tragic, but Cather's vitalistic scheme finally eclipses individual destinies: the bloodstained earth beneath the mulberry tree "told only half the story." "Above Marie and Emil, two white butterflies from Frank's alfalfa-field were fluttering in and out among the interlacing shadows; diving and soaring now close together, now far apart; and in the long grass by the fence the last wild roses of the year opened their pink hearts to die" (*OP* 270). The reckless passions of youth proceed from the same sort of biological impulses and repeat the same age-old stories, and Ivar's reaction to the deaths of the young ones as the catastrophe of sin is partial and narrow.

"The White Mulberry Tree" prepares the way for the concluding section, "Alexandra," a story that is in substance radically different from the tale that originally bore that title. The Alexandra story that became "The Wild Land" section of the novel was tragic. But in the novel that same character stands as the crowning achievement and last best effort of a primordial evolutionary cycle—not as its victim, as she had been when the story ended with the dream of a lover who might rescue her from fatigue and struggle, but as its heroine. The same dream figure reappears in this concluding section and by dramatic implication modifies the earlier tale. For the first time in her life, Alexandra recognizes him. He is not the "old illusion of her girlhood," the selfish dream of an earthly lover. He is as "strong as the foundations of the world," the "mightiest of all lovers" (*OP* 283); he is death. This final lover, however, offers neither rescue nor eternity.

Alexandra is the heroic figuring forth of an immanent organic impulse that through her defines the future. Like Whitman who, at the conclusion of "Song of Myself," bequeaths himself to the soil "to grow from the grass I love," Alexandra's ultimate revelation is that she will return to the rich land that mysteriously spawned her: "Fortunate country, that is one day to receive hearts like Alexandra's into its bosom, to give them out again in the yellow wheat, in the rustling corn, in the shining eyes of youth!" (*OP* 309). This is the concluding passage of *O Pioneers!*, and it properly elevates Alexandra's achievement and her significance to the land. It has been prepared for from the first time we meet her as a child possessed of an "Amazonian" fierceness and a vague, but determined, sense that she must soon "face something," that with all her might she must "grasp a situation" and deal with it (*OP* 10). From the beginning, Alexandra is made to adapt to situations in a way that defeats necessity.

Adaptation and assertion define Alexandra's personality. She envies Carl Linstrum's "freedom," mistaking escape from the routine of prairie life for the true freedom that expresses itself in concrete acts and the creation of new forms. Alexandra is herself an artist, and she brings to the land some-thing that has not existed before and that could not have been predicted for the shaggy wild beast who had defeated so many would-be pioneers.

So absorbed is she in adapting to the harshness of frontier life and transcending the inevitability and finality others see in things that she is least aware of her own creative achievement:

> Her personal life, her own realization of herself was almost a subcon-scious existence; like an underground river that came to the surface only here and there, at intervals months apart, and then sank again to flow on under her own fields. Nevertheless, the underground stream was there, and it was because she had so much personality to put into her enterprises and succeeded in putting it into them so completely, that her affairs prospered better than those of her neighbors.
>
> [OP 203]

The language and the concept expressed here are reminiscent of passages in *Creative Evolution*. Life is a "current sent through matter" (*CE* 265) and, like a river, in its course divides into distinct individualities that we may call "souls," but whose destinies are not separable from the larger vital impetus into which they are eventually reabsorbed. "On flows the current, running through human generations, subdividing itself into individuals. This subdivision was vaguely indicated in it, but could not have been made clear without matter. Thus souls are continually being created, which, nevertheless, in a certain sense pre-existed. They are nothing else than the little rills into which the great river of life divides itself" (*CE* 269–70).

Passages such as these prompted some critics to assign to the Bergson-ian philosophy a certain pantheistic character. His point, however, is that if one separates the life of the spirit from the acts of the body and the requirements of matter, the effect is to "suspend" the soul above the earth where it is free from attack but exposes itself as a mere "mirage" (*CE* 268). As we have seen, Cather once dramatized the salvation of the soul (par-ticularly the artist's soul) as a retreat into the garden. In *O Pioneers!* she was to endorse what Wallace Stevens calls the "necessary angel of the earth," through whom one sees the earth again cleared of its "man-locked set" and whose spiritual idealizations are revealed in and through creative response to the near at hand.

The biological adaptations of Alexandra are, in Bergson's language, active rather than passive, a "replying" to a situation rather than a "repeating" of customary responses (*CE* 58). Such relentless adaptation exacts its price, however. In Alexandra, it results in fatigue and a too early serious-ness that creates in her a "blindness" to the passions of youth. She is hard because she has grown up in hard times—a "vine" that has been cut back again and again until it "grows hard like a tree" (*OP* 171). But she does continue to grow. By contrast, her brothers are "stumps" (*OP* 172), so defined by original tendencies that have become ingrained habits that year by year they grow "more and more like themselves" (*OP* 55). They are familiar instances of arrested development who, unlike their sister, hate "experiments" (*OP* 45) and are meant to follow in paths "already marked out for them, not to break trails in a new country" (*OP* 48). But Cather found the means to accept these individuals as playing a part in an evolu-tionary scheme, and she conveys her tolerance of them through Alexandra who comes to realize that "we are not all made alike" (*OP* 305) and who is enlarged by sympathies that extend even to Frank Shabata, the murderer of her beloved Emil.

Like other characters in the book, Lou and Oscar are part of an evolu-tionary process, but they have "turned short." "Our freedom," writes Bergson, "in the very movements by which it is affirmed, creates the growing habits that will stifle it if it fails to renew itself by a constant effort; it is dogged by automatism" (*CE* 127). Oscar's love of routine "amounted to a vice"; "he worked like an insect, always doing the same thing over in the same way, regardless of whether it was best or no" (*OP* 55). Lou, on the other hand, is flighty, incapable of seeing any job to completion. The first, in Bergson's system, is an "automaton" (*MM* 201) whose acts so completely fill his consciousness that he is incapable of contemplation and, as a result, denies his own possibilities and latent freedom (*CE* 144). The second is a "dreamer" (*MM* 198) whose effects are scattered and ineffectual. Lou and Oscar are only the most extreme in-stances of arrested development, however. Habit is also strong in Alex-andra's mother, but her "unremitting efforts to repeat the routine of her old life" (*OP* 28) do provide a certain continuity for her family. Carl Linstrum, even as a boy, looks to the past and is afraid of the wild land about him. Frank Shabata is a bitter man because the gaiety of his youth has been withdrawn. Ivar's primitive Christianity moves him to resist all manner of temptation, but it also makes him a hermit in whom the wish to go "without defiling the face of nature" (*OP* 36) denies the spirituality of a life urge seeking progressively to realize itself in the future. Alexandra alone is that specimen of "perfect humanity" (*CE* 267) in whom intellect and intuition have freely developed, and she alone looks to the future of her country.

When Alexandra commits herself to the future of the land, the act establishes her epic proportions—"For the first time, perhaps, since that land emerged from the waters of geologic ages a human face was set toward it with love and yearning." And the land responds in kind: "Then the Genius of the Divide, the great, free spirit which breathes across it, must have bent lower than it ever bent to a human will before. The history of every country begins in the heart of a man or a woman" (*OP* 65). Again, the language and thought have their analogues in *Creative Evolution*: Sometimes, "in a fleeting vision, the invisible breath that bears them [particular manifestations of the living principle] is materialized before our eyes. We have this sudden illumination before certain forms of maternal love, so striking, and in most animals so touching, observable even in the solicitude of the plant for its seed. This love, in which some have seen the great mystery of life, may possibly deliver us life's secret. It shows us each generation leaning over the generation that shall follow. It allows us a glimpse of the fact that the living being is above all a thoroughfare, and the essence of life is in the movement by which life is transmitted" (*CE* 128).

Alexandra is such a thoroughfare, one who fulfills the deathbed request of her father and bequeaths herself to the soil, and she exhibits the encompassing and mysterious sympathy of maternity. Though childless herself, she is continually adopting the men and women around her. She treats Emil as a son and Marie and the servant Signa as daughters; even the homeless Ivar receives her protection. Her natural sympathies extend finally to Frank Shabata, whom she visits in his cell. But Alexandra's maternal sympathies are not compensatory, for her knowledge is finally mystical. She loved to "reflect upon the great operations of nature" (*OP* 70) and one night has an intuition about the desires of the land that installs within her a "new consciousness of the country" (*OP* 71) and her relation to it. Her innermost self is mysteriously tied to the potency of the soil— "She had felt as if her heart were hiding down there, somewhere, with the quail and the plover and all the little wild things that crooned or buzzed in the sun. Under the long shaggy ridges, she felt the future stirring" (*OP* 71).

This is the most comprehensive of Alexandra's insights, but her life is a record of such intuitions. She knows how much it had cost to fatten a steer and can guess the weight of a hog before it goes on the scales (*OP*

23). She knows the future belongs to the high ground, not the river land. She urges her brothers to mortgage their homestead and buy more land, but Lou objects:

> "But how do you *know* that land is going to go up enough to pay the mortgages and—"
> "And make us rich besides?" Alexandra put in firmly. "I can't explain that, Lou. You'll have to take my word for it. I *know*, that's all. When you drive about over the country you can feel it coming."
>
> [*OP* 67]

Her intuitions even extend to what Bergson described as an "organic memory" (*CE* 19), an intuition that discloses to her the true nature of death. Alexandra grieves over the grave of Emil, and a fall rain chills her to the bone. "After you once get cold clear through," she tells Ivar, "the feeling of the rain on you is sweet."

> "It seems to bring back feelings you had when you were a baby. It carries you back into the dark, before you were born; you can't see things, but they come to you, somehow, and you know them and aren't afraid of them. Maybe it's like that with the dead. If they feel anything at all, it's the old things, before they were born, that comfort people like the feeling of their own bed does when they are little."
> "Mistress," said Ivar reproachfully, "those are bad thoughts. The dead are in Paradise." [*OP* 281]

To that, Cather might respond with Stevens's narrator in "Sunday Morning," "The tomb in Palestine / Is not the porch of spirits lingering. / It is the grave of Jesus, where he lay."

At any rate, the "metaphysician" Bergson insisted each of us carries within is particularly strong in Alexandra and provokes in her a sense of a past that drives back beyond her birth and of a future that reaches beyond her death. She drags behind her not only her personal past but the bequest of her father, who entrusts her with the future, and of her father's father (who in his own way had "come up from the sea himself" [*OP* 24])—a primordial past that includes the prehistoric races who made their "feeble scratches on the stone" (*OP* 19–20) and the larks who "have been singing the same five notes over for thousands of years" (*OP* 119), the records of glaciers and the land itself when it first emerged from the waters.

It is this quality that makes *O Pioneers!* a biological epic and establishes Alexandra as its heroine. This second "first" novel was as ambitious and comprehensive as *Alexander's Bridge*, and for its author, as it has been for its readers, far more satisfying. Cather never again wrote a novel that might be properly described as vitalistic, but the effects Bergson had upon her art were permanent and reveal themselves in the aesthetic attitude she eventually adopted and, more importantly, in her own later fiction.

FOUR

Fragments of Desire

I

IN THE PREVIOUS CHAPTER, I traced in the contours of Cather's early career a movement away from imitative modes and a conventionally naturalistic view to a more natural literary manner, one that, in *O Pioneers!*, may be described as a kind of literary vitalism. In part, this shift in sensibility grew out of a deep and abiding interest in and concern with the relations of art and life. In *O Pioneers!*, Willa Cather exchanged a mechanistic view of the world for an organic one and implicated her narrative in a remote evolutionary past that still worked in the present moment. This transformation can be explained by (though it cannot be said to have been wholly caused by) her adoption of the new philosophy. For Cather, as for T. E. Hulme, Bergson provided, in the "dialect of the time," a way out of the nightmare of mechanism, but his influence upon her was no doubt due to a disposition that already existed in embryo. *Creative Evolution* affected Cather profoundly and enabled her to coordinate and integrate imaginative materials in a way that allows one to describe her first significant novel as a biological epic. But the Bergsonian influence was a permanent one and entered into her thinking about life and literature in ways that help us to identify the intellectual interests of her mature fiction and to measure and define her artistic achievement.

How systematic a reader of Bergson Cather was is unclear, but she did revise her aesthetic principles in the years following the publication of *O Pioneers!* and found a way to use her own best talents in the service of an art that was significantly more subtle and confident than that of her apprentice years. In that, she was much like the painter Don Hedger in her story "Coming, Aphrodite!" By 1913 she, too, had "outlived a succession of convictions and revelations" about her art (*YBM* 9). Hedger found himself "groping his way from one kind of painting into another, . . . and he was chiefly occupied with getting rid of ideas he had once thought very fine" (*YBM* 10). Cather, too, groped her way toward a satisfactory art; the reconception of artistic principles, which she no doubt once thought very fine, are observable in the several aesthetic statements she made in essays, lectures, and interviews. The worth of these reformations is proved by her accomplished fictions, but they are revealed as well in another novel that participates in the same prewar optimism she had shown in *O Pioneers!*— *The Song of the Lark* (1915).

In that novel she dramatizes the growth of the artist Thea Kronborg. The story is at several points largely autobiographical and reaches back to Cather's early years in Red Cloud, but the aesthetic and psychology she employed in her rendering of the life of her artist heroine were only recently acquired. Cather enjoyed writing *The Song of the Lark* and wrote quickly and expansively—it is by far the longest and baggiest of her books. Though she did not regret the experience of having written this novel, she would later disparage the artistic mistakes she made in it. Edith Lewis believed that the faults Cather later found in *The Song of the Lark* "came in part from working too directly from immediate emotions and impressions."[1] But Cather also appears to have been working from an immediate intellectual stimulus and applying redefined notions of art and psychology to her narrative before they had settled into an enabling point of view. For this reason, it is instructive to linger over this novel before briefly examining her later critical statements and fiction and to discern in it an aesthetic attitude taking shape, one that, in the diffuse excitements that characterized it, was more often expressed than suggested.

II

The Song of the Lark is an American success story, a theme that always fascinated Cather. Later, recognizing that "success is not so interesting as struggle" (*PSL* i), she would regret that she had not ended her story before Thea's final achievement, but American society and the place of the creative personality within it had long preoccupied her. *Alexander's Bridge* explored the spiritual losses of the conventionally self-made man, and *O Pioneers!* celebrated the nearly mythic triumph of a pioneer woman for whom material success was almost incidental. When Cather agreed to help S. S. McClure write his autobiography in 1913, she was, in effect, committing herself to write yet another.

By this time, as well, Cather had effectively severed her ties with *Mc-*

Clure's, but (in addition to the serialized autobiography) she had promised to supply the magazine with five journalistic pieces. The second of these was entitled "Three American Singers: Louise Homer, Geraldine Farrar, Olive Fremstad" and sought to reveal in its successive accounts of their rise to operatic dominance "one of the most interesting stories in the history of American achievement."[2] Cather's interviews with these women coincidentally supplied her with fresh literary material. Louise Homer, in her thoroughly "professional personality" (*YBM* 79), may have contributed something to the character of Cressida Garnet in the short story "The Diamond Mine" (1916), although Garnet was modeled, perhaps too exactly, after the soprano Lillian Nordica.[3] Both Homer and Garnet are reliable but matter-of-fact artists at any rate. As Cather wrote in the *Mc-Clure's* article, Louise Homer "worked hard, but goading ambitions never kept her awake. . . . she set for herself no goal that it would break her heart to lose." Geraldine Farrar, on the other hand, may have served in some measure as a model for the vivacious and mischievous Kitty Ayrshire of "The Gold Slipper" (1917) and "Scandal" (1919), two other stories Cather wrote soon after completing *The Song of the Lark*. Farrar, wrote Cather, has "a hold on the baseball type of American"; she, like Ayrshire, makes a "direct appeal" to the "popular imagination" (*YBM* 60).

For Farrar, claimed Cather, art is too exclusively a thing of feeling, and she has neither the will nor the desire to reach the "frozen heights" of her art. Olive Fremstad, however, is an intellectual who attains those same heights Farrar refuses to attempt. Fremstad is the artist par excellence, for whom "artistic experiences are always mental experiences" and who is willing to take the risks necessary to attain her highest idea. Fremstad, wrote Cather, enjoyed neither the complacency of Homer nor the simple luck of Farrar: "Circumstances never helped Mme. Fremstad. She grew up in a new, crude country where there was neither artistic stimulus nor discriminating taste."

Fremstad's story of struggle epitomized the "artist's quest," but the rewards of her success were "pursued alone" and, for the most part, "enjoyed alone." Her voice, nevertheless, "has its roots deep in human nature, it follows the old paths of human yearning, it repeats the habits of mind and body which, by repeating themselves, define human nature." Fremstad's lonely determination enabled her to wring "from fortune the one profit which adversity sometimes leaves with strong natures—the power to conquer." As Cather concluded in her article, the example of this Swedish-born immigrant makes her "the most interesting kind of American. As

Roosevelt once said, Americanism is not a condition of birth, but a condition of spirit." In Olive Fremstad, Cather found the inspiration for the heroine of her next novel, a woman whose story served as much as an occasion to render this special example of Americanism as an opportunity for Cather to explore the nature of artistic growth.

Cather's title (she had originally wanted to call it "Artist's Youth") came from an indifferent painting she had seen at the Chicago Art Institute, but her book would be about the American spirit, realized and triumphant, in the figure of Thea Kronborg. She began her new novel in October 1913, and from the beginning Fremstad's story had blended with Cather's own history. Cather so identified with Thea Kronborg, in fact, that, according to Elizabeth Sergeant, "when the book came out and the close inner tie was severed, she felt the pang and emptiness of one deserted."[4] For Cather had set out to tell the story of an artist's growth and recorded along the way her own feelings of struggle and progress. E. K. Brown found it curious that the book in which Cather was "most engaged with artists and the artistic process is the least artistic of her works" and laments the fact that she felt so strongly an impulse "to drive an idea deep into presumably inattentive heads."[5] But the author seems to have been as captivated by her newly acquired thoughts about the artistic process as she was absorbed by her subject, and she felt compelled to express rather than suggest her meanings. It is true, at any rate, that the several conversations about art and the sometimes excessive commentary on the same subject obtrude upon her narrative, but these same inartistic excesses have a special interest for us here because they best reveal the philosophical interest of the book.

The intellectual qualities of Cather's fiction have too often been neglected, even by her most ardent admirers. Cather was, of course, an artist of feeling, but she was an artist of ideas as well. She once wrote Zoë Akins that any good story must be guided and sustained by strong and authentic feeling or directed by an intellectual interest of a sufficiently high order to save it from excess or peculiarity.[6] Often in her mature work, especially in her historical novels, both qualities are superbly combined and properly controlled by a technical assurance and quiet detachment. But *The Song of the Lark* is the product of a more excitable imagination. Although Cather sometimes drew upon her earliest memories in writing it, Thea's story of artistic growth conformed to certain Bergsonian notions of art and metaphysics that Cather herself had only recently adopted.

Critics have sometimes groped for an adequate term to describe *The Song of the Lark*. Susan Rosowski has deemed it Cather's equivalent to

Wordsworth's *Prelude*, a *bildungsroman* that treats of the growth of Thea's creative powers. Similarly, David Stouck has called it a *künstlerroman*, a novel about an initiation "conceived entirely in terms of an artist's mastery of his craft." And E. K. Brown identified the novel as an *entwicklungs-roman*, in which the artist gradually unfolded within herself and ripened into the great artist she was to become.[7] Each of these identifications is accurate enough, but they focus too exclusively on the separate and separable strivings of the heroine of the book. Howard Mumford Jones recognized the social implications of Thea's story, though he likewise gave it a rather narrow focus when, borrowing a term from Robert Schumann, he characterized it as a *Davidsbündler*—the "League of David against the Philistines"—a mystery cult with Thea as its centerpiece.[8]

Cather's interests were more conventionally democratic, however, and she had been severely critical of all forms of aestheticism. She sought instead to connect the resources and achievements of her artist to the life of the republic, not its cultural life merely but its capacity to aspire and to dream. Though she may have later regretted that she did not end Thea's story before the interest of her struggle paled and the richness of her personality became absorbed by its own artistic performances, her heroine's final achievement and, more importantly, her epilogue were necessary to the social vision Cather wished to convey.

The story of Thea Kronborg chronicles the life of an extraordinarily talented woman who grew up in Moonstone, Colorado (based on Cather's own Red Cloud). Thea has to reckon with her father's good-willed but limited expectations of her and with her active detractors. But Thea has her admirers and supporters as well—her mother; the restless but joyous Spanish Johnny; the unhappy but encouraging Dr. Archie; the simple but decent suitor, Ray Kennedy; her cynical music teacher, Wunsch; and her vapid Aunt Tillie, whose behavior is embarrassing but whose intuitive faith in her niece is finally justified. These, as the title of the first section suggests, are the "Friends of Childhood." Each contributes to Thea's destiny, and each recognizes in this local girl a nascent possibility that they themselves have forfeited. In 1932, Cather would say of *The Song of the Lark* that "what I cared about, and still care about, was the girl's escape; the play of blind chance, the way in which commonplace occurrences fell together to liberate her from commonness. She seemed wholly at the mercy of accident; but to persons of her vitality and honesty, fortunate accidents will always happen" (*PSL* iii).

Thea's success does indeed seem to be guided by many ordinary accidents—Ray Kennedy's life insurance money enables her to study music in Chicago; her casual mention that she sings in a church leads her teacher Andor Harsanyi to discover that her true instrument is her voice, not the piano; Fred Ottenberg's offer to send her to his father's ranch in Arizona puts her in mysterious contact with an ancient people and renews her determination to succeed. These, and a dozen incidents like them, seem to mark Thea's destiny and to make her one of fortune's favorites. Her rise, superficially considered, is as inadvertent and fortuitous as Carrie Meeber's. But the naturalism of *The Song of the Lark* is not the naturalism of *Sister Carrie*, and Cather's vision was not Theodore Dreiser's. Thea's story is rather an affirmation of human freedom in a world still in the making, and she, like Alexandra Bergson, completes and promotes desires as old and eternal as those of the ancient people who once inhabited the cliff dwellings in Panther Canyon.

Thea Kronborg is a kind of populist überdame, created in the days when Cather, as she recalled in 1931, thought people "just as they were" were not good enough and had to be "trimmed up" a bit (*WCP* 123). And the provincial life Thea heroically sought to escape is finally responsible for her triumph. Her potent personality is diminished by each successive achievement, however, and in the final sections of the book Thea is as "dry and preoccupied" (*PSL* ii) as Cather said she was. Part 6, "Kronborg," takes place in New York ten years after Thea left to study in Germany and to perfect her art. This section presents a recognized artist in full possession of her powers, but one whose inner life has been sacrificed to her achievement. Her consolation and continuing resource are the memories and dreams of youth. "They save me: the old things," she tells Dr. Archie, "things like the Kohler's garden. They are in everything I do" (*SL* 460). Recollections of Moonstone contribute an inestimable share to her finest performance, a performance improbably witnessed by those who believed in her from the beginning—by Dr. Archie and Fred Ottenberg, Mr. and Mrs. Harsanyi, and, remote in the top gallery, an aged Spanish Johnny.

The imaginative life one is able to get into one's art, Cather once observed, is "cremated youth" (*WCP* 36). The raw and undirected experience and desire of childhood supply Thea with the creative energy she has to master and control, but in her maturity that same desire is only intermittently realized in her art. "A child's attitude toward everything is an artist's attitude," Thea says. "I am more or less of an artist now, but then I was nothing else" (*SL* 460). It is fitting, then, that Cather returns to Moonstone in the epilogue, for Moonstone is both the origin and (because it is the place of her youth) the active cause of Thea's special and uncompromised success. "Money and office and success are the consolations of impotence," wrote Cather. A truer sort is reserved for the young "who are the Future, and who possess the treasure of creative power" (*SL* 265).

By returning her story to Moonstone, Cather returned as well to Thea's earliest and most undoubting admirer, to her queer old Aunt Tillie. The success of the diva popularly known as "Kronborg" is general and complete, but in her hometown Thea is remembered as the young girl who sang at Maggie Evans's funeral twenty years ago. That "little settlement of quiet people" is brightened and refreshed by Tillie's news and stories about her niece, and Thea gives back to her own people what she herself experienced many years before when she heard Antonín Dvořák's *New World Symphony*: "first memories, first mornings long ago; the amazement of a new soul in a new world; a soul new and yet old, that had dreamed something despairing, something glorious, in the dark before it was born; a soul obsessed by what it did not know, under the cloud of a past it could not recall" (*SL* 199). In a word, she gives them what her old music teacher Wunsch had told her was the secret of art—desire. Or, as Cather herself chose to conclude her novel, Thea's success and her art bring "to the old, memories, and to the young, dreams" (*SL* 490).

Cather may have borrowed her vision of the uses of art to the common life from Emerson or from Whitman (who had contributed something to the writing of *O Pioneers!*) or perhaps from Leo Tolstoy, whose *What Is Art?* she had read and admired. If she derived her aesthetic mysticism from any of these, however, it was Bergson who provided the psychological and philosophical foundation for her portrait of the artist and of the creative process. *The Song of the Lark* is saturated with Bergsonian notions, and to the advantage of discerning them, if not to the artistic advantage of the novel itself, they are more often expressed than convincingly dramatized or suggested. I have indirectly touched upon three such notions already but now need to reconsider them in their Bergsonian context.

First, art derives its power from the consolidated memories of youth before the necessity of deliberate action coordinates and subordinates past experiences to the practical interests of meaningful activity. Often, as is evident in *O Pioneers!*, the ordinary uses of life restrict the free play of perception and memory and solidify them; habit unceasingly dethrones the authority of freedom. Thus, a second, socialized self preempts the urges of a primary self, a *moi fondamentale*. Ordinarily we are content with this "shadow self" (*TFW* 128) because it is better adapted to the requirements of social life, but a primary self is ever with us and blazes up from time to time, notably in childhood, in dreams, and in aesthetic feeling. Dr. Archie recognizes this when, despite his financial success, he laments, "the only things we cherish are those which in some way met our original want; the desire which formed in us in early youth, undirected, and of its own accord" (*SL* 401). This first point implies a second.

The bare basis for aesthetic feeling is the communication by suggestion of a deep-seated, authentic self lingering on the fringes of our consciousness. Great art returns us to the active presence of this primary self. From time to time, argued Bergson, and by "lucky accident," nature spawns individuals whose perceptions are "less adherent to life"; these persons are artists. They are born "detached" and perceive "not simply with a view for action; they perceive in order to perceive" (*CM* 138).[9] Because perceptions become memories and the self is the whole of memory, that same detachment *is* the personality of the artist.

Cather had always been interested in the doubleness of human personality, but Bergson provided a metaphysic that enabled her to reconcile the opposing claims of the artistic soul and the uninspired, socialized self and thereby to give the artist a special yet somehow common dignity. By implication, since the child's attitude is essentially the artist's attitude, Cather was able to believe that the artistic soul was a common possession but one that had atrophied in most because they lacked the means or the desire to gratify it.

Thea ponders her special desire and the unaccountable interest the friends of childhood have taken in her in part 2 of the novel. She recognizes that her voice, "more than any other part of her, had to do with that confidence, that sense of wholeness and inner well-being, that she had felt ever since she could remember" (*SL* 216). She recognizes, too, her special possibility:

> She remembered the way Ray had looked at her that morning. Why had he cared so much? And Wunsch, and Dr. Archie, and Spanish Johnny, why had they? It was something that had to do with her that made them care, but it was not she. Perhaps each of them concealed another person in himself, just as she did. Why was it that they seemed to feel and to hunt for a second person in her and not in each other? Thea frowned up at the dull lamp in the roof of the car. What

if one's second self could somehow speak to all these second selves? What if one could bring them out, as whiskey did Spanish Johnny's? How deep they lay, these second persons, and how little one knew about them, except to guard them fiercely. It was to music, more than to anything else, that these hidden things in people responded.

[*SL* 217]

This is the deep appeal of art, and it cements the activities of the artist with the uses of life. Art justifies itself in its several acts and restores and heals the divisions in those separated from the wholeness of youth, and it reveals itself in those odd moments when one feels the liberating presence of continuous identity. This is what Wallace Stevens meant when he wrote, "Poetry is a health" (*Opus* 176). How can the suggestive power of music be explained, asks Bergson, unless by repeating to ourselves the sounds heard, we carry ourselves "back into the original psychic state, which nothing will express, but which something may suggest, viz., the very motion and attitude which the sound imparts to our body?" (*TFW* 44). The bold novelist, Bergson insists elsewhere, encourages us to "put aside for an instant the veil which we interposed between our consciousness and ourselves. He has brought us back to our own presence" (*TFW* 134). This is the ambition that Cather put into the mind and heart of Thea, and it is the artistic premise that the author herself meant to dramatize in her story of the development of creative power. As we will see in the next chapter, it is the same aesthetic understanding that Wallace Stevens discovered and, at about the same time, sought to disclose in his poem "Peter Quince at the Clavier."

A third Bergsonian notion is related to the other two. Thea's determination derives from the makeup of her character. Other people believe in her because "she had both imagination and a stubborn will, curiously balancing and interpenetrating each other. . . . She had the power to make a great effort, to lift a weight heavier than herself" (*SL* 96).

H. L. Mencken praised *The Song of the Lark* for its vital "intellectual interest,"[10] and he may have detected in the book certain Nietzschean qualities that suited his temperament. However, Cather made her own übermensch out of conspicuously Bergsonian materials. For man, as a species and as an individual, acts by a willed contraction and condensation of consciousness, carves out some portion of perception meant for him. Only by this route does the vital movement seek to establish itself in the future, but such assertions exact a price: "*It is as if a vague and formless being, whom we may call, as we will,* man *or* superman, *had sought to realize himself, and had succeeded only by abandoning a part of himself along the way"* (*CE* 266).

In order to conquer matter and "to reconquer its own self," "consciousness has had to exhaust the best part of its power." But intuitions re-invigorate the assault upon necessity. Intuition is a "lamp almost extinguished, which glimmers only now and then, and for a few moments at most. But it glimmers wherever a vital interest is at stake" (*CE* 267–68). Thea Kronborg's life, like Alexandra Bergson's, is punctuated by these intuitions, and they combine with a passionate will and a determination to preserve that vital interest. The world at large seems intent on stealing that exhilarating sense of self, but Thea resolves that they shall not have it: "As long as she lived that ecstasy was going to be hers. She would live for it, work for it, die for it; but she was going to have it, time after time, height after height" (*SL* 201).

The result of this fierce commitment is artistic triumph. That same success, however, steals what she would not lose, for her personality becomes lost in its own operatic impersonations. Cather had learned from Bergson that the evolution of character participates in the same tendencies as the evolution of species, and the assertions of personality and freedom require a sacrifice:

Each of us glancing back over his history, will find that his child-personality, though indivisible, united in itself divers persons, which could remain blended just because they were in a nascent state: this indecision, so charged with promise, is one of the greatest charms of childhood. But these interwoven personalities become incompatible in course of growth, and, as each of us can live but one life, a choice must perforce be made. We choose in reality without ceasing; without ceasing, also, we abandon many things. The route we pursue in time is strewn with the remains of all that we began to be, of all that we might have become.   [*CE* 99–100]

This is the quality Cather isolated for attention in her 1932 preface to the novel: As Thea's "artistic life grows fuller and richer, it becomes more interesting to her than her own life. . . . Her artistic life is the only one in which she is happy, or free, or even very real. . . . But the free creature, who retains her youth and beauty and warm imagination, is kept shut up in the closet, along with the scores and wigs" (*PSL* ii). Youth, vitality, that "biological force" Cather detected in Arnold Bennett and exhibited in her own novel, is finally exhausted in its own efforts.

It would be pointless to recount all of the parallels that exist between *The Song of the Lark* and Bergson. Cather's story of artistic unfolding had been inspired by the impression Olive Fremstad left on her and guided by the author's sense of her own development as an artist. For the intellectual justification of the story, however, she had turned to the new reality of the age as it had been articulated in *Creative Evolution* and elsewhere. And the aesthetic she formulated in the book, perhaps was formulating even as she wrote, is nowhere more exact or memorable than in part 4, "The Ancient People." This constitutes the mystical and aesthetic center of her novel.

Cather had visited Walnut Canyon in 1912; it was to become the Panther Canyon of her novel. Her experience there, as her experience in the Southwest generally, deeply affected her. The light and air, the strong simplicity of the landscape, the ruins of a vanished race—everything about it seemed to ratify and clarify her thinking about art and life. The Anasazi cliff dwellings in Walnut Canyon provided the locus for dramatizing her current convictions about the nature and significance of creative activity.

Almost as soon as Thea arrives in Arizona, she feels a release from the "stream of meaningless activity and undirected effort" (*SL* 299) that she had found in Chicago, but she is absorbed by another stream—an élan vital that she perceives in everything around her and feels within her as a "driving power in the blood" (*SL* 307). A "persistent affirmation" moves in her and eventuates in an overwhelming "desire for action" (*SL* 307). She decides then that she will go to Germany to study—to take life by storm and to risk everything for her art. In so doing, she resolves to slip the bonds of necessity mapped out by complacency or habit but not by design. No "kindly Providence" directs her: "One's life was at the mercy of blind chance. She had better take it in her own hands and lose everything than meekly draw the plough under the rod of parental guidance" (*SL* 307). For in Panther Canyon Thea discovers that she labors under a deep and persistent responsibility. "The Cliff-Dwellers had lengthened her past. She had older and higher obligations" (*SL* 308).

What is disclosed to Thea in the canyon is a world of unceasing life and change (blind chance, perhaps, but not mechanistic determination), and her revelation is prepared for by a series of perceptions or, more accurately, by a giving of herself to perception itself. "The faculty of observation was never highly developed in Thea Kronborg," we are told. "A great deal escaped her eye as she passed through the world. But the things which were for her, she saw; she experienced them physically and remembered them as if they had once been a part of herself" (*SL* 301). In Panther Canyon she begins to see as she has not seen since childhood. The images of swallows, juniper, the canyon walls join those earlier recollections, such as the moon flowers over Mrs. Tellamantez's door or the mint in Mrs. Kohler's garden, and become a part of her personality. In Panther Canyon "there were again things which seemed destined for her" (*SL* 301), and she could become "a mere receptacle for heat, or become a color . . . she could become a continuous repetition of sounds, like the cicadas" (*SL* 300).[11]

There is nothing mystical about her experience. These epistemological disclosures are grounded in what Bergson insisted was the common sense view of reality but with this important difference—Thea, as a born artist, spawned by nature itself, "perceives in order to perceive" (*CM* 138). Released from the enslaving desire to get on in the world, she is able to cleanse her vision of the ready-made understandings of tradition and reason and to experience a certain rebirth of sensation. No longer does she perceive according to the representations of the intellect. Instead, she partakes in what Bergson called "pure perception" (*MM* 26)—a quality of affective sensation that is nevertheless an "internal state" and arises within the body itself. Such perception is, in fact, a "part of things" and is not represented to the mind at all; rather, it is an absorption in duration before the intellect represents to consciousness the false and static reality of symbols. This, in Bergson's system, is the foundation of metaphysics, that "science which claims to dispense with symbols" (*IM* 9), and is a process already familiar to the creative artist. Thus can Thea "lie for half a day undistracted, holding pleasant and incomplete conceptions in her mind—almost in her hands. They were scarcely clear enough to be called ideas. They had something to do with fragrance and color and sound, but almost nothing to do with words" (*SL* 299).

Cather's description of Thea's experience is as clear and succinct a rendering of Bergsonian intuition as one could wish. The singer's "power to think seemed to be converted into a power of sustained sensation" (*SL* 300), and she sometimes believes she could remain in this dreamlike state forever. But her destiny is not to dream but to act, and her purpose is confirmed by her mysterious commerce with the past and with the ancient people. It is in Thea's relation to this past that the mysticism of the book resides.

In *Matter and Memory* Bergson hints at the possibility of a union between mind and matter in positing what he calls pure perception, the sort of perception Thea experiences in Panther Canyon. Because such perception is "mind without memory" and because it is bodily reaction rather than understanding, it is, in his special sense of the term, matter itself. His argument is complicated, but his conclusion is simple enough: "If matter does not remember the past, it is because it repeats the past unceasingly," and thus the past is "truly given in its present" (*MM* 297).[12] But a freely evolving being borrows from matter perceptions that will direct its future, and as such cannot read the past in the present. "The past should be *acted* by matter, *imagined* by mind" (*MM* 298). Randolph Bourne put the matter more clearly in *Youth and Life*, a book that by this time Cather had likely read: "It is only the Past that we really make. . . . For the Past is really the child of the Present. We are the authors of its being, and upon it we lavish all our thoughts, our interests, and our delight."[13] This connection is an important one because memory and the past are so much a part of all of Cather's later fiction and fully connected to her artistic vision.

In *The Song of the Lark*, this interest takes a particular and quasi-mystical form. In the canyon, Thea hears "a voice out of the past, not very loud, that went on saying a few simple things to the solitude eternally" (*SL* 302). There is a fusion between her body and her perceptions—a series of "intuitions" about the ancient people (*SL* 302). She begins to understand these people; certain feelings are "transmitted" to her that were "not expressible in words, but seemed rather to translate themselves into attitudes of body, into degrees of muscular tension or relaxation" (*SL* 303).

"We shall never know the past unless we frankly place ourselves within it," wrote Bergson (*MM* 313). Thea begins to understand the voice of this past and to feel its recurring rhythms, and she discovers in the artifacts of the Indians an ancient desire to create. Cather was fascinated by the fact that the Indian women so exactingly decorated their pottery, for they obviously struggled with only the necessities of life: "This care, expended upon vessels that could not hold food or water any better for the additional labor put upon them, made her heart go out to those ancient potters. . . . Food, fire, water, and something else—even here, in this crack in the world, so far back in the night of the past! Down here at the beginning that painful thing was already stirring; the seed of sorrow, and of so much delight" (*SL* 305).

The eternal struggle of the life urge to assert and formalize itself is ample testimony to an atavistic desire and to the possibility of human freedom. "The stream and the broken pottery: what was any art but an effort to make a sheath, a mould in which to imprison for a moment the shining, elusive element which is life itself,—life hurrying past us and running away, too strong to stop, too sweet to lose. . . . In singing, one made a vessel of one's throat and nostrils and held it on one's breath, caught the stream in a scale of natural intervals" (*SL* 304). Through her voice, Thea will, to use Bergson's word, "canalize" the life force and, through her presence, give back to others a sense of themselves, a sense as essential and as old as desire itself.

For Cather, as for Bergson, great art is created by a correspondingly great personality, one whose productions and forms suggest a considerable part of one's own history and suggest as well the quality and intensity of feeling that engendered it. Suggestion is the foundation of a Bergsonian aesthetic because art, like the immanent dynamism of creation itself, is at once form and unforeseeability. "The feeling of the beautiful is no specific feeling, but that every feeling experienced by us will assume an aesthetic character, provided that it has been *suggested* and not *caused*" (*TFW* 17–18). Through the character Landry, Cather attributes Thea's unique gifts as an artist to just those qualities. "What she does is interesting because she does it," he says. "Even the things she discards are suggestive." Her performance in the role of Elizabeth in *Tannhäuser* is "full of the thing every plain creature finds out for himself, but that never gets written down. It's unconscious memory, maybe; inherited memory, like folk-music. I call it personality" (*SL* 449).

Landry's equation of personality and inherited memory is interesting because it yokes together, by implication, a primordial past and present identity in a single, timeless reality. Thea Kronborg succeeds because she promotes and carries into the future ancient truths, and she carries them to great, even frozen, heights. She envies the grace and ease of the swallows in Panther Canyon but finds it sad that they are timid and "lived their lives between the echoing cliffs and never dared to rise out of the shadow of the canyon walls" (*SL* 301). She finally identifies her destiny with the eagle that momentarily dropped into the shadowy gulf and then soared into the light of the sun: "O eagle of eagles! Endeavor, achievement, desire, glorious striving of human art! From a cleft in the heart of the world she saluted it. . . . It had come all the way; when men lived in caves, it was there. A vanished race; but along the trails in the stream, under the spreading cactus, there still glittered in the sun the bits of frail clay vessels, fragments of their desire" (*SL* 321).

III

The Song of the Lark is a passionate and, perhaps, overly confident statement of the relevance of creative power to the uses of life. It dramatizes
and localizes the most ancient and fundamental energies and desires—
emergent in Thea Kronborg, underwritten by the example of the cliff
dwellers, and passed on to the future and to youth. Cather had believed in
the new generation, but youth, as youth has a way of doing, disappointed
her. Her novel was written during an era when, as she recalled in 1936,
"the world was changing" (*WCOW* 24). She had participated in the enthusiasms of the age, though in later years she would become increasingly
embittered by the nation's appetite for the commercial and material. Nevertheless, she had adopted the new philosophy and persisted in this vision
long beyond the heyday of its popular appeal. *The Song of the Lark* expressed her vision unmistakably, but subsequent fictions were informed by
her new aesthetic in ways that are far more sophisticated and not as obvious. Cather's later critical writings, because they seek to define rather than
to embody her artistic vision, are more useful in demonstrating how permanently affected she was by the new philosophy and, particularly, by
Bergson.

The world was indeed changing in these prewar years, and there were,
she claimed, a company of promising young men just graduated from the
university who meant to play a part in the change. They were anxious to
bring about a "renaissance" in a decade or so, but "the only new thing
they offered," she wrote with her own full measure of contempt, "was
contempt for the old" (*WCOW* 25). This newness she found discouraging. "The theme of true poetry, of great poetry, will be the same until all
the values of human life have changed and the strongest emotional responses have become different—which can hardly occur until the physical
body itself has fundamentally changed" (*WCOW* 28).[14] The "new poetry,"
she thought, rejected the old themes and confined itself "to regarding the
grey of a wet oyster shell against the sand of a wet beach through a drizzle
of rain." The effect was not memorable, even when the craft was expert,
even "when a beat in the measure was unexpectedly dropped here and
there with what one of the poet's admirers calls a 'heart-breaking effect.'
Certainly the last thing such poetry should attempt is to do anything
heart-breaking" (*WCOW* 28).

If we can trust Cather's recollection in 1936 of her own sense of things
twenty years before, then almost as soon as she had consolidated and

dramatized her newly adopted aesthetic in *The Song of the Lark*, she began to feel that the new generation was passing her by. She had located the source and pleasure of art in the biological organism of the human animal itself and had identified the need to create as one of the necessities of life. She had found as well that creative desire was fully connected to the historical and social life of the individual and to the vital and enduring element in an evolutionary movement that still sought to realize itself and still whispered a few simple things in the solitude. In the larger-than-life characters of Alexandra Bergson, Thea Kronborg, and, later, Ántonia Shimerda, Cather created figures whose free acts involved them in eternity—not a "conceptual eternity," which, as Bergson said, "is an eternity of death," but an eternity of life, "a living and therefore still moving eternity in which our own particular duration would be included as the vibrations are in light" (*IM* 63–64). Willa Cather had felt as intensely as had Wallace Stevens that, as he said, "art must fit with other things; it must be a part of the system of the world" (*LWS* 24). Cather herself said, "Art springs out of the very stuff that life is made of" (*WCP* 47).

Cather rejected as ardently in the twentieth century as she had in the nineteenth the quantifying and enumerative explanations of scientists who might claim to read the desires of the soul in the ticker tape of sensation. And she spoke bitterly through Professor St. Peter of the "superficial" "amazements" of a science whose "sleight of hand" would take away the sins of the world in the laboratory (*PH* 68). She rejected, as she rejected Freud, those behaviorists or biologists who sought to explain the nature of man as somehow made rather than in the making. Human nature could be better explained, she believed, by someone like Thomas Mann, whose *Joseph and His Brothers* treated Abraham's seed not as the chosen people but as *"the people who chose"* (*NUF* 104).

Cather's essay on Mann was included in a volume with the cautionary title *Not under Forty* (1936), and the volume was dedicated to the "backward," among whom she rather proudly counted herself. Willa Cather is herself largely responsible for the widespread view that she was at odds with the modern world and bitterly nostalgic for past grandeurs. Her critical writings, particularly her tributes to such women as Sarah Orne Jewett, Madame Grout (niece of Gustave Flaubert), and Mrs. James T. Fields (wife of the famous nineteenth-century American publisher and minor poet), and her turn to historical romances in which genuine heroism seemed possible or to bitter portrayals of modern life (such as *A Lost Lady, My Mortal Enemy,* or *The Professor's House*) in which it did not—all

these served to substantiate the view that she was indeed an "antiquarian,"[15] ignorant of or indifferent to the struggles of her own time. But the
problem of modern life and art was for Cather, as it was for Wallace
Stevens, finding "what will suffice" (*CP* 239). And, like Stevens, she found
in the new philosophy that prospered in the prewar years a view sufficient
to her art, one that served not merely as a congenial aesthetic attitude but
as a vision of life and history and human nature.

In 1942, Stevens defined the problem of the modern spirit in "Of Modern Poetry." The old theater of human activity had disappeared, and the
artist must "construct a new stage." One's art has to be "on that stage,"
and the artist must speak to the mind the words "it wants to hear" and
write to an "invisible audience" who listens "Not to the play, but to itself,
expressed / In an emotion as of two people, as of two / Emotions becoming one" (*CP* 240). Cather had expressed the same commitment thirty
years before when she had Thea wish to speak with her most authentic
being to all those other second selves in the world willing to listen. And
she restated it in 1932 in the story "Two Friends" when she had her narrator remark how strangely revealing it was to listen to these two business-
men talk about plays and actors one had never seen. They "merely reminded each other of moments here and there in the action. But they saw
the play over again as they talked of it, and perhaps whatever is seen by the
narrator as he speaks is sensed by the listener, quite irrespective of words"
(*OD* 218). It is true that Cather, like Stevens, often spoke what she
"wanted to hear," but this was a principle not an indulgence. "So long as a
novelist works selfishly for the pleasure of creating character and situation
corresponding to his own illusions, ideals and intuitions," she said, "he
will always produce something worth while and natural" (*WCP* 59). To
create fictions that corresponded to the truth of intuition was for Cather,
as it was for Stevens, an ideal she had derived from a vitalistic vision of the
world, and she kept an unwavering allegiance to it.

In essays, lectures, and interviews, Cather was to repeat again and again
her beliefs about the nature and function of art. It was a simple faith, and
a mundane one, but she believed in it. She hoped she did not take herself
too seriously, she once wrote Zoë Akins, but she knew that she took her
convictions seriously indeed.[16] The purpose of art was not to instruct,
expose, or reform; that was the business of the pamphleteer or social
worker. Artists are "useful" only insofar as they can "refresh and recharge
the spirit," she said (*WCOW* 20). In that, too, she was following Bergson.
Artists grasp in themselves the "living law" of reality, "varying with each

individual," and communicate it to us; they "impel us to set in motion, in the depths of our being, some secret chord which was only waiting to thrill" (*L* 161–62).

Such refreshment comes only from close contact with the living principle that a primary self knows and responds to. In the presence of great art, one repossesses one's own inner life; a primary self surfaces, if only for a moment, under the spell of almost hypnotic suggestion. The whole business of art and creation is to enfold the reader in a coherent form that is nevertheless unforeseeable, to create a fictional world that may be suggested but that can never be expressed because language tends to solidify that same dynamic reality it seeks to reveal. Cather wrote Akins in 1932 that the interest of life typically resides in its unanticipated qualities. The surprise of events is logical and the effect of certain causes, but this is something we never realize until afterward. This quality in fiction has nearly vanished from modern writing, she wrote, but it was nevertheless her kind of writing. She added that she wished that she could do away with the atmospheric quality in her fiction and be another kind of writer for a while.[17] But she could not, and it is doubtful that she really wanted to.

Cather often wrote about the atmospheric effects of good writing. She praised in Thomas Mann the "dreamy indefiniteness" he got into his story of Joseph and his brothers, a people "without any of the relentless mechanical gear which directs every moment of modern life toward accuracy" (*NUF* 99). The lasting appeal of Nathaniel Hawthorne's *The Scarlet Letter*, she wrote in "The Novel Démeublé" (1936), consists in the "material investiture" of the tale, its mood of "twilight melancholy" (*WCOW* 41), not in anything one might learn about Puritan manners. In Tolstoy, who had as great a love of "things" as Balzac, there is nonetheless the rendering of the feelings of his characters that gives an "emotional penumbra" (*WCOW* 39–40) to the literalness of his treatment. She also saw in the work of some of the younger writers of the time a willingness and desire "to present their scene by suggestion rather than enumeration" (*WCOW* 40).

How nice it would be, she thought, to have unfurnished novels once again, to "throw all the furniture out the window; and along with it, all the meaningless reiteration concerning physical sensation . . . and leave the room as bare as the stage of a Greek theatre, . . . leave the scene bare for the play of emotions" (*WCOW* 43). For Cather, this was not the wistful expression of regret, it was part and parcel of her convictions about the metaphysical nature of the creative process: "Whatever is felt upon the page without being specifically named there—that, one might say, is created. It is the inexplicable presence of the thing not named, of the overtone divined by the ear but not heard by it, the verbal mood, the emotional aura of the fact or the thing or the deed, that gives high quality to the novel or the drama, as well as to poetry itself" (*WCOW* 42). Perhaps Cather never thought of herself, as did Stevens, as a "metaphysician in the dark" (*CP* 240), but the art of suggestion was her art, and it was grounded in a species of metaphysics she had discovered in Bergson. At all events, her testimony about the creative process at several points echoes a Bergsonian epistemology.

John Randall is right to say that Cather's art, at its best, "represented an escape into reality instead of an escape away from it."[18] Of what that reality consists, however, he does not say. Leon Howard comes closer when he observes that her best books (most notably *Death Comes for the Archbishop*) bear witness to "a sense of the past not as history but as life."[19] Reality is duration, the past moving into the future. Thea Kronborg knew that the immanent world of change was "too strong to stop, too sweet to lose." What Thea feels inside her is a double movement—her "happiness consisted of that backward and forward movement of herself. The something [in her] came and went, she never knew how" (*SL* 79). The same movement is the course of Frost's "West-Running Brook" that "runs counter to itself"—back to the "beginning of beginnings":

> It is this backward motion toward the source,
> Against the stream, that most we see ourselves in,
> The tribute of the current to the source.[20]

Reality is perpetual growth and change, as is consciousness; but, according to Bergson, while consciousness "does indeed move in the same direction as its principle, it is also continually drawn the opposite way, obliged, though it goes forward, to look behind" (*CE* 237).

The remounting of the slope of consciousness that is the work of intuition is, as well, the whole effort and effect of art. One can never attain to the truth of duration through an assemblage of so many points of view, the massing of planes, or the determination of a number of psychic states, no more than (to borrow Bergson's example) an infinite number of photographs of Paris can give us the knowledge of being in Paris. Analysis always remains external to the thing it contemplates; intuition places one within the thing itself. This is one of the reasons Cather objected to the grubby auctioneering kind of writing that, piling detail upon detail, presented itself as "realism." This is also why she complained of D. H. Lawrence's mere cataloguing of physical sensations in *The Rainbow*. "Characters can be almost dehumanized by a laboratory study of the behavior of their bodily organs under sensory stimuli—can be reduced, indeed, to mere animal pulp" (*WCOW* 42).

The living character or event is got by other means. Cather faulted Daniel Defoe's *The Fortunate Mistress* as a bare-boned narrative written by a man of "ready invention but no imagination" (*WCOW* 78). Particularly, the novel lacks the evocative quality of suggestion and scene:

> The "scene" in fiction is not a mere matter of construction, any more than it is in life. When we have a vivid experience in social intercourse, pleasant or unpleasant, it records itself in our memory in the form of a scene; and when it flashes back to us, all sorts of apparently unimportant details are flashed back with it. When a writer has a strong or revelatory experience with his characters, he unconsciously creates a scene; gets a depth of picture, and writes, as it were, in three dimensions instead of two. The absence of these warm and satisfying moments in any work of fiction is final proof of the author's poverty of emotion and lack of imagination.   [*WCOW* 79–80]

The psychological and epistemological process Cather describes here is thoroughly Bergsonian. Memory records perceptions in the form of images (or scenes) and mysteriously stores them for future use. In ordinary life, the resemblance of present perception to past experience calls forth these images to serve as tutors to intelligent action in the present. Often the memory installs within individuals stabilized and ready-made concepts to deal with present experience, but by definition these concepts are not identical with the present moment. The bond is resemblance, but there is no real reason why any perception should not, potentially, resemble in some feature or characteristic any or all past experiences. (The psychology of resemblance, as we shall see in Stevens, is the basis and motive for metaphor.) It is convenient in ordinary life that the ready-made response should be recalled, though this tends to make one's life mere sensorimotor reaction rather than true freedom existing in the full duration of its becoming. The inner life or personality, which collects those images that most appeal to it, is usually obscured because it does not serve well the necessities of social life or the requirements of the intellect. Consciousness (except in its hypothetical forms as pure perception or pure memory) is, therefore, always a blend of memory and perception. In that sense, the past is always a part of the present and makes practical activity possible.

This same process obtains for the artist, but with the important difference already noted. Because artists are by nature "absentminded" (*L* 160)—that is, detached from the compulsion to sift and order experience with an eye always toward concrete and effective action—they know how to value the useless. They recall in intuitive flashes images of sensory detail in the fullness of their original movement and embody them in imaginative forms. True artists possess a "natural detachment, one innate in the structure of sense or consciousness" (*L* 160), perceive reality for its own sake, and see into the "inner life of things" (*L* 161). That Willa Cather thought of herself in these Bergsonian terms is evident in a comment she made in an interview in 1921: "It happened that my mind was constructed for the particular purpose of absorbing impressions and retaining them" (*WCP* 44). She is, in a word, a "born" artist.

Those same impressions, properly managed by craft and form, give vitality to one's art and, at the same time, remain an expression of the personality of the artist. Such memories cannot be sought or forced up, for they come unbidden and in intuitive flashes. This was both a stated principle and, judging from her letters, an actuality in Cather's experience as a creative artist.[21] "Life began for me," she told Elizabeth Sergeant, "when I ceased to admire and began to remember."[22] When she was writing hard, driving for the main episodes, she trusted her memory to supply the details. Striking the right note, selecting out of the swarm of recollection the right detail, is a natural process for the writer who has given herself "absolutely to her material" (*WCOW* 51). Sarah Orne Jewett was such a writer: "She early learned to love her country for what it was. What is quite as important, she saw it as it was. She happened to have the right nature, the right temperament, to see it so—and to understand by intuition the deeper meaning of all she saw" (*WCOW* 56). To the extent that Jewett understood her native environment (its country, its speech and manners, and its attitudes toward life) by means of her intuitions, she was a metaphysician of the real. And, so Cather believed, to the extent that Jewett restored these deeper meanings in her fiction, her sketches and stories were a gift from "heart to heart" and reveal in her the artist's greatest gift—"the gift of sympathy" (*WCOW* 51).

This phrase is often cited in reference to Cather's own peculiar talents as a novelist. This is appropriate, of course, but her use of the expression, I think, is more suggestive than some have supposed. Certainly, this gift is more than simple sensitivity. Finally, it has to do with a way of knowing the world. The writer who has the gift of sympathy "fades away into the landscape and people of his heart":

> he dies of love only to be born again. The artist spends a lifetime in loving the things that haunt him, in having his mind "teased" by them, in trying to get conceptions down on paper exactly as they are to him and not in conventional poses supposed to reveal their character; trying this method and that, as a painter tries different lightings and different attitudes with his subject to catch the one that presents it more suggestively than any other. [*WCOW* 51]

Sympathy for Willa Cather is intuition and creates living character rather than sociological types. To understand life as it is lived rather than as it is represented to the intellect requires the metaphysical operations of intuition, which, according to Bergson, corresponds to a "divining sympathy" (*CE* 175):

> Instinct is sympathy. If this sympathy could extend its object and also reflect upon itself, it would give us the key to vital operations—just as intelligence, developed and disciplined, guides us into matter. For— we cannot too often repeat it—intelligence and instinct are turned in opposite directions, the former toward inert matter, the latter towards life. . . . [Intelligence] goes all around life, taking from outside the greatest possible number of views of it, drawing it into itself instead of entering into it. But it is to the very inwardness of life that *intuition* leads us—by intuition I mean instinct that has become disinterested, self-conscious, capable of reflecting upon its object and enlarging it indefinitely.
>
> That an effort of this kind is not impossible, is proved by the existence in man of an aesthetic faculty along with normal perception. Our eye perceives the features of the living being, merely as assembled, not as mutually organized. The intention of life, the simple movement that runs through the lines that binds them together and gives them significance, escapes it. This intention is just what the artist tries to regain, in placing himself back within the object by a kind of sympathy, in breaking down, by an effort of intuition, the barrier that space puts up between him and his model. [*CE* 176–77]

I quote this passage at length not merely because it gives fuller significance to Cather's expression but also because it identifies several of the
preoccupying interests Cather had in the creative process and in the art of
fiction.

For Willa Cather, more often than not, the barrier between herself and
her subject was not space but time. As a child (and she remarked more
than once that as an author she got all of her essential themes before the
age of fifteen), she loved to listen to her Nebraska neighbors, to hear them
talk and to watch them work and to imagine their lives. Several of her
childhood acquaintances found their way into her fiction, not as versions
of real people, but as the imaginative recovery of the author's own youthful intuitions and feelings about them.[23] The novelist of emotions has a
mind filled with "ghosts, for which he has always tried to find bodies"
(*WCP* 79). But entering into the living reality of created characters and
giving them imaginative substance provided Cather with one of her greatest satisfactions. Nothing can compare to the joy of entering into "the
very skin" of another person, she told Elizabeth Sergeant.[24] This is the
work and the satisfaction of sympathy or intuition, and it is as well, at least
in Bergson's estimation, a "true empiricism" (*IM* 36) that is, at the same
time, a true metaphysics—undeluded by the snapshots the intellect takes
of reality, untempted by the analytic method forever external to its object.

The inwardness of life was what Cather sought to convey in her art.
David Stouck recognized that one of the greatest concerns and most persistent themes in Cather is the relation between art and life. As I have tried
to show, she could not, or at least did not, write truly memorable fiction
until the opposition between art and life was reconciled in her own mind.
But nothing could be more foreign to the later Cather than Stouck's
characterization of the object of art: "The goal of art . . . is to transcend
the human condition—to create something permanent, immutable, outside the world of time and chance—and the commitment required for
artistic creation often excludes the artist from a full participation in and
enjoyment of life."[25] Not only is this untrue of Cather herself—she felt
most alive when she was creating—but it is contrary to her practice and
antithetical to her mature beliefs about the function and special significance of art. She did not wish to transcend the human condition but to
enter wholly into it, at the expense of art if necessary. She acknowledged
the technical defects in *My Ántonia*, for example; as a work of art it has
many structural faults—"I know they are there, and made them knowingly, but that was the way I could best get my squint at her [Ántonia].

With those faults I did better than if I had brought them together into a more perfect structure. Sometimes too much symmetry kills things" (*WCP* 79).

True art stems from the fierce upwelling of an emotion mastered by craft and discipline, and in the sensitive reader, because that emotion is recreated and shared, it becomes a living thing. As such, it conveys life itself—the "stuff" that art is made of. Even when she spoke of the permanence of great fictions, her critical statements were informed by a conception of the evolutionary character of reality. Even those books she felt were assured a long life—*The Scarlet Letter*, *Huckleberry Finn*, *The Country of the Pointed Firs*—cannot defeat change or contingency. Instead, they register an emotional poise in the face of change that is continually appealing: "I can think of no others [American books] that confront time and change so serenely" (*WCOW* 58). They are works, because of their directness and simplicity, likely to be among those few works time spares.

Human values will not change until the human body changes, and these same values provide the essential themes of art—jealousy and strife, desire and hope. It was the human condition that Cather hoped to embody, not transcend, and part of the psychology of that condition is the groundless faith that we are inclined to place in an immutable reality outside of time. In fiction, as in life, she was fond of saying, "The end is nothing. The road is all. In fact the road and the end are literally one" (*NUF* 99). But she recognized, nevertheless, in such characters as Myra Henshawe, Godfrey St. Peter, or Euclide Auclair, the natural desire for something imperishable and solidly true.

"Eternity," as A. O. Lovejoy observed in 1909, is an obsolete concept,[26] and reality forever eludes the exact discriminations of the intellect. This was one of the most disturbing implications of the new reality. But the *desire* for certainty and the immutable, whether in art or religion, was more permanent, and *that* might be dramatized. Cather had found in *Creative Evolution* that the imagination was absolutely central to evolutionary development and, by implication, that the artist was likewise central to an understanding of the real. In *O Pioneers!*, she had shown the artistic element operating in the pioneer woman, Alexandra Bergson. In *Song of the Lark*, she reversed the process, for Thea Kronborg's worldly success as an artist derives from her Moonstone memories. But Cather seems to have instinctively pushed her belief in a world of duration and the place of the creative imagination within it still further.

If reality is inaccessible to the intellect and only intermittently available to the gleamings of intuition; if no distinguishable difference exists between an imagined memory and an actual one; if language has essentially connotative, not denotative, power; and if language, like any symbol system, interposes a veil between man and the fundamental reality of duration—if these Bergsonian premises are pursued in the extreme, the conclusion one must draw is that any understanding of the real is, by necessity, a fiction.

There is no evidence that Cather ever thought in quite these terms, but Wallace Stevens did. In "The Pure Good of Theory," he contemplates "the mind that knows it is destroyed by time" (*CP* 329). Adam, the first parent, slept and "woke in a metaphor: this was / The metamorphosis of paradise" (*CP* 331). The fall represents an alteration of consciousness and perception: "It is never the thing but the version of the thing" we see. The modern age is a world without the security of firm belief, yet the possibility of felicity remains nonetheless:

Yet to speak of the whole world as a metaphor
Is still to stick to the contents of the mind
And the desire to believe in a metaphor.
It is to stick to the nicer knowledge of
Belief, that what it believes in is not true. [*CP* 332]

If Cather ever came to believe that her atmospheric fictions were superior and truer versions of the real than the more precise and accurate fictions of sociologists or scientists, I do not know. But she did believe that men and women lived and were guided by their own lights. She had Myra Henshawe say somewhat heretically in *My Mortal Enemy*, "Religion is different from everything else; *because in religion seeking is finding*" (*MME* 94). And Cather told Fanny Butcher that *Death Comes for the Archbishop* did not deal in folklore but in legend, and legend is a "sort of interpretation of life by faith."[27] Her later novels, at any rate, are filled with the stuff of local legend, forms of fiction that, unlike science, myth, or creed, do not require belief to be of use. One can believe in heroes and legends and still retain that nicer knowledge that what one believes is not true.

Cather's turn to the historical novel was but an extension of this fabled faith. As we have seen, the so-called new history of Woodbridge and Robinson (and implicit in Bourne) recognized that the re-creation of historical circumstance was an imaginative process, and Carl Becker, after them, linked the historian to the bards and priests that all cultures have had. The historian's job, said Becker, is, with the soothsayers of the tribe, to keep alive the useful myths. Whether or not Cather shared this philosophy of history, she at least recognized, perhaps unconsciously, that the past is a living reality and that the simple faith of Father Joseph in *Death Comes for the Archbishop* or Cécile Auclair in *Shadows on the Rock* was useful to them and, just possibly, to her readers. She had, at any rate, a natural antipathy to the "machine-made" historical novels (*NUF* 90) that were so much in fashion. History was organic growth, and the story of history must be a living thing as well.

Willa Cather was committed to those fictions that were true. The past, whether it appeared as simple memory or in its extended form as history, was life itself. Her mature critical statements made over a period of thirty years are ample testimony to an artistic faith that exceeded art. And they owe much of their expression and a degree of their resolve to the vision of the world she had absorbed around 1912. She never abandoned that vision, though she was often sorry that the world at large had. More importantly, this was an enabling point of view, one that permitted a writer to believe in the "game of make believe" that is art (*WCOW* 125). It is not important, finally, whether what she believed is "true" but only that it encouraged fictions that were also art. And it is the fiction we need now to consider.

IV

There is neither space nor need to examine Cather's later fiction in any detail. Her mature art proceeded from the same imaginative vision she had forged in the years before the Great War, and though she acquired a certain personal bitterness and regret, her aesthetic stance and its philosophical foundation, if not its accompanying optimism, remained pretty much intact. And Cather's aesthetic is particularly important to an understanding of her fiction because the psychology of art is, for her, the psychology of human experience as well. Santayana meant to diminish the appeal and significance of Bergsonism by labeling it a literary psychology, but for the imaginative writer that was one of its most attractive features. The creative imagination was fully connected to the common life and, in a way, constituted its best hope.

"The world has a habit of being in a bad way from time to time," Cather wrote in 1936, "and art has never contributed anything to help matters—except escape" (*WCOW* 19). There was nothing conciliatory, or even defensive, in the remark—she was familiar with the desires of reform-ers and pamphleteers from her days at *McClure's*, and the political zeal of the 1930s did not strike her as much different. Art outlives social engineering and institutional reform; it persists not because it answers the practical needs of the present but because it springs from an "unaccountable predilection of the one unaccountable thing in man" (*WCOW* 19). The source and the use of art is desire.

In *The Professor's House*, she has the urbane Godfrey St. Peter speak the philosophy of desire: "A man can do anything if he wishes to enough. . . . Desire is creation, is the magical element in that process" (*PH* 29). A few years earlier in *A Lost Lady*, she had had the pioneering Captain Forrester, from out of a more rugged experience, say the same, "What you think of and plan for day by day, in spite of yourself, so to speak—you will get" (*LL* 54). "A thing that is dreamed of in the way I mean, is already an accomplished fact. . . . We dreamed the railroads across the mountains, just as I dreamed my place on the Sweet Water. All these things will be everyday facts to the coming generation, but to us—"(*LL* 55). This was but a way of reaffirming her belief that "the road is all," that the world is incessant change, always in the making, always about to be. The creative intelligence draws its strength from a living principle, as remote as a prehistoric people and as near at hand as one's own shadow, and propels one's desires into the future.

In 1913, Cather wrote that she thought that youth (considered as a biological force) is "the only power that will drive the world ahead. It makes the new machine, the new commerce, the new drama; it is Fecundity." Youth, however, will not linger beyond its appointed hour. "People are in many ways more interesting after they have lost their rocket quality," she added. "But the world *could* get on without the old; without the young it can not."[28] In later years, she would be drawn to portraits of those who had lost their "rocket quality" (such as Godfrey St. Peter or Bishop Latour) or of those who, to the distress or dismay of those around them, mysteriously did not (such as Oswald Henshawe in *My Mortal Enemy*, Father Joseph in *Death Comes for the Archbishop*, or Marian Forrester in *A Lost Lady*) or sometimes of those who died before they had to face that prospect (such as Claude Wheeler in *One of Ours*, Tom Outland of *The Professor's House*, or Lucy Gayheart in the novel of the same name). In a way, all of Cather's fiction is about the relation of age and youth— tradition and hope, habit and invention, a remembered past and present circumstance. Again and again, she was to test her own convictions in created fictions. Far from being nostalgic indulgence, her dramas of memory were the creations of a tough-minded realist measuring the claims of a disappointing present against the potency of memory and the possibility of desire and dramatizing her belief that the past itself is life.

For Gertrude Stein, as for Cather, the problem of writing was "to try to find out just what it is that what happens has to do with what is."[29] But they chose distinctly different literary means. "Is there any way," Stein asked, "of making what I know come out as I know it, come out not as remembering?"[30] What Stein attempted to avoid, Cather attempted to refine, and she might have asked herself, "Is there any way of making what I knew come out as I know it, come out as remembering?" At any rate, when Cather came to write *My Ántonia*, she abandoned the full-blooded method she had used in *The Song of the Lark*. Rather than articulating Bergsonian notions as she had in the earlier novel, she imbedded them in her approach toward her subject from the beginning, and they constituted the informing atmosphere of her drama of memory.

Cather told the story of her own warm memories of Annie Sadilek, a childhood friend, from the point of view of Jim Burden, a man whose romantic disposition made him funny as a child but had contributed to his personal success as a lawyer. Like Thea's, his memories of youth served him well in the present, for the capacity to remember was also the capacity to dream. Burden's story is the narrative of warm remembrance, and his fondness for the country of his childhood is epitomized by the memory of one Bohemian girl, Ántonia Shimerda, a girl who seemed to "mean" "the country, the conditions, the whole adventure of childhood" (*MA* ii). As James E. Miller notes, the novel is not about the real Ántonia but about the feeling for her that exists in that narrator and is shared with the reader.[31] One might go further and say that her persistence in the memory of the narrator is, for Burden, the real Ántonia, for her memory penetrates his real present and colors his perceptions and gives them meaning. It also enlarges his past—for she "lent herself to immemorial attitudes which we recognize by instinct as universal and true." She was a "rich mine of life, like the founders of the early races" (*MA* 353). Burden was Cather's "squint" on her subject, and in order to obtain this view, she abandoned familiar literary conventions and justified her fiction by imposing yet another fiction upon it—that Jim Burden "simply wrote down pretty much all that her name recalls to me. I suppose it hasn't any form" (*MA* iii).

The form of *My Ántonia*, however, as with many of Cather's novels, is less a matter of artistic structure than a vessel through which the living quality of feeling and the evocations of memory might flow. Imaginative form, that is to say, was an intuitive matter for her and came of its own accord, or not at all, and enclosed and conveyed to readers something of that original feeling. Cather, as Edward and Lillian Bloom observed, "was incapable of rendering personal experience or emotion literally, and she sought a new way of communicating. That is, experimentation with form was as integral to her as was the moral substance of the theme she wished to narrate."[32] Her imaginative forms had to remain pliable enough to preserve the spirit and vitality of the recollections that emerged in the process of composing. "Too much symmetry kills things," she said (*WCP* 79).

Her critics often reacted to the apparent formlessness of Cather's novels—each succeeding book was unpredictable from the last, and they sometimes found her narratives loose and undirected. They were like the readers of the early volumes of Godfrey St. Peter's history entitled *Spanish Adventurers*: "Nobody saw that he was trying to do something quite different—they merely thought he was trying to do the usual thing, and had not succeeded very well" (*PH* 32). But Cather's experimentation was not that of a literary trickster or charlatan;[33] she sought always the proper mode for the evocation of living feeling. She wanted Ántonia to stand out like a rare jar upon a table, she explained to Elizabeth Sergeant, so that one may "examine her from all sides."[34] *The Professor's House* was meant to generate in her readers the same feeling that one gets from Dutch paintings in which a crowded domestic scene is relieved by a square window through which one sees fleets of ships or a wide stretch of sea (*WCOW* 31). In *Shadows on the Rock*, she took "the incomplete air and tried to give it what would correspond to a sympathetic musical setting . . . a series of pictures remembered rather than experienced" (*WCOW* 15). *Death Comes for the Archbishop* was to be written in the "style of legend, which is absolutely the reverse of dramatic treatment." She wanted to achieve in prose the same quality she had detected in the Puvis de Chavannes frescoes she had seen in Paris (*WCOW* 9). *Lucy Gayheart* was meant to be read at full tilt, but *Shadows on the Rock* required the settled and patient attitude one gets when reading by firelight.[35] In every instance, Cather addressed her fictions to the consciousness of her readers, for she meant to give them something of that original feeling that inspired their creation. This was an artistic ambition fully consonant with her stated critical principles and one that fulfilled the role of the artist as Bergson had identified it.

True art, he had maintained in *Le Rire* (1900; translated as *Laughter*), is always "*individual*": "What the artist fixes on his canvas is something he has seen at a certain spot on a certain day, at a certain hour, with a colouring that will never be seen again. What the poet sings of is a certain mood which was his, and his alone, and which will never return. What the dramatist unfolds before us is the life-history of a soul, a living tissue of feeling and events—something, in short, which has once happened and can never be repeated" (*L* 164). The whole appeal of art is not made of the universal but of the individual. Art is accepted as true by "the very effort it forces us to make against our predispositions in order to see sincerely. Sincerity is contagious." In short, the artist's attempt to lift the veil "compels our imitation" (*L* 165). By virtue of its sincerity, art succeeds in "laying bare a portion of ourselves," and we catch a glimpse of a "whole host of ghostly feelings, emotions and events that would fain have come into real existence. . . . It also seems as if an appeal had been made within us to certain ancestral memories belonging to a far-away past—memories so deep-seated and so foreign to our present life that this latter, for a moment, seems something unreal and conventional, for which we shall have to serve a fresh apprenticeship" (*L* 164).

Cather did not expect her readers *to know* the women who inspired Ántonia Shimerda or Marian Forrester, of course; nor did she wish (as she had in her early fiction) to give her readers case studies or even heroic examples. Nor, finally, did she seriously expect of them a retreat into a pioneering past. She did indeed identify herself as "backward," but such backwardness was not, as Morton Zabel insisted, "the condition of her existence as an artist." If that were so, then her subjects would indeed have become, as Zabel claimed they did, mere "abstractions" and therefore "unworkable, in any critical or moral sense."[36] The moral quality of the work of imagination, for Cather as for Henry James, depends ultimately "on the amount of felt life concerned in producing it." The "high price" of the novel is, in fact, to preserve the "freshness and straightness" of a sincere vision of life.[37] The contagion of such sincerity might indeed make her readers serve a "fresh apprenticeship" to their own peculiar present.

A vitalistic vision of life, as we have seen, supplied Cather with a warrant for her own vocation as an artist—it gave her confidence to consult the muse of memory and to trust to her own artistic intuitions. And that vision was a part of both her creative method and her fictional subjects. Bergsonian notions about a *moi fondamentale*, memory, intuition, and time are everywhere observable in Cather's later fiction and serve to underscore her commitment and indebtedness to the new reality, which as early as 1920 had become for many old-fashioned and irrelevant, in a word, backward.

"Two Friends" (1932) is the story, as it is remembered by a disillusioned narrator, of a valuable friendship dissolved by a quarrel of "principle." It begins with this passage: "Even in early youth, when the mind is so eager for the new and untried, while it is still a stranger to faltering and fear, we yet like to think that there are certain unalterable realities, somewhere at the bottom of things. These anchors may be ideas; but more often they are merely pictures, vivid memories, which in some unaccountable and very personal way give us courage" (*OD* 193). The seemingly imperturbable friendship of two of the town's leading citizens is one of those unalterable realities, and its rupture constitutes a permanent loss for the narrator. She remembers them talking into the night, lighted only by moonlight, and in later years when the narrator comes upon a white road drinking up the moonlight, it brings on a sudden sadness. Only later does the narrator realize that in this moment of perception a "scar" had been touched that brought on "the feeling of something broken that could so easily have been mended" (*OD* 230). As with so much of Cather's fiction, this little drama of memory reveals the persistence of memory in the present moment. The vivid pictures of youth blend mysteriously with the present and—just as Thea Kronborg had always measured the tall buildings of New York against the standpipe in her native Moonstone—provide its standard of measurement.

The original self of youth, because it is a fund of vivid memories that slumber beneath the habits and compromises of age, is a constant and sometimes accusing companion. Cather's novels are densely populated with characters who lead double lives or lead lives so singularly cautious and proper that one only suspects a deeper self at work. Lucy Gayheart's sister Pauline always "put up a front" as though she were pushing a "mannikin" before her: "no one had ever seen the pusher behind that familiar figure, and no one knew what the second person was like" (*LG* 168). The sensitive, but unimaginative, Claude Wheeler in *One of Ours* still wants something more from life than the security of three meals a day and the assurances of eternal salvation. He senses that "inside of living people, too, captives languished. Yes, inside of people who walked and worked in the broad sun, there were captives dwelling in darkness—never seen from birth to death" (*OO* 178). Jim Burden believes that the ordinary life that goes on in Black Hawk is made up of evasions and negations: "Every individual taste, every natural appetite, was bridled by caution. The people asleep in those houses, I thought, tried to live like the mice in their own kitchens; to make no noise, to leave no trace, to slip over the surface of things in the dark" (*MA* 219). Godfrey St. Peter, from the days of his adolescence, had lived out the life of a "secondary social man" (*PH* 265). He knew that the "complexion of a man's life was largely determined by how well or ill his original self and his nature as modified by sex rubbed on together," but he did not know until late in life that a man's "first nature" (*PH* 267) might return to him virtually untouched by all the experiences of his adult life and reveal to him how truly external to him were his family, house, and accomplishments.

Many of Cather's characters, like Godfrey St. Peter, recognize within themselves that they have led thwarted lives because they have adapted their original desires to conventional expectations, whether social, religious, or domestic. Others, like Claude Wheeler, view with contempt and fear the compromised lives of those around them. The lives these secondary men and women lead are external to the life they desired and meant to have. Ready-made ideas are inherited rather than absorbed and, as Bergson remarked in *Time and Free Will*, float on the surface of consciousness "like dead leaves on a pond" (*TFW* 135). At one time, this fact was for Cather a matter of tragedy or contempt, but later in life she came to accept this as a condition of existence, not as lamentable mischance or the result of cowardice.

This is why those "curious survivals" (*MA* 258) of the past have such significance in Cather's fiction. They were acquired when life was whole; a child's attitude toward everything is an artist's attitude, she said. And because those intuitive moments survive as memory images, as Jim Burden discovers, "the figures of my old life seemed to be waiting for me in the new" (*MA* 258). Even in the excitement of new ideas and unfamiliar experiences, Burden's destiny is marked out by old roads: "I suddenly found myself thinking of the places and people of my own infinitesimal past. They stood out strengthened and simplified now, like the image of the plough against the sun. . . . They were so much alive in me that I scarcely stopped to wonder whether they were alive anywhere else, or how" (*MA* 262). Burden's true life is in the mind, composed of that mixture of the past and the present that is itself but a fiction after all, but one that he believes in. And the curious survivals of his past are instances of spontaneous memory, not of the lesson learned nor of the habit acquired. Only when one is able to "value the useless," observed Bergson, does one have the power to dream (*MM* 94). For Burden, such memories are all he has to "answer the new appeal" (*MA* 262); he has found that in the flux of the modern world the memory of Ántonia is "what will suffice."

Jim Burden's experience with his past is luckier than Godfrey St. Peter's, but the psychology is the same. Burden, whatever else he had missed or suffered, including a bad marriage, knows that he and Ántonia "possessed together the precious, the incommunicable past" (*MA* 372). The professor is reunited with a boy he thought he had left behind—"the original, unmodified Godfrey St. Peter" (*PH* 263). These two had once planned to live out "some sort of life together," but that had not happened. "But now that the vivid consciousness of an earlier state had come back to him, the Professor felt that life with this Kansas boy, little as there had been of it, was the realest of his lives, and that all the years between had been accidental and ordered from the outside. His career, his wife, his family, were not his life at all, but a chain of events which had happened to him" (*PH* 264). The professor knows at last that he is a "solitary" and will remain so; he recognizes that he "was earth and would return to earth" (*PH* 265). The recognition is happy enlightenment, and thereafter he delights in sensuous perception of clouds and trees or drifts among the "long forgotten, unimportant memories of his early childhood" (*PH* 266).

The Professor's House is the story of a man who comes to understand how disparate are the life he has lived and the life he desired. Loretta Wasserman has discussed the Bergsonian influence in this work and has shown how interestingly and provocatively it can be enlisted to interpret the novel.[38] Our interest here, however, is merely to suggest how pervasively and persistently that Bergsonian vision affected Cather's later fiction. Godfrey St. Peter, sensing that his own death is near, finds that he has fallen out of love, has somehow lost his place in the "human family" (*PH* 275). As Cather herself explained it in the inscription she wrote in the copy of the novel she gave Robert Frost, St. Peter's story is about "letting go with the heart."[39] St. Peter does not die, but he knows that he will have to learn how to live without "delight" and to face the future with a quiet fortitude (*PH* 282).

In her next novel, *My Mortal Enemy*, she would probe the same problems of despair, and it would be her darkest book. Myra Henshawe undergoes the same sort of struggle as St. Peter. She too has fallen out of love and discovers herself a solitary. The recollections of her youth set her to crying an "anachronistic" tear for the "long dead time" of her life (*MME* 79). But she is only partly stoical. Her embittered present is made the more unbearable by a husband who has somehow kept the dreams of youth and their love alive, and she hates him for it. Oswald Henshawe is her "mortal enemy." She knows it is sad to "reach out a grudging hand and try to spoil the past for anyone. Yes, it's a great cruelty. But I can't help it. He's a sentimentalist, always was; he can look back on the best of those days when we were young and loved each other, and make himself believe it was all like that" (*MME* 88).

Oswald is comforted by the fiction that is memory. Myra broods on her own mortality and resents her past, but she does turn with hope to the religion of her youth. She abhors all but candle light, guards her ebony crucifix, and receives daily visits from the young and naive Father Fay, who thinks some of the saints of the early church must have been like her. Out of her own bitter and violent nature, she seeks the repose and security, not of the immemorial attitudes of an Ántonia, but of the rite and ritual of the church.

Something of the absolution and serenity Myra Henshawe found in the faith of her own childhood informed Cather's next novel, but from neither *My Mortal Enemy* nor *The Professor's House* could one have predicted so tranquil a novel as *Death Comes for the Archbishop*. Like those American books she admired, this novel faces the future and change with an equanimity and emotional poise that is registered in virtually every sentence. It was to be a book written in "the style of legend" and was to give an accounting of life "interpreted by faith." *Death Comes for the Archbishop* was her first historical novel and was set in the country she had learned to love. The American Southwest had once impressed her as a place for God not man, but at least six times she had returned to it and had used it for important episodes in *The Song of the Lark* and "Tom Outland's Story" in *The Professor's House*. In *Death Comes for the Archbishop*, she made it the scene for a novel about belief and the believing spirit.

When Bishop Jean Latour first enters that country, he finds it unfinished, monotonous, a "geometrical nightmare" (*DCA* 18). But after forty years there, building his church in Santa Fe and establishing his diocese, he decides not to return to his native France but to die in the peculiar air that only a new country has. It is the air of possibility. "He had come back to die in exile for the sake of it. Something soft and wild and free, something that whispered to the ear on the pillow, lightened the heart, softly, softly picked the lock, slid the bolts, and released the prisoned spirit of man into the wind, into the blue and gold, into the morning, into the morning!" (*DCA* 276).

Death Comes for the Archbishop is only generically a historical novel and only incidentally a religious one. Cather had, of course, done the historical research necessary to give her subject a narrative continuity and the feel of authenticity, and she had drawn particularly from William Joseph Howlett's *The Life of the Right Reverend Joseph P. Machebeuf* (1908).[40] But much of the folklore and legend in the novel she had gathered firsthand, and the plentiful and evocative descriptions of place and landscape derived from her own experience there. She especially wanted to capture the "direct expression of some very real and lively human feeling" (*WCOW* 5) that she had gotten from contemplating the mission churches of the Southwest. Cather, in short, was rendering her own feeling for the country and conveying its present reality as it had been enlarged and enriched by imagining its past.

In "Joseph and His Brothers," Cather wrote that there are two ways to approach a theme set in the distant past. One may, as did Gustave Flaubert in *Salammbô*, look backward, regard the past with the detachment of one's own present. This method only accentuates the alienation and distance one feels about a historical subject. The other method (which she discerned in Mann's novels and which was her own) is to get "behind the epoch of his story" and to look forward (*NUF* 98). Willa Cather followed this method in all of her historical novels—*Death Comes for the Archbishop*, *Shadows on the Rock* (1931), and *Sapphira and the Slave Girl* (1940). Far from retreating into the past, she meant to give some portion of that excitement Thea Kronborg felt when she imagined the living past of the ancient people, for the present is rich in proportion to the past it possesses. Surely, there is an amusing and perhaps an intended irony in the fact that Bishop Latour despises the "improvements" of the 1870s and 1880s and longs for an earlier time, for these were the years of Cather's own precious childhood. But Latour never deceives himself about the past—his church, though it is built in an architectural style out of fashion, belongs, nevertheless, to the future. Cather must have felt much the same about her novel, for it was written in an earlier and now discarded manner but was addressed, nevertheless, to a living present.

She sought in *Death Comes for the Archbishop* what Hawthorne had sought in *The House of the Seven Gables*—to give the feeling of a place by presenting it through the "grey legendary mist of the past." Willa Cather wrote about the New Mexico she knew and loved in historical terms, and she wanted to show how its enchanted history still clung to its palpable present. And just as this novel is not a conventional historical novel, it is not a religious one, though it was widely accepted as that and many of her readers in fact believed the author was herself a Catholic. The final emphasis of the book, however, is a wholly secular one.

In the last weeks before the archbishop's death, he is released from the felt necessity to act in the present, and as a consequence, his memories tend to have more force for him. As Bergson observed, memory blends with present perception, in fact attempts to drive out perception. This is precisely what happens when Latour attends Father Vaillant's funeral. He does not see a shriveled old man in the coffin, though he sees him as clearly as he sees those around him. Instead, he sees his friend as he appeared when they first arrived in New Mexico some forty years before: "It was not sentiment; that was the picture of Father Joseph his memory produced for him, and it did not produce any other" (*DCA* 288).

In the last scenes that prefigure Latour's own death, Cather's interest is not in a transcendent and immortal future but in a very human past. Even Latour is not interested in his future, which he believes will take care of itself, and his interest in his own dying is merely how it affected his beliefs about life:

> More and more life seemed to him an experience of the Ego, in no sense the Ego itself. This conviction, he believed, was something apart from his religious life; it was an enlightenment that came to him as a man, a human creature. . . .
>
> He observed also that there was no longer any perspective in his memories. He remembered his winters with his cousins on the Mediterranean when he was a little boy, his student days in the Holy City, as clearly as he remembered the arrival of M. Molny and the building of his Cathedral. He was soon to have done with calendared time, and it had already ceased to count for him. He sat in the middle of his own consciousness; none of his former states of mind were lost or outgrown. They were all within reach of his hand, and all comprehensible. [*DCA* 289–90]

Life as concentrated action directed toward the future has ceased to matter for the dying man. And except for a difference in attitude and circumstance, Latour's recognition is identical to Godfrey St. Peter's. Cather's description of Latour's psychic state is what Bergson called the condition of "pure memory"—"when our mind retains in all its details the picture of our past life" (*MM* 322), which is also, for him, the domain of the spirit. "If almost the whole of our past is hidden from us because it is inhibited by the necessities of present action, it will find strength to cross the threshold of consciousness in all cases where we renounce the interests of effective action to replace ourselves, so to speak, in the life of dreams" (*MM* 199). In such a state, Bergson goes on to say, we may live over again "in all their detail, forgotten scenes of childhood" (*MM* 200).

Willa Cather had so perfectly sympathized with the religious point of view, had so woven into the texture of her narrative stories, miracles, and legends, and had so nicely emulated the literary manner of *The Golden Legend* (whose stories of the lives of the saints never hold the note but "touch and pass on" [*WCOW* 9]) that she created in *Death Comes for the Archbishop* a book that everywhere suggests the activity and fortitude of life interpreted by faith but is nowhere mastered by it. She attempted the same sort of treatment in her next novel, *Shadows on the Rock*, a book even more crowded by legend and fable.

Again, she rendered present feeling colored by the shadows of an ancestral past. This story of a father and daughter in seventeenth-century Quebec examines the lives of Euclide Auclair, who yearns for the peace and security of the Old World of his native France, and the young Cécile, who discovers that she is not her father's daughter but a Canadian of the future. Each borrows something from the other: Cécile recognizes that out of commonplace traditions, out of coppers and brooms and brushes, one made a "climate within a climate," "one made life" (*SR* 198). Euclide comes to believe that he is fortunate after all to live in a new land and to see his grandsons grow up in a country "where the death of the King, the probable evils of a long regency, would never touch them" (*SR* 280).

Shadows on the Rock is not as fine a book as *Death Comes for the Archbishop*, but it too possesses an atmosphere suffused with legend and miracle. In it, Cather recognized that the mind has a kind of "blood"—"in common speech we call it hope" (*SR* 257). The Sisters of Quebec are just as near the realities of their lives as their neighbors, they are neither nostalgic nor vulgarly contemptuous of the common life. "They were still in their accustomed place in the world of the mind (which for each of us is the only world), and they had the same well-ordered universe about them." In this God-created universe, the stars beautified the heavens and served as clock and compass for man. "And in this safe, lovingly arranged and ordered universe (not too vast, though nobly spacious), in this congenial universe, the drama of man went on at Quebec just as at home" (*SR* 97). The capacity for belief is the subject of this novel, but it is belief engendered and ordered by the human imagination: "The people have loved miracles for so many hundred years, not as proof or evidence, but because they are the actual flowering of desire. In them the vague worship and devotion of the simple-hearted assumes a form. From being a shapeless longing, it becomes a beautiful image. . . . the experience of a moment, which might have been a lost ecstasy, is made an actual possession and can be bequeathed to another" (*SR* 137). Religion and art, Cather had said in a letter to the *Commonweal*, "spring from the same root and are close kin" (*WCOW* 27). Artistic form and religious ritual are the public and formalized inheritance of unceasing desire in a world of incessant flux.

In 1936, she wrote of Thomas Mann that he believes every legend has "a fact behind it," is an "occurrence of critical importance to the breed of man" (*NUF* 98). It is uncertain whether she actually discerned this quality in Mann or was attributing to him what Bergson had to say about the myth-making function (*fonction fabulatrice*) in his recently published *The Two Sources of Morality and Religion* (1932; translation in 1935); that is, that mythmaking is an analogue to instinct and necessary to the evolutionary development of communities. But she had anticipated both Mann and Bergson in her own historical novels. Like Wallace Stevens, Cather came to believe that we "live in the mind" and our lives are made the more inhabitable to the extent that the imagination composes and formalizes a reality that can only be known by intuition but can be secured and enlarged by memory and sympathy.[41]

At odd moments, the past may be recovered in the mind by sympathy— by the acts of memory or intuition. The image of the plow against the sunset in *My Ántonia* is such a moment. As Loretta Wasserman remarks, this scene suggests "the power of intuition to go beyond personal memory, to include all of human energy and endeavor and to perceive, however dimly, the wholeness of the universe behind the apparent disruptions of change."[42] Such a moment occurs as well in *The Professor's House* when Tom Outland acquires an intuitive understanding of the Cliff City on Blue Mesa. He had meticulously studied the ruin and its artifacts—analyzed them piece by piece—but not until he spends the night on the mesa and is there with his whole being do things come together for him: "Something had happened in me that made it possible for me to co-ordinate and simplify, and that process going on in my mind, brought with it great happiness. It was possession" (*PH* 250–51). This intuitive possession of the past energizes Outland. He is not tempted to "unravel" his understanding because he is afraid that the "whole" will be lost in its "parts" (*PH* 252).

In later years Cather would settle for more tranquil satisfactions than those experienced by Thea Kronborg or Tom Outland. But the power of imagination over events was still central to her thinking, and it was detectable in the simplest of human lives. In *Lucy Gayheart*, for example, she explored the debilitating effects of hero worship. Lucy rejects her hometown suitor, Harry Gordon, for a romance with the singer Clement Sebastian. Like other characters in the book, Lucy attaches her hopes and desires to another's fulfillment; and Sebastian, because he values some lost part of himself and because he had missed "the deepest of all companionships, a relation with the earth itself, with a countryside and a people" (*LG* 78), turns his attention to Lucy as a redeemer. Both die dramatically, by drowning, but Cather's final emphasis is on one who outlasts them but has not outlived his own romantic dreams, the hardheaded realist, Harry.

Beneath the "layers of caution" (*LG* 175), a real Harry Gordon exists, an original self he has kept locked up, ashamed to live out that part of himself in the open air. He believes that he might have lived that submerged life in Lucy had she consented to marry him (*LG* 107). But Lucy rejects him. Harry makes a quick and a bad marriage out of spite and has to continue to live as a secondary man. The final section of the novel takes place twenty-five years after Lucy's death. The local boy has lived a quiet and bitter life and has come to understand that one's hometown is but a place where one has had disappointments and has "learned to bear them" (*LG* 231). The memory of the vitality of Lucy has sustained him, nonetheless. Many years before, they had visited an exhibit of the French impressionists at Chicago together. Harry rejects the paintings out of hand as anatomically inaccurate: "facts," after all, "are at the bottom of everything." But Lucy, even so young, knows that they are meant "to express a kind of feeling merely," that accuracy "doesn't matter" (*LG* 101).

Harry remains the realist. But now and then his mind drifts back to the time he first met the little girl, Lucy Gayheart. She was playing in her front yard when suddenly, by impulse, she ran quickly over the wet slabs of concrete before her house. Those three swift steps secured in cement what Harry had sought to preserve in memory and in fact:

For Harry Gordon they did seem swift: the print of the toes was deeper than the heel; the heel was very faint, as if that part of the living foot had just grazed the surface of the pavement. Was there really some baffling suggestion of quick motion in those impressions,

Gordon often wondered, or was it merely because he had seen them made, that to him they always had a look of swiftness, mischief, and lightness? [*LG* 227]

Harry Gordon, in spite of himself, lives his life in the mind, in the fiction of his own composing. A memory trace of motion, escape, glad mischief, is captured in the wet concrete; it is this accidental impressionist image that sustains him and helps him bear his disappointments: "Nothing else seemed to bring her back so vividly into the living world for a moment. Sometimes when he paused there he caught for a flash the very feel of her: an urge at his elbow, a breath on his cheek, a sudden lightness and freshness like a shower of spring raindrops" (*LG* 227).

Willa Cather's critical writings give ample testimony to an artistic faith that exceeded art. Her fictions are so many fragments of desire that she constructed out of feeling and made vivid through craft. And both owe much of their expression to the vision of the world she had absorbed around 1912 and had clung to for the next thirty-five years. A detectable weakening of that resolve is evident in the last of her critical writings, but even here the old convictions shine through her age and fatigue.

"Light on Adobe Walls" is a reaffirmation of her aesthetic, but its tone is quiet, somehow resigned. It restates a version of artistic creation that is, once again, analogous to Bergsonian intuition. In *Introduction to Metaphysics*, Bergson had compared metaphysical intuition to literary composition. After steady and painstaking preparation, something else is needed to set to work—the often painful effort to place oneself in the heart of one's subject. But the impulse once started inaugurates a movement that is not a thing but a direction that, though "indefinitely extensible," is also "infinitely simple" (*IM* 90). Literary composition and metaphysical intuition are won by "long companionship" with the superficial manifestations of reality and finally have less to do with generalizations of facts than with the integrations of experience (*IM* 90–91).

"Light on Adobe Walls" echoes these notions, but Cather claims less for the significance of the artist than she had in her earlier critical writings. The artist cannot paint life, nor light, nor shadow, but only the emotion they give. "At bottom all he can give you is the thrill of his own poor little nerve—the projection in paint of a fleeting pleasure in a certain combination of form and colour, as temporary and almost as physical as a taste on the tongue" (*WCOW* 124). Perhaps those fleeting pleasures are not very great; "art is too terribly human to be very 'great,' perhaps" (*WCOW* 125).

Even very rare artists have outgrown their "toys" at last and have turned to the countryside to gratify their appetites for a people and a countryside they loved.

Perhaps Cather herself might have done so in time. But she was embarked on another historical novel at the time of her death in 1947. And in the last story she completed before she died, she recovered in the act of the imagination a reunion with the people and the country of her birth. In "The Best Years," she meant to convey something of the warmth that came from visiting her brother Roscoe in 1941. She was ill and could not even dress herself, so Edith Lewis accompanied her on the trip to California. On the way out, she traveled through the southwestern country that meant so much to her. She knew that it would be the last time she would see that landscape; she knew as well that she would never see her brother again. But the journey seemed to have been worth the effort.

"The Best Years" is a small tale meant to evoke a simple satisfaction. It deals with that "clan feeling, which meant life or death for the blood, not for the individual. For some reason or for no reason, back in the beginning, creatures wanted the blood to continue" (*FS* 134). Her belief in the life impetus coursing through the living world was still strong, but she was content to express it in muted statement. An élan vital pulsed through life. Life was its own excuse for being, and, perhaps for no reason at all, it coursed through the blood and was the foundation of desire. The "best years," she wrote, are those when "we're working hardest and going right ahead when we can hardly see our way out" (*FS* 147), but those years were behind her. The young schoolmistress, Lesley Ferguesson, is reunited with her family and gives herself to the feeling of simply being home. "A plant that has been washed out by a rain storm feels like that, when a kind gardener puts it back into its own earth with its own group" (*FS* 124). When Cather wrote this story, she knew that, like her archbishop, she was dying from having lived, and like him too, she knew it was "the Past that she was leaving"; the future, if there was one, would take care of itself. Like the Alexandra she had created so many years before, she knew that she would be restored to the earth that had borne her. She took her epitaph not from *O Pioneers!* but from *My Ántonia*, however: "That is happiness; to be dissolved into something complete and great."[43] If we may judge from the serenity of her last story, that was knowledge enough.

FIVE

Poetry and the System of the World

I

IN DECEMBER 1940, Wallace Stevens wrote Leonard C. Van Geyzel and, among other things, informed him that he had asked a New York book dealer to send his friend a copy of Willa Cather's most recent novel, *Sapphira and the Slave Girl*. The gift was meant to represent her art, but also, judging from the context of the letter, it was intended to convey the richness of a distinctly American talent. "Miss Cather is rather a specialty," he wrote. "You may not like the book; moreover, you may think she is more or less formless. Nevertheless, we have nothing better than she is. She takes so much pains to conceal her sophistication that it is easy to miss her quality. But the book will take you far away from Ceylon" (*LWS* 381). Above all else, one must conclude, Stevens admired Cather's craft, a craft that was anything but formless. Willa Cather's devotion to form in a way that made form itself seem altogether absent appealed to Stevens, as did her efforts to conceal her literary sophistication. But there would have been other reasons for his admiration that made her a specialty of his.

He shared with her a political conservatism and a feeling for an atavistic past (what Stevens termed the "primordia" of life) in which art was central, not peripheral. Like her, he had been preoccupied with the possibility, or rather, given the complexities and necessary compromises of modern life, the defeated possibility, of heroes and heroism.[1] Like her, too, he was a Francophile; he admired the French language and character so much that he recorded in his book of aphorisms, *Adagia*, the curious observation that "French and English constitute a single language" (*Opus* 178); in fact, he found the American sensibility much closer to that of the French than that of the English (*Opus* 176). Stevens, like Cather, read and responded to Bergson and William James and Santayana. Perhaps he read more deeply in philosophy than she; certainly his thoughts about his reading were more conspicuous. But Cather's interests in Bergson were more often scientific and psychological, whereas Stevens's were more conventionally philosophical. Too, he must have appreciated Cather's sense of place and the determining characteristics of place. The soul "is composed / Of the external world," he wrote in 1918 in "Anecdote of Men by the Thousand." "There are men of the East" who "are the East":

> There are men whose words
> Are as natural sounds
> Of their places
> As the cackle of toucans.
> In the place of toucans.   [*CP* 51]

But he believed, as did Cather, in the possibility of transcending the limitations of place, that the human imagination, "extended beyond local consciousness, may be an idea to be held in common by South, West, North and East" (*LWS* 370). These, and no doubt other qualities in her fiction, would have appealed to Stevens and contributed to his fondness for her writing.

However, Cather's art, and her devotion to it, would have most attracted Stevens. Both had been accused of a narrow, even stultifying, aestheticism, that their art was remote from the lives of their contemporaries as they were lived day by day. And somewhat contradictorily, they had been criticized for a vague and undisciplined formlessness as well. Yet, like Cather, Stevens was an experimentalist, one whose artistic inventiveness was commanded by inner impulse and aesthetic principle. As Helen Vendler has observed, if in Stevens we find a poet who "tries and discards mode after mode, genre after genre, form after form, voice after voice, model after model, topic after topic, we also find a marvelous sureness mysteriously shaping his experiments."[2] The record of Stevens's poetic development is not simply the search for an adequate voice or subject; it derives from a commitment to the transforming character of the poet's art. His experimentation, his creation of new, unexampled poetic forms and poetic language, proceeded from his vision of life itself as constant change and from the compensating belief in the role of the creative imagination as an instrument that might shape experience, as a defense against chaos if nothing more. Wallace Stevens was as fully a participant in the new romanticism as was Cather and, indeed, eventually became its most eloquent and insistent apologist.

Born in Reading, Pennsylvania, in 1879, Wallace Stevens was heir to the intellectual and cultural attitudes of the latter half of the nineteenth century. It was a double inheritance: a rugged, mechanistic worldview articulated and endorsed by a Spencer or a Haeckel prevailed on the one hand, and a feckless and delicate aestheticism epitomized by a Pater or a Beardsley on the other. Seemingly, Stevens had chosen between the two worlds, had opted for the world of Pater, when he enrolled as a special student at Harvard in 1897 to take a three-year course of elective study composed mostly of classes in English literature and composition and modern languages. While at Harvard, he met and was befriended by a young professor of philosophy, George Santayana, and though he enrolled in no courses taught by this poet/philosopher nor, for that matter, in any philosophy courses, he evidently was influenced by Santayana's thought. The record of their friendship, however, indicates that they were more often given to conversations about poetry than philosophy. In any event, it is implausible that, as Samuel French Morse has suggested, Stevens was familiar with the writings of Bergson during his years as an undergraduate and that he likely "had made their acquaintance through the recommendation of Santayana, who knew and admired them,"[3] since Santayana did not admire Bergson and seems to have had but slight acquaintance with the writings himself until later.

Literary interests, not philosophical ones, seemed to preoccupy Stevens during his college years. His journal entries during this period reveal a rich poetic sensibility, even if he found the record itself unsatisfactory: "Diaries are very futile. It is quite impossible for me to express any of the beauty I feel to half the degree I feel it: and yet it is a great pleasure to seize an impression and lock it up in words: you feel as if you had it safe forever" (LWS 30). Here, in embryo, is the attitude of the mature Stevens, a "connoisseur of chaos," who would arrest the flux of reality itself by the formal efforts of the imagination. For the moment, however, his impressions were as so many pressed flowers, mementos of a susceptible imagination, and many of his entries are simply jottings of ideas for future poems or prose sketches, inchoate notes for the poetic expression of beauty. Other journal entries declare vague convictions about the nature of beauty and the dignity of poetry and the poet; still others describe his walks in the country and detail his observations of nature. His journal during these years is the record of sensuous indulgence and enjoyment with occasional disclosures of self-scrutiny about his right to this joy. "The feeling of piety is very dear to me," he wrote. "I thoroughly believe that at this moment I get none of my chief pleasures except from what is unsullied." But the paragraph ends with self-admonishment: "We *must* come down, we *must* use tooth and nail, it is the law of nature: 'the survival of the fittest'; . . . I believe as unhesitatingly as I believe anything, in the efficacy of fact meeting fact—with a background of the ideal." That same background of the ideal provides him with the spiritual consolation in the next paragraph: "I'm completely satisfied that behind every physical fact there is a divine force. Don't therefore, look *at* facts but *through* them" (*SP* 53–54). This attitude is typical of the sort of bifocal vision at the turn of the century that allowed one to attend to facts but still have faith in an unknowable ideal, but it contrasts dramatically with the stance he would adopt in later years. Stevens might believe in a unitary and primordial force, an élan vital if you will, but he attended to facts as they presented themselves to an all-too-human consciousness, to "things as they are."

The quick vacillations of thought and feeling we find in this journal entry suggest a genuine, if slightly ill-defined, ambivalence. The practical claims of life in the marketplace competed with an unaffected delight in the beautiful. The resolution here is a typical transcendence of the terms of opposition. He had expressed the difficulty somewhat differently only a few months before, in March 1899:

> Art for art's sake is both indiscrete and worthless. It opposes the common run of things by simply existing alone and for its own sake, because the common run of things are all parts of a system and exist not for themselves but because they are indispensable. . . . Beauty is strength. But art—art all alone, detached, sensuous for the sake of sensuousness, not to perpetrate inspiration or thought, art that is mere art—seems to me to be the most arrant as it is the most inexcusable rubbish.
>
> Art must fit with other things; it must be part of the system of the world. [*LWS* 24]

Santayana's *Interpretations of Poetry and Religion* (1900), published the next year, is a book Stevens likely read, if in fact he had not already read the portions of it that had been published earlier. The concluding chapter of Santayana's book might have struck Stevens as especially pertinent to his own uncertainty about the worth of poetry and the relation of art to life. The role of true poetry, Santayana had argued, has a higher function than the world at large seems willing to grant it. "What is that [the doctrine of transubstantiation] but to treat facts as an appearance, and their ideal import as a reality? And to do this is the very essence of poetry, for which everything visible is a Sacrament—an outward sign of that inward grace for which the soul is thirsting." Poets aware of their mission as poets do just this, but those poets who have failed or have refused to recognize their function "have been willing to leave their world ugly as a whole, after stuffing it with a sufficient profusion of beauties." Poetry, at last, must "become an interpretation of life and not merely an irrelevant excursion into the realm of fancy."[4]

Stevens's own poetry during these years, published mostly in the *Harvard Advocate* (of which he was for a time the editor), betrays much of the ambition but little of the quality of this higher function of poetry. However, Santayana was sufficiently impressed by one of the young Stevens's sonnets to respond with a sonnet of his own. The first line of Stevens's poem reads "Cathedrals are not built along the sea," and the poem nicely develops the notion that the beauties of the cathedral and of the art within would be eclipsed by wind and tempest and the droning of the sea. Santayana's "Reply to a Sonnet" argued that the cathedral was "Earth's" response to the sea, that the church itself made the motions of sea and air coherent because it signified what they meant "eternally."[5]

They debated their differences one evening, but Stevens apparently remained uninstructed by Santayana's rebuttal—he wrote in his journal that "we both held our grounds" (*SP* 68)—and continued to explore the discrepancies between art and life in subsequent sketches. "Cathedrals are not built along the sea" is one of Stevens's better efforts during these years. More often, the poems display an artificial sentiment or a rarefied delicacy of feeling. Robert Buttel has traced the informing, if indeterminate, influences upon the young Stevens's poetry that was written during his years at Harvard—the poetry of the symbolists, the imagists, the Harvard poets, the Pre-Raphaelites—and has shown that each would contribute its share to the forging of the more mature and original manner of his first volume of verse, *Harmonium* (1923).[6]

Despite his emulation of poetic modes and his thoughtful contemplation of the role of the poet, Stevens left Harvard with the competing worlds of art and life unresolved in his own mind; they were as oil and water. The intensity of this common intellectual difficulty was exacerbated by his father's continual reminders throughout Stevens's college years that "you are not out on a pic-nic." Garrett Stevens, himself a self-made man, advised that his son prepare himself for "the campaign of life—where self sustenance is essential and where everything depends on yourself" (*LWS* 18). Whether through his father's advice that you are "bound 'to paddle your own canoe'" or the public celebrity of Theodore Roosevelt, who epitomized a manly response to the strenuousness of life, Stevens was reminded on all sides of the insoluble conflict between art and life. George Lensing and Joan Richardson have traced the inner conflicts in Stevens as an individual sensibility, but these struggles were mirrored, however imperfectly, in the common intellectual debates of the age as well.[7]

For the moment, at least, the young Wallace Stevens would not "come down." He moved to New York in 1900 and tried his hand at writing and journalism for a time, but the dream of the artist as hero against a world of tooth and nail was fast beginning to pale. His doubts may have been hurried along by his witnessing of the funeral service of Stephen Crane that first summer in New York. It was a "frightful" affair—the small church barely one-third full, the artists in attendance a ragtag lot, the remainder, it seemed, merely there to pass the time. The service was "absurd"—the music as uninspired as the sermon was cloying. For all that, he continued to believe Crane "lived a brave, aspiring, hard-working life" and deserved better than this "silly" service. He came away with the realization of something he had only "doubtfully suspected" before: "There are few hero worshippers. Therefore, few heroes" (*SP* 78).

Stephen Crane, a fated figure, an American Keats who had died for art, or so it was widely held, was only eight years older than Stevens himself, and the would-be poet had witnessed not only the general neglect of the world at large for this tough-minded realist and brilliant stylist but also the tawdry lot of artists who came to bury him. Years later, Stevens came to regard the artist as a soldier; perhaps in some way, he regarded Crane as such a one, one who, like the fallen combatant in "Death of a Soldier," "did not become a three-days personage / Imposing his separation." Stevens understood, at least, that "The clouds go, nevertheless, / In their direction" (*CP* 97). I do not wish to exaggerate the significance of this event. Although Stevens would contemplate the need for heroes and heroism in an age without the gods or myths to sustain them throughout his life, he eventually heeded his father's practical counsel to find a place in the world. He enrolled in the New York Law School the next year.

There elapsed, from the time his last poem was published in the *Harvard Advocate* until he would next publish a poem, some fourteen years. During those years he attempted, unsuccessfully, to make his way in the world first as a journalist and later as a partner in a New York law firm. He continued to write poetry and apparently wrote a play during this period, but most of the surviving manuscripts date from 1909, the year he married

Elsie Moll, to 1914. It was during these last few years before the war in Europe broke out, then, that Stevens began, again, to write with sufficient seriousness of purpose to impel him to publish his poetry, even if at the same time he confessed to his wife that there was something "absurd" about writing verse (*LWS* 180).

To suggest a lapsed interest in becoming a published poet during the first decade of this century is not to suggest the abandonment of his interest in the arts and in philosophy. Stevens read extensively during this period and probably continued to write poetry as well. He attended art exhibits and moved in artistic circles.[8] His friendships included Walter Arensberg, William Carlos Williams, Pitts Sanborn, Donald Evans, Alfred Kreymborg, and others. Part of the intellectual stimulation of the time and required reading for the Arensberg circle, as Joan Richardson notes, was the arts magazine, *Camera Work*, which, among other things, sought to define in theoretical terms the nature of the new art, particularly in painting. It also published, incidentally, excerpts from Bergson's *Creative Evolution* and *Laughter*, and many of its contributors cited Bergson in support of the aesthetic they were attempting to develop.[9] If Stevens participated in the cultural life of the time, he also seems to have participated in its enthusiasms.

Wallace Stevens was not so jaded in 1910, for example, that he would not contemplate attending the homecoming celebration for Theodore Roosevelt, just back from safari, and he did actually visit Hempstead, New York, instead to see the airships "thrilling beyond description" (*LWS* 168). He was as susceptible as most to the seductions of progress and optimism. Yet in the same letter in which he confessed to his interest in these attractions, he wrote to his wife in rather interesting terms of quieter satisfactions:

> Somehow I do not feel like reading. It isn't in the air in June. But I *do* like to sit with a big cigar and think of pleasant things—chiefly of things I'd like to have and do. I was about to say "Oh! For a World of Free Will!" But I really meant free will in this world—the granting of that one wish of your own: that every wish were granted.—Yet so long as one keeps out of difficulty it isn't so bad as it is. For all I know, thinking of a roasted duck, or a Chinese jar, or a Flemish painting may be quite equal to having one. Possibly it depends on the cigar. And anyhow it doesn't matter.   [*LWS* 168]

In this passage Stevens's mind moves effortlessly in and among several attitudes, in a sense, among antithetical premises. He is necessitarian when he attributes his lassitude to the June air; romantic when he hankers for unencumbered free will; realistic, even stoical, when he says that things are not really so bad as long as one "keeps out of difficulty"; idealistic when he speculates that thinking of a roasted duck may be equal to having one; again deterministic in his suggestion that it all may depend on the cigar; and pragmatic, rather than fatalistic, in the end when he abandons the line of inquiry altogether as promising no practical consequence. Here reality and imagination combine, compete, and recombine in casual contemplation. The passage suggests the terms, if not the sophistication, of Stevens's maturest thinking about the possible and right relation between life and art. If he had "come down" and was now working to improve his estate, he had not suspended his awareness of the uneasy truce between the attractions of art and the practical claims of life that existed in American culture and presumably in himself. He had begun at Harvard, as Robert Buttel has shown, a "life long meditation"[10] on the interrelationship between imagination and reality, of how poetry fit in the system of things; the meditation would not abate, for it is the central preoccupation of all of Stevens's verse and criticism.

However seriously Stevens may have regarded this dilemma, his poetry (in its often lavish imagery and seeming whimsy of diction and syntax, its frequently flamboyant rhythms and gaudy and antic poses) retained something of the flavor of a fin de siècle decadence. And certain critics would label him aesthete and hedonist. When, for example, Yvor Winters, who had responded favorably to Stevens's first volume of verse, described him in 1940 as a "Paterian hedonist," the poet expressed his reaction to the attribution in a letter to Theodore Weiss: "I need not say that what is back of hedonism is one thing and what is back of a desire for agreement with reality is a different thing. There is also the possibility of an acceptable fictive alternative" (*LWS* 463).

If this were a distinction with a difference, it is uttered with a degree of confident conviction that we should not mistake for self-satisfaction, for it was a hard-won attitude. The problem of the relation of the imagination to reality, or of art to life, or of the poet to society, was the problem of "finding / What will suffice." And as Stevens further observed in "Of Modern Poetry," "It has not always had / To find: the scene was set; it repeated what / Was in the script" (*CP* 239). Then the theater was changed to "something else," and the modern poet became a "metaphysician in the dark" (*CP* 240), standing, as it were, on the verge of an as yet to be created world. Or, as Stevens put it in "July Mountain,"

> We live in a constellation
> Of patches and pitches
> Not in a single world, . . .
> Thinkers without final thoughts
> In an always incipient cosmos. [*Opus* 114–15]

To some extent we may regard this complaint as characteristic of the modernist dilemma, but when the theater itself first changed to "something else," there was generally more relief than despair. It is misleading to collapse the distinction between a mode of thought that affirmed and celebrated an "always incipient cosmos" before the Great War and a more despairing consciousness that existed after the war, when the idea of a world of incessant flux remained but the optimistic expectations of progress and fulfillment had foundered, if not expired. Stevens, it appears, had been more inspired than troubled by the new vitalistic philosophy.

"When I was a boy," he wrote in 1940, "I used to think that things progress by contrasts, that there was a law of contrasts. But this was building the world out of blocks. Afterwards I came to think more of the energizing that comes from mere interplay, interaction" (*LWS* 368). This, as Stevens himself said, is a "crude illustration," but the shift in the way one thought about the world, a shift from Spencer's building block philosophy to an organic, interdependent one, was more general and pervasive than idiosyncratic. This view, as we have seen, was popularly received by many because it repudiated a vision of life marked by fang and claw, cog and gear; it proffered an answer to the disturbing vision of the cosmos as nothing more than "dark, cold, and shaking like a jelly." Stevens himself recalled the bouyant feeling of prewar America and its subsequent loss in a lecture, "The Irrational Element in Poetry":

> The pressure of the contemporaneous from the time of the beginning of the World War to the present time has been constant and extreme. No one can have lived apart in a happy oblivion. For a long time before the war nothing was more common. In those days the sea was full of yachts and the yachts were full of millionaires. It was a time when only maniacs had disturbing things to say. The period was like a stage-setting that since then has been taken down and trucked away. It had been taken down by the end of the war, even though it

took ten years of struggle with the consequences of the peace to bring about a realization of that fact.   [*Opus* 224]

We may trust that this statement reflected Stevens's own lingering hopes, if not his generation's. There were younger men than Stevens whose oblivion, if they dwelled apart, was anything but happy (T. S. Eliot's "Love Song of J. Alfred Prufrock" was published in 1915) or men, younger still (witness F. Scott Fitzgerald), who might at times believe beyond the time of belief that the seas were full of yachts. Insufficient evidence exists to determine the degree of Stevens's enthusiasm for Bergsonian vitalism before the war, but it is sure that Bergson was an important and lifelong influence upon Stevens, upon his poetry, and upon his thinking about poetry.

II

It is generally agreed that Bergsonism was a significant influence upon Stevens, that, along with Santayana and William James, Bergson instructed Stevens's vision and fortified his sense of the priority of the imagination and the significance of the creative act. Joan Richardson and Samuel French Morse have suggestively demonstrated the influence *Le Rire* had upon Stevens's verse and particularly on the legitimization of his antic poses. Frank Doggett and Joseph Riddell have examined Stevens's poetry of ideas in detail and have shown the extent to which Bergson and others figured forth a philosophy of flux and immanence that characterizes Stevens's sense of the world and, to a degree, defined his subject. In addition, Frank Kermode has noted the similarity between Stevens's notion of the poet as mythmaker, one whose imaginative fictions supplant the realm of faith, and Bergson's idea of *fonction fabulatrice*.[11] Without question, Bergson's writing affected Stevens's thinking and, inevitably, contributed something to his poetic idiom and his personal aesthetic. But more needs to be said about how fully Bergson contributed to Stevens's sense of the world and of his special privilege as a poet.

By his own admission, Stevens was not a philosopher and had never pretended to be one (as early as 1899, he wrote in the margins of his copy of James Russell Lowell's *Letters* that he liked his philosophy "smothered in beauty and not the opposite"),[12] and his reading in and thinking about philosophy had more to do with the poetic enterprise than with intellectual system. As he argued in his essay "A Collect of Philosophy," certain philosophical concepts are also poetic concepts, and these ideas may transform our sense of reality (*Opus* 183–89). Some philosophers may think like poets but do not write like them—Leibniz was such a one; he was "a poet without flash" (*Opus* 185). Other philosophers write as poets without having ideas that are "inherently poetic concepts" (Nietzsche, for example). Still others possess the qualities of both: "In the case of Bergson," wrote Stevens, "we have a poetry of language, which made William James complain of its incessant euphony. But we also have the *élan vital*" (*Opus* 187).

Stevens's genuine and abiding admiration for Bergson is unquestionable. He ranked him with Plato when he suggested that Bergson both thinks and writes like a poet, and Stevens obviously personally preferred the philosophy of Bergson to that of Plato. The philosopher Paul Weiss once wrote Stevens and asked why the poet insisted on founding his view of philosophy on William James and Bergson, why did he not "'grapple with a philosopher full-sized'" (*LWS* 476), such as Aristotle or Kant or Hegel, or perhaps even Bradley, Whitehead, or Peirce? Stevens's reaction to this suggestion, which he made to another correspondent, was that most modern philosophers impressed him as academic (he knew that to be the case with Whitehead), though he did confess to a certain curiosity about Peirce. It is doubtful that Stevens would have found Peirce congenial, however, for he likely would have deemed him, like Leibniz, a man who thought like a poet but did not write like one. In any event, by not disputing the notion that he founded his philosophical vision upon the thought of James and Bergson, he seems to have been acknowledging the truth of the suggestion.

Stevens often cited Bergson in his essays on the poetic imagination, displaying acquaintance not only with *Creative Evolution* but *Matter and Memory* and *The Two Sources of Morality and Religion* and suggesting a familiarity with other writings of Bergson as well as writings about Bergsonism. Additionally, he draws from the thought of Henri Brémond, who Stevens himself argued was following Bergson in his thought (*Opus* 221–22). Stevens instanced in other essays the aesthetic theories of Henri Focillon, whose *The Life of Forms in Art* (1948) he found to be "one of the really remarkable books of the day" (*NA* 46), and he approvingly cited Charles Mauron's *Aesthetics and Psychology* (1935) as an enlightening text on the irrational element in poetry. Focillon's book is heavily indebted to Bergsonian principles, I think, and Mauron's only slightly less so. Focillon attended Bergson's lectures in Paris, as did Jean Wahl, the French philosopher with whom Stevens corresponded and whom he cited in a lecture.

Wahl, as had others, ranked Bergson as one of the four greatest philosophers in the history of Western thought.[13] But the most suggestive remark Stevens made concerning Bergson was in the opening paragraph of his essay "The Figure of the Youth as Virile Poet."

Stevens begins this essay by citing three responses to Bergson. The first is a quotation from a letter by Henry Bradley, written in reply to a letter from Robert Bridges, in which the latter apparently commented approvingly on Bergson. Bradley, by contrast, expresses a skepticism for all philosophy. The second is a quotation from Valéry. Valéry, whom Stevens greatly admired, identified Bergson as one of the last men to think, to think seriously and profoundly in an age given less and less to thinking at all. "Bergson semble déjà appartenir à un âge révolu, et son nom est le dernier grand nom de l'histoire de l'intelligence europééne" (*NA* 39). Finally, Stevens cites William James's reaction to his reading of *Creative Evolution* in which James confessed to finding "the same aftertaste remaining after finishing *Madame Bovary*" (*NA* 40). The rhetorical purpose of these three quotations is to demonstrate that "what is central to philosophy is its least valuable part." Stevens's comment on the variety of reactions is this: "if any considerable number of people feel this way about the truth and about what may be called the official view of being . . . we cannot expect much in respect to poetry, assuming that we define poetry as an unofficial view of being" (*NA* 40). If the larger purpose of the essay is to explore the essential differences in philosophical and poetic pursuits of truth and being, there is nevertheless considerable presumption, which in turn reveals a conviction, in having Bergson stand as the putative representative of truth and the official view of being. The example testifies to more than Stevens's simple admiration for Bergsonian vitalism; it establishes the French philosopher as one whose thought had, to borrow the language of "A Collect of Philosophy," "transformed reality." We shall see later in what ways this transformation affected Stevens's poetry and his aesthetic, but for the moment it is more instructive to discern this transformation in the concrete assumptions implicit in three poems that, together, describe the contours of the historical moment in which that transformation occurred.

One of Stevens's feeblest poetic efforts published during his Harvard years is "Song" (1900). In it, the forlorn speaker imagines a time when "beyond these barren walls / Two hearts shall in a garden meet":

And out above these gloomy tow'rs
   The full moon tenderly shall rise
To cast its light upon the flow'rs
   And find him looking in her eyes.[14]

Quite apart from the embarrassingly trite emotion and the poetic archaisms, the quality of thought itself is encased in a transcendent sentimentality—the use of "beyond," "out," "above," "shall" points to an ethereal realm of essence where the background of the ideal might actually exist and the despairing lover finds love's transmundane satisfactions and glories among the mercies of moonlight and flowers.

Written nine years later and included in Stevens's "Little June Book" (a volume of verse written for his fiancée, Elsie Moll), we find this only slightly superior piece:

He sang, and in her heart, the sound
Took form beyond the song's content.
She saw divinely, and she felt
With visionary blandishment.

Desire went deeper than his lute.
She saw her image, sweet and pale,
Inside her to simplicity,
Far off, in some relinquished vale.[15]

The differences in attitude are noteworthy. Instead of the abstract desire in "Song," located in homogenous space and time, albeit projected into some indefinite future, the location of desire in this second poem is within the auditor. The sound of the song, not its content, enables the woman to see "divinely" and to evoke her own image. The psychological process whereby the woman perceives a simpler and lost version of herself in some relinquished vale is akin to Bergson's remark on the prolongation of images drawn up from the past: "To call up the past in the form of an image, we must be able to withdraw ourselves from the action of the moment, we must have the power to value the useless. Man alone is capable of such an effort. But even in him the past to which he returns is fugitive, even on the point of escaping him" (*MM* 94).

The logic of the poem may be represented in this way: the song, having the power of suggestion, evokes a form, intensely personal, and summons the resource of memory. The free-floating suggestiveness of the music evolves an image (and there is no real distinction between an imagined memory and an historically accurate one) of the *moi fondamentale*. Stevens, in the much later "Owl's Clover" (1936), would refer to this Bergsonian self as a "second self" or the "subman" (*Opus* 66). That *moi fondamentale* is at once fugitive and forsaken, argued Bergson, because it grows up alongside a diminished, socialized self, is constantly in flux and not to be fixed. It is neither a Kantian transcendental ego nor a Freudian unconscious. Rather, it is an uncompromised empirical ego that is identifiable with the whole of memory and experience. This self-consciousness evoked by music is necessarily momentary, though Stevens does not here reveal the transitory quality of the implicit relation between the duration of the song and the image itself, but it is authentic and real, not imagined.

Some years later, Stevens would return to this theme in more explicit terms in "Anglais Mort à Florence" (1936), a poem in which an aging man turns to Brahms as his "alternate" in speech and becomes "that music and himself. / They were particles of order, a single majesty." The Englishman (much like Godfrey St. Peter in *The Professor's House*) would remember a time when he "stood alone," when "to be and delight to be seemed to be one" (*CP* 149). More immediately, however, Stevens would develop the same sort of psychological transactions in fuller and more poetic detail than in "He sang, and in her heart, the sound" in "Peter Quince at the Clavier."

Published in *Others* (a small magazine edited by Stevens's friend Alfred Kreymborg) in 1915, this, as Joseph Riddell has remarked, is Wallace Stevens's first really noteworthy poem.[16] If "Song" was composed during the fin de siècle era when Victorian sureties still ruled, when, as Stevens recalled in a lecture delivered in 1942, reality was "taken for granted" (*NA* 26), "Peter Quince" was composed after the intellectual and social "minorities" had had their influence and had converted "our state of life into something that might not be final": "This much more vital reality made the life that preceded it look like a volume of Ackermann's colored plates or one of Töpfer's books of sketches in Switzerland. I am trying to give the feel of it. It was the reality of twenty or thirty years ago" (*NA* 26). These passages recollect the emotional and psychological revolution attendant to the displacement of a familiar, sturdy reality by one fluid and vital. As we have seen, however, such an upheaval was also accompanied by a new way of looking at the world, by a revolution of thought and feeling. As Stevens was later to argue in an essay, a poet's subject is dictated by a private sense of the world, and, as he was also to say, reality is in the mind. But the new vital reality was not a Berkeleyean nor even an Hegelian idealism, because "things as they are" (to use Stevens's language) possess a materiality and self-supporting existence essential to human knowing and, by implication, to the making of poetry. "Reality is the central reference for poetry" (*NA* 71), insisted Stevens in a lecture, and to a material reality must poets return again and again for their subjects. Nevertheless, reality is ever and again imagined (or imaged) and therefore exists in the mind. This is the vitalistic, ontological view of Bergson: the world is in constant flux, and our perception of it, despite the arguments of rationalists or realists, is, to use Bergson's term, a "common sense" view in which matter exists as an "aggregate of images," existing halfway between "representations" and "things" (*MM* xi–xii).

Bergson developed this epistemology most explicitly in *Matter and Memory*, a book in which he attempted to affirm the reality of spirit and matter and determine the relation between the two: "For common sense, then, the object exists in itself and, on the other hand, the object is, in itself, pictorial, as we perceive: image it is, but a self-existing image" (*MM* xii). This, in substance, is the same meliorist position, neither tough minded nor tender minded, that William James adopted in his *Pragmatism* and later in his *Essays in Radical Empiricism*, but for a creative writer Bergson's argument and his conceptual emphases are more attractive postulates, for they emphasize the image-making process and intuition (which Stevens identified as the "imagination") as essential to knowledge.

The material world, so conceived, is a heterogeneous mass that is invested with order, not by a Kantian rational synthesis composed of categories of understanding, but by the deeply and uniquely personal qualities of individual experience. The capacity to perceive resemblance and difference, Bergson maintained, is a force rather than a mental act and is related always to the necessities of life. The mind is as a plant that selects nutrients from the soil. Man, as a superior biological organism, possesses the enabling resources of memory, which blend with present perception and make possible a harmonious ordering of experience. The region of sensations, wrote Bergson, is like a "keyboard" (*MM* 165), and the external object plays upon it, converting sensation to images by virtue of the resemblance of present perception to remembered experience.

By merely placing Peter Quince before a clavier rather than before any particular keyed instrument, Stevens may have intended to convey just this sort of association. But whether or not the poet had Bergson's analogy in mind when he wrote "Peter Quince," this concept (which is at once philosophical and poetic) has a substantive relation to the opening lines of the poem:

> Just as my fingers on these keys
> Make music, so the selfsame sounds
> On my spirit make a music, too.
> Music is feeling, then, not sound;
> And thus it is that what I feel,
> Here in this room, desiring you,
> Thinking of your blue-shadowed silk,
> Is music. [CP 89–90]

This is the dramatic occasion of the poem—Peter Quince playing music and analyzing his desire for the woman in blue silk; and he does so by examining that desire in terms of his memory of the parable of Susanna of the Apocrypha, which the music of sound and feeling has summoned. In fact, the story of Susanna among the elders becomes the ostensible subject of the remainder of the poem, but the biblical story is always qualified and informed by Quince's recollection of it, a remembering provoked and modulated by his immediate perceptions. These opening lines possess the force of syllogism, are rigorously analytical, and serve as both analogue and counterpoint to the biblical story of illicit passion and false accusation.

The making of music is, according to the Bergsonian psychology, a mental act: sounds play upon the ear, but music upon the spirit. The perception of sound is sensorimotor, but the perception of music is affective sensation; for sound is composed of the vibratory disturbances of the air, a natural physical property, but nature does not possess the resources of rhythm. Music is, in a word, feeling, and, likewise, Stevens seems to be saying, feeling is a kind of music as well. How, asked Bergson, are we ever to account for the suggestive power of music except that we repeat the sounds (external sensation) to ourselves "so as to carry ourselves back into the psychic state out of which they emerged, an original state, which nothing will express, but that something may suggest, viz., the motion and attitude which the sound imparts to the body?" (*TFW* 44).

Stevens himself seems to be referring to this process in his lecture "Three Academic Pieces" when he argues that resemblance is the very "base of appearance" and the enabling condition of metaphor. In metaphor, resemblance may establish a relation between reality and imagination in several ways. A resemblance may, for instance, be established "between something real and something imagined or, what is the same thing, between something imagined and something real, as for example, between music and whatever may be evoked by it" (*NA* 72). Music is imagined, but the physiological and psychological state it evokes, in terms of recollected images, is real. This is a clear echo of the Bergsonian position. It is also the aesthetic discovery of Thea Kronborg in *The Song of the Lark*, published in the same year. This is the epistemological foundation and hence the structural mode upon which "Peter Quince" is built.

Surely Riddell is correct when he asserts that "Peter Quince" is a poem about poetry and, more particularly, "pays homage to the problems of the poet in a post-transcendental world, to the problems of adjusting poetic vision to the world's incoherent but sensuous body."[17] But he is mistaken, I think, when he remarks that the aesthetic premise proffered here focuses on an old paradox, that "the ideal must take body, and thus become less than ideal before man can know it."[18] Stevens speaks in this poem with the assurance of one already converted to a philosophy of immanence, and although such a paradox may exist for others, the logic of his poem works to affirm a principle rather than to define a dilemma. As William James argued in his *Pragmatism*, experience is not validated by ideas, quite the reverse. "Truth *happens* to an idea. It *becomes* true, is *made* true by events."[19] In Stevens's own example, music is the imagined condition that evokes something real and supremely personal, but the evocation works by suggestion not expression. The real in this case is the unreifiable condition of Peter Quince's sensuous apprehension of the woman in blue silk, but it is rendered in terms of and transformed by its suggestiveness and resemblance of the parable of Susanna.

The rhythm and language of "Peter Quince" aspire to the quality of music and replicates the mental tones of thought and feeling, but the metaphysical presuppositions governing the poem also parallel the evocative, that is to say, the suggestive, power of music. Quince's feelings *are* the music of the poem. The music of his desire resembles the parable, and it is the poetic rendering of this biblical story, rather than the unshaped and chaotic desire itself, that is played upon the keyboard of his sensibility and dramatized in the poem. His desire, we are told, "is like the strain / Waked in the elders by Susanna" (*CP* 90). That is, the passion of the elders resembles his own and is called forth by this resemblance, and this evocation presides over the remainder of the poem, though it has constant reference to the speaker's dynamic emotional state.

It is just this identified, analogous relation between immediate desire and the parable that makes "Peter Quince" a poem about poetry. Throughout Stevens's criticism, one finds reference to the notion of resemblance as the bare basis of poetry. "Poetry," he writes, "is a satisfying of the desire for resemblance" (*NA* 77). Or, "Poetry is almost incredibly one of the effects of analogy" (*NA* 117). But poetry is more, as well, because in the very act of satisfying this desire poetry intensifies one's sense of reality. Indeed, the forging of effective analogies is, in a manner, to enter into the structure of reality itself and to deliver, by way of authentic communication, one's sense of the world. "When one speaks of images," he argued, "one means analogies": "If, then, an emotional image or, say, an emotional analogy communicates the emotion that generates it, its effect is to arouse the same emotion in others" (*NA* 111). "Peter Quince" lays bare the poetic operations of mind; Quince in the discovery of an adequate analogy to the emotion that generates it discovers the very nature of beauty itself.

It would falsify the poem to say that Quince's present desire gives way to a reverie about Susanna or even that the two parts of the poem are merely juxtaposed and mutually inform one another. Rather, the evocation, or his memory's summoning of this story as bearing upon immediate perception, mirrors rhythmically and substantively his own affective state. The story of the beautiful Susanna, who repulses the assault of the lustful elders and who, in turn, is spitefully accused of adultery by the same men, floats upon the speaker's consciousness and refracts his own emotional music. If the "red-eyed elders" "felt / The basses of their beings throb / In witching chords and their thin blood / Pulse pizzicati" (*CP* 90) when they spied Susanna at her bath, the motions of their blood resemble Quince's affections. Crashing cymbals, roaring horns, the noise of tambourines—all record the symphonic emotional reaction of Peter Quince to the woman in blue silk in terms of the Susanna story. The consciousness dramatized here derives its force from the poet's concentration upon effects rather than causes. William James had identified in his *Principles of Psychology* the nature of emotion when he argued that one is never conscious of emotions as such but only of the physiological changes occasioned by the reaction to perception, which we may afterward name as the emotion that possessed us.[20] Similarly, Stevens renders the rhythms of Quince's reactions to perception in a way that artfully avoids naming the emotion at all.

The poem intends, in other words, to suggest rather than to express a dynamism of feeling, and to the degree that the speaker himself becomes aware of his own state (to the degree that he becomes self-conscious) and composes it in the act of recollection, the poem deals with the relation of reality to the imagination. Surely, the beginning lines of the final section of the poem are meant to be a statement of Peter Quince's own revelation and not an obtrusive formulation of an idea addressed to the reader:

Beauty is momentary in the mind—
The fitful tracing of a portal;
But in the flesh it is immortal.   [*CP* 91]

As A. Walton Litz has observed, this is a "startling reversal of our everyday assumption that earthly beauty is an evanescent reflection of the 'ideal form' in the mind."[21] Beauty itself derives its force from perception and is dependent upon it. Sensation gives way to the harmonized aggregate of images and evocations (themselves rhythmic, or musical). Memory summons the image of Susanna as an analogue to the beauty of the woman in blue silk, and her beauty is abstracted from the fleshly beauty of the woman in blue, just as the elder's lust is summoned and abstracted from Peter Quince's own immediate desire. As Bergson argued in *An Introduction to Metaphysics*, memories adhere to perceptions and serve to interpret them: "These memories have been detached, as it were, from the depths of my personality, drawn to the surface by the perceptions which resemble them; they rest on the surface of my mind without being absolutely myself" (*IM* 10).

The poem works as poem, then, not by the power of literary allusion, but in and through the dynamic force of evocation and suggestion, as in music. But it deals as well, if only by implication, with knowing in its most immediate experiential context. How different are the gardens and the moonlit evenings in this later poem from those in "Song":

So evenings die, in their green going,
A wave, interminably flowing.
So gardens die, their meek breath scenting
The cowl of winter, done repenting.   [*CP* 92]

This is the voice of a "poet of the earth," and it describes a universe of immanent, not transcendent, beauty. The world in its interminable flowing recedes before us in our very contemplation of it. What remains is Susanna's beauty, or rather the music of her beauty, and "in its immortality, it plays / On the clear viol of her memory [the memory of her], / And makes a constant sacrament of praise." The music of feeling, then, transformed into the recollected image of Susanna, finally plays upon the imagination and, those turbulent, erotic moments passed, or rather composed and formalized, plays clearly. The present experience has been given form by the harmonizing efforts of memory and music, and by the poem itself. But the sacrament is contingent upon present perception.

Here is no background of the ideal. Susanna's divine beauty is the effect of, is caused by, the fleshly beauty of the woman in blue silk. Indeed, Susanna's is verified by hers, for the truth of present experience has happened to the idea of Susanna's beauty. "Peter Quince at the Clavier" is as far removed from "Song" as "Nude Descending a Staircase" (which Stevens no doubt saw at the Armory Show in 1913) is removed from Ackermann's colored plates. And the later poem exhibits the revolution in thinking that made for the vital reality of Stevens's poetics.

What is intended by this brief and limited exploration of Stevens's poetic development from 1899 to 1915, from the saccharine and conventionalized attitude of "Song" to the accomplished "Peter Quince at the Clavier," is not to offer an explication per se nor to account for the latter's success as a result of Stevens's appropriation of a vitalistic worldview. The advance in sensibility is attributable to the poet's own personal maturity, and the superiority of execution is the result of his own development as an artist. Nor, for that matter, do I intend to inquire into the "meaning" of the poem so much as to examine the epistemological and ontological presuppositions as prior and enabling acts that inform the poems and make sense of them as attitudes rather than as linguistic constructions. As Stevens was himself to say, poets' subjects are given to them by their sensibility, which is nothing more, or less, than their individual sense of the world: "The truth is that a man's sense of the world dictates his subjects to him and that this sense is derived from his personality, his temperament, over which he has little control and possibly none, except superficially. It is not a literary problem. It is the problem of his mind and nerves. . . . A poet writes of twilight because he shrinks from noon-day" (*NA* 122).

To the extent that Stevens's sense of the world was transformed by prewar changes not in thought alone but in how one thinks, his poetry reflects that transformation. To the extent that that sense of the world was informed by his absorption of the writings of James, Bergson, and others, that sense is, as well, significantly, if only incidentally, a philosophical one. Years later Stevens would identify the poet as a "chanting brooder":

Seeking the acutest end
Of speech: to pierce the heart's residuum
And there to find music for a single line,
Equal to memory, one line in which
The vital music formulates the words.   [CP 259]

This is a vitalistic aesthetic uttered with undiminished confidence in the poet's purpose, but it is more pensive than celebratory. In Stevens's first volume of verse, he was more chanter than brooder, however, and those poems participated emotionally as well as intellectually in the optimism of the age. *Harmonium* (1923), therefore, deserves special attention, for by Stevens's own reckoning, the recognition that the Great War had thrust America into an era of unexampled confusion and complexity was delayed by a decade. In this sense, the poems of *Harmonium*, despite its publication date, were composed when the author was still excited by prewar enthusiasms.

III

Stevens resisted for some time the urgings of friends and associates to collect a volume of his poetry. When *Harmonium* at last appeared, the poet was forty-four years old. Yet the book bears little trace of the middle-aged—it is alternately playful and flamboyant, sensuous and celebratory, mocking and comic; to use one of Stevens's favorite terms, it is "gaudy." Most of the poems were composed during an era when only "maniacs" had discouraging things to say, during that time when the public (or at least Stevens) did not yet realize that the theater of "happy oblivion" had been dismantled and carted off. Unless one makes the sorts of historical adjustments that accommodate lingering hopes and aspirations beyond their appointed time, Stevens must appear slightly ridiculous. In the aftermath of the Great War, after Europe had been ravaged, when war-related casualties numbered some eight million, Stevens was writing and publishing poems with such titles as "Hymn from a Watermelon Pavilion," "Floral Decorations for Bananas," "The Emperor of Ice Cream," and "Stars at Tallapoosa" and writing such lines as: "Chieftain Iffucan of Azcan in caftan / Of Tan with henna hackles, halt!" (*CP* 75). But the endorsements and affirmations of *Harmonium* were deliberate. Stevens included in this volume only one of the poems from *Lettres d'un Soldat*, a collection of poems that together sensitively and movingly respond to the thought and feeling, as they are recorded in his letters, of the French soldier Edward LeMercier, who had died in the war. Even in the 1931 edition of *Harmonium*, Stevens would add only three poems from this series. He meant for the poems of *Harmonium* to conform to the mood suggested by the title.

Harmonium may indeed represent Stevens's finest achievement, as many critics are disposed to believe. It is, at all events, his most healthy-minded book, if by "healthy-minded" one means to convey something of that quality William James found in the expression when he applied it to the poetry of Walt Whitman. Whitman, James believed, systematically expunged from his writings all "contractile" elements; he is an "expansive" poet, and a "passionate and mystic ontological emotion suffuses his words, and ends by persuading the reader that men and women, life and death and all things are divinely good."[22] Perhaps, to suggest the comparison and then to withdraw it would be more accurate, for Stevens actively discouraged any comparison between his thoughts about poetry and the mystical; and Frank Kermode has aptly described Stevens as something of an "agnostic Blake."[23] Too, those healthy-minded features of *Harmonium* are observable only in parts of the volume, although observable frequently enough to tip the scales in their favor.

"The great poems of heaven and hell have been written," observed Stevens in 1948, "and the great poem of the earth remains to be written" (*NA* 142). Clearly Stevens, even so much earlier, meant to speak as a poet of the earth in this book and to celebrate the gross materiality of the new vital reality as irreverently as Whitman himself. Thus, "Ploughing on Sunday":

Remus, blow your horn!
I'm ploughing on Sunday,
Ploughing North America.
Blow your horn!

Tum-ti-tum,
Ti-tum-tum-tum!
The turkey-cock's tail
Spreads to the sun.   [*CP* 20]

Broadly farcical and openly defiant, "Ploughing on Sunday" is as boisterous and reckless a poem as any of several parts of "Song of Myself." By contrast, "Domination of Black" describes somber and more despairing moments—the color of "heavy hemlocks," fallen leaves, and twilight prevailing. But, even here (as with many of Stevens's poems), in the midst of morose contraction and apprehension, the antidote for such depression is the recollection of a feathered and gaudy boast:

> I saw how the night came,
> Came striding like the color of the heavy hemlocks.
> I felt afraid.
> And I remembered the cry of peacocks.   [CP 8–9]

These two poems establish, more or less, the emotional range of *Harmonium*. The poetry, however, is always tinged with an intellectual conviction that makes of his lyrics something more than simply the corralling of a sentiment. As Samuel French Morse has remarked, something of the "doctrinal" is always present in Stevens's poetry (even in poems that at first glance appear slight),[24] and the variety of means he sought in this first volume to write a poetry of the earth gives to his verse a certain weight and substance, even ponderousness, that quite eclipses a rather monochromatic emotional scale. Much of the energy of Stevens's poetry derives from his willingness to be, even his insistence upon being, a sort of sage of the quotidian, a "Socrates of snails" (*CP* 27). "Imagination applied to the whole world," he wrote in *Adagia*, "is vapid in comparison to imagination applied to a detail" (*Opus* 176). This sort of devotion to singular experience is analogous to, perhaps emerges out of, James's insistence that truth is composed of several separate truths and that truth and reality are always in the making. Stevens expressed this thought in the adage, "Reality is not what it is. It consists of the many realities which it can be made into" (*Opus* 178). He would eventually conclude that one could only get at reality by means of attending to pure experience and applying the resources of metaphor and suggestion. To use the phrase of Kenneth Burke, with whom Stevens shares many interesting similarities, one might find one's orientation in the world by forging a certain "perspective by incongruity," which is the very nature of metaphor.

Harmonium offers many such perspectives. In "Depression before Spring" Stevens writes,

> The hair of my blonde
> Is dazzling
> As the spittle of cows
> Threading the wind.   [CP 63]

In this image there is no trace of an intervening intelligence measuring and adapting, making mental adjustments according to conventionalized attitudes toward the "real," toward either the hair of one's love or the spittle of cows. Neither does it possess the crystalline resolution of an imagist poem; it is, without ever ceasing to be an image, an analogy as well. Stevens has distilled a rawer perception into an image that insists, by virtue of the isolable features of resemblance, that we perceive the hair of his blonde as a filament of light trailing in the wind.

To force this sort of perception upon a reader requires a certain imaginative violence and exacts a compensating price in the poet's credibility, as Stevens well recognized. As he noted in "The Comedian as the Letter C," it required him to be at times an "aesthetic tough"—"diverse, untamed / Incredible to prudes" (*CP* 31). Like the Crispin of that poem, Stevens vastly preferred "text to gloss," though this might make of him a "clown," but at least he would be "an aspiring clown" (*CP* 39). If Stevens were willing to play the fool in the service of his anti-intellectualism, it was something of a mischievous, Shakespearean fool. His antic poses enabled him to lampoon and otherwise satirize rationalists and idealists in several ways.

Sharing with James and Bergson a contempt for the intellectualism of the day, or more likely borrowing it since philosophers and scientists were in no way his daily professional adversaries, Stevens would make the intellectual a figure of fun. Indeed, the rationalist became something of a symbol for him. In the last of "Six Significant Landscapes," he ridicules rationalists hemmed in by the geometric precision of their thought: "Rationalists, wearing square hats, / Think, in square rooms."

If they tried rhomboids,
Cones, waving lines, ellipses—
As, for example, the ellipse of the half-moon,
Rationalists would wear sombreros.   [*CP* 75]

The capacity for such comic derision comes from secure conviction. The cooped-up philosopher who renounces or ignores the fluid perfection of a world whose movements perpetually escape the rationalist's analytic intelligence is life denying, a mockery. Such is the case with the emotionally landlocked "Doctor of Geneva," who "stamped the sand," "patted his stove-pipe hat and tugged his shawl." "Lacustrine man" (that is, one whose mind can accommodate lakes but not oceans) cannot account for the "long-rolling opulent cataracts" of the sea—"Lakes are more reasonable than oceans," wrote Stevens in a later poem (*CP* 325). The Doctor of Geneva is not fearful, but neither does he feel a vitalizing awe "Before these visible, voluble delugings." His "simmering" mind spins and hisses "with oracular / Notations of the wild ruinous waste":

> Until the steeples of his city clanked and sprang
> In an unburgherly apocalypse.
> The doctor used his handkerchief and sighed.   [*CP* 24]

Here the contractile and confining operations of the good doctor's intellect (which reduces percepts to concepts, makes notations of perpetual flux) act in opposition to an immanent world of incessant change. The diction of the poem is one of compression and underscores the anxious pressure of his teakettle mind; yet, no more than the steam in the pot will the undulations of the sea be denied. And Stevens displays a special degree of sardonicism toward the doctor by the fact that the experience of immediate and absolute duration is somehow relieved by the mechanical clanking of the steeple clocks.

One other example of Stevens's ridicule of intellectualists will suffice. In "Homunculus et la Belle Étoile," Stevens puts in dramatic opposition the "young emerald, evening star" and "Homunculus" (that man of chemicals that Paracelsus the alchemist wished to create). The evening star provides a fitting light for "drunkards, poets, widows, / And ladies soon to be married" (*CP* 25), and it would be nice to think that this "prinking" star might charm philosophers "Until they became thoughtlessly willing / To bathe their hearts in later moonlight" and know that they might "bring back thought" and reflect "this thing and that" before sleep (*CP* 25–26). The satire here is multilayered, and in part it is a satire of the mechanistic, building block philosophy Stevens had grown up on. The poet is at once ridiculing the notion of an individual as merely chemical compound and the analytic mind that should attempt to fashion such a being. Even philosophers may from time to time become "thoughtlessly willing" rather than reflect sensuous apprehension through the alembic of intellect, but it is better for them that they should keep indoors lest they discover, like the Doctor of Geneva, that the universe does not abide by their genteel conceptions of it.

It is better that, as scholars,
They should think hard in the dark cuffs
Of voluminous cloaks
And shave their heads and bodies.

It might well be that their mistress
Is no gaunt fugitive phantom.
She might, after all, be a wanton,
Abundantly beautiful, eager. [*CP* 26–27]

One finds the same sort of comedy in other *Harmonium* poems—such as the "Anecdote of Canna" (which Frank Doggett identifies as a poem about the discrepancy between dream and reality)[25] or "Last Looks at the Lilacs" in which a man ("Poor buffo!" [*CP* 49]) scratches his buttocks and with a caliper anatomizes sensation, indifferent to his quivering paramour. One finds this humor too in Stevens's contempt for "Funest philosophers and ponderers" in "On the Manner of Addressing Clouds." "Funest" (mournful or fatal) is by punning implication a word that connotes, as well as mortality, the fun and playfulness that somehow escape "Gloomy grammarians," whose sterile music is an "exhaltation without sound." The proclamations of these grammarians—idealized, immutable—are actually the music of "meet resignation" (*CP* 55–56). One also finds a scorn for the desiccating operations of reason in "The Bird with the Coppery Keen Claws," where the etherealized "parakeet of parakeets prevails." This idealized form of parakeet is not a "paradise of parakeets." It has but a taxonomic domination over the real birds; it necessarily "broods" above them and is "still":

But though the turbulent tinges undulate
As his pure intellect applies its laws,
He moves not on his coppery keen claws.

He munches a dry shell while he exerts
His will, yet never ceases, perfect cock,
To flare, in the sun pallor of his rock. [*CP* 82]

Only through the artificial efforts of will and intellect does the idealized form of parakeet so tyrannize over the real, but the emotional costs for such reification and eternalizing are despair and anger and deprivation.

Again and again Stevens satirizes rationalists and idealists who brood and munch a dry shell as life denying and artificial. Yet for all this, Stevens's pity mollifies his contempt: funest philosophers and ponderers are pathetic rather than truly pernicious. If he mocks them, his is the laughter of secure conviction. The parakeet of parakeets has been deposed, and the things of the earth have resumed their rights. As William James said of Bergson in a letter Stevens read and cited, the Frenchman has delivered the death wound to intellectualists of every stripe. These poems, for all their affectation, are spoken with the confidence of one who can afford to laugh.

Stevens would continue to mock the rationalist throughout his life, but over the years his humor became more acid, I think, and lacks the large tolerance of *Harmonium*. In one of his finest late poems, "Notes toward a Supreme Fiction" (1942), he would note sardonically that

> The President ordains the bee to be
> Immortal. The President ordains. But does
> The body lift its heavy wing . . . ?
>
> The President has apples on the table.
> And barefoot servants round him, who adjust
> The curtains to a metaphysical t.
>
> And the banners of the nation flutter, burst
> On the flag-poles in a red-blue dazzle, whack
> At the halyards. [CP 390]

For all its humor, there is a stridency here that is clearly lacking in *Harmonium*. The realm of essence and the preoccupations of gloomy grammarians are bureaucratized and sustained by magisterial pomp and trivial rite. The "metaphysical t" to which the president's curtains are so nicely and fastidiously adjusted has punning reference to the italicized and likewise metaphysical *t* that Bergson eloquently and rigorously criticized as both scientific delusion and Platonic deception and argued, instead, for the preeminent reality of felt duration. Just so, and in opposition to insipid presidential proclamation, Stevens celebrates the vitality of sensuously perceived flux in the conclusion of the section: the warmth of spring "is for lovers at last accomplishing / Their love, this beginning, not resuming, this / Booming and booming of the new-come bee" (*CP* 391).

This is the assertion of the poet as the unofficial interpreter of being with all the zest displayed in the earlier verse. The playful punning with the concepts of *bee* and *be*, of *being* and *bee-coming*, "booming and booming" in springtime, is especially sprightly and antic in its flamboyant affirmations; in his declamations, however, Stevens became increasingly acerbic. His quarrel with the hypostatization of the natural world was developed early, persisted, and took many forms. Among them was his quarrel with the idealizations of conventional religion.

Stevens's faith, or his lack of it, is a complex question and has only peripheral interest for us here. Adelaide Kirby Morris, among others, has examined these complexities in detail, and she may well be right that Stevens derived some portion of his atheism from Nietzsche.[26] He found little in vitalistic doctrine to actively support his doubts—not in Driesch or Bergson, at any rate—though vitalism might engender and encourage a scepticism about traditional religious convention. Perhaps it is enough to know finally that Stevens considered himself a "dried-up Presbyterian" (*LWS* 792). More pertinent is his contempt for a rarefied faith in the immutable that diverts one from the manifold richness of the world at hand. He expressed this contempt in several ways.

Stevens bristles in "Of Heaven Considered as a Tomb," rejects those "men / Who in the tomb of heaven walk by night." The stars in the sky are equated with the "freemen" of death; are they "about and still about / To find whatever it is they seek?," he asks. The question is rhetorical; they provide no answer, nor do they respond from their "icy Élysée" (*CP* 56). Similarly, in "Cortège for Rosenbloom," "the infants of misanthropes," the "infants of nothingness," bear the dead Rosenbloom to the sky and bury him there "Body and soul / In a place in the sky" (*CP* 80–81). The funeral cortège of the wry Rosenbloom ("rose in bloom") is nought but the worms that feed on his decay, much as the processional in "The Worms at Heaven's Gate" bear away, part by part, the princely remains of Badroulbadour.

In his address to "A High-Toned Old Christian Woman," Stevens notes the mental transactions that accomplish such a heaven:

Poetry is the supreme fiction, madame.
Take the moral law and make a nave of it.
And from the nave build haunted heaven. Thus,
The conscience is converted into palms.

The high-toned woman builds a heaven by virtue of the operation of the imagination upon a fixed principle, a moral law, but this kind of abstraction is life denying. One may as well create fictions out of the rawer, impermanent stuff of life is his polite rebuttal, and

> Thus, our bawdiness,
> Unpurged by epitaph, indulged at last,
> Is equally converted into palms,
> Squiggling like saxophones. [CP 59]

If such rhetoric might prove incredible to prudes, Stevens had nevertheless expressed this theme, happily free from the sardonicism of "A High-
Toned Old Christian Woman," in "Sunday Morning." "Sunday Morning"
is in fact suffused with an authentic sympathy that tempers his rhetoric
and makes this poem of the earth something of an agnostic hymn. The
question, however, is the same: why should this woman, in passive viola-
tion of the Sabbath, settled amidst the contentment of "late / Coffee and
oranges in a sunny chair," offer up her "bounty to the dead?" (CP 66–67).

> What is divinity if it can come
> Only in silent shadows and in dreams?
> Shall she not find in comforts of the sun, . . .
> In any balm or beauty of the earth,
> Things to be cherished like the thought of heaven?
> Divinity must live within herself: . . .
> All pleasures and all pains, remembering
> The bough of summer and the winter branch.

> These are the measures destined for her soul. [CP 67]

Throughout, the poetic voice gives tender answer to her fears and long-
ings. A. Walton Litz is perfectly right to say that "Sunday Morning"
ought not to be approached as "disguised philosophy."[27] Sympathy, not
cant, makes this poem something unexampled in the Stevens canon. Nevertheless, if the articulation of the woman's fears and desires derives from
the poet's identification with her, Stevens's endorsements of a life com-
pounded of perception and imagination still derive from the undiluted
conviction that the new, vital reality offers its own consolations. Indeed,
he speaks of her destiny as though it were a spiritual calling grounded in
the energy of the soul itself. He recommends, in short, a "fictive alternative," no less divine for its perishable nature, to the woman's dreams of
"imperishable bliss." His response to her need for the eternal and immutable is simple and direct: "Death is the mother of beauty; hence from
her, / Alone, shall come fulfillment to our dreams" (CP 68–69).

"The honey of heaven may or may not come," Stevens wrote in "Le
Monocle de Mon Oncle," "But that of earth both comes and goes at once"

(*CP* 15). To recognize and embrace the truth of incessant change is to recognize that birth and death, the past and the future, are inextricably bound up together in duration. It is a primitive recognition, he suggested in "Sunday Morning," one that stirs the blood if not the brain:

> Shall our blood fail? Or shall it come to be
> The blood of paradise? And shall the earth
> Seem all of paradise that we shall know?   [*CP* 68]

The paradise of earth celebrated by the poet is near and constantly available. A passage from *Creative Evolution* is pertinent to the emotional complex dramatized in Stevens's poem:

> The mystery that spreads over the existence of the universe comes in great part from this, that we want the genesis of it to have been accomplished at one stroke or the whole of matter to be eternal. Whether we speak of the creation or posit an uncreated matter, it is the totality of the universe that we are considering at once. . . . Once this prejudice is eradicated, the idea of creation becomes more clear, for it is merged in that of growth. But it is no longer then of the universe in its totality that we must speak.   [*CE* 240–41]

The intellect may apply more general and eternal laws to the universe and creation, but life tells us that "we depend on the planet on which we are, and on the sun that provides for it, but on nothing else" (*CE* 241). A more primitive and local relation to the world is to provide entrance back into the very nature of the spirit as it works within us: "When we put back our being into our will, and will itself into the impulsion it prolongs, we understand, we feel that reality is a perpetual growth, a creation pursued without end. Our will already performs this miracle" (*CE* 239).

To adopt this attitude of temporality is to become as that ring of men in section 7 of "Sunday Morning" who sing and celebrate the sun "Not as a god, but as a god might be, / Naked among them, like a savage source. / Their chant shall be the chant of paradise." To realize that the "tomb in Palestine / Is not the porch of spirits lingering" but merely a tomb is to recognize that

> We live in an old chaos of the sun,
> Or old dependency of day and night,
> Or island solitude, unsponsored, free,
> Of that wide water, inescapable.   [*CP* 70]

Our transient pleasures shall be instead in the deer that walk the mountains, the sound of quail, berries ripening in the wilderness, the descent of pigeons. If we live "unsponsored," a paradise of the blood makes a truce of the hostility and despair existing between the woman and her environment and a mockery of a haunted heaven.

> The sky will be much friendlier then than now,
> A part of labor and a part of pain,
> And next in glory to enduring love,
> Not this dividing and indifferent blue.   [CP 68]

Acceptance of the new, vital reality means becoming at one with the world as it is in the fullness of its becoming. It means as well abandoning vain hopes for an immutable empyrean, which is but the imaginative projection and hypostatization of a common, human longing that effectively separates us from the lives we live and were meant to live.

In no other poem in *Harmonium* is Stevens's advocacy so eloquent and self-assured. There is an emotional poise in "Sunday Morning" that is lacking in the simple complaint of, say, "Gubbinal":

> That strange flower, the sun,
> Is just what you say.
> Have it your way.
>
> The world is ugly,
> And the people are sad.   [CP 85]

A positivistic vision, shorn of the features and the feel of the familiarly human, is unfriendly and depressing because it lacks the appropriative and associative quality imagination brings to the world. "Imagination is the will of things" (*CP* 84), Stevens has his Polish aunt say in the poem immediately preceding "Gubbinal." Without the imagination, we are divided against ourselves, longing for the immutable and eternal or the static and predictable and laboring against the perception and acceptance of incessant change that make beauty possible.

Imagination is intuition. Stevens himself equated the terms in his lecture, "A Collect of Philosophy" (*Opus* 200). As with the intuition, the imagination seizes and composes the world without substituting fixed concepts for fluid realities. Again and again, Stevens celebrates the imagination as an enabling power and value, a notion he would reaffirm years later in his lecture on the "Imagination as Value." We shall consider that prose statement of the nature and significance of the imagination in the next chapter. Here, it is sufficient to note that the imagination, for Stevens, is a power, a "power of the mind over the possibilities of things" (*NA* 136), a "power that enables us to perceive the normal in the abnormal, the opposite of chaos in chaos" (*NA* 153). As value, the imagination is a human faculty and, strictly speaking, has neither ontological nor logical substance. Imagination is not being, but the "magnificent cause of being . . . the one reality / In this imagined world" (*CP* 25).

The imagination, for all its primacy in the most essential functions of life, may nevertheless be lost or abandoned, attenuated or bastardized. "To the One of Fictive Music" is the secularized invocation of an earthly muse, a plea for the ancient power and resource of the imagination. Like "Sunday Morning," it shuns the eternalized and rigidly symbolic sphere of essence and rejects conventional muses as a "sisterhood of the living dead." Their divinity originated as an act of the imagination and sprang from a human origin, but their formal perfections have now become steady mirrors of humanity, self-enclosed, masturbatory.

> Now of the music summoned by the birth
> That separates us from the wind and sea,
> Yet leaves us in them, until earth becomes,
> By being so much of the things we are,
> Gross effigy and simulacrum   [*CP* 87]

The traditional muse that descends from above insists that we despise the earth. Hers is a music that "vaunts the clearest bloom" and "apprehends the most which sees and names, / . . . an image that is sure." Through her, "We give ourselves our likest issuance" (*CP* 88).

The poet of the earth requires, by contrast, a music "not too like":

> yet not so like to be
> Too near, too clear, saving a little to endow
> Our feigning with the strange unlike, whence springs
> The difference that heavenly pity brings.   [*CP* 88]

Instead of the "arrant spices of the sun," an earthly muse ought "bear other perfumes" and on her head wear a band "set with fatal stones." Such a muse knows that death is the mother of beauty. The muse, any muse, is a fiction, unreal; but a divine and transcendent muse encourages faith in a hypostatized beauty, remote and immutable. Stevens's final plea is for a return to a vital imagination: "Unreal, give back to us what once you gave: / The imagination that we spurned and crave" (*CP* 88). In other words, Stevens asks, as he did in "Sunday Morning," for a primitive muse, a "savage source," who moves among men and women and inspires a music that ascends to the sky rather than descends from heaven.

One cannot overemphasize the significance that the role of the human imagination plays in Stevens's poetic vision—throughout his career he opposes this capacity to the currents of popular opinion and political contest. Only through the vitalizing operations of the imagination may one break through the crust of stultifying habit and seize in all its richness the reality of life as force and movement. Only through the recognition of this power is the final function of poetry and the poet realized. To solidify impressions, to substitute for life as lived a set of symbols, or to place one's belief in ideas about the thing above the thing itself is to deny the movement of duration that is the current of life. In a sense, imagination and motion are inextricably bound up together, as for Bergson are intuition and duration. Indeed, Bergson spoke of motion as the "living symbol" of duration (*TFW* 110).

And *Harmonium* is everywhere in motion; the poet celebrates movement and change not as hectic distraction but as the truest of poetic subjects. Such poems as "Earthy Anecdote," "Life Is Motion," or "The Curtains in the House of the Metaphysician" are lyrics in praise of sheer movement. But, for Stevens, as for Bergson, motion is a psychological not a physical fact; the very concept of motion presupposes a synthetic mental act and as such is potentially poetic. Thus, in such a poem as "The Wind Shifts," the poet links motion and change to the motive springs of thought. The wind shifts "Like a human without illusions, / Who still feels irrational things within her" (*CP* 83). "Poetry," Stevens would write in *Adagia*, "must be irrational" (*Opus* 162) because it encourages the imaginative or intuitive impulse to look on life directly rather than to filter perceptions through the intellect. Here, as elsewhere, it is the rationalist who is self-deceived, who harbors illusions. In "The Place of Solitaires," Stevens pleas for "perpetual undulation" as the prompter of thought and speech:

> There must be no cessation
> Of motion, or of the noise of motion,
> The renewal of noise
> And manifold continuation;

And, most, of the motion of thought
And its restless iteration.   [*CP* 60]

However strongly Stevens may have felt that poetry and the imagination represented salvation, an alternative to the loss of the gods, however
ardently he celebrated the imaginative, he recognized from the beginning
the recalcitrance of convention and custom. Stevens's lyrics praise the
potency of the imagination; his rhetoric anatomizes the costs of its loss. In
"Stars at Tallapoosa," he distinguished between the astronomer's impulse
and a more human, earthly plaint:

The lines are straight and swift between the stars.
The night is not the cradle that they cry,
The criers, undulating the deep-oceaned phrase.
The lines are much too dark and much too sharp.   [*CP* 71]

As Bergson had argued in several places, astronomical calculation pretends to foreseeability, but life (and art) is unmade and incalculable.
(Bergson instanced a Beethoven symphony as "unforeseeability itself.")
True art replicates the rhythms of life, which is duration. The intellect may
describe lines between the stars ("the mind herein attains simplicity"), but
the sacrifice is great: There is "no moon, on single, silvered leaf. / The
body is no body to be seen / But is an eye that studies its black lid" (*CP*
71). Better that earthbound humanity wades "sea-lines," "moist and ever
mingling"; "earth-lines," "long and lax, lethargic." These lines too are
swift and "fall without diverging"; they fall to earth but embrace, at least,
the "melon flower" (*CP* 72) and supply abundant, if temporary, pleasure.
But this is only one way to forfeit the imagination; to study the eye's black
lid is an intellectual mistake merely.

Another is to submit to the "malady of the quotidian" (*CP* 96). "The
Man Whose Pharynx Was Bad" was, to Marianne Moore's regret, excluded from the first edition of *Harmonium*,[28] but the tone is somewhat
shrill and out of keeping with the mood of the majority of poems in the
volume. In that poem Stevens speaks of the poet whose voice is ruined
because "I am too dumbly in my being pent." The wind does not stir the
poet in his sleep; it tolls only "The grand ideas of villages" (*CP* 96). These
grand ideas are the clichéd utterances of the villagers, men and women like
the Doctor of Geneva or the high-toned old Christian woman. By contrast, the poetic and, by implication, the human ideal is, as he expressed it

in *Adagia*, "To live in the world but outside existing conceptions of it" (*Opus* 164). To live wholly within rigid and solidified abstractions is the malady of the quotidian—the blight of the insufferable and stifling ready-made. These prepared ways of thinking make one indifferent and insensitive to the season. The man whose pharynx was bad is voiceless because all things are alike in the routine of his life.

Another danger to the imagination, and related to the other two, is easy submission to necessity and indulgence in complacency. This is the implication of the puzzling little poem, "Frogs Eat Butterflies. Snakes Eat Frogs. Hogs Eat Snakes. Men Eat Hogs." The title suggests a cyclical naturalism that does not evolve but simply repeats determined patterns, and in the context of the poem, the terms of the title could be extended to read "Time Eats Men." But the title itself is obscure. Stevens meant to suggest that evolution and progress may be rendered inert through indolence. As the rivers tug at their banks, "nosing like swine," so does time's river tug at the man who

> erected this cabin, planted
> This field, and tended it awhile,
> Knew not the quirks of imagery. [*CP* 78]

Like the realist Crispin in section 5 of "The Comedian as the Letter C," this man is inured to the possibilities of things—"For realist, what is is what should be" (*CP* 41). The quotidian "saps" the will and intent to "track the knaves of thought" (*CP* 43). As a realist intent on nothing more than creature comfort, the man in "Frogs Eat Butterflies" is resistant to the quirks of imagery. His failure is the failure of the imagination, and "the imagination is man's power over nature" (*Opus* 179). Thus,

> the hours of his indolent, arid days, . . .
> Seemed to suckle themselves on his arid being,
> As the swine-like rivers suckled themselves
> While they went seaward to the sea-mouths. [*CP* 78]

This indolent planter labors to the extent of convenience merely. His life is otherwise torpid; his days are arid, though the "rattapallax" of thunder can be heard in the distance. The hours suckle themselves on his dry being—that is, he is inert, little more than matter in his obtuse self-satisfaction. Knowing nothing of the vitalizing power of the imagination, he draws nothing from the ocean of life toward which the rivers flow.

If poems such as these describe the dangers to and the loss of the imagination, a greater number by far celebrate its peculiar power, not by rhetoric, but by the lyrical example of luxuriant and fantastic metaphoric transformation. "My titillations have no foot-notes," wrote Stevens, "And their memorials are the phrases / Of idiosyncratic music" (*CP* 79). Stevens's verse was never supplied with such belated and collateral clarifications as the footnotes Eliot appended to "The Waste Land" or the genealogy Faulkner added to *The Sound and the Fury*, nor does it require such amplification. Stevens's aim was to offer up a "vivid apprehension":

Of bliss submerged beneath appearance
In an interior ocean's rocking
Of long, capricious fugues and chorals. [*CP* 79]

Much of his poetry is neither referential nor self-referential but phenomenal—joyful disclosures of the world of appearance as appearance. These vivid apprehensions testify to the sincerity of Stevens's conviction, recorded in *Adagia*, that "The poem reveals itself only to the ignorant man" (*Opus* 160). More often than not, he meant to render an immanent world of flux rather than to argue it, and though one cannot gainsay the obscure and fantastic qualities of *Harmonium*, though he confessed to Harriet Monroe that he meant to keep his poems "obscure" until such time as he might develop an "authentic and fluent" speech (*LWS* 231), his motive impulse was more democratic than mysterious. Stevens was neither imagist nor surrealist (in fact, he registered his objections to both movements). Instead, his poetic was grounded more in theory than in personal indulgence or aesthetic trend, but it was a theory that had its humanistic and anti-intellectual aspirations. His poems were so many attempts to return his readers to the realm of feeling, an intuitively grasped reality as familiar as it is remote.

The opening poem of *Harmonium*, "Earthy Anecdote," serves as a prelude to the volume and was surely meant as an address to the reader, an invitation to enter into the book in the terms implicit there. The poem describes the movement of bucks "clattering" over the plains of Oklahoma and arranging themselves in "swift, circular lines" as they swerve away from the "firecat." Their composition is *caused* by the firecat that "bristled in the way" (*CP* 3). Stevens concludes the poem with, "Later, the firecat closed his bright eyes / And slept." As in the familiar anthology piece, "Anecdote of the Jar," this poem describes the ordering and composing of a world in flux, and the firecat here is meant to represent the poet's function in the book—to compose without arresting, to provide "vivid apprehension" of the submerged undulations of the sensible world. Like "Life Is Motion" (of which it was originally a companion piece), "Earthy Anecdote," Stevens claimed, has no symbols; "there is a good deal of theory about it, however" (*LWS* 204).

The theory dramatized in this lyric, one must suppose, reflects the effort to seize and compose unsolidified moments of change—it is, in the Bergsonian sense, a metaphysical attempt, insofar as metaphysics is the attempt to do away with symbols, to apprehend and to represent the world as one of confluence and divergence, erosion and decay, restitution and repair. A supplementary doctrinal point is conveyed by the short poem entitled simply "Theory":

I am what is around me.

Women understand this.
One is not duchess
A hundred yards from a carriage.   [*CP* 86]

This is a statement of the local habitation of the human sensibility, and it is founded upon a psychology of resemblance and affiliation. Taken together, these two theoretical positions encompass the range and tension of Stevens's own version of particulars and universals. He expressed the dichotomy succinctly in an aphorism: "The stream of consciousness is individual; the stream of life is total" (*Opus* 157). Like Willa Cather, Stevens was something of a cosmopolitan regionalist, one whose local color was perforce implicated in the larger currents of the totality of life, indeed could only be so implicated through the individual consciousness. These are points we shall return to, but for the moment it is enough to say that the fantastic figures of *Harmonium* emerge from the struggle between these opposing impulses. When Stevens wrote that "it is life that we are trying to get in poetry" (*Opus* 158), he meant for the word *life* to connote both a Jamesian presentational immediacy and a Bergsonian immanent biological impulse. And he speaks of the imagination as just that kind of power or impulse when he notes that "the imagination wishes to be indulged" (*Opus* 159). The imagination is, perhaps, Stevens's own version of the élan vital.

In any event, much of *Harmonium* is the record of this indulgence. In the "Apostrophe of Vincentine," for example, the speaker "figures" Vincentine "as nude between / Monotonous earth and dark blue sky." In consequence, the monotonous earth became "Illimitable spheres of you" (*CP* 52). In "Floral Decorations for Bananas," in conformity with the aesthetic principle identified in "Theory," the selection of bananas for the table is an epistemological as well as an aesthetic mistake. Whoever planned the table was an "ogre" who had his eye on an "outdoor gloom" rather than on the occasion as it is, or should be. Because bananas are "hacked and hunched," the women at the table "will be all shanks / And bangles and slatted eyes" (*CP* 54).

Again and again, Stevens asserts the transforming power of the imagination over and against the hackneyed and codified representations of reality. But his transformations are not, strictly speaking, metamorphoses as much as they are, to use once again Burke's terms, so many "perspectives by incongruity." They are meant to provide a new orientation through "methodical misnaming"²⁹ in order to enable the reader to see afresh what is already there and constantly available to the intuition, to make one's perceptions pure through analogue. It is an effort to overthrow, through an imaginative violence, the habitual intellectualist tendency to wedge between percipient and percipiens an idea or concept or a physiological or psychological state, an attempt to get at things as they are in the full richness of their sensory content. The intellect acts as a cleaver, separating humanity from the natural world. Thus the fifth of Stevens's "Six Significant Landscapes":

> Not all the knives of the lamp-posts,
> Nor the chisels of the long streets,
> Nor the mallets of the domes
> And high towers,
> Can carve
> What one star can carve,
> Shining through the grape-leaves.   [*CP* 74–75]

Or, the second landscape:

> The night is of the color
> Of a woman's arm:
> Night, the female,
> Obscure,
> Fragrant and supple,
> Conceals herself.

A pool shines
Like a bracelet
Shaken in a dance.   [*CP* 73–74]

Lyrics such as these are the outcroppings of a sensibility that participates fully in the philosophical vision of the new reality, but they are not philosophical statements. As Frank Doggett observes, Stevens often "inverts the usual relationship of experience and ideas in a poem."[30] However, it is just that sort of inversion that James detected in Bergson and that led him to assert that once one adopted the Bergsonian point of view one could never again return to that previous and ancient attitude of mind that characterized the mode of thought of the nineteenth century. If Stevens is a poet of ideas, his use of ideas is frequently meant to clarify the relation between humanity and things and not to invest experience with some superadded ideational or cognitive content. For this reason, there is little of the dialectic in Stevens's verse (virtually none in *Harmonium*), and he is not a philosophical poet in any conventional sense.

"The poet must not adapt his experience to that of the philosopher," wrote Stevens (*Opus* 170). The reason, presumably, is that such adaptation is privative. The accordance and accommodation of experience to rational understanding deprives the poet of primary experience, of a personal sense of the world. Stevens's familiar "Thirteen Ways of Looking at a Blackbird" seems almost in open defiance of Kantian rationalism. Instead of twelve categories of understanding, Stevens gives us a baker's dozen of modes of apprehension of the blackbird, and no doubt there could be more. At least Stevens was not above such bold gestures.

Crispin of "The Comedian as the Letter C" may be a "profitless philosopher" bragging his "green brag"; he may be indulging a "fancy gorged / By apparition," illuminating "plain and common things" (*CP* 46). The weeping burgher may, with a "strange malice," "distort the world" (*CP* 61). The dew of Florida may bring forth "hymn and hymn / From the beholder" and, in the possession of a felt reality, "So in me, come flinging / Forms, flames, and the flakes of flames" (*CP* 95). Even so, exuberant poetic gesture has therapeutic value, for "in excess continual / There is cure of sorrow" (*CP* 61). Stevens believed that poetry is a "health" (*Opus* 176) and, by implication, that the poet is a healer. Nothing mystical is intended by the representation of the poet as healer, at least nothing more mystical than the biological metaphysics Bergson advocated. By recalling the reader to the reality of felt life through the transmutations and incantations of poetry, the poet assists in repairing the wound that separates men and women from their world. And if there is an indefinite number of realities, "the most provocative of all realities is that reality of which we never lose sight, but never see solely as it is" (*Opus* 214).

Because one never perceives the present as such, but the past moving into the future, the reality nearest to hand is continually withdrawn from immediate apprehension. Poetry's highest function, so Stevens believed, is to "increase the feeling for reality" (*Opus* 162), and it performs this task through metaphoric transformation. The reality Stevens found most provocative is the reality of duration that can never be expressed but only suggested. Poetry, then, is the art of suggestion. A consensus vision of the world constitutes a version of reality, but such a reality is "a cliché from which we escape by metaphor. It is only *au pays de la métaphore qu'on est poète*" (*Opus* 179). The poetic transmutations of *Harmonium* serve to assist in that escape. The overarching achievement of Stevens's first volume of poetry was the comic and gaudy insistence that we return to the earth, for its grace and its music and for our own salvation.

SIX

The Makings of a Self

I

IN THE LAST CHAPTER we examined *Harmonium* at length because its poetry issued from a vision congruent with widespread prewar enthusiasms for and assurances of a new, vital reality. The philosophical foundations of this new worldview were peculiarly appropriate and congenial to the efforts of the creative imagination. To the extent that Stevens was in agreement with and participated in the intellectual currents of his day, his poetry is historically conditioned, and to that extent, too, the poems of *Harmonium* radiate outward from the poet's own sense of the world, which, as Stevens would claim, is the poet's richest and truest and most authentic subject. His antagonism toward late nineteenth-century intellectualism, his hymns in praise of the incessant change of the natural world, his exuberant attempt to redirect the attention to the things of the earth, his celebration of the transmuting power of the imagination as an active and enabling principle—all these contributed to the emotional coherence of *Harmonium*. How complete was Stevens's engagement in the rendering of this reality, how totally and adequately *Harmonium* represented what he had to say at a time especially conducive to his saying it, may be suggested by the fact that after its publication in 1923 he would not publish another poem for several years. How central to and representative of his poetic vision it was may be suggested by the fact that Stevens at one time thought his first volume should be entitled "THE GRAND POEM: PRELIMINARY MINUTIAE" (*LWS* 237–38).

When he resumed publication of his poetry, his productivity was prodigious. In addition to the revised edition of *Harmonium* (1931), he published five more volumes of verse—*Ideas of Order* (1936), *The Man with the Blue Guitar* (1937), *Parts of a World* (1942), *Transport to Summer* (1947), and *Auroras of Autumn* (1950)—and *The Collected Poems* (1950) included a final section entitled "The Rock" that amounted to yet another volume of poetry. But whether the Stevens corpus constitutes such an integrated poetic whole, as some have argued,[1] is a question unrelated to our concerns here. More pertinent is the fact that a continuity of Stevens's poetic vision is discernible throughout the poet's career, not as overarching aesthetic achievement, but as a familiar and abiding habit of mind. He found in later years that the substance of his objections to a neo-Lamarckian "blind Creator" (*CP* 97) (indifferent to the creative acts of individuals), as they had been expressed in an early poem like "Negation," might be transferred to a Marxist social utopianism and that logical positivists, rather than Spencerian naturalists, had become an anathema to the creative imagination. In 1948, he observed that "a generation ago we should have said that the imagination is an aspect of the conflict between man and nature. Today we are more likely to say that it is an aspect of the conflict between man and organized society" (*NA* 150). And he addressed in poetic as well as expository detail the nature of this conflict.

But Stevens was temperamentally, and somewhat romantically, disposed to retain a livelier interest in the earlier conflict between humanity and nature. He recorded an especially interesting self-assessment of his private difficulty with the times when he wrote in *Adagia*, "Life is an affair of people not of places. But for me life is an affair of places and that is the trouble" (*Opus* 158). The conflict of the individual living in a natural habitat, rather than the citizen functioning under political arrangements, continued to possess Stevens's most enduring interest. He complained that "Marx has ruined nature," yet he would append to this remark his skepticism—he has ruined it only "for the moment" (*CP* 134)—and Stevens persisted in his disposition to "live by leaves" (*CP* 134). If the poet's concerns and complaints varied and his rhetoric acquired an argumentative edge over the years, if he became more conspicuously a poet of ideas, his fundamental poetic vision did not alter significantly: he remained a poet of the earth whose worldview had been forged under the favorable influences of William James and, more significantly, of Henri Bergson.

How profoundly and permanently Bergsonism affected Stevens's poetics and how completely his response epitomizes the influence Bergson had upon American artists may be discerned most succinctly and clearly by an examination of his prose statements about poetry and the imagination. Through an examination of Stevens's theory of poetry, we may form a consolidated view of his later work and, as well, sketch the contours of his poetic achievement. Most of these statements were delivered as public lectures and written without intention to publish them as essays. Nevertheless, most were published in journals, and Stevens eventually acceded to the request to collect several of them in a book. A poet's feelings about what constitutes poetry as these are expressed in individual poems, he would insist in the introduction to that book—*The Necessary Angel: Essays on Reality and the Imagination* (1951)—are finally the disclosures of poetry, "not disclosures of definitions of poetry." The essays in this volume are, by contrast, "intended to disclose definitions of poetry" (*NA* vii). Stevens modestly denied that the essays in *The Necessary Angel* were criticism or philosophy; instead he deemed them literary "pages." Indeed, they neither answer to the evaluative function of criticism nor to the systematic rigor of philosophy. But these essays, along with those later published in *Opus Posthumous* and the succinct statements of *Adagia*, reveal Stevens's maturest thinking about the nature and function of poetry and the imagination.

Whatever else these "pages" may reveal, what they ultimately disclose is a mind alert and devoted to the poetic enterprise as "one of the enlargements of life" (*NA* vii). Perhaps no artist has ever been more unjustly accused of hedonism or aestheticism than Wallace Stevens. Unlike a Yeats, say, or an Emily Dickinson, who strove to make, and largely succeeded in making, their lives poems, Stevens's strivings were directed toward the more general application of poetry to life itself.[2] Several of Stevens's adagia testify to this aspiration: "It is life that we are trying to get in poetry" (*Opus* 158). "Art, broadly, is the form of life or the sound or color of life. Considered as form (in the abstract) it is often indistinguishable from life itself" (*Opus* 158). "The theory of poetry is the theory of life" (*Opus* 178). These aphorisms argue, if such argument is needed, for Stevens's longstanding commitment to the belief recorded while still an undergraduate at Harvard that "art must fit with other things; it must be part of the system of the world" (*LWS* 24).

II

Art most significantly and profoundly fits in the larger system of things, insofar as it embodies and epitomizes the transforming power of the imagination, because the imagination is a faculty that functions in the larger operations of life. This was the explicit theme of Stevens's lecture on the "Imagination as Value," and he acknowledged there that the imagination plays a more important role in life than in arts and letters (*NA* 146). Nevertheless, if poetry has any intrinsic value it is just this—that it exemplifies the value of "imaginative activity that diffuses itself throughout our lives": "I say exemplify and not justify, because poetic value is an intuitional value and because intuitional values cannot be justified" (*NA* 149). They cannot be justified because only the reason could justify them, but the very nature of reason is to reify consciousness and to solidify impressions and translate them into concepts. The reason continually eclipses the intuition. Stevens would also claim, and for much the same reason, that the poem "reveals itself only to the ignorant man." The disclosures of poetry are disclosures of the irrational (that is, the intuitional) activity.

The most difficult and, to some extent, the foredefeated task of the poet is not to "sing jubilas at exact, accustomed times" (*CP* 398).

> the difficultest rigor is forthwith,
> On the image of what we see, to catch from that
>
> Irrational moment its unreasoning,
> As when the sun comes rising, when the sea
> Clears deeply, when the moon hangs on the wall
> Of heaven-haven. These are not things transformed.
> Yet we are shaken by them as if they were.
> We reason about them with a later reason.   [*CP* 398–99]

The art of poetry is, in short, the "art of perception" (*Opus* 191), and Stevens's repeated endorsements of the primacy and power of the imagination as a faculty are not so much special pleading as an effort to establish the epistemological basis of the poetic act for writer and reader alike. Poetry is a kind of mundane metaphysics available and valuable, in greater or lesser degree, to all. As such, poetry, or rather the imagination, is a part of life, for the imagination is the "sum of our faculties" (*NA* 61). In the routine of ordinary life, the intellect necessarily intervenes between the intuitive apprehension of things as they are in the fullness of duration (that irrational moment) and the real. Only the reason stands between the imagination and reality, and the two are engaged in an unrelenting "struggle" to possess the real (*NA* 41). For Stevens, this struggle has "heroic" aspects we seldom recognize. It may well be, he suggests, that in this perpetual combat "the spirit is at stake"; the loss of the imagination "may involve the loss of the world" (*NA* 141).

Stevens later in the same essay mollifies the dramatic opposition of imagination and reason when he writes "the imagination is the power that enables us to perceive the normal in the abnormal" (*NA* 153). The normal is that primary relation between humanity and the world; the abnormal is the excess of imaginative transformation that renews our capacity to see things as they are. The imagination in its lavishness returns one to a refreshed sense of the world, a world of the mind but nevertheless a world prior to the concepts and extrasensual postulates of reason. But in the last analysis, it is not possible to distinguish between the operations of reason and the operations of the imagination because they work in tandem:

> The truth seems to be that we live in concepts of the imagination before the reason has established them. If this is true, then reason is simply the methodizer of the imagination. It may be that the imagination is a miracle of logic and that its exquisite divinations are calculations beyond analysis, as the conclusions of the reason are calculations wholly within analysis. If so, one understands perfectly the remark that "in the service of love and imagination nothing can be too lavish, too sublime or too festive." In the statement that we live in concepts of the imagination before the reason has established them, the word "concepts" means concepts of normality. Further, the statement that the imagination is the power that enables us to perceive the normal in the abnormal is a form of repetition of this statement. One statement does not demonstrate the other. The two statements together imply that the instantaneous disclosures of living are disclosures of the normal. [*NA* 154]

This passage clearly reflects the Bergsonian epistemology. The intuitively apprehended world of flux and heterogeneous particularity is stabilized by the image. The intellect formalizes this image when it establishes concepts and, in so doing, delocalizes and eternalizes the perception. The intellect wrenches the self away from pure experience and inserts a socialized version of the world that is at once clichéd and ready-made. It is the all-too-human tendency to believe in reason's postulates at the expense of perception that Stevens sardonically dramatizes in the psychic poverty of the "anti-master-man" of "Landscape with Boat." The man who "wanted to see" denies perception in his yearning for the truth. Unable to recognize that the truth "lay where he thought," he is given to unceasing supposition: Truth had to be "supposed,"

> a thing supposed
> In a place supposed, a thing that he reached

In a place that he reached, by rejecting what he saw
And denying what he heard. He would arrive.
He had only not to live, to walk in the dark,
To be projected by one void into
Another.   [*CP* 242]

Stevens examines here the man's tendency to suppose—to substitute a transcendent and absolute reality for a perceived one and, thereby, to forfeit the claims of the normal and immanent for the promise of the rational but remote, the transcendentally secure but invisible. Ironically, the man is unable to suppose that he himself might be the truth, that the eye "played / Upon by clouds, the ear so magnified / By thunder" (*CP* 242) are truths. In his anxiousness to see, the anti-master-man denies perception itself.

The fate of the anti-master-man is no less than a "loss of the world." But if he is adrift in the nothingness of his own desire for the real, his is essentially a private loss. The operations of the imagination also have a public dimension that contributes to those social forms we commonly know as the rites and rituals and fashions of ordinary life—as, say, to give Stevens's own examples, a wedding, a baptism, a funeral (*NA* 145). These are the residual and familiar imaginative forms that have their origins in ancient fictions, but to the degree that their acceptance is familiar, habitual, and normalized, the loss is more general and imperceptible:

> Costume is an instance of imaginative life as social form. At the same time it is an instance of the acceptance of something incessantly abnormal by reducing it to the normal. It cannot be said that life as we live it from day to day wears an imaginative aspect. On the other hand, it can be said that the aspects of life as we live it from day to day conceals the imagination as social form.   [*NA* 146]

The socialized forms of the imagination make their appeal to, indeed shape, those socialized selves that obscure authentic fundamental selves suppressed by routine and habit. The availability of so-called normal life conceals a more general loss.

"Most men's lives are thrust upon them" (*NA* 147), wrote Stevens. They mechanically perform the routines of the ready-made and socially ordained. Bergson argued in *Time and Free Will* that consciousness prefers the conventionalized self, which is but a shadow of the fundamental self, because it is better adapted to the requirements of social life (*TFW* 128).

This second self is the result of our tendency to substitute the symbol for reality and to cultivate attendant sensorimotor reactions, and little by little we become divided and lose sight of that deep-seated self wherein resides our capacity for freedom. Stevens described the origins of the divided self in his own terms in "An Ordinary Evening in New Haven":

> Why, then, inquire
> Who has divided the world, what entrepreneur?
> No man. The self, the chrysalis of all men
>
> Became divided in the leisure of blue day
> And more, in branchings after day. One part
> Held fast tenaciously in common earth
>
> And one from central earth to central sky
> And in moonlit extensions of them in the mind
> Searched out such majesty as it could find.   [CP 468–69]

The intellect claimed the sky, the transcendent and absolute, as its realm; the intuition held fast to the unreasoning and earthly reality of duration. The self of intuition, the *moi fondamentale*, though obscured, is nevertheless constantly present to consciousness and exists as the whole of human memory. Of that fundamental self, Stevens wrote variously and to diverse ends throughout his life. It is the "sub-man" of "Sombre Figuration," an "anti-logician," the "man below" who imagines the truth (*Opus* 66); or it is the "sibyl" of the self in "The Sail of Ulysses," a "true creator," a "luminous companion" (*Opus* 100); it is the interior paramour of "Final Soliloquy of the Interior Paramour," "a light, a power, the miraculous influence" (*CP* 524); it is implicit in Crispin's recognition that "shrewd noviates / Should be the clerks of our experience" (*CP* 39).

In the expressions of this fundamental self, one finds the sources of poetry, but also the resources of freedom and hope. Free acts, argued Bergson, occur when they express the whole of personality, "when they have that indefinable resemblance to it that one sometimes finds between the artist and his work" (*TFW* 172). The source of art, then, is located in the soul, and the efforts of art are, like the metaphysical efforts of philosophy, so many attempts to consult the interior voice of intuition. Thus it is that Crispin became an "introspective voyager," confronting at last the "veritable ding an sich," "free / From the unavoidable shadow of himself" (*CP* 29); or, again echoing the language of Bergson, Stevens has the man with the blue guitar declare, "Nothing must stand / Between you and the shapes you take / When the crust of shape has been destroyed" (*CP* 183). Yet for the imagination to break through the crust of the conventional is unavailing because the poem is always limited by its connotative possibilities. Language, like number, intervenes between the imagination and reality because it is the symbolic substitute for things as they are experienced in pure duration. The man with the blue guitar may throw away the "definitions" and repudiate the "rotted names" (*CP* 183), but as a poet he can never bring things "quite round" and give us "things as they are." In "Notes toward a Supreme Fiction," Stevens wonders whether the poet ought speak his own "gibberish" or that of the masses. Is he the speaker

> Of a speech only a little of the tongue?
> It is the gibberish of the vulgate that he seeks.
> He tries by a peculiar speech to speak
>
> The peculiar potency of the general
> To compound the imagination's Latin with
> The lingua franca et jocundissima.   [*CP* 397]

Faced, on the one hand, with the recognition of the insufficiency of language to express the real and, on the other, with an insistent desire to compose experience (a "Blessed rage for order" [*CP* 130]), the poet's dilemma is that of finding voice at all. Stevens's means were extreme. He used language with a lexical precision often mistaken for gaudiness and pretense,[3] but he was driven also to the sheerest invention, to Whitmanesque neologism, or, at times, to exultant sound, to the mere noise of "Ohoyaho, / Ohoo . . . " or "rattapallax." These strivings represent the poet's imaginative attempts at a communication beyond the words out of which his poems are built. "There is always an analogy between nature and the imagination," Stevens argued in "Effects of Analogy," "and possibly poetry is merely the strange rhetoric of that parallel: a rhetoric in which the feeling of one man is communicated to another in words of the exquisite appositeness that takes away all their verbality" (*NA* 118).

The strange rhetoric of poetry may send us to that ineffable first syllable that constitutes, in Emerson's phrase, "an original relation" with the universe. It sends us to the gods that are but our projections upon the world —"Phoebus was / A name for something that never could be named" (*CP* 381)—and beyond them to the mind itself, to the source of our human fictions in the imagination:

The poem refreshes life so that we share
For a moment, the first idea. . . . It satisfies
Belief in an immaculate beginning

And sends us winged, by an unconscious will,
To an immaculate end.   [*CP* 382]

The poem does this through the resources of suggestion, not expression.
The power of art, its priority over nature, resides in its power to suggest
feelings whereas nature is restricted to merely expressing them, argued
Bergson. "The poet is he with whom feelings develop into images, and
the images themselves into words which translate them while obeying the
laws of rhythm. In seeing these images pass before our eyes, we in our
turn experience the feeling which was, so to speak, their emotional equivalent" (*TFW* 15). Surely Stevens had this notion of the creative process, or
something like it, in mind when he copied in his commonplace book this
passage from W. G. Moore's book on Molière: "And in comedy, as in
other forms of poetry, suggestion is enough."[4]

The poetic translation of feelings is what Stevens sometimes termed
"rhetoric"—that portion added to experience that arrests and arranges
change. He wrote in "Add This to Rhetoric":

In the way you speak
You arrange, the thing is posed,
What in nature merely grows.   [*CP* 198]

Nature's changes outlast such posings, however. Tomorrow the sun comes
up as itself, and "Your images will have left / No shadow of themselves."
What is left to artists is not nature as such—though they must return to it
again and again for their subjects because it is the world in which they
move and breathe—but their sense of the world. Thus the poet may
conclude his poem:

The sense creates the pose.
In this it moves and speaks.
This is the figure and not
An evading metaphor.   [*CP* 199]

An authentic sense of the world is the only true source of poetry; it is an
attitude characterized not so much by idiosyncrasy or iconoclasm as by
natural disposition. Bergson observed in *Le Rire* that nature from time to
time spawns artists, men and women who are "detached" from life. The

term is somewhat misleading for it is meant to connote a "virginal" gift of perception that is immune to the tendency to read the labels of the world or to filter perception according to the immediate practical interests of life. Bergson is actually identifying the naïveté of the artistic attitude, free from custom and convention, rather than the subjectivism science so meticulously avoids. With this understanding, Stevens may claim at once that "poetry is not personal" (*Opus* 159) and that "poetry is a process of the personality of the poet" (*NA* 45). There is no real contradiction involved in these two statements. The composing of one's experience in artistic form involves an externalization and a distancing from the immediate interests of life. This very detachment enables the artist to summon the whole of memory, which is ever present and constitutes the authentic self, and to notice resemblance and difference, free from those natural selections of memory that bear upon immediate perception and individual interest. Poems are as so many extrusions that originate from the poet's feelings and perceptions but are nevertheless impersonal. Bergson's statement also helps to explain why Stevens claims that "poets are born not made" (*NA* 122) and, elsewhere, that poets may be viewed as "biological mechanisms" (*NA* 120).[5]

To recognize Stevens's conviction that the imagination and the real interpenetrate and are interdependent, and that though we act in the world we nevertheless live in the mind, is to recognize the psychological dimensions of Stevens's art as they are integrated with matters of perception and expression. In "The Noble Rider and the Sound of Words," Stevens cites first a passage from Bergson about the effects of memory upon mistakenly termed "stable" internal states. Even in the most straight-jacketed perception of an object, the vision of that object alters because "my memory is there, which conveys something of the past into the present" (*NA* 25). Stevens then cites C. E. M. Joad's comment on the passage that extends Bergson's observation into the external realm of physical reality. "How, then," asks Joad somewhat skeptically, "does the world come to appear to us as a collection of solid, static objects extended in space? Because of the intellect which presents us with a false view of it" (*NA* 25). Stevens seems to be expressing a greater interest in the internal and essentially humanistic province that Bergson describes when he responds to the passage from Joad: "The subject matter of poetry is not that 'collection of solid, static objects extended in space' but the life that is lived in the scene it composes; and so reality is not that external scene but the life that is lived in it. Reality is things as they are" (*NA* 25).

Nowhere else is Stevens more explicit about the concerns of poetry or about his adherence to the Bergsonian conception of the real as a blending of the memory with present perception. In another lecture, he would note that "we never see the world except for the moment after. Thus we are constantly observing the past" (*Opus* 190). So conceived, the world instantly becomes "immaterial": "It has become an image of the mind. . . . What we see is not an external world but an image of it and hence an internal world" (*Opus* 191). Imagination and memory work in concert (indeed, in a way they are indistinguishable), but the activities of both enable us not only to recover the world but to live in it. In ordinary living, the memory is consulted always with an eye toward future action upon matter, but in art, one learns to value the useless and to face reality directly. Yet the artistic imagination participates in the same power of the imagination applied to the business of life. Within us is an "operative force," a "constructive faculty" (Stevens might have said an élan vital) "that derives its energy more from the imagination than from the sensibility" (*NA* 164). This force "retains experience" and "makes its own constructions out of that experience"—in other words, it creates a world that we may inhabit.

One need not rehearse the Bergsonian epistemological position to reveal the parallels (more, the restatement) of that position in Stevens's aesthetic. Unlike the associationist psychology, the psychology of James and Bergson insisted that consciousness has a sensory content manifested as an image that is at once private and coherent; the operations of the human psyche cannot be reduced to the association of ideas. Our thoughts, argued James, are of "things," not "ideas."[6] The blendings of past and present are projected into an indeterminate future—they are imagined. The most authentic and free of these projections issue from a fundamental self (which is nothing less than the whole of human memory present at every moment), uncodified, unnormalized. Thus, Stevens may write these lines in "Sombre Figuration" from "Owl's Clover":

The man below beholds the portent poised,
An image of his making, beyond the eye. . . .
The future must bear within it every past. . . .
The portent may itself be memory;
And memory may itself be time to come,
And must be, when the portent, changed, takes on
A mask up-gathered brilliantly from the dirt.   [*Opus* 69–70]

Or these in "Like Decorations in a Nigger Cemetery":

> If ever the search for a tranquil belief should end,
> The future might stop emerging out of the past,
> Out of what is full of us; yet the search
> And the future emerging out of us seem to be one.   [*CP* 151]

The future, or the "possible," is a "mirage" (*CM* 119) of the present in the past. Nevertheless, the future constitutes an indispensable part of the contents of consciousness. For this reason, among others, Bergson might separate himself from associationists and determinists alike and argue that evolution is creative. Moreover, the image has experiential priority over the concept (whether that concept be expressed as word or number). And the image that consciousness holds before it has a sensory content that does not eclipse the real; it is the real.

Reality, in other words, is "abstracted" from perception. The word *abstract* is an important term in Stevens's poetic, and he most often uses it in its radical sense of to draw from or to separate. The relation of this notion to Stevens's poetic theory as a form of metaphysics and to matters of perception and expression may be further clarified by Arthur Szathmary's comments on Bergson's theory of art and its relation to philosophy:

> The emphasis upon immediate intuition does not mean, however, that philosophy is to dispense with abstractions. Bergson has realized fully that our thought proceeds naturally by a series of abstraction from presented objects. He wishes to insist, nevertheless, upon the recognitions of such derivations as abstractions. It is just this recognition which the aesthetic approach will offer to philosophy. The artist, for example, starts with what we may term "first abstractions." He tries to make these first abstractions coincide as much as possible with the actual presentations before him—to make them "real abstractions." Such a process involves rigor and accuracy of observation; and such a process should be native to philosophy as well as to art.[7]

Ultimately, Bergson believed, philosophy, properly practiced, would exceed the arts in legitimate metaphysics. Stevens, on the other hand, was to assert that poetry was finally superior to both science and philosophy, not only in enabling us to live our lives, but in providing metaphysical insight into the real.

Only with this special understanding of abstraction may one appreciate the fact that the first note in "Notes toward a Supreme Fiction" is that "*It Must Be Abstract.*" "The first idea," Stevens asserts in that section of the poem, "is an imagined thing" (*CP* 387), and as such, the imagination establishes itself as the agent that cuts through false abstraction and renders by suggestion and music an immediate apprehension of reality. Such renderings are typically partial, but as he noted in "The Ultimate Poem Is Abstract," they nevertheless avoid the "cloud pole / Of communication" offered by an intellect that pretends to be "present / Everywhere in space at once" (*CP* 430).

Parts of a World, as the title indicates, is a volume that predominantly deals with the artistic forms of abstraction. Poems, such as "Extracts from Addresses to the Academy of Fine Ideas," "The Well Dressed Man with a Beard," or "Woman Looking at a Vase of Flowers," treat of "parts" of the world, the local habitation of an abstraction that is not everywhere in space at once. "Contrary Theses (II)" explicitly renders a version of a Wordsworthian spot of time without the accompanying transcendent explanation. In this poem, a man walks one autumn afternoon carrying his one-year-old boy upon his shoulders.[8] He searches for a "final refuge" from the onset of winter and from the martyrdom of enduring patience. What he finds instead, happens upon really, is "An abstract, of which the sun, the dog, the boy / Were contours."

> The abstract was suddenly there and gone again.
> The negroes were playing football in the park.
> The abstract that he saw, like the locust-leaves, plainly:
>
> The premiss from which all things were conclusions,
> The noble, Alexandrine verve. The flies
> And the bees still sought the chrysanthemums' odor.   [*CP* 270]

Stevens's thesis is contrary because it goes against the conventional notion of abstraction as general precept applicable broadcast to a multitude of occasions and manifestations of the real. The man's experience of this abstract is tied to the conditions of experience and not separable from them. Stevens poeticizes another abstract moment in a very late poem, "Reality Is an Activity of the Most August Imagination." He observes on an evening's drive home "the visible transformations of summer night." The moment is

> An argentine abstraction approaching form
> And suddenly denying itself away.

There was an insolid billowing of the solid.
Night's moonlight lake was neither water nor air.   [*Opus* 110–11]

All this is to say, as Stevens himself says in "An Ordinary Evening in New Haven," that

The poem is the cry of its occasion,
Part of the res itself and not about it.
The poet speaks the poem as it is,

Not as it was.   [*CP* 473]

At such privileged moments (those moments when, according to Bergson, the interposing veil between the artist and reality is lifted), a whole relation between men and women and their world is established. At such moments, even the swirling leaves resemble the "presences of thought, as if,"

In the end, in the whole psychology, the self,
The town, the weather, in a casual litter,
Together, said words of the world are the life of the world. [*CP* 474]

Still, the presences of thought and the life of the world are at best coordinated resemblances. And this fact points to another dimension of the psychology of Stevens's art.

We have earlier alluded to the psychology of resemblance as part and parcel of Stevens's poetic. Nevertheless, to elaborate upon this psychology (endorsed with some slight differences by both James and Bergson) is appropriate here, for it is to be distinguished from a nineteenth-century associationist psychology, from Freudianism—which Stevens thought inimical to poetry[9]—and from twentieth-century phenomenology.[10] Two of Stevens's lectures ("Three Academic Pieces" and "Effects of Analogy") undertake to clarify the relation of poetry to reality through an examination of resemblance as "one of the significant components of the structure of reality" (*NA* 71). As such, these lectures represent further attempts to have poetry "fit" with the system of the world.

Indeed, Stevens's wish to integrate poetry with a larger system became increasingly confident and ambitious over the years. It was, and is, a bold assertion he made in 1947 at Harvard in his lecture "Three Academic Pieces" when he said that "the structure of poetry and the structure of reality are one or, in effect, that poetry and reality are one, or should be" (*NA* 81). He could make this claim because he was convinced that human reality is substantively metaphoric. Resemblance "binds together" reality; it is the "base of appearance" (NA 72) and therefore constitutes the world in which we will and act. A world of resemblance is, in a sense, our fated condition because it betrays the most fundamental way we may attempt to know and understand our universe directly.

Stevens is careful to distinguish between resemblance and identity, on the one hand, and resemblance and imitation, on the other. Identity, as one might expect, is for Stevens a delusion; it is essentially the "vanishing-point" of resemblance (NA 72). His reason for making this claim is explicit—nature is never identical with itself. "Nature is not mechanical," he insists. Its things and events are multiform and unique: "Its prodigy is not identity but resemblance and its universe of reproduction is not an assembly line but an incessant creation. Because this is so in nature, it is so in metaphor" (NA 73). This view, we recognize, derives its intellectual force from the argument of *Creative Evolution*. Resemblance is not imitation because imitation, even as it announces its failure, presupposes a correspondence theory of truth. Imitation is nothing more than "identity manqué" (NA 73).

Stevens makes further discriminations in the essay. There is a level of resemblance "which is the level of nature" (NA 73), by which he seems to mean that there is a natural mode of resemblance invoked to insure survival and expedient action in the world. But in metaphor, no such level exists because that would delimit the possibilities of the imagination, and the imagination cannot be so limited. The activity of resemblance in nature, as Bergson several times explained, has as its constant aim a biological utility (MM 206). A cow vaguely discerns the resemblance of grass in one meadow to that in another according to sensorimotor mechanisms. The faculty for dissociation, for discerning in sensory details differences and peculiarities as well as unexpected similarities, is, by contrast, reserved for the higher animals (MM 205). For the most part, human beings too perceive resemblance according to practical need and emotional tendency, but the artist has the privilege of valuing the useless. That does not mean that art is useless, however. Quite the contrary.

There is a natural desire for resemblance, a desire poetry satisfies (NA 77), but this tendency has two extreme forms in our mental life. The first is practicality itself. The mind detects analogues in experience; it stiffens memory images and converts them into the ready-made, makes of them motor habits that are stored up and available for future action (MM 214–16). The second approaches the level of dream. On this plane, where consciousness is removed from the realm of action, perception is at once more detached and more personal; for, since anything may in one way or another resemble any other thing, the whole of human memory is evoked and seeks to attach and enlarge itself, in all of its particularity, in the present (*MM* 218–24). William James makes a related observation in his *Principles of Psychology* when he says that *"minds of genius may be divided into two main sorts, those who notice the bond* [of resemblance] *and those who merely obey it."*[11] To this second class belong the poets and artists, those men and women of intuitions. Gertrude Stein, who had studied under James, was such an artist. She had an acute ear for the resemblances of common speech and discerned in it the "rhythm of anybody's personality": "If listening was talking and talking was listening then and at the same time any little movement any little expression was a resemblance, and a resemblance was something that presupposed remembering."[12]

Stevens's manner was very different from Stein's, but surely he had these sorts of discriminations in mind when he argued the preeminent value of poetry, though he likely derived them more immediately from his reading of Charles Mauron's *Aesthetics and Psychology*[13] than from Bergson or James. If poetry accomplished nothing more than satisfying our desire for resemblance, the poet's significance would be common, and poetry would not provide any greater satisfaction than many other things. However, argued Stevens, the poet accomplishes a great deal more: The "singularity" of poetry is that "in the act of satisfying the desire for resemblance it touches the sense of reality, it enhances the sense of reality, heightens it, intensifies it" (*NA* 77). This is but another way of saying what Bergson said in "The Perception of Change," that "the poet is a revealing agent" (*CM* 159). The poet enlarges and deepens our consciousness of the real, and that, according to Bergson, should be the proper aim of philosophy. Suppose philosophy, like the arts, were to plunge into perception of the real with the purpose of expanding our vision of things; what would be the result? "To the multiplicity of systems contending with one another armed with different concepts, would succeed the unity of a doctrine capable of reconciling all thinkers in the same perception—a perception which moreover would grow ever larger, thanks to the combined efforts of philosophers in a common direction" (*CM* 158–59).

Stevens reserves for poetry the province Bergson urges upon philosophers. The poet, not the philosopher, may unite us in a common perception, for poetry adds its inimitable voice to reality that the unreal may become the real: "What our eyes behold may well be the text of life but one's meditations on the text and the disclosures of these meditations are no less a part of the structure of reality" (*NA* 76). That structure is literally an "adult make-believe" (*NA* 75). The poetry of earth begins at that point of contact with the real where connotation, resemblance, appositiveness, and ambiguity abide. The point where the objects of our perception may be extended and enlarged by metaphor is the "point at which ambiguity has been reached. The ambiguity that is so favorable to the poetic mind is precisely the ambiguity favorable to resemblance" (*NA* 79).

A "gradus ad Metaphoram" (*NA* 81) reaches toward perfection and touches poetry at its source. The terminus of this process, of course, is that Supreme Fiction we call God.[14] Perhaps, suggested Stevens in a tone more tentative that he probably felt, it is not too extravagant to think of "resemblances and the repetitions of resemblances as the source of the ideal" (*NA* 81). If so, it is vain to think that we have outlived the ideal. "The truth is that we are constantly outliving it and yet the ideal itself remains alive with an enormous life" (*NA* 82).

By way of collateral argument, Stevens chose to read two poems after his lecture. These are the second and third of his three "academic" pieces and, therefore, enjoy the status of argument. In the first, "Someone Puts a Pineapple Together," a man contemplates, by way of a particular pineapple, "a wholly artificial nature, in which / The profusion of metaphor has been increased" (*NA* 83).[15] The poem records the mental and emotional transactions attendant to this imaginative act, and the result is something of a program for the imagination. The man must "say nothing of the fruit that is / Not true, nor think it less. He must defy / The metaphor that murders metaphor" (*NA* 84). That is to say, as Stevens himself said in one of his adagia, "There is no such thing as a metaphor of a metaphor. . . . reality is the indispensable element in each metaphor" (*Opus* 179). The man must recognize the pineapple as a tangent of himself, "of human residence" (*NA* 84). If he would resist "false metaphor" (*NA* 83), then he might conceive at least a dozen true ways to put a pineapple together. The twelve numbered metaphors for the pineapple that Stevens supplies in the poem are "casual exfoliations" of "the tropic of resemblance," "Apposites, to the slightest edge, of the whole / Undescribed composition of the sugar cone" (*NA* 86). The pineapple on the table, in all its metaphoric possibilities, is "everybody's world." "Here the total artifice reveals itself / As the total reality" (*NA* 87).

If the first poem comments upon the desire for resemblance as a common property of our mental life, the second, "Of Ideal Time and Choice," serves as a footnote to Stevens's statement that we might think of "resemblances and the repetitions of resemblances as the source of the ideal." Thirty mornings are required to make the day we desired because the repetitions of resemblance allow us to imagine a "day of blank, blue wheels." Thirty summers for "counting and remembering" are needed to "fill the earth with young men centuries old" (*NA* 88), men who have displaced the unique possibilities of life with the formulas of the habitual and clichéd. They are old and lack vitality because "what they have chosen is their choice / No more and because they lack the will to tell / A matin gold from gold of Hesperus" (*NA* 88). In a way, they are old because they have seen it all before and therefore see nothing any more; they lack the imaginative power to discern similarity and difference in the details of experience. From repeated and remembered experiences, which resemble one another but are neither identical nor imitate a transcendent time or place, emerges the "pale pole of resemblances / Experienced yet not well seen" (*NA* 88). The ideal time and choice are abstracted from life's desires and disappointments and derived from repeated analogous experience. Who shall speak and celebrate "thought's compromise, resolved / At last, the center of resemblance found / Under the bones of time's philosophers?," asks Stevens (*NA* 89). The answer, by implication, is the poet. The poet will serve as that orator of the ideal: "The orator will say that we ourselves / Stand at the center of ideal time, / The inhuman making choice of a human self" (*NA* 89).

The source of the ideal is the source of poetry, but the ideal is a common enough wish. It is the desire of the man in "This Solitude of Cataracts" who "wanted his heart to stop beating and his mind to rest / In a permanent realization" (*CP* 425). This man wanted just once to know how it would feel to be a "bronze man," "Breathing his bronzen breath at the azury centre of time" (*CP* 425). It is the desire for final belief in "Asides on the Oboe," though one knows that final belief "Must be a fiction," as much a fiction as the belief in the "impossible possible philosopher's man" whom we project (*CP* 250). It is the proposal of "The Pure Good of Theory." Time may be "a horse that runs in the heart, a horse / Without a rider on a road at night" (*CP* 329). To retard the battering of time, we may propose "A large-sculptured, platonic person, free from time." This form then may mature, and "A capable being may replace / Dark horse" (*CP* 330). And we may believe in him, for "the desire to believe in a metaphor" is "to stick to the nicer knowledge of / Belief, that what it believes in is not true" (*CP* 332). The human capacity to extrapolate the ideal from resemblance and the repetition of resemblance is the revelation of "The Man on the Dump," who recognizes that

> Between that disgust and this, between the things
> That are on the dump (azaleas and so on)
> And those that will be (azaleas and so on),
> One feels the purifying change. One rejects
> The trash.   [*CP* 202]

To believe and to know that what one believes is not true is the nicer knowledge of resemblance and metaphor. It is belief in the impossible ideal that prevents us from becoming so absolutely what we are.

In 1948, one year after delivering "Three Academic Pieces," Stevens read the lecture "Effects of Analogy" at Yale. It is a less ponderous effort than "Three Academic Pieces," though it concludes by making the same sort of overarching claims for poetry's relation to life. The writings of great poets are but analogies forged out of their sense of the world, he contended. Their poems are the "pictorializations of men, for whom the world exists as a world and for whom life exists as life, the objects of their passions, the objects before which they come and speak, with intense choosing, words that we remember and make our own. Their words have made a world that transcends the world and a life livable in that transcendence" (*NA* 129–30). This is but a restatement of the conviction in "Someone Puts a Pineapple Together" that the "incredible" has its own truth and that "the incredible gives him a purpose to believe" (*NA* 85).

The more immediate intention of the lecture was less grandiose, however—it meant to examine the effects of analogy and by that examination to disclose the fact that poetry is "almost incredibly one of the effects of analogy" (*NA* 117)—and its assumptions are likewise grounded in a psychology of resemblance. From his analysis of lines from John Bunyan, Jean de La Fontaine, Virgil, Allen Tate, St. Matthew, and others, Stevens derives three generalizations about analogy: that "every image is the elaboration of a particular of the subject of the image" (*NA* 127), that "every image is a restatement of the subject of the image in the terms of an attitude" (*NA* 128), and that "every image is an intervention on the part of the image-maker" (*NA* 128).

Together, these two essays, in their subtlety and relative rigor and straightforwardness, answer to the self-criticism delivered in "An Ordinary Evening in New Haven." "A more severe"

More harassing master would extemporize
Subtler, more urgent proof that the theory
Of poetry is the theory of life,

As it is, in the intricate evasions of as,
In things seen and unseen, created from nothingness,
The heavens, the hells, the worlds, the longed-for
    lands.   [*CP* 486]

Yet, as Stevens recognized, poetry is not the place for the sort of severity and proof that would define poetry. The disclosures of poetry are not the disclosures of definitions of poetry. "Effects of Analogy" yielded perhaps the most adequate definition of poetry of any of Stevens's prose statements on that subject: "Poetry becomes and is a transcendent analogue composed of the particulars of reality, created by the poet's sense of the world, that is to say, his attitude, as he intervenes and interposes the appearances of that sense" (*NA* 130).

The appearances of the poet's sense of the world are to be located in the proliferation of metaphors as they are generated out of the poet's contact with and attitude toward reality. The world exists as world, in all of its lavishness and brute facticity; the poet's analogies do not displace that world, they add to it. For as Stevens noted in *Adagia*, "To be at the end of a fact is not to be at the beginning of imagination but it is to be at the end of both" (*Opus* 175). We must turn our facts into fiction in order to possess them, and the metaphors of Stevens's poetry are attempts to possess and repossess the world. Yet were one, however improbably, to discount the metaphoric quality of his verse, one would still be struck by how replete with the "intricate evasions of as" is Stevens's verse. One need only glance at the concordance of his poetry to establish the fact—there are nearly seven hundred entries for the word *as* and over five hundred for *like*. Clearly, he meant for his poetry to attain to a kind of Bergsonian metaphysics—an unofficial metaphysics, to be sure, but one that attended as closely as possible to experience, attempted through appositiveness to reach beyond the limits of "verbality," and sought to create a poetry supremely useful to life as it is lived.

The interests of life and of nature provide a common ground where poet and poetry, reader and writer, fit within the larger operations of the world. In "Academic Discourse in Havana," Stevens identifies the poet's function as something more than to "stuff the ear" with the music.

As a part of nature he is part of us.
His rarities are ours: may they be fit
And reconcile us to our selves in those
True reconcilings, dark, pacific words,
And the adroiter harmonies of their fall.   [*CP* 144]

If nature has, by "lucky accident" (*CM* 162), produced the poet, it is to nature—nature not exclusively as subject matter but also as biological organization and organic impulse—that the poet is finally responsible; for it is nature, and life, that underwrites the poet's existence and defines the poet's function.

So little has been made of the biological aspects of Stevens's poetics that perhaps I may, without objection, risk stating the obvious. When Stevens declared that poets are born not made, he was being neither evasive nor wry, nor was he invoking poetic license. Rather, he was identifying a biological and philosophical justification for the significance of the poet. In 1942, he attempted to clarify that role in the concluding section of his lecture, "The Noble Rider and the Sound of Words."

The poet is under neither moral nor social obligation; poetry is called forth by the pressure of the contemporaneous, but that pressure does not constitute social responsibility: "the all-commanding subject-matter of poetry is life, the never-ceasing source. But it is not a social obligation," Stevens wrote (*NA* 25). Rather, the poet's function is to make his imagination "the light in the minds of others. His role, in short, is to help people live their lives" (*NA* 29). How the poet accomplishes this Stevens expresses through several aphorisms. Those aphorisms are: "That the artist transforms us into epicures; that he has to discover the possible work of art in the real world, then to extract it, when he does not himself compose it entirely; that he is *un amoureux perpétuel* of the world that he contemplates and thereby enriches; that art sets out to express the human soul; and finally that everything like a firm grasp of reality is eliminated from the aesthetic field" (*NA* 30).

Stevens realizes that these generalizations may be interpreted as so many characterizations of poetry as a form of escapism. Indeed, he, like Cather, insists that the poetic process is an "escapist process" (*NA* 30). Stevens adds that escapism is a pejorative term only when the poet is not attached to reality. "Life," he observed in *Adagia*, "is the elimination of what is dead" (*Opus* 169); the elimination of a firm grasp of reality from the aesthetic field, he seems to be saying, is an analogous activity. In other words, life (and poetry) continually escapes from the already made into the being made, from being to becoming, through creative evolution and imaginative transformation. That there should be no mistake on this point, Stevens returns in his lecture to the passage he had cited earlier from Joad that the world is but a collection of "solid, static objects extended in space." Such a conception of the world is impoverishing and exerts but a "mournful power" over the soul. If, however,

we hear a different and familiar description of the place:

This City now doth, like a garment, wear
The beauty of the morning, silent[,] bare,
Ships, towers, domes, theatres, and temples lie
Open unto the fields, and to the sky;
All bright and glittering in the smokeless air;

if we have this experience, we know how poets help people live their lives. [*NA* 31]

The transfigurations of the poet, as they are so self-evidently disclosed in these lines from Wordsworth, are neither evasions nor adornment. The imagination, like the spirit, resists the coercions of the ready-made and the pressures of reality. Its resistance is a violence from within, a violence that "protects us from the violence from without. It is the imagination pressing back against the pressure of reality. It seems, in the last analysis, to have something to do with our self-preservation" (*NA* 36). "Self-preservation" is here meant in the evolutionary sense.[16]

Stevens characterizes the imagination as a somewhat more benign force in another lecture. The imagination may be viewed as a power within the poet "not so much to destroy reality at will as to put it to his own use. He comes to feel that his imagination is not wholly his own but that it may be part of a much larger, much more potent imagination, which it is his affair to get at" (*NA* 115). That more potent imagination is the poetic equivalent of the unitary, primordial life impetus, and this, according to Stevens, is the sort of imaginative power Valéry cultivated as he attempted to live on the "verge of consciousness." This larger imagination is also analogous to Jung's collective unconscious, and Jung himself recognized the affinities between his theories and Bergson's élan vital.[17] To participate in a larger and more potent imagination is to at least suspect, as Stevens expressed it in "Final Soliloquy of the Interior Paramour," that "God and the Imagination are one" (*CP* 524). It is to feel the strength of the "Latest Freed Man" who, having attained to the "centre of reality," finds the "ant of the self changed to an ox / With its organic boomings" (*CP* 205). The puny individual, joined to a creative power that lives and moves in all organic becoming, prolongs a large and living past and propels it into the future. To identify God with the imagination is not simply to say that God is a Supreme Fiction; it is also to maintain that the imagination participates in and is actuated by a larger life force. It is to say as well that the imagination as it is realized in poetry—a poetry that celebrates a god even as it creates that god—needed what it had created (*NA* 51), that the ecstasy of the poem that accomplishes its purpose is, in its own way and to a significant degree, a sanctifying act.

Stevens establishes this connection even more explicitly in "The Figure of the Youth as Virile Poet" (1943). Poetry is a matter of nerves and feeling, he argues. Poets are born not made; poetry is their inheritance and their vocation. They possess a certain type of consciousness that implicates them in a "technical destiny," a "vocation of mind" (*NA* 48). The poet experiences in the accomplishment of the poem a metaphysical attainment, and Stevens cites Bergson's *The Two Sources of Morality and Religion* as providing a clue to the poet's feeling and an understanding of the transcendent significance of the creative process. The feelings of aspiration and liberation familiar to mystics and saints are familiar to the poet as well. Those men and women who have written their first essential poems are like the person looking in a mirror who has suddenly discovered in the reflected image an "unsuspected genealogy" (*NA* 50). They have discovered in their achievement a sudden liberation from the clichéd.

The power of the imagination works within each and all—"In the world of words, the imagination is one of the forces of nature" (*Opus* 170). A certain unaccountable "poetic energy" (*Opus* 219) produces the irrational element in poetry, for that energy drives beyond and through intellectual representations of the real to the intuitional knowledge of a world in flux. The resources of the imagination help men and women to slip the net of necessity. As such, the raw operations of the material world and the irrational transformations of the imagination absorb us in a mystery near at hand. "Your knowledge is irrational. In that sense life is mysterious; and if it is mysterious at all, I suppose that it is cosmically mysterious" (*Opus* 226).

This was something of a concession for Stevens to make since he was primarily interested in the irrational intuitions of the real as constant flux, not in discovering transcendent and absolute certainty. He had little patience with the mystical mind, and these vague intimations of an operant force in nature were as far as Stevens was willing to go in declaring himself in converse with a transcendent power.[18] Nevertheless, he wrote to Sister Beretta Quinn that he was not an "atheist," "although I do not believe to-day in the same God in whom I believed when I was a boy" (*LWS* 735). Stevens might have said what William Faulkner in fact did say—that the only sort of God that might command his belief is neither mechanical nor personal but "the most complete expression of mankind," "a deity very close to Bergson's."[19] Stevens was a poet of the earth, and his angel was of reality. In "Angels Surrounded by Paysans," he has that angel say,

I am one of you and being one of you
Is being and knowing what I am and know.

Yet I am the necessary angel of earth,
Since, in my sight, you see the earth again,

Cleared of its stiff and stubborn, man-locked set.   [*CP* 496–97]

Thus, too, he would record in *Adagia*, and in succession, these thoughts upon a power from within: "This world is myself. Life is myself." "God is in me or else is not at all (does not exist)." "The world is a force, not a presence" (*Opus* 172).

This last adage is of special interest because in his humorous and humanistic poem, "Saint John and the Back-Ache," he put in the mouth of Saint John the converse formulation. "The mind is the terriblest force in the world, father, / Because, in chief, it, only, can defend / Against itself," says the back-ache. Saint John replies, "The world is presence and not force. Presence is not mind" (*CP* 436). The poem is Stevens's own witty version of the philosopher's toothache, and it is clear from his own view recorded in *Adagia* that he meant John's otherworldly religiosity to appear slightly ridiculous. Saint John argues that presence (though it "fills the being before the mind can think") is delusion. A sudden color on the sea or the changes wrought upon the landscape by autumn are not "that big brushed green" or the unraveling of a "yellow shift" (*CP* 437). He claims to speak "below the tension of the lyre" and to reveal that earth's transitory beauties are not angels. Presence is the delusion of sense; our poetic and imaginative transformations are useful only insofar as "They help us face the dumbfounding abyss / Between us and the object, external cause." But the back-ache has the last word:

It may be, it may be. It is possible.
Presence lies far too deep, for me to know
Its irrational reaction, as from pain.   [*CP* 437]

The voice of the back-ache is the voice of an earthly pain that does not owe its existence as a felt quality to a presence or to an external cause. Pain (as any other intense affective sensation) is not, according to Bergson, the "inward echo of an outward cause" (*TFW* 34), because it prefigures and calls forth a resistance to an automatic reaction that might otherwise be destructive to life. Pain is interrupted action that allows us to avoid through choice the damages that would result should that action be pursued. Pain is, in a word, "nascent freedom" (*TFW* 34), nature's gift, if not its blessing, rather than nature's punishment. It allows the child to withdraw a finger from the candle's flame and to choose another possible action, rather than to follow out the motions of dangerous discovery. As with pain, the world beyond or beneath pure presence, prior to the image, is a biological force, not extrasensual substance.

The problem of pain in the larger context of evil as a part of the natural world called forth a different set of responses in the longer poem, "Esthétique du Mal." His broodings and disturbances there are more serious and, finally, pursued at the expense of the poem, the tone of which is irregular and somewhat anxious. Yet Stevens is able to make solid, even Whitmanesque, affirmations in his contemplation of suffering and death.[20] "The mortal no / Has its emptiness," it is true, but one must say yes at last "because under every no / Lay a passion for yes that had never been broken" (*CP* 320). This is a difficult position for the poet to adopt, for the spirit that endures suffering receives no personal redemption, finds its consolations only in a life that persists. Suffering might not be so grave if one knew that pain was not the punishment of life. Understanding "That he might suffer or that / He might die was the innocence of living, if life / Itself was innocent" (*CP* 322), might suffice; this consolation might finally be enough.

Those individuals whose suffering makes of their lives individual tragedies are but "secondary characters." They command our sympathy, but their tragedy is "fragmentary" "Within the universal whole":

> The son
> And the father alike and equally spent,
> Each one, by the necessity of being
> Himself, the unalterable necessity

Of being this unalterable animal.
This force of nature in action is the major
Tragedy. This is destiny unperplexed,
The happiest enemy.   [*CP* 324]

Such a condition, after all, may be transformed by the imagination. One
may establish a time to watch the "fire-feinting sea" and declare it good,
"The ultimate good." The "force that destroys us" may be endured; one
may feel with invigorating passion its "action moving in the blood" (*CP*
324).

Life may be a "bitter aspic" (*CP* 322), but it may also be an adventure of
the blood, a moving and living in the physical world. "The adventurer / In
humanity has not conceived of a race / Completely physical in a physical
world," Stevens wrote. This conception provides its own assurances, for
the "greatest poverty is not to live in a physical world" (*CP* 325). Such a
world, its evil notwithstanding, is a miracle. He had asked in an earlier
poem, "How can / We chant if we live in evil and afterward / Lie harshly
buried there?" His answer there had been the purely intellectual assurance
that "If earth dissolves / Its evil after death, it dissolves it while / We live"
(*CP* 259). His answer at the conclusion of "Esthétique du Mal" is more
deeply felt and more properly a chant:

One might have thought of sight, but who could
    think
Of what it sees, for all the evil it sees . . . ?
Of what one feels, who could have thought to make
So many selves, so many sensuous worlds,
As if the air, the mid-day air, was swarming
With the metaphysical changes that occur
Merely in living as and where we live.   [*CP* 326]

III

These several ingredients in Stevens's poetic combine and establish, at
least to the satisfaction of the poet, a unified vision of the role of the
imagination in modern life. Stevens's belief in an immanent world in
which a life force strives against material necessity and the pressures of
reality reveals and justifies the cultural, even biological, significance of the
role of the creative imagination in general and of the poet in particular.

The artist's participation in a comprehensive and more potent imagination connects him vitally to this impetus, allows Stevens at length to say that God and the imagination are one. He insisted that poetry emanates from the individual artist's sense of the world and that that sense is conveyed through the apposite and suggestive power of a language that reaches beyond the limitations of words and involves the poet in an unofficial metaphysics. This insistence, as I have argued, was fortified by and grounded in an adherence to the assumptions of a psychology of resemblance in which consciousness possesses its own sensory content; poetic images are generated from the elaboration of the particulars of reality, and poetry thereby becomes a transcendent analogue of the real. The poetically intuitive act is an act of abstraction in its radical sense and derives its power from the apprehensions of feeling and intuition rather than from the hypostatizations of reason.

If the creative act issues from the deepest processes of the personality of the poet, it in turn proceeds from a fundamental and authentic self that restores the real by circumnavigating the clichéd symbolic substitutes for reality (whether they be expressed as political program, religious dogma, philosophical system, or social form) and delivers metaphoric transformations of reality that heighten and contribute to our sense of the world. This heightening constitutes the poet's foremost obligation—the responsibility to the imagination as power and value. The composite nature of these elements of Stevens's poetic, as they are revealed in his prose statements about poetry and the arts, at once stamps him as a neoromantic and identifies him as the most articulate and ambitious advocate of a vitalistic poetic, for he claimed for poetry a preeminent role in a constantly evolving world, seeking through its own best resources the means of self-preservation. Surely he had something like this in mind when he wrote, "The whole race is a poet that writes down / The eccentric propositions of its fate" (CP 356).

There is little novelty in arguing for the romanticism of Wallace Stevens. Harold Bloom, Northrop Frye, A. Walton Litz, and George Bornstein, to name but a few, have done so in essentially critical terms.[21] They have located Stevens within a romantic tradition extending back to Coleridge and Wordsworth and beyond. Roy Harvey Pearce has placed Stevens in the American romantic tradition on the basis of a cultural history that finds its most eloquent voice in Emerson.[22] Pearce's argument is an insightful and useful example of cultural historicism that simultaneously reveals the continuity of American poetic tradition and locates Stevens within that tradition. My own aims and interests have been more narrowly historical. Stevens's "sense of the world" was profoundly altered by the philosophical currents so popular in prewar America and Europe. He gladly abandoned his belief in a Spencerian building block universe in favor of the pluralism and radical empiricism of William James and the vitalism of Henri Bergson, and in so doing, he adopted a philosophical vision especially congenial to the creative imagination and essentially romantic in its tendencies. Yet, as Joseph N. Riddell advises, one ought not confuse Stevens's brand of romanticism with a Coleridgean or, by extension, Emersonian version of the romantic because Stevens explicitly rejects any transcendental idealism as providing the metaphysical ground for the power of the imagination.[23]

Nevertheless, as we have seen, Bergson was characterized, often in the most severe and disparaging terms, as a romantic by A. O. Lovejoy, George Santayana, Irving Babbitt, John Burroughs, and others. The neo-romanticism of Bergsonism was a philosophy of immanence, not transcendence. And Santayana, writing in 1911, described William James as a "genuine and vigorous romanticist."[24] Neither James nor Bergson was free from the imputation of the romantic. Indeed, twenty years later than his essay on James, Santayana, and with a great deal less sympathy for the times than he had had for his friend and colleague, identified the tendencies of romanticism with the tendencies for the modernist age: "Romance is evidently a potent ingredient in the ethos of the modern world; and I confess that I can hardly imagine in the near future any poetry, morality, or religion not deeply romantic."[25] Santayana, at least, did not discern the incongruities between the romantic and modern in the world at large, and in fact, he added that he would be happy to be counted among the moderns if only they were "modern enough, and dared to face nature with an unprejudiced mind and clear purpose."[26]

Whether or not Stevens was "modern enough" to satisfy the requirements of a Santayana, he did attempt to clarify his own purposes and to assign the task of art in a modern age. Surely, Santayana could not complain of a lack of courage in those artists who would make their own "vital self-assertions" in an age of disbelief and indifference. To such artists belongs the special dignity that comes with authenticity, an authenticity that, argued Stevens, need not be realized only in orphic works:

It should be enough for him that that to which he has given his life should be so enriched by such an access of value. Poet and painter alike live and work in the midst of a generation that is experiencing essential poverty in spite of fortune. The extension of the mind beyond the range of the mind, the projection of reality beyond reality, the determination to cover the ground, whatever it may be, the determination not to be confined, the recapture of excitement and intensity of interest, the enlargement of spirit at every time, in every way, these are the unities, the relations, to be summarized as paramount now. It is not material whether these relations exist consciously or unconsciously. One goes back to the coercing influences of time and place. It is possible to be subjected to a lofty purpose and not to know it. [NA 171–72]

These are grand claims and sentiments. They are, as well, romantic pronouncements made by one who looks upon modern disbelief face-to-face.

Yet for all his recorded thoughts on the subject, Stevens resists, without qualification, simple labeling as romantic or as modern, partly because he was often critical of both and partly because he had refined his own understanding of a romanticism that is at once authentic, intelligible, and serviceable to a modernist age. He would say, for instance, that the romantic "belittles" the imagination and is "incapable of abstraction" (NA 138), that the romantic's achievements are limited to "minor wish-fulfillments" (NA 139). He complained that "the ideal is the actual become anaemic. The romantic is often pretty much the same thing" (Opus 164). In addition, "romanticism is to poetry what the decorative is to painting" (Opus 169). On the other hand, he approved of the poetry of Samuel French Morse because it is "realistic" and insisted that Morse is not the "ghost of a Transcendentalist." "If he has any use at all for Kant, it is to keep up the window in which the cord is broken. He is anti-transcendental. His subject is the particulars of experience" (Opus 265). Stevens might have said the same of himself.

To the extent that the romantic is to be identified with the transcendental or sentimental or idealistic, Stevens is no romantic. However, this identification, according to Stevens, is restrictive and "pejorative" and applies, or should apply, only to a phase of the romantic that has become stale. There is another sort of romanticism to which Stevens responded and attached himself. "The whole effort of the imagination is toward the production of the romantic," he wrote. "When, therefore, the romantic is in abeyance, when it is discredited, it remains true that there is always an unknown romantic and that the imagination will not be forever denied"

(*Opus* 215). The romantic, like the imagination, constantly reasserts itself. Refusing to be too exactly oneself or to be too content with the popularly accepted reality, the romantic imagines the world otherwise. In short, the impulsions of the romantic are toward a renewal of the world.

To the extent that Stevens was in agreement with Ezra Pound's modernist credo to "Make it new," Stevens was a modern. He was himself constantly engaged in the creative evolving of poetic forms and busy in the poetic "renovation of experience" (*Opus* 177). Yet on the whole, Stevens displayed little interest in or sympathy with modernism—"One cannot spend one's time in being modern when there are so many more important things to be" (*Opus* 175). He variously describes modern art as "uncompromising" (in the sense of being belligerent) and "plausible" (in the sense of being ratiocinative and canny) (*NA* 167). The modern poet's exploitation of form, he sardonically observed, too often "involves nothing more than the use of small letters for capitals, eccentric line-endings, too little or too much punctuation, and similar aberrations. These have nothing to do with being alive" (*NA* 168). The efforts of the creative imagination for Stevens always have to do with life, and it is with life that Stevens's criticism and verse is principally concerned. His estimation of the abuses and tendencies of a modernist aesthetic is effectively suggested by a note in his commonplace book. Above a passage copied from the *Apollo* magazine, Stevens wrote "A just placing of Picasso." Among other things, the unidentified critic complained in the passage that Picasso "is not a painter"; he is an "over-intellectual designer who moves us to thought but not to feeling."[27] Stevens, as anti-intellectualist, meant for his poetry to move his readers to feeling, to life, to the imagination and the intuition, in a word, to the romantic.

In accepting the National Book Award in 1951, Stevens spoke of the word modern in more general terms, believing it to be little more than a "sense of modishness." (This, one recalls, is the way the term was typically defined forty years earlier—the way the church defined it, essentially, when it denounced the modernist heresy.) Stevens elaborated upon his intentional vagueness and reluctance to define the modern in ways that ultimately defend his own special sense of the modern: a modern poet desires above all else "to be nothing more than a poet of the present time" (*Opus* 241). Through individual thought and feeling, available only through an awareness of the thoughts and feelings of others, the poet "derives himself and through himself his poetry." In turn, the poet gives back to his or her generation that which has been borrowed from it—a sense of the world at the present time, a sense of being alive. This awareness may not be conscious on the part of the poet and may, in fact, be "limited to instinct" (*Opus* 242), but it nevertheless provides the unavoidable foundation of a truly modern poetry that moves us to feeling and heightens our sense of the real.

Those meanings of modern and romantic acceptable to Stevens are finally synonymous, the last in fact comprehending the first. The romantic in a nonderogatory sense, "meaning always the living and at the same time the imaginative, the youthful, the delicate . . . , constitutes the vital element in poetry" (*Opus* 248–49). The romantic always means the living element in poetry, for life itself means extending the mind and feelings beyond the realm of both, beyond calculation and inherited form. The romantic is a vitalizing agency that makes realism possible—"Something of the unreal is necessary to fecundate the real," he noted (*Opus* 253). And this overarching understanding of the romantic allows Stevens (no doubt with admiring mischief in mind) to identify as a romantic William Carlos Williams because he has "rejected the accepted sense of things" (*Opus* 252), or T. S. Eliot because he "incessantly revives the past and creates the future" (*Opus* 249), or Marianne Moore because of her authenticity and truthfulness (*Opus* 250–51). Stevens reserves for these poets the tribute of a romanticism that he denies to the pseudoromanticism of the surrealists, for example, who impress him as inventing without discovering: "To make a clam play an accordion is to invent not to discover. The observation of the unconscious, so far as it can be observed, should reveal things of which we have previously been unconscious, not the familiar things of which we have been conscious plus imagination" (*Opus* 177).

The enlargement and heightening of consciousness through the efforts of the artist may indeed be romantic. It is, at all events, consistent with a Bergsonian vision. The artist aims to show us, "in nature and in the mind, outside of us and within us, things which did not explicitly strike our senses and our consciousness[.] The poet and the novelist who express a mood certainly do not create it out of nothing; they would not be understood by us if we did not observe within ourselves, up to a certain point, what they say about others" (*CM* 159). This is but another way of saying that the true artist discovers rather than invents and returns to us what is most authentically our own—things as they are. Only through the falsifications of the romantic may the poet direct our attention to the availably true and real. The authentic romantic poet restores and reclaims the earth for our habitation. Such an artist (Marianne Moore is Stevens's example, and the lines are hers) gives us what we most want and need: "imaginary gardens with real toads in them" (*Opus* 250).

A casual reading of Stevens's prose statements about the nature of poetry may strike us as so many vaporous effusions—ill-defined and singularly lacking in intellectual firmness, argumentative rigor, and distinct rhetorical purpose. His distinction between the honorific and pejorative senses of the romantic is a case in point. One understands him well enough. The romanticism he asserts may serve as an adequate token of his convictions about the vitalizing function of the imagination, but it is so generalized a distinction that it is virtually useless for critical discourse. Similarly, Stevens's use of ideas, especially philosophical ideas, in his critical writings, as in his poetry, often seems obtrusive rather than supportive. He was by his own admission no philosopher, and surely Frank Doggett is right when he suggests that Stevens does not offer sufficient elaboration to make a "search for philosophic affinities worthwhile."[28] I have not here been engaged in such a search, however. My concern in this and in the previous chapter has been with the foundations of the poet's sense of the world insofar as it was fortified and informed by a shift in the reigning epistemological, metaphysical, and ontological assumptions about life and human possibility.

How securely and profoundly this sense is fastened to a demonstrable philosophical sophistication is surely debatable. The more one attends to the conceptual designs of his essays and lectures, however, the more it becomes evident that he is not at all diffuse or muddled in his thinking and that his argument is subtle and well crafted. His seeming tentativeness and his reluctance to offer poetic dogma are the result of a conscious avoidance in prose of what he sometimes ridicules in poetry—namely, the petrifactions and hypostatizations of the intellect. As for Stevens's philosophical sophistication, a careful reading of the essays discloses that what philosophy Stevens knew and was engaged by he knew very well and that he was deeply committed to certain philosophical assumptions. To say that is to say nothing more, or less, than that the writings of James and Bergson were a familiar part of his sense of the world.

The accuracy or validity of Stevens's thought vis-à-vis definable philosophical issues, the comprehensiveness and systematic quality of his poetry of ideas, the congruence of expressed opinion and identifiable philosophical ideas—these are finally beside the point. What matters is that his values and interests, ultimately his poetic vision, participated in the shift away from the mechanistic worldview of Spencer and toward the dynamic vitalism of Bergson and that he persisted in this latter attitude. This shift represented an alteration in the way one understands the nature of reality and human awareness. What matters still more is that this alteration encouraged him to write a different kind of poetry—a poetry that, happily, has outlasted the coercions of time and place, has outlasted the historical moment in which that new poetic vision was forged.

Bergsonism was enabling to the poet in several ways: it established the preeminent dignity and importance of the creative imagination and the significance of the artist in modern life; it endorsed the imagination (or intuition) as a fundamental way of metaphysical knowing; it encouraged origination and experimentation and the proliferation of poetic forms; it supported the exploitation of experience of the personal and the local as a species of metaphysics; it supplied a psychology congenial to metaphoric transformation; it legitimized the broadly romantic inclinations of the artist; and finally, it allowed the creative imagination, more particularly the poetic imagination, to fit in the system of the world. In short, and quite independent of its philosophical substance or the refinement of Stevens's understanding of philosophy, it articulated and made available a vision of the world and supported the creative writer's instrumental place within that world. For that reason, if for no other, Bergsonism constituted an opportunity and a temptation for the modern artist; it validated the significance of poetic intuition and dignified the artist's vocation.

Wallace Stevens provides us with a most interesting example of the influence of Bergsonism upon the American literary sensibility. Stevens can in no way be seen as the spokesman for other significant American writers who were likewise influenced. As I have argued, Willa Cather's fiction represents the most exemplary embodiment and the finest achievement of a vitalistic aesthetic in the novel. But influence distributes itself unevenly among individuals, and this is particularly true of individual creative temperaments. It combines and competes with other unique circumstances and inclinations. Nevertheless, Wallace Stevens's poetic offers a detailed glimpse of the mental transactions and artistic decisions of a writer who was deeply committed to his art and who proposed to define and justify it, both in theory and in practice. Bergsonism contributed its portion to the making of genuinely significant and original works of literature, and Wallace Stevens provides a case study, so to speak, of how that influence might be articulated. From his example, we may infer the sorts of encouragements and consolations Bergson offered to the artist;

from it, as well, we may infer the intellectual dimensions and aesthetic and psychological assumptions that were often grounded in a reading of Bergson and converted to aesthetic purpose.

For Stevens's part, persistence in the philosophical optimism that once invigorated prewar America but that had since been abandoned may have impelled him to lament in "Sailing after Lunch" that he was "A most inappropriate man / In a most unpropitious place" (*CP* 120). And he muttered a poet's prayer:

> The romantic should be here.
> The romantic should be there.
> It ought to be everywhere.
> But the romantic must never remain,
>
> Mon Dieu, and must never again return.   [*CP* 121]

The restraining forces of the heavy "historical sail" may be relieved by imaginative effort and minor achievement. This may be enough for the poet.

> To expunge all people and be a pupil
> Of the gorgeous wheel and so to give
> That slight transcendence to the dirty sail,
> By light, the way one feels, sharp white,
> And then rush brightly through the summer air.   [*CP* 121]

The romantic for Stevens, even in the mid-1930s when he wrote "Sailing after Lunch," was the accomplishment of that "slight transcendence" of necessity, not minor wish fulfillments nor bold declarations of an infinite I AM.

Many years later, near the end of his life, Stevens wrote "The Planet on the Table." "Ariel was glad that he had written his poems," it begins. "They were of a remembered time / Or of something seen that he liked":

> His self and the sun were one
> And his poems, although makings of his self,
> Were no less makings of the sun.
>
> It was not important that they survive.
> What mattered was that they should bear
> Some lineament or character,

Some affluence, if only half-perceived,
In the poverty of their words,
Of the planet of which they were part.   [*CP* 532–33]

Stevens was first to last a poet of the earth—that was enough. To write a living poetry for a living people was his object, and his best poems achieve the artistic ambitions he identified in "Of Modern Poetry":

Sounds passing through sudden rightnesses, wholly
Containing the mind, below which it cannot descend,
Beyond which it has no will to rise.   [*CP* 240]

Unlike his Saint John, Stevens had no ambition to speak below the tension of the lyre. Rather, he wished to write of the affluence that comes of living in a physical world. Sorrow, wrote Bergson, is the impoverishment of sensation when we perceive the future "stopped up" (*TFW* 11). Joy, by contrast, is alive with a sense of the future: "our perceptions and memories become tinged with an indefinable quality, as with a kind of heat or light, so novel that now and then, as we stare at our own self, we wonder how it can really exist" (*TFW* 10). Stevens was a poet of joy. Randall Jarrell once observed of his fellow poet that "in an age when almost everybody sold man and the world short, he never did, but acted as if joy *were* 'a word of our own,' as if nothing excellent were alien to us."[29] The times may often be unpropitious for such a faith, but can such a man ever be "inappropriate"?

NOTES

INTRODUCTION

1. Wilder, "Thornton Wilder," p. 105.
2. William James, *Pragmatism and Four Essays from "The Meaning of Truth,"* pp. 18–19.
3. Becker, *The Heavenly City of the Eighteenth-Century Philosophers*, pp. 72–73.
4. Boorstin, "The Myth of an American Enlightenment," p. 65.
5. Bergson published *Durée et simultanéité: à propos de la théorie d'Einstein* (1922) as a defense of views expressed in *Creative Evolution* that he believed Einstein's theory of relativity challenged. For a full discussion of Bergson's relation to physics see Gunter, *Bergson and the Evolution of Physics*.
6. Kern, *The Culture of Time and Space*, pp. 11–12.
7. Tuchman, *The Guns of August*, pp. 31–32.
8. Bloom, *Wallace Stevens*, p. 168.
9. The advantage of adopting an interpretive vocabulary from a historical context may be suggested by Bloom's difficulty with what he calls the "most problematic element" in Stevens's "Notes toward a Supreme Fiction"—what Stevens terms in the poem a "later reason" (*CP* 399). Bloom enlists Freud, Lacan, Derrida, Wordsworth, Coleridge, and Tetens to help him come to grips with this concept (see Bloom, *Wallace Stevens*, pp. 168–71). But the concept, as will become clear in chapters 5 and 6, is a simple one, and its origins, historically rather than critically considered, are not at all difficult or obscure.

CHAPTER ONE

1. Hulme, "The International Philosophical Congress at Bologna," pp. 399–400. Hulme of course was predisposed to favor Bergson, for he had studied under Bergson, who had also done him a personal service in helping him to be readmitted to Cambridge. Hulme's reaction to Bergsonism is discussed in fuller detail in chapter 2.
2. Eucken's philosophical method was itself a historical method. He conceived of historical facts as consisting of systematic wholes (syntagma) that could be studied both reductively and "noologically"—i.e., as possessing their own inner

dialectical movement. Eucken's speech is published as "Naturalism or Idealism?," pp. 74–87 (hereafter cited in the text by page number).

3. Eucken describes the new idealism he proposes in *Main Currents of Modern Thought*, pp. 113–15. Labels are tricky during this era, and some preferred to treat Eucken as a vitalist (for example, Mead in *Movements of Thought in the Nineteenth Century*). But, insofar as his philosophy lacks the pervasive biological character of a purer vitalist such as Hans Driesch, idealist seems a more satisfactory term and the one he preferred.

4. William James, *The Will to Believe*, p. 181n.

5. Cecelia Tichi gives an interesting account of the emblem of the machine and its cultural importance from 1890 through 1920 in *Shifting Gears*; and Howard Mumford Jones's invaluable history of the era, *The Age of Energy*, gives particular attention to energy and the machine in chapters 3 and 4, pp. 100–178.

6. Lovejoy, *Bergson and Romantic Evolutionism*, p. 30.

7. Perhaps it is relevant, at least it is interesting, that Clarence Day, Jr., author of the popular *Life with Father* (1935), published *This Simian World* only a few years before the Scopes trial. In that book, Day treated the subject of evolution in a jocular and undisturbed mood as he moved toward seemingly disturbing conclusions: "It is possible that our race may be an accident, in a meaningless universe, living its brief life uncared-for, on this dark, cooling star: but even so—and all the more—what marvelous creatures we are!" (p. 91).

8. Ronald E. Martin, *American Literature and the Universe of Force*, p. 30 (hereafter cited in the text by page number).

9. Jones, *The Age of Energy*, p. 23.

10. Mead, *Movements of Thought in the Nineteenth Century*, p. 263.

11. Spencer, *First Principles*, p. 396.

12. Royce, *Herbert Spencer*, p. 115.

13. Quoted in Introduction to Perry Miller, *American Thought*, p. xxxv.

14. Noted in Jay Martin, *Harvests of Change*, p. 8n.

15. Lears, *No Place of Grace*, p. 22.

16. See Ronald E. Martin, *American Literature and the Universe of Force*, pp. 56–57 on this point.

17. William James, *Pragmatism and Four Essays from "The Meaning of Truth,"* p. 76.

18. Steele, *Fourteen Weeks in Natural Philosophy*, p. 158n. (hereafter cited in the text by page number).

19. William Vaughan Moody, "The Menagerie," p. 580.

20. Edwin Arlington Robinson, *Collected Poems of Edwin Arlington Robinson*, p. 64 (hereafter cited in the text by page number).

21. See Kaplan, *Philosophy in the Poetry of Edwin Arlington Robinson*, esp. pp. 25–34.

22. Twain, "What Is Happiness?," p. 337.

23. Quoted in Watt, *Conrad in the Nineteenth Century*, p. 153.

24. Watt discusses fin de siècle pessimism in *Conrad in the Nineteenth Century*, pp. 147–68.

25. William James, *The Will to Believe*, pp. 165–66.

26. Foreword to Chapple, *Heart Throbs in Prose and Verse*, n.p.

27. Zola, *The Experimental Novel*, pp. 25–26 (hereafter cited in the text by page number).

28. Quoted in Bosanquet, *The Distinction between Mind and Its Object*, p. 7. The new realists included two former students and disciples of James, Horace Kallen and Ralph Barton Perry; and the school was promoting what Bosanquet called "the doctrine of the open door," wherein reality was treated as what it seems to be—"bright, warm, responsive" (p. 21). In that sense, the new realists were, as Bosanquet recognized, materialists who did not envision the world as a cold jelly.

29. Eucken, *Knowledge and Life*, pp. 55–56 (hereafter cited in the text by page number).

30. Oron J. Hale, *The Great Illusion, 1900–1914*, p. 93. Hale discusses the transactions of the Third Congress on pp. 92–93.

31. Adams, *The Education of Henry Adams*, p. 457. For an instructive and sympathetic account of the emotional disturbances occasioned by the breakdown of classical physics, see Russell McCormmach's well-documented novel, *Night Thoughts of a Classical Physicist*, about the German physicist Jakob (an invented, composite figure representative of the attitudes of several scientists). Jakob, writes McCormmach, was "out of sympathy" with the new physics; he could accept quantum mechanics insofar as it possessed a logical construction, but he could not believe "that the innermost workings of nature were ruled by indeterminacy" (p. 162).

32. Haeckel, *The Riddle of the Universe*, p. 91 (hereafter cited in the text by page number).

33. See Oron J. Hale, *The Great Illusion, 1900–1914*, p. 122n.

34. See Cochran and Miller, *The Age of Enterprise*, p. 128.

35. Hoernlé, *Matter, Life, Mind, and God*, p. 87.

36. Quoted in Perry's *The Thought and Character of William James*, p. 288.

37. Scoon, "The Rise and Impact of Evolutionary Ideas," p. 29.

38. Josiah Royce actually approved the common usage of the term insofar as it meant a certain loyalty to large ideals; see May, *The End of American Innocence*, p. 14.

39. Eucken, *Main Currents of Modern Thought*, p. 337 (hereafter cited in the text by page number).

40. It is a great curiosity that Eliot adopted the term modernism in 1916, aware as he was of its popular connotations. His adoption of this label is similar to an iconoclastic literary movement in our own time willingly adopting the name yuppies.

41. See Eucken, *Main Currents of Modern Thought*, pp. 462–77, for a discussion of the preference for philosophies of immanence such as Bergson's.

42. Wohl's *The Generation of 1914* is a thorough collective biography of the younger generation in France, Germany, England, Spain, and Italy. Youth was itself a social category, representing to its members the possibilities of the future and the hope of the present. The "ideology of youth" was vitally active and compelling during this era; "the organization of youth and the challenging of adult values by younger men and women," writes Wohl, "is one of the most striking aspects of the prewar period. . . . It operated with the premise that youth was a superior and privileged stage of life, beyond which lay degeneration" (p. 205).

43. See May, *The End of American Innocence*, pt. 1, chaps. 2, 3, and 4, pp. 9–51.

44. William James, *Pragmatism and Four Essays from "The Meaning of Truth,"* p. 86.

45. Brooks, "America's Coming of Age," p. 32 (hereafter cited in the text by page number).

46. Jones's chapter on the genteel tradition in *The Age of Energy*, pp. 216–58, is very instructive.

47. Lears, "From Salvation to Self-Realization," p. 9.

48. William James, *The Will to Believe*, p. 181.

49. William James, *Principles of Psychology*, vol. 1, p. 196 (hereafter cited in the text by page number).

50. Perry, *The Thought and Character of William James*, p. 194.

51. James's radical empiricism held that the final criterion of knowledge is experience and, more importantly, that the relations between and among things are as much a part of experience as the things themselves. Thus, he explicitly rejected both the association of ideas of British empiricism and the transcendental categories of Kantian idealism.

52. Perry, *The Thought and Character of William James*, p. 275.

53. William James, *The Will to Believe*, p. 177.

54. Hartog, *Problems of Life and Reproduction*, p. 234.

55. Driesch, *The Problem of Individuality*, pp. 4–5.

56. See Driesch's *The History and Theory of Vitalism*, pp. 146–47.

57. Driesch, *The Problem of Individuality*, p. 18 (hereafter cited in the text by page number).

58. See Driesch, *The Science and Philosophy of the Organism*, vol. 2, pp. 80 and 224.

59. Ibid., p. 192.

60. For a technical explanation of the vitalistic criticism of the second law of thermodynamics see Johnstone, *The Philosophy of Biology*, pp. 366–76.

61. Driesch, *The Science and Philosophy of the Organism*, vol. 2, p. 373.

62. Some of Driesch's most interesting work began as lectures in England and Scotland, including *The Science and Philosophy of the Organism*, and there were

several notable English vitalists, Johnstone and Hartog among them. C. K. Ogden translated Driesch's *The History and Theory of Vitalism*, and some of Ogden's interest in vitalism may have entered into *The Meaning of Meaning*, which he coauthored with I. A. Richards.

T. E. Hulme's literary theory had developed the notion of "intensive manifolds," and though he describes the concept as an extension of Bergson, the term at least was Driesch's invention.

63. See the author's Preface to the essay "The Meaning of Truth" in William James, *Pragmatism and Four Essays from "The Meaning of Truth,"* p. 199.

64. Douglass in *Bergson, Eliot, and American Literature*, Schwartz in *The Matrix of Modernism*, and Menand in *Discovering Modernism*, to name only three recent studies, have shown how Bergsonism affected the formulations of modernism.

65. William James, *A Pluralistic Universe*, pp. 265–66.

66. Lovejoy, *Bergson and Romantic Evolutionism*, pp. 33–34.

67. See Hartshorne, *Creativity in American Philosophy*.

68. William James, *The Will to Believe*, p. 181n. Bertrand Helm discusses James's philosophical conceptions of time in his *Time and Reality in American Philosophy*, pp. 39–52. Throughout the book, Helm shows how centrally interested the principal figures of America's Golden Age of Philosophy (Peirce, James, Royce, Santayana, Dewey, and Whitehead) were in the problem of time. James rejected the notion of the existence of a single, all-inclusive time. Time, for James, occurs in "drops" or "buds," and to that extent he was in agreement with Bergson that time is in its very nature heterogeneous.

69. See Bergson, *Le Rire* (1900; translated as *Laughter*). Bergson's *The Meaning of the War* (1914) was a propaganda piece that argued that the French were guaranteed victory in the Great War because Germany had organized itself mechanically and drew its finite energies from mechanical sources, whereas France was organically organized and therefore could replenish the energies expended in the war effort.

70. Bergson spelled out his metaphysical method most lucidly in his *Introduction dè la métaphysics* (1903).

71. Perry, *The Thought and Character of William James*, p. 340.

72. Quoted in Behrman's *Portrait of Max*, pp. 146–48.

CHAPTER TWO

1. William James letter to Bergson, 13 June 1907, in Perry, *The Thought and Character of William James*, pp. 345–46.

2. William James, *A Pluralistic Universe*, p. 214 (hereafter cited in the text by page number); quote taken from the lecture "Compounding of Consciousness."

3. May, *The End of American Innocence*, p. 228.

4. "Professor Bergson at the City College," p. 467.

5. Levine, "The Philosophy of Henri Bergson and Syndicalism," pt. 5, p. 4.

6. Riley, *American Thought*, pp. 408–9.

7. William James letter to Bergson, 13 June 1907, in Perry, *The Thought and Character of William James*, p. 346.

8. For a fuller treatment of Bergson as an influence on the cultural life of America, see Quirk's "Bergson in America," pp. 453–90.

9. Santayana, *Winds of Doctrine*, pp. 73–74 (hereafter cited in the text by page number).

10. Lindsay, *The Philosophy of Bergson*, p. vi.

11. Willcox, "Some Implications of Bergson's Philosophy," p. 448 (hereafter cited in the text by page number).

12. Sanborn, "Henry Bergson Pronounced 'The Foremost Thinker in France,'" p. 173.

13. Johnston, "Where Bergson Stands," p. 16.

14. Burroughs, "A Prophet of the Soul," p. 120.

15. Whittaker, "Bergson," p. 414.

16. See Russell, *The Autobiography of Bertrand Russell*, p. 166; and Nathan G. Hale, *Freud and the Americans*, p. 197.

17. A writer for the *North American Review* complained in April 1913 that Bergson had never "grappled with Christ, or recognized the stimulus—the creative evolution—of Gethsemane" (see Douglas, "Christ and Bergson," p. 440); and Santayana wrote sarcastically in *Winds of Doctrine* that "we are fortunate that at least her [Nature's] darling is all mankind and not merely Israel" (p. 73).

18. Babbitt, "Bergson and Rousseau," p. 455.

19. Lovejoy, "The Metaphysician of the Life-Force," p. 299 (hereafter cited in the text by page number). Lovejoy wrote extensively about and even corresponded with Bergson. See Gunter, *Henri Bergson*, items 470, 2665–77.

20. Huneker, "Playboy of Western Philosophy," p. 258.

21. "Pascendi Dominici Gregis," p. 94 (hereafter cited in the text by page number).

22. See Kallen, *William James and Henri Bergson*; and Perry, *The Present Conflict of Ideals*, chap. 24, or *The Thought and Character of William James*, chap. 36.

23. Riley, *American Thought*, pp. 422–23.

24. Perry, *The Present Conflict of Ideals*, p. 348.

25. Nathan G. Hale, *Freud and the Americans*, p. 241.

26. Putnam, *James Jackson Putnam and Psychoanalysis*, p. 94.

27. Nathan G. Hale, *Freud and the Americans*, p. 243.

28. Bergson's *Dreams* was published as a two-part English translation in the *Independent* in October 1913 and printed separately as a book the following year. Bergson foresaw in the psychoanalytic probings of the unconscious discoveries as

wonderful and as important "as have been in the preceding centuries the discoveries of the physical and natural sciences" (*D* 57).

29. Balfour, "Creative Evolution and Philosophic Doubt," pp. 1–23. Summarized in "Balfour's Objections to Bergson's Philosophy," pp. 659–61.

30. Johnstone, *The Philosophy of Biology*.

31. Elliot, *Modern Science and the Illusions of Professor Bergson*, p. 4 (hereafter cited in the text by page number).

32. Lodge, "Balfour and Bergson," p. 291 (hereafter cited in the text by page number).

33. Carr, *The Philosophy of Change*, p. 10 (hereafter cited in the text by page number).

34. Slosson, "Twelve Major Prophets of Today," p. 1257.

35. Preface to James McKeller Stewart, *A Critical Exposition of Bergson's Philosophy*, n.p.

36. "Bergson's Reception in America," p. 226.

37. Ibid.

38. "Freedom," p. 379.

39. Tyrell, "Bergson," pp. 520–21.

40. Cox, "Bergson's Message to Feminism," p. 548 (hereafter cited in the text by page number).

41. Willcox, "Impressions of M. Bergson," p. 6.

42. See Flewelling, "Bergson, Ward, and Eucken in Their Relation to Bowne," pp. 374–82; and Flewelling, *Bergson and Personal Realism*.

43. Underhill, "Bergson and the Mystics," pp. 668–75. Ironically, Bergson's impressions of Americans, delivered in a lecture, "Discours au Comité—France-Amérique," after his return from his first visit to America in 1913, included the observation that Americans were possessed of an idealism that bordered on mysticism; see Bergson, *Écrits et Paroles*, pp. 381–82.

44. Roosevelt, "The Search for Truth in a Reverent Spirit," pp. 819–26.

45. Hermann, *Eucken and Bergson*, pp. 162–63 (hereafter cited in the text by page number).

46. Lippmann, *A Preface to Politics*, p. 219 (hereafter cited in the text by page number).

47. Björkman, *Is There Anything New under the Sun?*, p. 219 (hereafter cited in the text by page number).

48. Becker, "Some Aspects of the Influence of Social Problems and Ideas upon the Study and Writing of History," p. 664 (hereafter cited in the text by page number).

49. See the essay "The New History" in James Harvey Robinson, *The New History*, p. 20.

50. Randolph Bourne had studied under Woodbridge, and both had been

deeply influenced by James and Bergson. John Dewey, Bourne, and John Burroughs (whom Bourne had brought with him) attended Bergson's lectures at Columbia University in February 1913, and Woodbridge probably attended as well (see Bourne, *The Letters of Randolph Bourne*, p. 85).

51. Woodbridge, *The Purpose of History*, p. 89.

52. See Becker's address "Every Man His Own Historian" in Becker, *Every Man His Own Historian*, p. 240 (hereafter cited in the text by page number).

53. See Becker's essay "Juliette Fronet and Victor Hugo" in ibid., p. 257.

54. See Becker's essay "Frederick Jackson Turner" in ibid., pp. 229–30.

55. See Becker's essay "Every Man His Own Historian" in ibid., p. 246.

56. "The Banning of Bergson," p. 86.

57. Lippmann, *A Preface to Morals*, p. 107.

58. Perry, *The Thought and Character of William James*, p. 340.

59. The literature tracing the influence of Bergson upon modern writers is extensive. Four excellent general studies are: Poulet, *Studies in Human Time*; Kumar, *Bergson and the Stream of Consciousness Novel*; Church, *Time and Reality*; and Pilkington, *Bergson and His Influence*.

A selective list of studies dealing with Bergson's influence on particular writers includes: Church's chapter entitled "Bergson and Proust" in her *Time and Reality*, pp. 3–20; Pilkington's chapter 4, "Proust," in his *Bergson and His Influence*, pp. 146–77; Friedman's chapter entitled "Bergson and Kazantzakis" in his *To Deny Our Nothingness*, pp. 63–79; Pilkington's chapter 3, "Valéry," in his *Bergson and His Influence*, pp. 99–145; Fernandat, "Bergson et Valéry," pp. 122–46; Delattre, "La durée bergsonienne dans le roman de Virginia Woolf," pp. 97–108; Pfister, *Zeit und Wirklichleit bei Thomas Wolfe*; for Wallace Stevens, Riddell, *The Clairvoyant Eye*; Klawitter, "Henri Bergson and James Joyce's Fictional World," pp. 429–37; and also see references to Joyce in Kumar's *Bergson and the Stream of Consciousness Novel*. Interesting studies of Bergson and Faulkner include Conder's *Naturalism in American Fiction*, pp. 160–95, and Douglass's *Bergson, Eliot, and American Literature*, esp. chaps. 6 and 7, pp. 118–65. Douglass should also be consulted for Bergson's influence on Eliot, chaps. 3 and 4, pp. 49–105, along with Skaff's *The Philosophy of T. S. Eliot*, pp. 23–35, for a differing view of Eliot's relation to Bergsonism. The several studies of Frost and Bergson include Bieganowski's "Sense of Time in Robert Frost's Poetic," pp. 184–94, and "Robert Frost's *A Boy's Will* and Henri Bergson's *Creative Evolution*"; Poirier, *Robert Frost*; and Sears, "William James, Henri Bergson, and the Poetics of Robert Frost," pp. 341–61. For Willa Cather, see Wasserman, "The Music of Time," pp. 226–39; Hulme speaks for himself and his relation to Bergson in essays to be discussed later in this chapter; for Wyndham Lewis, see Campbell, "Equal Opposites," pp. 351–69. The researches of Riddell and Wasserman are particularly relevant to this study.

60. See Allegra Stewart, "The Quality of Gertrude Stein's Creativity," pp. 488–506.

61. Wharton, *A Backward Glance*, p. 170.

62. Noted in Bruccoli's *Some Sort of Epic Grandeur*, p. 77.

63. Fitzgerald, *The Beautiful and the Damned*, p. 48 (hereafter cited in the text by page number).

64. See Douglass, *Bergson, Eliot, and American Literature*, esp. pp. 27–48.

65. Murry, "Art and Philosophy," p. 56 (hereafter cited in the text by page number). For a general study of British modernism, see Levenson, *A Genealogy of Modernism*.

66. Hulme's essay "Bergson's Theory of Art" is reprinted in Hulme, *Speculations*, pp. 141–69; his "Notes on Bergson" and "A Lecture on Modern Poetry" are reprinted in Hulme, *Further Speculations*, pp. 28–63 and 67–76, respectively (hereafter cited in the text by page number).

67. Noted in Matthews, *Great Tom*, p. 33.

68. The essay "Francis Herbert Bradley" is found in Eliot's *Selected Prose of T. S. Eliot*, p. 197.

69. Eliot, *A Sermon Preached in Magdalene College Chapel*, p. 5.

70. See Matthiessen, *The Achievement of T. S. Eliot*, p. 183; A. D. Moody, *Thomas Stearns Eliot*, pp. 26–29; and Douglass, *Bergson, Eliot, and American Literature*, esp. chap. 3, pp. 49–82.

71. Eliot, "Eeldrop and Appleplex," pt. 1, pp. 7–11, pt. 2, pp. 16–19.

72. Skaff, *The Philosophy of T. S. Eliot*, pp. 25–26.

73. Eliot, "Eeldrop and Appleplex," pt. 1, p. 10 (hereafter cited in the text by page number).

74. For a well-documented account of Lewis's resentful indebtedness to Bergson, see Campbell, "Equal Opposites," pp. 351–69.

75. Wyndham Lewis, *Time and Western Man*, p. 162 (hereafter cited in the text by page number).

76. Quoted in Campbell, "Equal Opposites," p. 354.

77. See the essay "Notes on Bergson" in Hulme's *Further Speculations*, p. 61 (hereafter cited in the text by page number).

78. The lecture "Mr. Bennett and Mrs. Brown" is found in Woolf's *The Captain's Death Bed and Other Essays*, p. 96 (hereafter cited in the text by page number).

79. Williams, *Autobiography*, p. 138.

80. See the essay "A Lecture on Modern Poetry" in Hulme's *Further Speculations*, p. 72.

81. Williams, *Selected Essays*, pp. 11–12.

82. Dell, *Homecoming*, p. 217 (hereafter cited in the text by page number).

83. See Hoffman, *The Twenties*, esp. pp. 21–33.

84. Eliot's *Syllabus of a Course of Six Lectures on Modern French Literature* is reproduced in A. D. Moody, *Thomas Stearns Eliot*, pp. 41–49. In the second lecture, "The Reaction against Romanticism," Eliot wrote that neo-Catholicism is

not to be confused with modernism, "which is a purely intellectual movement."

85. See Hoffman's *Freudianism and the Literary Mind*, esp. chaps. 2 and 3, pp. 43–84.

CHAPTER THREE

1. From the inscription in the copy of *O Pioneers!* that Cather gave to Carrie Miner (Sherwood). Quoted in full in Bennett's *The World of Willa Cather*, pp. 200–201.

2. See Higham, "The Reorientation of American Culture in the 1890s," pp. 77–88; and Lears, *No Place of Grace*, esp. pp. 117–39.

3. For a portrait of Willa Cather during her university days see Cather's *Writings from Willa Cather's Campus Years*, esp. pp. 115ff, a collection of letters commenting on Willa Cather's appearance and attitudes during these years.

4. Reported in Woodress, *Willa Cather: A Literary Life*, p. 52.

5. See Slote, "The Kingdom of Art," pp. 31–112; and Rosowski, *The Voyage Perilous*, esp. pp. ix–xiii and 3–18.

6. See Woodress, *Willa Cather: A Literary Life*, esp. chaps. 4, 5, and 6, pp. 64–136.

7. Randall, *The Landscape and the Looking Glass*, pp. 1–6.

8. Cather gives a variant account of this letter in the 1913 interview. Not only is the quotation slightly different (which may be the result of quoting from memory), but Cather gives the impression that the letter was not written to her but that she found it among Jewett's papers in South Berwick, Maine, after Jewett's death (*KA* 447).

9. See Woodress, *Willa Cather: A Literary Life*, p. 41.

10. Arnold in *Willa Cather's Short Fiction*, pp. 41–42 and 83–86, identifies many of the parallels between these stories and the novels.

11. Woodress uses the phrase in his *Willa Cather: Her Life and Art*, p. 207, but the autobiographical elements are dealt with more completely in the later *Willa Cather: A Literary Life*, see esp. pp. 367–71. See also Edel, "A Cave of One's Own," pp. 200–217, for a psychoanalytic view of this relation between the author and her book.

12. Woodress, *Willa Cather: A Literary Life*, p. 150.

13. Letter to Carrie Miner Sherwood, 29 April 1945, in the Willa Cather Pioneer Memorial Museum and Education Foundation, Red Cloud, Nebraska. Stipulations in Cather's will prohibit direct quotation from her letters.

14. The theme of arrested development may have been more widespread among women writers of the period than is commonly known. C. J. Wershoven, at any rate, has made a convincing case that Edna Pontelier and Lily Bart are instances of this condition (see Wershoven, "*The Awakening* and *The House of Mirth*," pp. 27–

41). The term *arrested development* itself was, according to the *OED*, first used by Thomas Huxley in 1859 and by Darwin in 1871. Cather, and indeed Chopin and Wharton, may have been applying a biological, evolutionary concept to a literary program.

15. The other stories are: "Flavia and Her Artists," "The Garden Lodge," "A Death in the Desert," "The Marriage of Phaedra," and "Paul's Case."

16. E. K. Brown, *Willa Cather*, p. 87.

17. In the preface to the 1922 edition of *Alexander's Bridge*, Cather writes that one of the few really "helpful words" she ever received from an older writer was when Jewett told her, "Of course, one day you will write about your own country. In the meantime, get all you can. One must know the world *so well* before one can know the parish" (*AB* 1922 vii).

18. For an interesting and perceptive discussion of Cather's classicism, see Sutherland's "Willa Cather," pp. 123–43.

19. Rosowski, *The Voyage Perilous*, p. x.

20. William James, *Pragmatism and Four Essays from "The Meaning of Truth,"* p. 116. On 16 September 1932, Willa Cather wrote Zoë Akins and said that the interest of life typically resided in its unanticipated qualities. The surprises of events are logical and causally consistent, but we never realize that until afterward. This atmospheric quality had almost vanished in modern fiction but was, nonetheless, her kind of fiction. Cather added that she wished she could do away with atmosphere in her fiction and be another sort of writer for a time. That her wish was genuine is doubtful, for one of Cather's strongest talents was for getting such a convincing sense of the "perceptual weather" of things into her fiction. (The letter to Akins is in the Huntington Museum and Library, San Marino, California.)

21. Ammons, "The Engineer as Cultural Hero and Willa Cather's First Novel, *Alexander's Bridge*," pp. 748–60.

22. See Quirk's "Cather and Fitzgerald," pp. 576–91.

23. See Stouck, *Willa Cather's Imagination*, pp. 12–19.

24. For a fuller discussion of this influence see Skaggs, "Poe's Shadow on *Alexander's Bridge*," pp. 365–74.

25. Trilling, "Willa Cather," p. 155.

26. Recorded in Sergeant's *Willa Cather*, p. 86.

27. O'Brien, *Willa Cather*, p. 381.

28. Edith Lewis, *Willa Cather Living*, p. 83.

29. Sergeant, *Willa Cather*, p. 116.

30. Quoted in Bennett, *The World of Willa Cather*, p. 200.

31. Sergeant, *Willa Cather*, p. 92.

32. Cather, "Plays of Real Life," pp. 63–72.

33. Letter to Elizabeth Sergeant, 12 September 1912, in the Pierpont Morgan Library, New York City, New York.

34. Sergeant, *Willa Cather*, p. 203.

35. See Howard, *Literature and the American Tradition*, p. 254; Bloom and Bloom, "The Genesis of *Death Comes for the Archbishop*," pp. 479–506; and Wasserman, "The Music of Time," pp. 226–39.

36. Seibel, in "Miss Cather from Nebraska," recalls that Cather was a "devoted disciple" of William James (p. 202).

37. Cather did not have much patience for the highly technical side of philosophy. She admired Santayana, for instance, and recommended his *Soliloquies in England* (1922) to Zoë Akins, but she said that a more ponderous work like *The Realm of Matter* (1930) was too much for her. (Letter to Zoë Akins, 28 April 1936, in the Huntington Museum and Library, San Marino, California.)

Wallace Stevens, though he had a greater patience and a larger appetite for philosophy than Cather, was not so very different in this respect. Both admired good writing wherever they might find it and were apt to find a great deal of it in James, Bergson, and Santayana. They both recognized that some philosophical ideas are also poetic ideas, but neither was a philosopher. In a word, Cather and Stevens were artists with strong intellectual interests, and to attempt to reduce that art to philosophy in fancy dress is a mistake.

38. Whether *O Pioneers!* is an epic novel (see for example Stouck, *Willa Cather's Imagination*, pp. 23–32) or a pastoral novel (see for example Rosowski, *The Voyage Perilous*, pp. 45–61) is a generic question. I am less concerned with matters of genre than with questions of literary motivation, and part of the originality of *O Pioneers!* seems to reside in the fact that Cather successfully embodied pastoral and regional materials in an overarching, cosmic scheme.

39. Wasserman speculates that Cather might have become aware of Bergson during her travels to England for *McClure's*, but if so, this awareness had no remarkable effect on *Alexander's Bridge*. Besides, Bergson was so popular a phenomenon in America (more popular than in England, in fact) that she would have hardly needed to travel beyond the local newsstand to become acquainted with him.

40. Bergson's, not Einstein's, "fourth dimension" (duration) was "deranging" people in these years.

41. Fisher and Alexander were Cather's fellow students at the University of Nebraska, and Fisher remained her friend afterward. Cather corresponded with and seems to have been on good terms with Edwin Björkman.

As we have already seen, Björkman advocated a Bergsonian literary program in his books and essays. Fisher's interest in Bergson is uncertain, but she did translate Adriano Tilgher's *Homo Faber* in 1930. Tilgher had published *Io libertà, e moralità nella filosofia di Enrico Bergson* in 1912, and Fisher may have been familiar with that book. Alexander, a professional philosopher and a member of the faculty at the University of Nebraska, published an essay on Bergson (see Alexander, "Socratic Bergson," pp. 32–43).

The relation between Cather and Alexander is intriguing but will no doubt remain mysterious. He perhaps was in her mind subconsciously when she wrote *Alexander's Bridge*, for she gave her central character an altered version of his name. Jasper Hunt recalls that Cather was "tied in" with members of the Union Literary Society at the University of Nebraska, which included Alexander (see Cather, *Writings from Willa Cather's Campus Years*, p. 127). Alexander's wife, Nelly, gave a copy of his *The Mid-Earth Life* (1907) to the Cather family (see Rosowski, *The Voyage Perilous*, p. 253 n. 11). This book, according to Rosowski, contains passages similar to passages in *Death Comes for the Archbishop*. Rosowski also notes that Alexander's actions when he was a professor of philosophy at the University of Nebraska (which he joined in 1908) were similar to those dramatized in Godfrey St. Peter of *The Professor's House*.

42. Letter to Elizabeth Sergeant, 25 June 1915, in Bourne, *The Letters of Randolph Bourne*, p. 306.

43. Letter to Carrie Miner (Sherwood), 11 February 1919, in the Willa Cather Pioneer Memorial Museum and Education Foundation, Red Cloud, Nebraska.

44. Bourne, *Youth and Life*, pp. 178–79.

45. Ibid., p. 182.

46. For example, the reviewer for the *Boston Transcript*, 16 July 1913, wrote that *O Pioneers!* was, "indirectly perhaps, an embodiment of feminist theory" (p. 18). And a reviewer for the *New York Times*, 14 September 1913, wrote that "possibly some might call it a feminist novel, but we are sure Miss Cather had nothing so inartistic in mind" (p. 466).

47. This image is borrowed from Bergson. See *MM*, p. 211.

48. Quoted in Sergeant, *Willa Cather*, p. 84.

49. Reprinted in Bloom, *Modern Critical Views: Willa Cather*, p. 147.

CHAPTER FOUR

1. Edith Lewis, *Willa Cather Living*, p. 93.

2. Cather, "Three American Singers," pp. 33–48.

3. H. L. Mencken turned the story down because he thought it might be libelous since it was so obviously patterned after Nordica. See Woodress, *Willa Cather: A Literary Life*, pp. 279–80.

4. Sergeant, *Willa Cather*, p. 137.

5. E. K. Brown, *Willa Cather*, p. 144.

6. Letter to Zoë Akins, n.d., 1947, in the Huntington Museum and Library, San Marino, California.

7. See respectively, Rosowski, *The Voyage Perilous*, p. 69; Stouck, *Willa Cather's Imagination*, p. 184; and E. K. Brown, *Willa Cather*, p. 144.

8. Jones, "Excerpt from *The Bright Medusa*," p. 241.

9. Bergson also defines the artist as a biological phenomenon in *Laughter* (*L* 241).

10. Mencken, Review of *The Song of the Lark*, pp. 7–8.

11. In *Time and Free Will*, Bergson notes that nature is all simultaneity and therefore does not possess the resources of rhythm (p. 16). Soon after Thea has absorbed the buzz and hum of the cicadas—their incessant repetition of sounds—a song begins to develop inside her. As an artist, she begins to supply rhythm to what is otherwise simple and spontaneous repetition.

12. In Bergson's system "matter" is what it appears to be—not things that change but change itself. The body is the primary image of matter each individual has; it is a thing that endures and is felt from within. As matter, the body repeats within itself the processes of bodily attitudes conjoined to its primary perceptions. To the extent that these patterns have developed in the course of evolution, they are repetitions of a primordial past speaking in the immanent present.

13. Bourne, *Youth and Life*, p. 218.

14. In 1931, Kenneth Burke, in *Counter-Statement*, advanced a similar notion when he wrote that the potentialities for aesthetic appreciation "seem to be inherent in the very germ-plasm of man, and which, since they are constant, we might call innate forms of mind" (see Burke, *Counter-Statement*, p. 46). I mention this because, so far as I know, no one has ever accused Burke of being remote, quaint, or antiquarian, though he seems to have held an aesthetic view similar to Cather's.

15. Henry Seidel Canby, for example, in "Fiction Sums Up a Century," wrote that Willa Cather "is preservative, almost antiquarian, content with much space in little room—feminine in this and in her passionate revelation of the values which conserve the life of the emotions" (vol. 2, p. 1216).

16. Letter to Zoë Akins, 18 January 1937, in the Huntington Museum and Library, San Marino, California.

17. Ibid., 16 September 1932.

18. Randall, *The Landscape and the Looking Glass*, p. 372.

19. Howard, *Literature and the American Tradition*, p. 254.

20. Frost, *The Poetry of Robert Frost*, pp. 259–60.

21. Cather often said that her art was not so much the product of invention as it was recollection and rearrangement (see her letter to Carrie Miner Sherwood, 29 April 1945, in the Willa Cather Pioneer Memorial Museum and Education Foundation, Red Cloud, Nebraska). She once insisted that her stories had to shape themselves on the paper before her like a picture or a drawing (ibid., 17 November 1941).

22. Sergeant, *Willa Cather*, p. 107.

23. Her Red Cloud characters, she wrote Carrie Miner Sherwood, 29 April 1945, were not to be precisely identified because they were made up of her emotions about them and not modeled after the physical types that engendered those feelings. The Paul of "Paul's Case," she said, was the combination of certain feelings

she had had about the glittering fascination of New York and her recollection of a romantic and pretentious young man she had had as a student. The combination of feelings and remembrance was how all creation works, she said.

24. Sergeant, *Willa Cather*, p. 111.

25. Stouck, *Willa Cather's Imagination*, p. 171.

26. Lovejoy, "The Obsolescence of the Eternal," pp. 479–502.

27. Reported in Butcher's *Many Lives—One Love*, p. 358.

28. Cather, "Plays of Real Life," pp. 63–72.

29. Stein, "Portraits and Repetition," p. 206.

30. Ibid., p. 181.

31. James E. Miller, "*My Ántonia*," pp. 476–84; reprinted in Bloom, *Modern Critical Views: Willa Cather*, pp. 51–59.

32. Bloom and Bloom, *Willa Cather's Gift of Sympathy*, p. 200.

33. In a letter to Irene Weisz, 6 June 1945, Cather expressed her enthusiastic appreciation of a letter she had received from Weisz. Her friend, Cather believed, recognized how much feeling went into her books, and Cather was especially glad that Weisz understood that the author's effects came from living feeling, not from artifice or cheap writerly tricks. The letter is in the Weisz collection at the Newberry Library in Chicago.

34. Sergeant, *Willa Cather*, p. 139.

35. She made this comparison in a letter to Akins, 10 October 1935, which is in the Huntington Museum and Library, San Marino, California.

36. See the essay by Zabel entitled "Willa Cather: The Tone of Time" in Bloom, *Modern Critical Views: Willa Cather*, pp. 41–49.

37. Henry James, Preface to *The Portrait of a Lady*, pp. 6–7.

38. See Wasserman, "The Music of Time," esp. pp. 232–39.

39. Reported in Sergeant, *Willa Cather*, p. 215.

40. For a discussion of Cather's use of sources, see Bloom and Bloom, "The Genesis of *Death Comes for the Archbishop*," pp. 479–506.

41. In "Joseph and His Brothers," Cather quoted the following passage from Mann:

> Indifference to the inner life of other human beings, ignorance of their feelings, display an entirely warped attitude toward real life, they give rise to a certain blindness. . . . Imagination, the art of divining the emotional life of others—in other words, sympathy—is not only commendable inasmuch as it breaks down the limitations of the ego; it is always an indispensable means of self-preservation. [*NUF* 115–16]

The equation of imagination and sympathy here wins Cather's complete approval. Wallace Stevens, as we will see, made an equivalent assertion when he identified the imagination with intuition. And for both, the operations of the imagination are instrumental in self-preservation and human evolution.

42. Wasserman, "The Music of Time," p. 230.
43. Quoted in Sergeant, *Willa Cather*, p. 281.

CHAPTER FIVE

1. Stevens copied in his commonplace book "Sur Plusiers Beaux Sujets" this passage of a letter from Henry Adams to Henry Osborn Taylor of 15 February 1915 that was quoted in the *Kenyon Review* (Winter 1940): "I need badly to find one man in history to admire. I am in near peril of turning Christian and rolling in the mud and in the agony of human mortification" (vol. 2, p. 1). This commonplace book is in the Huntington Museum and Library, San Marino, California. Stevens examined exhaustively the question of heroes and heroism in his "Examination of the Hero in a Time of War" (*CP* 273–81).
2. Vendler, *On Extended Wings*, p. 6.
3. Morse, *Wallace Stevens*, p. 115.
4. Santayana, *Interpretations of Poetry and Religion*, pp. 285–86.
5. Stevens's sonnet is reprinted in Buttel, *Wallace Stevens*, pp. 17–18; Santayana's sonnet is unpublished and is in the Huntington Museum and Library, San Marino, California.
6. Buttel, *Wallace Stevens*, passim, see esp. chaps. 1–3.
7. Joan Richardson in her *Wallace Stevens* describes Stevens's insecurities about his own masculinity and the inner divisions within him concerning the practical life and the life of the imagination (see particularly chaps. 4 and 5, "The Opposing Law, 1901–1904" and "It Will Exceed All Faëry, 1904–1907," pp. 159–265). George S. Lensing in his *Wallace Stevens* discusses Stevens's struggles with the conflict between the world of fact and the world of the ideal during his Harvard period, particularly in the chapter "Early Life and College Years," pp. 3–31.
8. See MacLeod, *Wallace Stevens and Company*, passim, see esp. chap. 2, pp. 19–44.
9. See Richardson, *Wallace Stevens*, p. 409. *Camera Work* featured any number of essays on the ambitions and characteristics of the new art. Some of the essayists continued to cite Herbert Spencer and Claude Bernard and to argue for the analytic and intellectual virtues or the positivistic and scientific character of cubism, for example. Others, like John Weischel in his piece "Cosmism or Amorphism?," insisted that the new artist "declares his more comprehensive point of view: all cosmos must be distilled in the eternal soul-depths of a full man." The ambition of the new artist, he continued, is "a positive attempt to embody in a plastic master-work the complete immanence, in man's perception, of all materiality and reality of the universe." Weischel cited Bergson as underwriting the new art: "The end of last century and our epoch shows science, in the hands of Ostwald and Bergson, unmistakably descending towards the domain of art; for such is the

position of their nature philosophies" (pp. 69–82). And Benjamin De Casseres in his essay "The Renaissance of the Irrational" avowed that "today the world is going back to Heraclitus." The new world exhibits "the sense of the Irrational as [the] principle of existence. It is the divination of Chance. It is the apotheosis of the Intuitive." He goes on to observe that "paradox of paradoxes! The new atheism is optimistic. Chance is a beneficent god! The Irrational has become a faith!" De Casseres further instanced Emerson, Thoreau, and Whitman (because they reported what they felt rather than what they saw) as the fathers of cubists and futurists (pp. 22–24).

10. Buttel, *Wallace Stevens*, p. 7.

11. See Richardson, *Wallace Stevens*, pp. 408–10; Morse, "Wallace Stevens, Bergson, Pater," pp. 1–34; Doggett, *Stevens' Poetry of Thought*, esp. pp. 35–36, 67–72; Riddell, *The Clairvoyant Eye*, pp. 37–38, 271–74; and Kermode, *Wallace Stevens*, pp. 80–83.

12. Stevens acquired the two-volume edition of Lowell's *Letters of James Russell Lowell* on 19 November 1898. Stevens wrote his comment in the margin of p. 73, vol. 1, beside this passage: "The proof of poetry is, in my mind, that it reduce to the essence of a single line the vague philosophy which is floating in all men's minds, and so render it portable and useful and ready to hand." Stevens continued his commentary: "I wonder what would be the fate of a poet who ventured to hang philosophy and stop guessing at truths that are as far off as ever." Stevens's copy of the *Letters* is in the Huntington Museum and Library, San Marino, California.

13. See the untitled lecture by Wahl in Hanna, *The Bergsonian Heritage*, p. 153.

14. The poem is reprinted in Buttel, *Wallace Stevens*, p. 15.

15. The poem is reprinted in ibid., p. 56.

16. Riddell, *The Clairvoyant Eye*, p. 73.

17. Ibid., p. 76.

18. Ibid., p. 75.

19. William James, *Pragmatism and Four Essays from "The Meaning of Truth,"* p. 133.

20. See William James, *Principles of Psychology*, vol. 2, pp. 442–85.

21. Litz, *Introspective Voyager*, p. 43.

22. William James, *Varieties of Religious Experience*, p. 84.

23. Kermode, *Wallace Stevens*, p. 58.

24. Morse's Introduction to Stevens's *Opus Posthumous*, p. xxxv.

25. Doggett, *Stevens' Poetry of Thought*, p. 159.

26. Morris, *Wallace Stevens*, p. 46.

27. Litz, *Introspective Voyager*, p. 45.

28. Moore, "Well Moused, Lion," p. 27.

29. Burke, *Permanence and Change*, p. 69.

30. Doggett, *Stevens' Poetry of Thought*, p. 208.

CHAPTER SIX

1. See esp. Baird's *The Dome and the Rock*.

2. Stevens expressed his desire to participate in the common life in a letter to Hi Simons dated 12 January 1940: "About the time when I, personally, began to feel round for a new romanticism, I might naturally have been expected to start on a new cycle. Instead of doing so, I began to feel that I was on the edge: that I was isolated, and that I wanted to share the common life." The common life for Stevens was epitomized by a photograph of "a lot of fat men and women in the woods, drinking beer and singing Hi-li Hi-lo" (*LWS* 352).

3. R. P. Blackmur disputed the linguistic preciousness attributed to Stevens and showed how precisely (though that very precision might inaugurate ambiguities) Stevens's vocabulary works within his verse (see Blackmur, "Examples of Wallace Stevens," pp. 52–80).

4. Stevens, "Sur Plusiers Beaux Sujets," vol. 2, p. 17, in the Huntington Museum and Library, San Marino, California.

5. Bergson expands upon this notion in "Perception of Change":

The auxiliary of action, it [perception] isolates that part of reality as a whole that interests us; it shows us less the things themselves than the use we can make of them. It classifies, it labels them beforehand; we scarcely look at the object, it is enough for us to know to which category it belongs. But now and then, by a lucky accident, men arise whose senses or whose consciousness are less adherent to life. Nature has forgotten to attach their faculty of perceiving to their faculty of acting. When they look at a thing, they see it for itself, and not for themselves. . . . In regard to a certain aspect of their nature, whether it be their consciousness or one of their senses, they are born *detached*; and according to whether this detachment is that of a particular sense, or of consciousness, they are painters or sculptors, musicians or poets. [*CM* 162–63]

6. William James, *Principles of Psychology*, vol. 1, p. 554.

7. Szathmary, *The Aesthetic Theory of Bergson*, pp. 73–74. B. J. Leggett in his *Wallace Stevens and Poetic Theory* argues persuasively that I. A. Richards's *Coleridge on Imagination* contributed a great deal to Stevens's use and understanding of the term abstraction. Abstraction, conceived as Richards found it in Coleridge, argues Leggett, assisted Stevens in dissolving what Leggett calls the "imagination reality conflict" because abstraction is the necessary condition of language and even the most particularized sensuous detail comes from this process. Leggett's argument, though it derives from different sources, so far as I can see, in no way conflicts with my own. Clearly, however, Stevens had dissolved the conflict Leggett identifies a long time before he came to prepare his lectures on the relation of reality and

the imagination (see Leggett's book, esp. pp. 26–41).

8. This may be an example of Stevens's adaptation of a philosophical and poetic concept. In "A Collect of Philosophy," Stevens quotes a summary of Schopenhauer from "A Student's History of Philosophy": "Reality, then, is will. . . . We must leave out of our conception of the universal will that action for intelligent ends which characterizes human willing. . . . The will is thus far deeper seated than the intellect; it is the blind man carrying on his shoulders the lame man who can see" (*OP* 192–93). In any event, the man in "Contrary Theses (II)" who carries an infant on his shoulder sees beyond the intellect with an innocent eye.

9. Stevens characterizes Freud as a "realist" (*NA* 15). He also notes that Nicolas Boileau's remark that "Descartes had cut poetry's throat is a remark that could have been made respecting a great many people during the last hundred years, and of no one more aptly than of Freud" (*NA* 15).

10. Phenomenological criticism offers a rich critical vein for interpreting and assessing Stevens's poetic achievement. Joseph Riddell approvingly points to this possibility in the conclusion of *The Clairvoyant Eye*, pp. 271–72. Critics, such as J. Hillis Miller in *Poets of Reality*, Michel Benamou in "Wallace Stevens and the Symbolist Imagination," pp. 92–120, and Richard Macksey in "The Climates of Wallace Stevens," pp. 185–223, have investigated some of these possibilities.

In 1951, Stevens quoted in his lecture "A Collect of Philosophy" from a letter by Jean Wahl a suggestive assessment of Edmund Husserl's *Méditations Cartésiennes*, but no evidence exists that Stevens ever read Husserl firsthand. In 1952, he did attempt to acquire a copy in French of Martin Heidegger's work on Friederick Hölderin (*LWS* 758) and otherwise expressed a curiosity about the man and his works (*LWS* 839, 846). Evidently that curiosity was never satisfied. At any rate, even if Stevens had acquired the writings of Husserl or Heidegger, his acquaintance with phenomenology would have come too late to have had more than a belated and tributary influence upon him. Nevertheless, several interesting parallels appear between Bergsonism and phenomenology. See, for example, Ingarden, "L'Intuition bergsonienne et le problème phénoménologie de la constitution," vol. I, pp. 163–66; Marneff, "Bergson's and Husserl's Concepts of Intuition," pp. 169–80; Seyppel, "A Criticism of Heidegger's Time Concept with Reference to Bergson's 'durée'," pp. 503–8.

11. William James, *Principles of Psychology*, vol. 2, p. 361.

12. Stein, "Portraits and Repetition," pp. 174–75.

13. Stevens's copy of Mauron's *Aesthetics and Psychology* is in the Huntington Museum and Library, San Marino, California. The work is heavily annotated, but the annotations remind one of a conscientious student cramming for an exam and are hardly revealing except, perhaps, for his copying a sentence from p. 69 on the inside cover: "Art sets out to express the human soul." He uses the statement as his own in "The Noble Rider and the Sound of Words" (*NA* 30). And Leggett has

found several echoes of the book in Stevens's "Notes toward a Supreme Fiction" (see Leggett, *Wallace Stevens and Poetic Theory*, esp. pp. 72–109). Stevens scored this passage on p. 90 of Mauron's book: "If I wished to give this discussion all the philosophic breadth of which it is capable, I should point out that the search for resemblances is an essential characteristic of the human mind." And he underlined this Bergsonian statement on p. 91: "In active life the intellect looks for resemblances because it wishes to foresee efficiently; in art this aim disappears but the intellect still looks for analogies—that is its function—and now, it seems, for the pure pleasure of finding them."

14. Kenneth Burke strikes a similar note when he argues that language "logologically" insists upon greater and greater abstraction, that language searches for a "title of titles" that "is technically a 'god-term'," (see Burke, *The Rhetoric of Religion*, p. 33).

15. Stevens's selection of a pineapple as the subject for this poem may have been a deliberate and sly allusion to John Locke. Locke had instanced the pineapple as an object of which we can have no sensation except by sense impressions. Sensations, though not so certain as intuitive knowledge or the demonstrations of reason, yield knowledge of an external world that causes those sensations, Locke argued. Sense organs do not cause perceptions; otherwise, "the eyes of a man in the dark would produce colors, and his nose smell roses in winter; but we see nobody gets the relish of a pineapple till he goes to the Indies, where it is, and tastes it" (see Locke, *An Essay Concerning Human Understanding*, vol. 2, p. 328). Stevens's poem repudiates this sort of empiricism.

16. Stevens's identification of the imagination's resistance to the pressures of reality recalls a passage from the concluding paragraph of *Creative Evolution*:

> matter, the reality which *descends*, endures only by its connection with that which *ascends*. But life and consciousness are this very ascension. . . . it is within the evolutionary movement that we place ourselves, in order to follow it to its present results. . . . Such seems to us to be the true function of philosophy. So understood, philosophy is not only the turning of the mind homeward, the coincidence of human consciousness with the living principle whence it emanates, a contact with the creative effort: it is the study of becoming in general, it is true evolutionism. [*CE* 369–70]

17. In reading Bergson, Jung discovered to his "great pleasure" that everything he had worked out practically was contained in Bergson's writings "but expressed by him in consummate language and in wonderfully clear philosophical style" (see Jung, "The Content of Psychoses, Part II, 1914," p. 351).

18. Lenora Woodman, for example, argues that Stevens is a "deeply religious poet" and that his subject is not natural man but, finally, "transcendental man" (see Woodman, *Stanza My Stone*, p. 4).

19. Quoted in Blotner's *Faulkner*, vol. 2, p. 1441.

20. In section 4 of "Esthétique du Mal," Stevens speaks of "B." at the piano. "Did he play / All sorts of notes," Stevens asks.

> Or did he play only one
> In an ecstasy of its associates,
> Variations in the tones of a single sound,
> The last, or sounds so single they seemed one? [*CP* 316]

The relevance of these lines to the poem's subject, pain, may be clarified by comparing them to a passage from *Time and Free Will*:

> The intensity of affective sensations might thus be nothing more than our consciousness of the involuntary movements which are being begun and outlined, so to speak, within these states, and which would have gone on in their own way if nature had made us automata instead of conscious beings.
> If such be the case, we shall not compare a pain of increasing intensity to a note which grows louder and louder, but *rather to a symphony, in which an increasing number of instruments make themselves heard.* [*TFW* 35; italics mine]

21. Bloom maintains that "any analysis" of Stevens's poetic stances "must rely upon some account of the way in which the Romantic dialectic of *ethos, logos,* and *pathos* in Wordsworth, Shelley, Keats, and Tennyson was modulated by Emerson into an American dialectic that he called Fate, Freedom, and Power" (see Bloom, *Wallace Stevens,* p. 3); Frye claims Stevens's poetry is "centrally" in the romantic tradition (see Frye, "The Realistic Oriole," p. 163); Litz takes Stevens at his word that he wished to fashion a new romanticism and says that Stevens wanted to "restate" the romantic (see Litz, *Introspective Voyager,* p. 190); and Bornstein maintains that Stevens both "extended romantic literary theory and reshaped romantic mental action into the poems of our climate" (see Bornstein, *Transformations of Romanticism in Yeats, Eliot, and Stevens,* p. 163).

22. Pearce finds in the poetry of Stevens a reemergence of the "Adamic" phase in American poetry that is a continuation of the poetics in the Emersonian tradition. Stevens, according to Pearce, explores the aboriginal source of our being, but with a difference. "But where Emerson was driven in the end to postulate a nature beyond nature, a supernatural, Stevens would postulate a reality within reality, an intranatural, or an infranatural" (see Pearce, *The Continuity of American Poetry,* pp. 413 and 376–419 passim).

23. Riddell, *The Clairvoyant Eye,* pp. 29–31.

24. See Santayana's essay entitled "The Genteel Tradition in American Philosophy" that was reprinted in his *The Genteel Tradition,* p. 55.

25. See Santayana's essay entitled "The Genteel Tradition at Bay" in his *The Genteel Tradition at Bay,* p. 162.

26. Ibid., p. 163.

27. Stevens, "Sur Plusiers Beaux Sujets," vol. 2, pp. 21–22. The notebooks are in the Huntington Museum and Library, San Marino, California. As early as 1913, similar objections to Picasso's cubism had been registered in *Camera Work*, a journal with which Stevens was probably familiar.

28. Doggett, *Stevens' Poetry of Thought*, p. 213.

29. Jarrell, "The Collected Poems of Wallace Stevens," p. 352; reprinted in Brown and Haller, *The Achievement of Wallace Stevens*, p. 190.

BIBLIOGRAPHY

A bibliographical listing of the works of Henri Bergson, Willa Cather, and Wallace Stevens cited in this study can be found in A Note on Texts and Abbreviations, pp. xi–xiv.

Adams, Henry. *The Education of Henry Adams*. Edited by Ernest Samuels. Boston: Houghton Mifflin Co., 1973.

Alexander, Hartley Burr. "Socratic Bergson." *Mid-West Quarterly* 4 (October 1913): 32–43.

Ammons, Elizabeth. "The Engineer as Cultural Hero and Willa Cather's First Novel, *Alexander's Bridge*." *American Quarterly* 38 (Winter 1986): 748–60.

Arnold, Marilyn. *Willa Cather's Short Fiction*. Athens: Ohio University Press, 1984.

———, ed. *Willa Cather: A Reference Guide*. Boston: G. K. Hall and Co., 1986.

Babbitt, Irving. "Bergson and Rousseau." *Nation* (1 November 1912): 452–55.

Baird, James. *The Dome and the Rock: Structure in the Poetry of Wallace Stevens*. Baltimore: Johns Hopkins University Press, 1968.

Balfour, Arthur J. "Creative Evolution and Philosophic Doubt." *Hibbert Journal* (October 1911): 1–23.

"Balfour's Objections to Bergson's Philosophy." *Current Literature* (December 1911): 659–61.

"The Banning of Bergson." *Independent* (20 July 1914): 85–86.

Bates, Milton J. *Wallace Stevens: A Mythology of Self*. Berkeley and Los Angeles: University of California Press, 1985.

Becker, Carl. *Every Man His Own Historian: Essays on History and Politics*. New York: F. S. Crofts and Co., 1935.

———. *The Heavenly City of the Eighteenth-Century Philosophers*. New Haven, Conn.: Yale University Press, 1932.

———. "Some Aspects of the Influence of Social Problems and Ideas upon the Study and Writing of History." *American Journal of Sociology* 18 (March 1913): 641–75.

Behrman, S. N. *Portrait of Max: An Intimate Memoir of Sir Max Beerbohm*. New York: Random House, 1960.

Benamou, Michel. "Wallace Stevens and the Symbolist Imagination." In *The Act of the Mind: Essays on the Poetry of Wallace Stevens*, edited by Roy Harvey Pearce and J. Hillis Miller, pp. 92–120. Baltimore: Johns Hopkins University Press, 1965.

Bennett, Mildred. *The World of Willa Cather*. Lincoln: University of Nebraska Press, 1961.

Bergson, Henri. *Durée et simultanéité: à propos de la théorie d'Einstein*. Paris: Félix Alcan, 1922.

————. *Écrits et Paroles*. Paris: Presses Universitaires de France, 1957–59.

"Bergson's Reception in America." *Current Opinion* (March 1913): 226.

Bieganowski, Ronald. "Robert Frost's *A Boy's Will* and Henri Bergson's *Creative Evolution*." *South Carolina Review* 21, no. 1 (Fall 1988): 9–16.

————. "Sense of Time in Robert Frost's Poetic: A Particular Influence of Henri Bergson." *Resources for American Literary Study* 13, no. 2 (Autumn 1983): 184–94.

Björkman, Edwin. "Henri Bergson: Philosopher or Prophet?" *Review of Reviews* (August 1911): 250–52.

————. "Henri Bergson: The Philosopher of Actuality." *Forum* (September 1911): 268–76.

————. *Is There Anything New under the Sun?* New York: Mitchell Kennerley, 1911.

Blackmur, R. P. "Examples of Wallace Stevens." In *The Achievement of Wallace Stevens*, edited by Ashley Brown and Robert S. Haller, pp. 52–80. Philadelphia: J. B. Lippincott Co., 1962.

Bloom, Edward A., and Lillian D. Bloom. "The Genesis of *Death Comes for the Archbishop*." *American Literature* 26 (January 1955): 479–506.

————. *Willa Cather's Gift of Sympathy*. Carbondale: Southern Illinois University Press, 1962.

Bloom, Harold, ed. *Modern Critical Views: Wallace Stevens*. New York: Chelsea House Publishers, 1985.

————. *Modern Critical Views: Willa Cather*. New York: Chelsea House Publishers, 1985.

————. *Wallace Stevens: The Poems of Our Climate*. Ithaca, N.Y.: Cornell University Press, 1976.

Blotner, Joseph. *Faulkner: A Biography*. 2 vols. New York: Random House, 1974.

Boorstin, Daniel. "The Myth of an American Enlightenment." In *America and the Image of Europe: Reflections on American Thought*, pp. 65–78. New York: World Publishing Co., 1960.

Bornstein, George. *Transformations of Romanticism in Yeats, Eliot, and Stevens*. Chicago: University of Chicago Press, 1976.

Boroff, Marie, ed. *Wallace Stevens: A Collection of Critical Essays*. Englewood Cliffs, N.J.: Prentice Hall, 1963.

Bosanquet, Bernard. *The Distinction between Mind and Its Object: The Adamson*

Lecture for 1913; With an Appendix. Manchester, England: The University Press, 1913.

Bourne, Randolph. *The Letters of Randolph Bourne: A Comprehensive Edition*. Edited by Eric J. Sandeen. Troy, N.Y.: Whitsun Publishing Co., 1981.

———. *Youth and Life*. Boston: Houghton Mifflin Co., 1913.

Brazeau, Peter. *Parts of a World: Wallace Stevens Remembered*. New York: Random House, 1983.

Brooks, Van Wyck. "America's Coming of Age." In *Essays on America*, pp. 15–112. New York: E. P. Dutton and Co., 1970.

———. *The Confident Years, 1885–1915*. New York: E. P. Dutton, 1952.

Brown, Ashley, and Robert S. Haller, eds. *The Achievement of Wallace Stevens*. Philadelphia: J. B. Lippincott Co., 1962.

Brown, Edward Killian. *Willa Cather: A Critical Biography*. Completed by Leon Edel. New York: Avon Books, 1953.

Bruccoli, Matthew. *Some Sort of Epic Grandeur: The Life of F. Scott Fitzgerald*. New York: Harcourt Brace Jovanovich, 1981.

Burke, Kenneth. *Counter-Statement*. Los Angeles and Berkeley: University of California Press, 1968.

———. *Permanence and Change: An Anatomy of Purpose*. New York: Bobbs-Merrill Co., 1965.

———. *The Rhetoric of Religion: Studies in Logology*. Boston: Beacon Press, 1961.

Burroughs, John. "A Prophet of the Soul." *Atlantic* (January 1914): 120–32.

Butcher, Fanny. *Many Lives—One Love*. New York: Harper and Row, 1972.

Buttel, Robert W. *Wallace Stevens: The Making of "Harmonium."* Princeton, N.J.: Princeton University Press, 1967.

Campbell, SueEllen. "Equal Opposites: Wyndham Lewis, Henri Bergson, and Their Philosophies of Time." *Twentieth-Century Literature* 29 (Fall 1983): 351–69.

Canby, Henry Seidel. "Fiction Sums Up a Century." In *Literary History of the United States: History*, edited by Robert Spiller, Willard Thorp, et al., vol. 1, pp. 1208–36. New York: Macmillan Co., 1948.

Carr, H. Wildon. *The Philosophy of Change: A Study of the Fundamental Principles of the Philosophy of Bergson*. London: Macmillan and Co., 1914.

Carroll, Joseph. *Wallace Stevens' Supreme Fiction: A New Romanticism*. Baton Rouge: Louisiana State University Press, 1987.

Cather, Willa. "Plays of Real Life." *McClure's* 40 (March 1913): 63–72.

———. "Three American Singers: Louise Homer, Geraldine Farrar, Olive Fremstad." *McClure's* 42 (December 1913): 33–48.

———. *Writings from Willa Cather's Campus Years*. Edited by John R. Shively. Lincoln: University of Nebraska Press, 1950.

Chapple, Joe Mitchell, ed. *Heart Throbs in Prose and Verse: The Old Scrap Book*. New York: Grosset and Dunlap, 1905.

Church, Margaret. *Time and Reality: Studies in Contemporary Fiction*. Chapel Hill: University of North Carolina Press, 1949.

Cochran, Thomas C., and William Miller. *The Age of Enterprise: A Social History of Industrial America*. Rev. ed. New York: Harper and Row, 1961.

Conder, John J. *Naturalism in American Fiction: The Classic Phase*. Lexington: University of Kentucky Press, 1984.

Cowley, Malcolm. "Naturalism in American Literature." In *Evolutionary Thought in America*, edited by Stow Persons, pp. 300–333. Hamden, Conn.: Archon Books, 1968.

Cox, Marion. "Bergson's Message to Feminism." *Forum* (May 1913): 548–59.

Day, Clarence, Jr. *This Simian World*. New York: Alfred A. Knopf, 1920.

De Casseres, Benjamin. "The Renaissance of the Irrational." *Camera Work* no. 43 (1913): 22–24.

Delattre, Floris. "La durée bergsonienne dans le roman de Virginia Woolf." *Revue Anglo-Américaine* 9 (December 1932): 97–108.

Dell, Floyd. *Homecoming: An Autobiography*. Port Washington, N.Y.: Kennikat Press, 1961.

Dodson, George Rowland. *Bergson and the Modern Spirit: An Essay in Constructive Thought*. Boston: American Unitarian Association, 1913.

Doggett, Frank. *Stevens' Poetry of Thought*. Baltimore: Johns Hopkins University Press, 1966.

Douglas, George William. "Christ and Bergson." *North American Review* (April 1913): 433–44.

Douglass, Paul. *Bergson, Eliot, and American Literature*. Lexington: University of Kentucky Press, 1986.

———. "The Gold Coin: Bergsonian Intuition and Modernist Aesthetics." *Thought: A Review of Culture and Idea* 58 (June 1983): 234–50.

Driesch, Hans. *The History and Theory of Vitalism*. Translated by C. K. Ogden. London: Macmillan and Co., 1914.

———. *The Problem of Individuality: A Course of Four Lectures Delivered before the University of London in 1913*. London: Macmillan and Co., 1914.

———. *The Science and Philosophy of the Organism: The Gifford Lectures Delivered before the University of Aberdeen in the Year 1907 and 1908*. 2 vols. London: Adam and Charles Black, 1908.

Edel, Leon. "A Cave of One's Own." In *Critical Essays on Willa Cather*, edited by John J. Murphy, pp. 200–217. Boston: G. K. Hall and Co., 1984.

Edelstein, J. M., ed. *Wallace Stevens: A Descriptive Bibliography*. Pittsburgh: University of Pittsburgh Press, 1973.

Eliot, T[homas] S[tearns]. "Eeldrop and Appleplex." 2 pts. *The Little Review* pt. 1 (May 1917): 7–11; pt. 2 (September 1917): 16–19.

———. *Selected Prose of T. S. Eliot*. Edited by Frank Kermode. New York: Harcourt Brace Jovanovich, 1975.

————. *A Sermon Preached in Magdalene College Chapel.* Cambridge, England: 1948.

Elliot, Hugh S. R. *Modern Science and the Illusions of Professor Bergson.* New York: Longmans, Green and Co., 1912.

Eucken, Rudolf. *Knowledge and Life.* Translated by W. Tudor Jones. New York: G. P. Putnam's Sons, 1913.

————. *Main Currents of Modern Thought: A Study of the Spiritual and Intellectual Movements of the Present Day.* Translated by Meyrick Booth. New York: Charles Scribner's Sons, 1912.

————. "Naturalism or Idealism?" In *Nobel Lectures: Including Presentation Speeches and Laureate's Biographies, Literature, 1907–1967,* edited by Horst Frenz, pp. 74–87. Amsterdam: Elsevier Publishing Co., 1969.

Fernandat, René. "Bergson et Valéry." *Vie Intellectuelle* 14, nos. 8–9 (August–September 1946): 122–46.

Fitzgerald, F. Scott. *The Beautiful and the Damned.* New York: Charles Scribner's Sons, 1922.

Flewelling, Ralph Tyler. *Bergson and Personal Realism.* New York: Abingdon Press, 1920.

————. "Bergson, Ward, and Eucken in Their Relation to Bowne." *Methodist Review* 96 (1914): 374–82.

"Freedom." *Craftsman* (January 1913): 379.

Friedman, Maurice. *To Deny Our Nothingness: Contemporary Images of Man.* London: Victor Gollancz, 1967.

Frost, Robert. *The Poetry of Robert Frost.* Edited by Edward Connery Lathem. New York: Holt, Rinehart and Winston, 1975.

Frye, Northrop. "The Realistic Oriole: A Study of Wallace Stevens." In *Wallace Stevens: A Collection of Critical Essays,* edited by Marie Boroff, pp. 161–76. Englewood Cliffs, N.J.: Prentice Hall, 1963.

Gerrard, Thomas. "Bergson and Divine Fecundity." *Catholic World* 98 (August 1913): 631–48.

————. "Bergson and Finalism." *Catholic World* 98 (June 1913): 374–82.

————. "Bergson and Freedom." *Catholic World* 97 (May 1913): 222–31.

————. "Bergson, Newman, and Aquinas." *Catholic World* 96 (March 1913): 748–62.

————. "Bergson's Philosophy of Change." *Catholic World* 96 (January 1913): 433–88.

————. "Bergson's Philosophy of Change: His Intuitive Method." *Catholic World* 96 (February 1913): 602–16.

Gunter, P[eter] A. Y., ed. *Bergson and the Evolution of Physics.* Knoxville: University of Tennessee Press, 1969.

————. *Henri Bergson: A Bibliography.* Bowling Green, Ohio: Philosophy Documentation Center, Bowling Green University, 1974.

Haeckel, Ernst. *The Riddle of the Universe: At the Close of the Nineteenth Century.* Translated by Joseph McCabe. New York: Harper and Brothers, 1900.

Hale, Nathan G. *Freud and the Americans: The Beginnings of Psychoanalysis in the United States, 1876–1917.* New York: Oxford University Press, 1971.

Hale, Oron J. *The Great Illusion, 1900–1914.* New York: Harper and Row, 1971.

Hanna, Thomas, ed. *The Bergsonian Heritage.* New York: Columbia University Press, 1962.

Hartog, Marcus. *Problems of Life and Reproduction.* London: John Murray, 1913.

Hartshorne, Charles. *Creativity in American Philosophy.* Albany: State University of New York Press, 1984.

Helm, Bertrand. *Time and Reality in American Philosophy.* Amherst: University of Massachusetts Press, 1985.

Hermann, Emily. *Eucken and Bergson: Their Significance for Christian Thought.* Boston: Pilgrim Press, 1912.

Higham, John. "The Reorientation of American Culture in the 1890s." In *Writing American History: Essays on Modern Scholarship*, pp. 77–88. Bloomington: Indiana University Press, 1973.

Hines, Thomas J. *The Late Poetry of Wallace Stevens: Phenomenological Parallels with Husserl and Heidegger.* Lewisburg, Pa.: Bucknell University Press, 1976.

Hoernlé, R. F. Alfred. *Matter, Life, Mind, and God: Five Lectures on Contemporary Tendencies of Thought.* London: Methuen and Co., 1923.

Hoffman, Frederick J. *Freudianism and the Literary Mind.* Baton Rouge: Louisiana State University Press, 1945.

———. *The Twenties: American Writing in the Postwar Decade.* New York: Free Press, 1949.

Howard, Leon. *Literature and the American Tradition.* Garden City, N.Y.: Doubleday and Co., 1960.

Hulme, T[homas] E[rnest]. *Further Speculations.* Edited by Sam Hynes. Minneapolis: University of Minnesota Press, 1955.

———. "The International Philosophical Congress at Bologna." *Nature: A Weekly Illustrated Journal of Science* 86 (18 May 1911): 399–400.

———. *Speculations: Essays on Humanism and the Philosophy of Art.* Edited by Herbert Read. New York: Harcourt, Brace and Co., 1936.

Huneker, James Gibbons. "Playboy of Western Philosophy." *Forum* (March 1913): 257–68.

Ingarden, Roman. "L'Intuition bergsonienne et le problème phénoménologie de la constitution." In vol. 1, *Actes du Xe Congrès des Sociétés de Philosophie de Langue Française*, pp. 163–66. Paris: Armand Colin, 1959.

"Is the Bergsonian Philosophy That of a Charlatan?" *Current Literature* (February 1912): 198–99.

James, Henry. Preface to *The Portrait of a Lady.* Edited by Robert D. Bamberg. New York: W. W. Norton and Co., 1975.

James, William. *A Pluralistic Universe: Hibbert Lectures at Manchester College on the Present Situation in Philosophy.* New York: Longmans, Green, and Co., 1912.
_____. *Pragmatism and Four Essays from "The Meaning of Truth."* Edited by Ralph Barton Perry. New York: World Publishing Co., 1955.
_____. *Principles of Psychology.* 2 vols. 1890. Reprint. New York: Dover Publications, 1950.
_____. *Varieties of Religious Experience.* New York: Modern Library, 1929.
_____. *The Will to Believe.* 1897. Reprint. New York: Dover Publications, 1956.
Jarrell, Randall. "The Collected Poems of Wallace Stevens." *Yale Review* 44 (March 1955): 340–53.
Johnston, Charles. "Where Bergson Stands: An Appraisement of the French Philosopher and His Contribution to Modern Thought." *Harper's Weekly* (15 March 1913): 16.
Johnstone, James. *The Philosophy of Biology.* Cambridge: University Press, 1914.
Jones, Howard Mumford. *The Age of Energy: Varieties of American Experience, 1865–1915.* New York: Viking Press, 1970.
_____. "Excerpt from *The Bright Medusa.*" In *Willa Cather and Her Critics,* edited by James Schroeter, pp. 235–48. Ithaca, N.Y.: Cornell University Press, 1967.
Jung, Carl Gustav. "The Content of Psychoses, Part II, 1914." In *Collected Papers in Analytical Psychology,* edited by Constance E. Long, pp. 336–51. London: Balliere, Tindall, and Cox, 1922.
Kallen, Horace. *William James and Henri Bergson.* Chicago: University of Chicago Press, 1914.
Kaplan, Estelle. *Philosophy in the Poetry of Edwin Arlington Robinson.* New York: Columbia University Press, 1940.
Kermode, Frank. *Wallace Stevens.* Edinburgh: Oliver and Boyd, 1960.
Kern, Stephen. *The Culture of Time and Space: 1880–1918.* Cambridge: Harvard University Press, 1983.
Klawitter, Robert. "Henri Bergson and James Joyce's Fictional World." *Comparative Literature Studies* 3, no. 4 (1966): 429–37.
Kumar, Shiv Kumar. *Bergson and the Stream of Consciousness Novel.* New York: New York University Press, 1963.
La Guardia, David M. *Advance on Chaos: The Sanctifying Imagination of Wallace Stevens.* Hanover, N.H.: University Press of New England, 1983.
Lears, T. J. Jackson. "From Salvation to Self Realization: Advertising and the Therapeutic Roots of the Consumer Culture, 1880–1930." In *The Culture of Consumption: Critical Essays in American History, 1880–1980,* edited by Richard Wightman Fox and T. J. Jackson Lears, pp. 3–38. New York: Pantheon Books, 1983.
_____. *No Place of Grace: Antimodernism and the Transformation of American Culture, 1880–1920.* New York: Pantheon Books, 1981.

Leggett, B. J. *Wallace Stevens and Poetic Theory: Conceiving the Supreme Fiction*. Chapel Hill: University of North Carolina Press, 1987.

Lensing, George S. *Wallace Stevens: A Poet's Growth*. Baton Rouge: Louisiana State University Press, 1986.

Le Roy, Éduoard Emmanuel. *The New Philosophy of Henri Bergson*. Translated by Vincent Benson. New York: Henry Holt and Co., 1913.

Levenson, Michael H. *A Genealogy of Modernism: A Study of English Literary Doctrine, 1908–1922*. Cambridge: Cambridge University Press, 1984.

Levine, Louis. "The Philosophy of Henri Bergson and Syndicalism." *New York Times* (26 January 1913): pt. 5, p. 4.

Lewis, Edith. *Willa Cather Living: A Personal Record*. New York: Alfred A. Knopf, 1953.

Lewis, Wyndham. *Time and Western Man*. Boston: Beacon Press, 1957.

Lindsay, A. D. *The Philosophy of Bergson*. London: J. M. Dent and Sons, 1911.

Lippmann, Walter. "The Most Dangerous Man in the World." *Everybody's Magazine* (July 1912): 100–101.

———. *A Preface to Morals*. New York: Macmillan Co., 1929.

———. *A Preface to Politics*. Ann Arbor: University of Michigan Press, 1962.

Litz, A. Walton. *Introspective Voyager: The Poetic Development of Wallace Stevens*. New York: Oxford University Press, 1970.

Locke, John. *An Essay Concerning Human Understanding*. 2 vols. New York: Dover Publications, 1959.

Lodge, Oliver. "Balfour and Bergson." *Hibbert Journal* (January 1912): 290–307.

Lovejoy, A[lfred] O[ncken]. *Bergson and Romantic Evolutionism: Two Lectures Delivered before the Union, September 5 and 12, 1913*. Berkeley: University of California Press, 1914.

———. "The Metaphysician of the Life-Force." *Nation* (30 September 1909): 298–301.

———. "The Obsolescence of the Eternal." *Philosophical Review* 18 (1909): 479–502.

Lowell, James Russell. *Letters of James Russell Lowell*. 2 vols. Edited by Charles Eliot Norton. New York: Harper and Brothers, 1894.

McCormmach, Russell. *Night Thoughts of a Classical Physicist*. Cambridge: Harvard University Press, 1982.

Macksey, Richard. "The Climates of Wallace Stevens." In *The Act of the Mind: Essays on the Poetry of Wallace Stevens*, edited by Roy Harvey Pearce and J. Hillis Miller, pp. 185–223. Baltimore: Johns Hopkins University Press, 1965.

MacLeod, Glen G. *Wallace Stevens and Company: The "Harmonium" Years, 1913–1923*. Ann Arbor, Mich.: UMI Research Press, 1983.

Marneff, J. "Bergson's and Husserl's Concepts of Intuition." *Philosophical Quarterly* 23, no. 3 (1960): 169–80.

Martin, Jay. *Harvests of Change: American Literature, 1865–1914*. Englewood Cliffs, N.J.: Prentice Hall, 1967.

Martin, Ronald E. *American Literature and the Universe of Force*. Durham, N.C.: Duke University Press, 1981.

Matthews, T. S. *Great Tom: Notes toward the Definition of T. S. Eliot*. New York: Harper and Row, 1974.

Matthiessen, F. O. *The Achievement of T. S. Eliot: An Essay on the Nature of Poetry*. 3d ed. New York: Oxford University Press, 1958.

Mauron, Charles. *Aesthetics and Psychology*. Edited by Roger Fry and Katherine Johns. London: Hogarth Press, 1935.

May, Henry F. *The End of American Innocence: A Study of the First Years of Our Own Time, 1912–1917*. New York: Oxford University Press, 1979.

Mead, George Herbert. *Movements of Thought in the Nineteenth Century*. Edited by Merritt H. Moore. Chicago: University of Chicago Press, 1936.

Menand, Louis. *Discovering Modernism: T. S. Eliot and His Context*. New York: Oxford University Press, 1987.

Mencken, H. L. Review of *The Song of the Lark*. In *Willa Cather and Her Critics*, edited by James Schroeter, pp. 7–8. Ithaca, N.Y.: Cornell University Press, 1967.

Miller, J. Hillis. *Poets of Reality*. Cambridge: Harvard University Press, 1965.

Miller, James E. "*My Ántonia*: A Frontier Drama of Time." *American Quarterly* 10 (Winter 1958): 476–84.

Miller, Lucius Hopkins. *Bergson and Religion*. New York: Henry Holt and Co., 1916.

Miller, Perry. Introduction to *American Thought: Civil War to World War I*, edited by Perry Miller, pp. ix–lii. New York: Holt, Rinehart and Winston, 1954.

Moody, A. D. *Thomas Stearns Eliot: Poet*. New York: Cambridge University Press, 1979.

Moody, William Vaughan. "The Menagerie." In *Nation and Region: 1860–1900*, edited by Milton R. Stern and Seymour L. Gross, p. 580. New York: Viking Press, 1962.

Moore, Marianne. "Well Moused, Lion." In *The Achievement of Wallace Stevens*, edited by Ashley Brown and Robert S. Haller, pp. 21–28. Philadelphia: J. B. Lippincott Co., 1962.

Morris, Adelaide Kirby. *Wallace Stevens: Imagination and Faith*. Princeton, N.J.: Princeton University Press, 1974.

Morse, Samuel French. "Wallace Stevens, Bergson, Pater." *ELH* 30 (March 1964): 1–34.

———. *Wallace Stevens: Poetry as Life*. New York: Pegasus, 1970.

Murphy, John J., ed. *Critical Essays on Willa Cather*. Boston: G. K. Hall and Co., 1984.

Murry, John Middleton. "Art and Philosophy." In *The Road from Paris: French Influences on English Poetry, 1900–1920*, edited by Cyrena Pondrom, pp. 54–57. Cambridge: Cambridge University Press, 1974.

O'Brien, Sharon. *Willa Cather: The Emerging Voice*. New York: Oxford University Press, 1987.

"Pascendi Dominici Gregis." In *The Papal Encyclicals: 1903–1939*, translated by Claudia Carlen, pp. 71–97. Wilmington, N.C.: McGrath Publishing Co., 1981.

Pearce, Roy Harvey. *The Continuity of American Poetry*. Princeton, N.J.: Princeton University Press, 1961.

Pearce, Roy Harvey, and J. Hillis Miller, eds. *The Act of the Mind: Essays on the Poetry of Wallace Stevens*. Baltimore: Johns Hopkins University Press, 1965.

Perry, Ralph Barton. *The Present Conflict of Ideals: A Study of the Philosophical Background of the World War*. New York: Longmans, Green, and Co., 1922.

———. *The Thought and Character of William James*. Briefer edition. Cambridge: Harvard University Press, 1967.

Persons, Stow, ed. *Evolutionary Thought in America*. Hamden, Conn.: Archon Books, 1968.

Peterson, Margaret. "*Harmonium* and William James." *Southern Review* 7 (July 1971): 658–82.

Pfister, Karin. *Zeit und Wirklichleit bei Thomas Wolfe*. Heidelberg: Carl Winter Universitätsverlag, 1949.

Pilkington, Anthony. *Bergson and His Influence*. Cambridge: Cambridge University Press, 1976.

Poirier, Richard. *Robert Frost: The Work of Knowing*. New York: Oxford University Press, 1977.

Pondrom, Cyrena, ed. *The Road from Paris: French Influence on English Poetry, 1900–1920*. Cambridge: Cambridge University Press, 1974.

Poulet, Georges. *Studies in Human Time*. Translated by Elliot Coleman. Baltimore: Johns Hopkins University Press, 1956.

"Professor Bergson at the City College." *Outlook* 103 (1 March 1913): 467.

Putnam, James Jackson. *James Jackson Putnam and Psychoanalysis: Letters between Putnam and Sigmund Freud, Ernest Jones, William James, Sandor Ferenezi, and Morton Prince, 1887–1907*. Edited by Nathan G. Hale. Cambridge: Harvard University Press, 1971.

Quirk, Tom. "Bergson in America." In *Prospects: An Annual Journal of American Cultural Studies*, pp. 453–90. Vol. 11-*Essays*. Cambridge: Cambridge University Press, 1987.

———. "Cather and Fitzgerald: *The Great Gatsby*." *American Literature* 54 (December 1982): 576–91.

Randall, John H. *The Landscape and the Looking Glass: Willa Cather's Search for Value*. Boston: Houghton Mifflin Co., 1960.

Review of *O Pioneers!*. *Boston Transcript* (16 July 1913): 18.

Review of *O Pioneers!*. *New York Times* (14 September 1913): 466.

Richardson, Joan. *Wallace Stevens: The Early Years, 1879–1923*. New York: William Morrow, 1986.

Riddell, Joseph N. *The Clairvoyant Eye: The Poetry and Poetics of Wallace Stevens*. Baton Rouge: Louisiana State University Press, 1965.

Riley, Woodbridge. *American Thought: From Puritanism to the Present*. New York: Henry Holt and Co., 1915.

Robinson, Edwin Arlington. *Collected Poems of Edwin Arlington Robinson*. New York: Macmillan Co., 1929.

Robinson, James Harvey. *The New History: Essays Illustrating the Modern Historical Outlook*. New York: Macmillan Co., 1912.

Roosevelt, Theodore. "The Search for Truth in a Reverent Spirit." *Outlook* (2 December 1911): 819–26.

Rosowski, Susan. *The Voyage Perilous: Willa Cather's Romanticism*. Lincoln: University of Nebraska Press, 1986.

Royce, Josiah. *Herbert Spencer: An Estimate and Review*. New York: Fox, Duffield and Co., 1904.

Russell, Bertrand. *The Autobiography of Bertrand Russell: 1872–1914*. New York: Bantam Books, 1967.

Sanborn, Alvan F. "Henry Bergson Pronounced 'The Foremost Thinker in France': Personality, Philosophy, and Influence." *Century* (December 1912): 172–76.

Santayana, George. *The Genteel Tradition*. Edited by Douglas L. Wilson. Cambridge: Harvard University Press, 1967.

————. *The Genteel Tradition at Bay*. New York: Charles Scribner's Sons, 1931.

————. *Interpretations of Poetry and Religion*. New York: Charles Scribner's Sons, 1900.

————. *Winds of Doctrine: Studies in Contemporary Opinion*. New York: Charles Scribner's Sons, 1913.

Schroeter, James, ed. *Willa Cather and Her Critics*. Ithaca, N.Y.: Cornell University Press, 1967.

Schwartz, Sanford. *The Matrix of Modernism: Pound, Eliot, and Early Twentieth-Century Thought*. Princeton, N.J.: Princeton University Press, 1985.

Scoon, Robert. "The Rise and Impact of Evolutionary Ideas." In *Evolutionary Thought in America*, edited by Stow Persons, pp. 4–42. Hamden, Conn.: Archon Books, 1968.

Sears, John F. "William James, Henri Bergson, and the Poetics of Robert Frost." *New England Quarterly* 48 (September 1975): 341–61.

Seibel, George. "Miss Cather from Nebraska." *New Colophon* 2 (September 1949): 195–208.

Sergeant, Elizabeth Shepley. *Willa Cather: A Memoir*. Lincoln: University of Nebraska Press, 1963.

Seyppel, Joachim H. "A Criticism of Heidegger's Time Concept with Reference to Bergson's 'durée'." *Revue Internationale de Philosophie* 10, no. 4 (1956): 503–8.

Skaff, William. *The Philosophy of T. S. Eliot: From Skepticism to a Surrealist Poetic, 1909–1927.* Philadelphia: University of Pennsylvania Press, 1986.

Skaggs, Merrill Maguire. "Poe's Shadow on *Alexander's Bridge.*" *Mississippi Quarterly* 35 (Fall 1982): 365–74.

Slosson, Edwin. "Twelve Major Prophets of Today: Henri Bergson." *Independent* (8 June 1911): 1246–61.

Slote, Bernice. "The Kingdom of Art." In *The Kingdom of Art: Willa Cather's First Principles and Critical Statements, 1893–1896,* edited by Bernice Slote, pp. 31–112. Lincoln: University of Nebraska Press, 1966.

Spencer, Herbert. *First Principles.* New York: D. Appleton and Co., 1894.

Steele, J. Dorman. *Fourteen Weeks in Natural Philosophy.* New York: A. S. Barnes and Co., 1875.

Stein, Gertrude. "Portraits and Repetition." In *Lectures in America.* Boston: Beacon Press, 1957.

Stewart, Allegra. "The Quality of Gertrude Stein's Creativity." *American Literature* 28 (January 1957): 488–506.

Stewart, James McKeller. *A Critical Exposition of Bergson's Philosophy.* London: Macmillan and Co., 1911.

Stouck, David. *Willa Cather's Imagination.* Lincoln: University of Nebraska Press, 1975.

Sutherland, Donald. "Willa Cather: The Classic Voice." In *Modern Critical Views: Willa Cather,* edited by Harold Bloom, pp. 123–43. New York: Chelsea House Publishers, 1985.

Szathmary, Arthur. *The Aesthetic Theory of Bergson.* Cambridge: Harvard University Press, 1937.

"Threatened Collapse of the Bergson Boom in France." *Current Opinion* (May 1914): 371.

Tichi, Cecelia. *Shifting Gears: Technology, Literature, Culture in Modernist America.* Chapel Hill: University of North Carolina Press, 1987.

Trilling, Lionel. "Willa Cather." In *Willa Cather and Her Critics,* edited by James Schroeter, pp. 148–55. Ithaca, N.Y.: Cornell University Press, 1967.

Tuchman, Barbara. *The Guns of August.* New York: Macmillan Co., 1962.

Twain, Mark [Samuel L. Clemens]. "What Is Happiness?" Parts reprinted in Walter Blair, *Mark Twain and Huck Finn,* p. 337. Berkeley and Los Angeles: University of California Press, 1960.

Tyrell, Henry. "Bergson." *Art World* (September 1917): 520–21.

Underhill, Evelyn. "Bergson and the Mystics." *Living Age* (16 March 1912): 668–75.

Vendler, Helen. *On Extended Wings: Wallace Stevens' Longer Poems.* Cambridge: Harvard University Press, 1969.

Wasserman, Loretta. "The Music of Time: Henri Bergson and Willa Cather." *American Literature* 57 (May 1985): 226–39.

Watt, Ian. *Conrad in the Nineteenth Century*. Berkeley and Los Angeles: University of California Press, 1979.

Weischel, John. "Cosmism or Amorphism?" *Camera Work* no. 42 (1913): 69–82.

Wershoven, C. J. "*The Awakening* and *The House of Mirth*: Studies in Arrested Development." *American Literary Realism* 19 (Spring 1987): 27–41.

Wharton, Edith. *A Backward Glance*. New York: Charles Scribner's Sons, 1961.

Whittaker, Albert L. "Bergson: First Aid to Common Sense." *Forum* (March 1914): 410–14.

Wilder, Thornton. "Thornton Wilder." Interview with Richard H. Goldstone, 14 December 1956. In *Writers at Work: The Paris Review Interviews*, edited by Malcolm Cowley, pp. 101–18. New York: Viking Press, 1959.

Willcox, Louise Collier. "Impressions of M. Bergson." *Harper's Weekly* (8 March 1913): 6.

―――. "Some Implications of Bergson's Philosophy." *North American Review* (March 1914): 448–51.

Williams, William Carlos. *Autobiography*. New York: New Directions, 1951.

―――. *Selected Essays*. New York: Random House, 1954.

Wohl, Robert. *The Generation of 1914*. Cambridge: Harvard University Press, 1979.

Woodbridge, Frederick J. E. *The Purpose of History*. New York: Columbia University Press, 1916.

Woodman, Lenora. *Stanza My Stone: Wallace Stevens and the Hermetic Tradition*. West Lafayette, Ind.: Purdue University Press, 1983.

Woodress, James. *Willa Cather: A Literary Life*. Lincoln: University of Nebraska Press, 1987.

―――. *Willa Cather: Her Life and Art*. Lincoln: University of Nebraska Press, 1970.

Woolf, Virginia. *The Captain's Death Bed and Other Essays*. New York: Harcourt, Brace and Co., 1950.

Young, David P. "A Skeptical Music: Stevens and Santayana." *Criticism* 7 (Summer 1965): 263–83.

Zabel, Morton. "Willa Cather: The Tone of Time." In *Modern Critical Views: Willa Cather*, edited by Harold Bloom, pp. 41–49. New York: Chelsea House Publishers, 1985.

Zola, Émile. *The Experimental Novel*. Translated by Belle M. Sherman. New York: Callell Publishing Co., 1893.

INDEX